A Concise Companion to
Postwar British and Irish Poetry

Blackwell Concise Companions to Literature and Culture
General Editor: David Bradshaw, University of Oxford

This series offers accessible, innovative approaches to major areas of literary study. Each volume provides an indispensable companion for anyone wishing to gain an authoritative understanding of a given period or movement's intellectual character and contexts.

Published

Modernism	Edited by David Bradshaw
Feminist Theory	Edited by Mary Eagleton
The Restoration and Eighteenth Century	Edited by Cynthia Wall
Postwar American Literature and Culture	Edited by Josephine G. Hendin
The Victorian Novel	Edited by Francis O'Gorman
Twentieth-Century American Poetry	Edited by Stephen Fredman
Chaucer	Edited by Corinne Saunders
Shakespeare on Screen	Edited by Diana E. Henderson
Contemporary British Fiction	Edited by James F. English
English Renaissance Literature	Edited by Donna B. Hamilton
Milton	Edited by Angelica Duran
Shakespeare and the Text	Edited by Andrew Murphy
Contemporary British and Irish Drama	Edited by Nadine Holdsworth and Mary Luckhurst
American Fiction 1900–1950	Edited by Peter Stoneley and Cindy Weinstein
The Romantic Age	Edited by Jon Klancher
Postwar British and Irish Poetry	Edited by Nigel Alderman and C. D. Blanton
Middle English Literature	Edited by Marilyn Corrie

Forthcoming

Terror and the Postcolonial	Edited by Elleke Boehmer and Stephen Morton
Postcolonial Literature	Edited by Shirley Chew and David Richards

A Concise Companion to
Postwar British and Irish Poetry

Edited by Nigel Alderman and
C. D. Blanton

WILEY-BLACKWELL

A John Wiley & Sons, Ltd., Publication

This edition first published 2009
© 2009 Blackwell Publishing Ltd

Blackwell Publishing was acquired by John Wiley & Sons in February 2007. Blackwell's publishing program has been merged with Wiley's global Scientific, Technical, and Medical business to form Wiley-Blackwell.

Registered Office
John Wiley & Sons Ltd, The Atrium, Southern Gate, Chichester, West Sussex, PO19 8SQ, United Kingdom

Editorial Offices
350 Main Street, Malden, MA 02148-5020, USA
9600 Garsington Road, Oxford, OX4 2DQ, UK
The Atrium, Southern Gate, Chichester, West Sussex, PO19 8SQ, UK

For details of our global editorial offices, for customer services, and for information about how to apply for permission to reuse the copyright material in this book please see our website at www.wiley.com/wiley-blackwell.

The right of Nigel Alderman and C. D. Blanton to be identified as the author of the editorial material in this work has been asserted in accordance with the Copyright, Designs and Patents Act 1988.

Wiley also publishes its books in a variety of electronic formats. Some content that appears in print may not be available in electronic books.

Designations used by companies to distinguish their products are often claimed as trademarks. All brand names and product names used in this book are trade names, service marks, trademarks or registered trademarks of their respective owners. The publisher is not associated with any product or vendor mentioned in this book. This publication is designed to provide accurate and authoritative information in regard to the subject matter covered. It is sold on the understanding that the publisher is not engaged in rendering professional services. If professional advice or other expert assistance is required, the services of a competent professional should be sought.

Library of Congress Cataloging-in-Publication Data

A concise companion to postwar British and Irish poetry / edited by Nigel Alderman and C.D. Blanton.
      p. cm. — (Blackwell concise companions to literature and culture)
   Includes bibliographical references and index.
   ISBN 978-1-4051-2924-4 (hardcover : alk. paper) 1. English poetry—20th century—History and criticism—Handbooks, manuals, etc. 2. English poetry—Irish authors—20th century—History and criticism—Handbooks, manuals, etc.
I. Alderman, Nigel. II. Blanton, C. D.
   PR603.C66 2009
   821'.91409—dc22
                                                                    2008033218

A catalogue record for this book is available from the British Library.

Set in 10.5/12pt Meridien by Graphicraft Limited, Hong Kong
Printed in Singapore by Fabulous Printers Pte Ltd

1   2009

Contents

state, including discussions of Derek Walcott, Kamau
Brathwaite, Lorna Goodison, Linton Kwesi Johnson,
Grace Nichols, Bernadine Evaristo, Louise Bennett,
Okot p'Bitek, Philip Larkin, Noel Coward,
Tony Harrison, Christopher Okigbo, and
Agha Shahid Ali.

Notes on Contributors

Nigel Alderman is Assistant Professor of English at Mount Holyoke College, having previously taught at Yale University. He has published on British poetry from John Milton to Philip Larkin and has co-edited, with C. D. Blanton, *Pocket Epics: British Poetry After Modernism* (*The Yale Journal of Criticism*, 2000). He is currently completing a book entitled, *Transitional Forms*, on British literature of the 1960s.

C. D. Blanton is Assistant Professor of English at the University of California, Berkeley, having previously taught at Princeton University. He writes on modernism and modern poetry generally, as well as aesthetic and cultural theory, and is currently completing a book on late modernist long poetic forms.

Stephen Burt is Associate Professor of English and American Literature and Language at Harvard University. He is the author of *Close Calls with Nonsense: Reading New Poetry* (Graywolf, 2009), *The Forms of Youth: Adolescence and Twentieth-Century Poetry* (Columbia, 2007), and *Randall Jarrell and His Age* (Columbia, 2003); and the editor of *Randall Jarrell on W. H. Auden* (Columbia, 2005). He is also the author of *Parallel Play* (Graywolf, 2006), a book of poems.

Eric Falci is Assistant Professor of English at the University of California, Berkeley. He is currently completing a study of contemporary Irish poetry.

Romana Huk is Associate Professor of English at the University of Notre Dame. She is the author of *Stevie Smith: Between the Lines* (Palgrave, 2005), the editor of *Assembling Alternatives: Reading Post-modern Poetries Transnationally* (Wesleyan, 2003), and with James Acheson, of *Contemporary British Poetry: Essays in Theory and Criticism* (SUNY, 1996).

Linda A. Kinnahan is Professor of English at Duquesne University. She is the author of *Lyric Interventions: Feminism, Experimental Poetry, and Contemporary Discourse* (Iowa, 2004) and *Poetics of the Feminine: Authority and Literary Tradition in William Carlos Williams, Mina Loy, Denise Levertov, and Kathleen Fraser* (Cambridge, 1994).

Peter Middleton is Professor of English at the University of Southampton. He is author of *Distant Reading: Performance, Readership, and Consumption in Contemporary Poetry* (Alabama, 2005), *The Inward Gaze: Masculinity and Subjectivity in Modern Culture* (Routledge, 1992), and, with Tim Woods, *Literatures of Memory: History, Time, and Space in Postwar Writing* (Manchester, 2000). He is also the author of *Aftermath* (Salt, 2003).

Drew Milne is the Judith E. Wilson University Lecturer in Drama and Poetry, in the Faculty of English, University of Cambridge. He edits the journal *Parataxis: Modernism and Modern Writing* (1991–) and is also the editor of *Modern Critical Thought: An Anthology of Theorists Writing on Theorists* (Blackwell, 2003) and, with Terry Eagleton, of *Marxist Literary Theory: A Reader* (Blackwell, 1996). He is the author of *Sheet Mettle* (Alfred David, 1994), *Bench Marks* (Alfred David, 1998), *The Damage* (Salt, 2001), *Mars Disarmed* (Figures, 2002) and *Go Figure* (Salt, 2003).

Jahan Ramazani is the Edgar F. Shannon Professor of English and Department Chair at the University of Virginia. He is the author of *Yeats and the Poetry of Death: Elegy, Self-Elegy, and the Sublime* (1990), *Poetry of Mourning: The Modern Elegy from Hardy to Heaney* (1994), which was a finalist for the National Book Critics Circle Award, *The Hybrid Muse: Postcolonial Poetry in English* (2001), and *A Transnational Poetics* (2009). He co-edited the third edition of *The Norton Anthology of Modern and Contemporary Poetry* (2003) and the eighth edition of *The Twentieth Century and After* in *The Norton Anthology of English Literature* (2006). He is a recipient of a Guggenheim Fellowship, an NEH

Fellowship, a Rhodes Scholarship, and the MLA's William Riley Parker Prize.

Vincent Sherry is Professor and Chair of English at Washington University in St Louis, having previously taught at Villanova University and Tulane University. He is author of *The Great War and the Language of Modernism* (Oxford, 2003), *James Joyce's Ulysses* (Cambridge, 1995), *Ezra Pound, Wyndham Lewis, and Radical Modernism* (Oxford, 1993), and *The Uncommon Tongue: The Poetry and Criticism of Geoffrey Hill* (Michigan, 1987). He is also editor of the *Cambridge Companion to the Literature of the First World War* (2005).

Michael Thurston is Associate Professor of English Language and Literature at Smith College, having previously taught at Yale University. He is the author of *Making Something Happen: American Political Poetry between the World Wars* (North Carolina, 2001) and editor, with Jani Scandura, of *Modernism, Inc.: Body, Memory, Capital* (NYU, 2001). His current project is *Going to Hell: The Underworld Descent in Twentieth-Century Poetry*.

John P. Waters is Clinical Assistant Professor of Irish Studies at New York University. He works broadly on British and Irish Literature from the eighteenth century to the present and has edited *Ireland and Irish Cultural Studies* (SAQ, 1996).

Acknowledgments

The editors and publisher gratefully acknowledge the permission granted to reproduce the copyright material in this book:

Excerpts from Simon Armitage, "Don't Blink," from *ZOOM!* (Bloodaxe Books, 1989) and Jean 'Binta' Breeze: "sisters celebration" from *The Arrival of Brighteye & Other Poems* (Bloodaxe Books, 2000). Reprinted by permission of Bloodaxe Books.

Alison Brackenbury, "Agenda" from *1829* (Carcanet, 1995); Gillian Clarke, excerpts from "Curlew," "Letter from a Far Country," and "Lunchtime Lecture," from *Collected Poems* (Carcanet, 1997); Donald Davie, excerpts from "The Nonconformist," and "Life Encompassed," from *Collected Poems* (Carcanet, 1990); and Peter Scupham, excerpt from "A Borderland" from *Collected Poems* (Carcanet, 2003). Reprinted by permission of Carcanet Press Ltd.

Ciaran Carson, "Turn Again," from *The Irish for No*, reprinted by permission of The Gallery Press, Loughcrew, Oldcastle, County Meath, Ireland and Wake Forest University Press.

Excerpt from Robert Conquest, "The Classical Poets," from *Poems* (Macmillan, 1955), reprinted by kind permission of the author.

Excerpts from "The Nonconformist," and "Life Encompassed," from *Collected Poems* (Chicago: University of Chicago Press, 1990), copyright © by Donald Davie 1990, reprinted by permission of University of Chicago Press.

Excerpt from "Foreign" is taken from *Selling Manhattan* by Carol Ann Duffy published by Anvil Press Poetry in 1987.

Excerpt from "Mrs Sisyphus," from *The World's Wife* by Carol Ann Duffy. Copyright © by Carol Ann Duffy 1999. Reprinted by permission of Pan Macmillan and Faber and Faber, Inc., an affiliate of Farrar, Straus and Giroux, LLC.

Excerpts from "Mr. Eliot's Sunday Morning Service" and "Airs of Palestine, No. 2" in *Inventions of the March Hare: Poems 1909–1917,* by T. S. Eliot, text copyright © 1996 by Valerie Eliot, reprinted by permission of Houghton Mifflin Harcourt Publishing Company.

Excerpt from "Rite, Lubitavish, Glenaan," John Hewitt, *The Selected Poems of John Hewitt*, ed. Michael Longley & Frank Ormsby (Blackstaff Press, 2007) reproduced by permission of Blackstaff Press on behalf of the Estate of John Hewitt.

Excerpt from "Respublica," from *New & Collected Poems 1952–1992* by Geoffrey Hill, copyright © 1994 by Geoffrey Hill, and excerpt from "LV," from *The Triumph of Love* by Geoffrey Hill, copyright © 1998 by Geoffrey Hill. Reprinted by permission of Houghton Mifflin Harcourt Publishing Company. All rights reserved.

Excerpt from "Respublica" from *Canaan* by Geoffrey Hill (Penguin Books, 1996), copyright © Geoffrey Hill, 1996, and excerpt from "LV" from *The Triumph of Love* by Geoffrey Hill (Penguin Books, 1999), copyright © Geoffrey Hill, 1998. Reproduced by permission of Penguin Books Ltd.

Excerpt from Tom Leonard, "Just ti Let Yi No." *Intimate Voices* (Galloping Dog Press, 1984). Reprinted by kind permission of the author.

Excerpt from Grace Nichols, "Of Course When They Ask for Poems About the 'Realities' of Black Women," *Lazy Thoughts of a Lazy Woman and Other Poems* (Virago, 1989). Copyright © Grace Nichols 1989 reproduced with permission of Curtis Brown Group Ltd.

Excerpt from Eiléan Ní Chuilleanáin, "River, with Boats," from *The Magdalene Sermon*, reprinted by permission of The Gallery Press, Loughcrew, Oldcastle, County Meath, Ireland, and from *The Magdalene Sermon & Earlier Poems*, reprinted by permission of Wake Forest University Press.

Acknowledgments

Ezra Pound: "In a Station of the Metro." By Ezra Pound, from *Personae*, copyright © 1926 by Ezra Pound. Reprinted by permission of New Directions Publishing Corp.

Excepts from Denise Riley, "Dark Looks" from *Mop Mop Georgette: New and Selected Poems 1986–1993* (Reality Street Editions, 1993). Reprinted with kind permission of Denise Riley and Reality Street Editions.

Reprinted by kind permission of Faber and Faber Ltd.:
Excerpts from "Mr. Eliot's Sunday Morning Service" and "Airs of Palestine, No. 2" in *Inventions of the March Hare: Poems 1909–1917*, by T. S. Eliot, text copyright © 1996 by Valerie Eliot. Excerpts from "Guidebook, to the Alhambra" and "What's Going On" from *A World Where News Travelled Slowly* by Lavinia Greenlaw. Copyright © 1997 by Lavinia Greenlaw. Excerpts from "The Beautician," "Elvis Presley," and "Tamer and Hawk" from *Collected Poems* by Thom Gunn. Copyright © 1994 by Thom Gunn. Excerpt from "At Toomebridge" from *Electric Light* by Seamus Heaney. Copyright © 2001 by Seamus Heaney. Excerpt from "Crowego" from *Collected Poems* by Ted Hughes. Copyright © 2003 by the Estate of Ted Hughes. Excerpts from "High Windows" and "Reference Back" from *Collected Poems* by Philip Larkin. Copyright © 1998, 2003 by the Estate of Philip Larkin. "In a Station of the Metro" from *Personae: The Shorter Poems of Ezra Pound* by Ezra Pound. Copyright © 1926 by Ezra Pound.

Reprinted by permission of Farrar, Straus and Giroux, LLC:
Excerpts from "The Beautician," "Elvis Presley," and "Tamer and Hawk" from *Collected Poems* by Thom Gunn. Copyright © 1994 by Thom Gunn. Excerpt from "At Toomebridge" from *Electric Light* by Seamus Heaney. Copyright © 2001 by Seamus Heaney. Excerpt from "Crowego" from *Collected Poems* by Ted Hughes. Copyright © 2003 by the Estate of Ted Hughes. Excerpts from "High Windows" and "Reference Back" from *Collected Poems* by Philip Larkin. Copyright © 1998, 2003 by the Estate of Philip Larkin.

Every effort has been made to trace copyright holders and to obtain their permission for the use of copyright material. The publisher apologizes for any errors or omissions in the above list and would be grateful if notified of any corrections that should be incorporated in future reprints or editions of this book.

Chronology

1945
German surrender; (UK) dissolution of War Cabinet under Winston Churchill, Prime Minister; Labour government: Clement Attlee, Prime Minister; Japanese surrender; United Nations (UN) chartered; beginning of Nuremberg trials; foundation of World Bank; beginning of widescale nationalization; Family Allowances Act.

Philip Larkin, *The North Ship*

1946
Winston Churchill's "Iron Curtain" speech; National Insurance Act; National Assistance Act; National Health Service Act; nationalization of the Bank of England; nationalization of coal industry; formation of British Arts Council.

Edwin Muir, *The Voyage and Other Poems*; Dylan Thomas, *Deaths and Entrances*

1947
Withdrawal of military aid to Greece and Turkey; announcement of Truman Doctrine; India and Pakistan become independent (partition); Jawaharlal Nehru becomes Prime Minister of India; UN partition of Palestine; Transport Act (nationalization of road and rail transport); nationalization of electrical industry; nationalization of Cable & Wireless.

1948
(Ire.) Éamon de Valera's Fianna Fáil government falls in Éire: first Inter-Party government, John A. Costello, Taoiseach; bread rationing ends in Britain; arrival of *Empire Windrush*, rise in West Indian immigration; launch of European Recovery Program (Marshall Plan); Burma (Myanmar), Sri Lanka (Ceylon) become independent; end of colonial rule in Trans-Jordan (Jordan), British Palestine, Egypt (excluding Suez); British Citizenship Act; beginning of Berlin blockade, airlift; assassination of Gandhi.

T. S. Eliot wins Nobel Prize for Literature; W. H. Auden, *The Age of Anxiety*; T. S. Eliot, *Notes towards the Definition of Culture*; Ezra Pound, *The Pisan Cantos*

1949
Republic of Ireland established, withdraws from Commonwealth; North Atlantic Treaty Organization (NATO); apartheid instituted in South Africa; India adopts constitution; nationalization of gas industry; devaluation of pound sterling.

1950
"Mother and Child Scheme" for public health care in Ireland fails; Britain recognizes People's Republic of China, Israel; London dock strike; nationalization of iron and steel industry; end of fuel rationing; British troops sent to Korea.

David Gascoyne, *A Vagrant, and Other Poems*

1951
(UK) Conservative government: Winston Churchill, Prime Minister; (Ire.) Fianna Fáil government: Éamon de Valera, Taoiseach; Festival of Britain; Guy Burgess and Donald Maclean defect to Soviet Union.

Keith Douglas, *Collected Poems*

1952
Death of George VI; Britain produces atomic bomb.

David Jones, *The Anathemata*

1953
Coronation of Elizabeth II; death of Stalin; London Conference of Commonwealth Prime Ministers.

Death of Dylan Thomas; D. J. Enright, *The Laughing Hyena and Other Poems*; Louis MacNeice, *Autumn Sequel*

1954
(Ire.) Second Inter-Party government: John A. Costello, Taoiseach; end of food rationing in Britain; Independent Television Authority established.

Thom Gunn, *Fighting Terms*; Jon Silkin, *The Peaceable Kingdom*

1955
(UK) Churchill resigns: Anthony Eden, Prime Minister; formation of European Union; Ireland joins United Nations, declines to join NATO; Bandung Conference; railroad and dock strikes.

D. J. Enright (ed.), *Poetry of the 1950s*; W. H. Auden, *The Shield of Achilles*; Austin Clarke, *Ancient Lights*; W. S. Graham, *The Nightfishing*; Elizabeth Jennings, *A Way of Looking*; Philip Larkin, *The Less Deceived*; Hugh MacDiarmid, *In Memoriam James Joyce*; R. S. Thomas, *Song at the Year's Turning*

1956
Suez crisis; beginning of the Border Campaign in Ireland; Twentieth Party Congress in Moscow: Nikita Khrushchev's "secret speech"; Soviet invasion of Hungary.

Robert Conquest (ed.), *New Lines*; Norman MacCaig, *Riding Lights*

1957
(UK) Eden resigns: Harold Macmillan, Prime Minister; (Ire.) Fianna Fáil government: Éamon de Valera, Taoiseach; Treaty of Rome (Formation of European Economic Community); Ghana, Malaya become independent; Wolfenden Report (on homosexuality and prostitution); Britain tests hydrogen bomb.

Donald Davie, *A Winter Talent and Other Poems*; Thom Gunn, *The Sense of Movement*; Ted Hughes, *The Hawk in the Rain*; Stevie Smith, *Not Waving But Drowning*

1958
Formation of West Indies Federation; Notting Hill race riots; London bus strike; opening of Preston bypass (M6, first motorway).

1959
(Ire.) de Valera resigns, elected President: Séan Lemass, Taoiseach; Singapore becomes independent; first section of M1 opened.

Geoffrey Hill, *For the Unfallen*; Elizabeth Jennings, *A Sense of the World*

1960
Cyprus, Nigeria become independent; *Lady Chatterley* trial.

Austin Clarke, *The Horse-Eaters*; Ian Hamilton Finlay, *The dancers inherit the party*; Ted Hughes, *Lupercal*; Charles Tomlinson, *Seeing Is Believing* (1958 in US)

1961
Construction of Berlin Wall; South Africa withdraws from Commonwealth.

Roy Fisher, *City*; Thom Gunn, *My Sad Captains and Other Poems*; Jon Silkin, *The Re-Ordering of the Stones*

1962
Commonwealth Immigrants Act; end of postwar National Service.

A. Alvarez (ed.), *The New Poetry*; Brian Coffey, *Missouri Sequence*; Thomas Kinsella, *Downstream*; Christopher Middleton, *Torse 3*

1963
(UK) Macmillan resigns: Alec Douglas-Home, Prime Minister; France blocks British entry into EEC; Kenyan independence; Profumo affair.

Death of Louis MacNeice; death of Sylvia Plath; Louis MacNeice, *The Burning Perch*; Charles Tomlinson, *A Peopled Landscape*; Rosemary Tonks, *Notes on Cafés and Bedrooms*

1964
(UK) Election of Labour government: Harold Wilson, Prime Minister; Tanzania, Zambia, Malawi, Congo, Malta become independent.

Donald Davie, *Events and Wisdoms*; Elizabeth Jennings, *Recoveries*; Philip Larkin, *The Whitsun Weddings*

1965
Gambia becomes independent; unilateral secession of Rhodesia; Death of Winston Churchill.

Death of T. S. Eliot; George Barker, *The True Confessions of George Barker*; Basil Bunting, *Loquitur*; Sylvia Plath, *Ariel*

1966
(Ire.) Lemass resigns; Jack Lynch, Taoiseach; wage and price controls; England wins World Cup.

Basil Bunting, *Briggflatts*; Austin Clarke, *Mnemosyne Lay in Dust*; Roy Fisher, *The Ship's Orchestra*; Seamus Heaney, *Death of a Naturalist*

1967
Sexual Offenses Act (repealing laws against homosexuality in Britain).

Death of Patrick Kavanagh; death of John Masefield; Cecil Day Lewis becomes Poet Laureate; Eavan Boland, *New Territory*; Andrew Crozier, *Loved Litter of Time Spent*; Veronica Forrest-Thomson, *Identikit*; Thom Gunn, *Touch*; Ted Hughes, *Wodwo*; Tom Raworth, *The Relation Ship*; John Riley, *Ancient and Modern*; Rosemary Tonks, *Iliad of Broken Sentences*

1968
Soviet invasion of Czechoslovakia; students and workers riot in Paris; Race Relations Act; Enoch Powell's "rivers of blood" speech against immigration.

Geoffrey Hill, *King Log*; Derek Mahon, *Night-Crossing*; Thomas Kinsella, *Nightwalker and Other Poems*; Edwin Morgan, *The Second Life*; J. H. Prynne, *Kitchen Poems*; C. H. Sisson, *Metamorphoses*; R. S. Thomas, *Not that He Brought Flowers*

1969
Riots in Derry; British troops sent to Northern Ireland; beginning of the Troubles.

George Mackay Brown, *The Year of the Whale*; Donald Davie, *Essex Poems*; Douglas Dunn, *Terry Street*; Seamus Heaney, *Door into the Dark*; Thomas Kinsella, *The Táin*; Michael Longley, *No Continuing City*; J. H. Prynne, *The White Stones*; Charles Tomlinson, *Way of a World*

1970
(UK) Election of Conservative government: Edward Heath, Prime Minister; dock strike, state of emergency declared; British Petroleum announces North Sea oil discovery; Tonga becomes independent.

W. S. Graham, *Malcolm Mooney's Land*; Tony Harrison, *The Loiners*; Ted Hughes, *Crow*; Peter Porter, *The Last of England*; John Riley, *What Reason Was*

1971
Currency reform: decimalization of British and Irish pound; beginning of detentions without trial in Northern Ireland; Commons votes to join EEC; Qatar independent.

Death of Stevie Smith; Fleur Adcock, *High Tide in the Garden*; Elaine Feinstein, *The Magic Apple Trees*; Veronica Forrest-Thomson, *Language Games*; Geoffrey Hill, *Mercian Hymns*; J. H. Prynne, *Brass*

1972
"Bloody Sunday," thirteen killed by British troops in Northern Ireland; British Embassy in Dublin burned; Parliament of Northern Ireland suspended; pound sterling allowed to float on open market; miners' strike.

Death of Cecil Day Lewis; John Betjeman becomes Poet Laureate; Donald Davie, *The Shires*; Seamus Heaney, *Wintering Out*; Thomas Kinsella, *Butcher's Dozen*; *Notes from the Land of the Dead and Other Poems*; Derek Mahon, *Lives*; John Montague, *The Rough Field*; R. S. Thomas, *H'm*

1973
(Ire.) Fine Gael government: Liam Cosgrave, Prime Minister; Britain and Ireland enter EEC; World oil crisis; IRA bombing campaign begins; Sunningdale Agreement for power-sharing in Northern Ireland (collapses 1974); beginning of coal miners' strike; Bahamas independent.

Death of W. H. Auden; D. J. Enright, *The Terrible Shears: Scenes from a Twenties Childhood*; Michael Longley, *An Exploded View*; Edwin Morgan, *From Glasgow to Saturn*; Paul Muldoon, *New Weather*; Peter Redgrove and Penelope Shuttle, *The Hermaphrodite Album*; John Riley, *Ways of Approaching*

1974
(UK) Labour government: Harold Wilson, Prime Minister; Local Government Act reforms administrative map; Prevention of Terrorism Act; Grenada independent; Ireland allows sale of contraceptives to married couples.

Death of Austin Clarke; death of David Jones; Allen Fisher, *Place*; Veronica Forrest-Thomson, *Cordelia: or, "A Poem Should Not Mean, But Be"*; Linton Kwesi Johnson, *Voices of the Living and the Dead*; Philip Larkin, *High Windows*; C. H. Sisson, *In the Trojan Ditch*; Anne Stevenson, *Correspondences: A family history in letters*

1975
Sex Discrimination Act, Equal Pay Act come into force.

Brian Coffey, *Advent*; Ulli Freer, *Rooms*; Seamus Heaney, *North*; Linton Kwesi Johnson, *Dread, Beat, and Blood*; Derek Mahon, *The Snow Party*; John Montague, *The Great Cloak*; F. T. Prince, *Drypoints of the Hasidim*; R. S. Thomas, *Laboratories of the Spirit*

1976
(UK) Wilson resigns: James Callaghan, Prime Minister.

Ciaran Carson, *The New Estate*; Thom Gunn, *Jack Straw's Castle*; Trevor Joyce, *The Poems of Sweeny Peregrine*

1977
(Ire.) Fianna Fáil government: Jack Lynch, Taoiseach; (UK) Labour–Liberal pact maintains Labour government; Silver Jubilee.

W. S. Graham, *Implements in Their Places*; Ted Hughes, *Gaudete*; Andrew Motion, *Pleasure Steamers*; Paul Muldoon, *Mules*; Tom Paulin, *A State of Justice*; Denise Riley, *Marxism for Infants*

1978
Beginning of "winter of discontent."

Death of Hugh MacDiarmid; Tony Harrison, *From the School of Eloquence and Other Poems*; Geoffrey Hill, *Tenebrae*; Ted Hughes, *Cave Birds*; Craig Raine, *The Onion, Memory*

1979

(UK) Conservative government: Margaret Thatcher, Prime Minister; (Ire.) Lynch resigns; Charles Haughey, Taoiseach; Irish pound joins Exchange Rate Mechanism; Scottish and Welsh devolution referenda fail; assassinations of Airey Neave and Lord Mountbatten; Warrenpoint ambush.

Fleur Adcock, *The Inner Harbour*; Douglas Dunn, *Barbarians*; Seamus Heaney, *Field Work*; Ted Hughes; *Moortown, Remains of Elmet*; J. H. Prynne, *Down where changed*; Craig Raine, *A Martian Sends a Postcard Home*; Jeremy Reed, *Saints and Psychotics*

1980

Steel strike; British Aerospace privatized; Zimbabwe becomes independent.

Eavan Boland, *In Her Own Image*; Linton Kwesi Johnson, *Inglan Is a Bitch*; Paul Muldoon, *Why Brownlee Left*; Tom Paulin, *The Strange Museum*; Jon Silkin, *The Psalms with Their Spoils*; Ken Smith, *Fox Running*

1981

(Ire.) Fine Gael–Labour coalition government; Garret Fitzgerald, Taoiseach; (UK) split in Labour party: formation of Social Democratic Party (SDP); British Nationality Act; Brixton riots; deaths of nine IRA hunger strikers in Maze Prison.

Douglas Dunn, *St Kilda's Parliament*; Tony Harrison, *Continuous: Fifty Sonnets from the School of Eloquence*; Christopher Logue, *War Music*; Andrew Motion, *Independence*

1982

Falklands War; (Ire.) Haughey returns as Taoiseach, succeeded again by Fitzgerald.

Andrew Motion & Blake Morrison (eds), *Penguin Book of Contemporary British Poetry*; Derek Mahon, *The Hunt by Night*; Medbh McGuckian, *The Flower Master*; Christopher Reid, *Pea Soup*

1983
(UK) General election returns Conservative government; escape of 38 prisoners from Maze Prison; mass demonstrations in London organized by Campaign for Nuclear Disarmament; Greenham Common Women's Peace Camp.

Jean "Binta" Breeze, *Answers*; George Mackay Brown, *Voyages*; James Fenton, *The Memory of War*; Geoffrey Hill, *The Mystery of the Charity of Charles Péguy*; John Montague, *The Dead Kingdom*; Andrew Motion, *Secret Narratives*; Paul Muldoon, *Quoof*; Grace Nichols, *i is a long memoried woman*; Tom Paulin, *Liberty Tree*

1984
Coal Miners' Strike; Trade Union Act; privatization of British Telecom; bombing of Grand Hotel, Brighton.

Death of John Betjeman; Ted Hughes becomes Poet Laureate; David Dabydeen, *Slave Song*; Seamus Heaney, *Station Island*; *Sweeney Astray*; Medbh McGuckian, *Venus and the Rain*; Grace Nichols, *The Fat Black Woman's Poems*; Craig Raine, *Rich*; Peter Reading, *C*.

1985
Anglo-Irish Agreement.

Death of Basil Bunting; death of Philip Larkin; Carol Ann Duffy, *Standing Female Nude*; Allen Fisher, *Brixton Fractals*; Tony Harrison, *v.*; Peter Reading, *Ukelele Music*; Christopher Reid, *Katerina Brac*; Denise Riley, *Dry Air*; Benjamin Zephaniah, *The Dread Affair*

1986
Riots in Brixton and elsewhere; London Stock Exchange deregulated; British Gas privatized.

Fleur Adcock, *The Incident Book*; Roy Fisher, *A Furnace*; Christopher Middleton, *Two Horse Wagon Going By*; Jon Silkin, *The Ship's Pasture*

1987
(Ire.) Fianna Fáil government: Charles Haughey, Taoiseach; Single European Act; British Airways privatized.

Andrew Crozier & Tim Longville (eds), *A Various Art*; Ciaran Carson, *The Irish for No*; Carol Ann Duffy, *Selling Manhattan*; Seamus Heaney,

The Haw Lantern; Kathleen Jamie, *The Way We Live*; Edwin Morgan, *Themes on a Variation*; Blake Morrison, *The Ballad of the Yorkshire Ripper and Other Poems*; Paul Muldoon, *Meeting the British*; Tom Paulin, *Fivemiletown*

1988
SDP merges with Liberal Party to form Social and Liberal Democratic Party; SAS shoot three unarmed IRA members in Gibraltar; transatlantic flight bombed over Lockerbie (Scotland).

Gillian Allnutt et al. (eds), *The New British Poetry*; Jean "Binta" Breeze, *Riddym Ravings and Other Poems*; David Dabydeen, *Coolie Odyssey*; Medbh McGuckian, *On Ballycastle Beach*; Jo Shapcott, *Electroplating the Baby*

1989
Opening of Berlin Wall; Release of Guildford Four; Iran places *fatwa* on Salman Rushdie.

Death of Samuel Beckett; Simon Armitage, *Zoom!*; Gillian Clarke, *Letting in the Rumour*; Selima Hill, *The Accumulation of Small Acts of Kindness*; George Macbeth, *Collected Poems 1958–1982*; E. A. Markham, *Towards the End of the Century*; Grace Nicholls, *Lazy Thoughts of a Lazy Woman and Other Poems*; Iain Crichton Smith, *The Village, and Other Poems*

1990
(UK) Margaret Thatcher resigns: John Major, Prime Minister; Poll Tax riots; pound sterling joins Exchange Rate Mechanism; Nelson Mandela released from Robben Island; reunification of Germany.

Eavan Boland, *Outside History*; Ciaran Carson, *Belfast Confetti*; Robert Crawford, *A Scottish Assembly*; Carol Ann Duffy, *The Other Country*; Paul Durcan, *Daddy, Daddy*; Elaine Feinstein, *City Music*; Thomas Kinsella, *Poems from Centre City*; Glyn Maxwell, *Tale of the Mayor's Son*; Paul Muldoon, *Madoc: A Mystery*

1991
Gulf War; release of Birmingham Six; Poll Tax replaced by Council Tax; official end of South African apartheid; dissolution of Soviet Union; Ireland agrees to sign Maastricht Treaty.

Lavinia Greenlaw, *The Cost of Getting Lost in Space*; Seamus Heaney, *Seeing Things*; Linton Kwesi Johnson, *Tings an' Times*; Jackie Kay, *The Adoption Papers*; Liz Lochead, *Bagpipe Muzak*; Michael Longley, *Gorse Fires*; Mebdh McGuckian, *Marconi's Cottage*; Andrew Motion, *Love in a Life*; Sean O'Brien, *HMS Glasshouse*

1992
(Ire.) Haughey resigns; Albert Reynolds, Taoiseach; Maastricht Treaty signed; sterling crisis; Britain withdraws from European Exchange Rate Mechanism; Irish voters approve a loosened abortion law, guaranteeing access to information and travel abroad

Simon Armitage, *Kid*; *Xanadu*; Jean "Binta" Breeze, *Spring Cleaning*; U. A. Fanthorpe, *Neck-Verse*; Thom Gunn, *The Man with Night Sweats*; Glyn Maxwell, *Out of the Rain*; Tom Raworth, *Catacoustics*; Peter Reading, *3 in 1*; Denise Riley, *Stair Spirit*; Benjamin Zephaniah, *City Psalms*

1993
Downing Street Declaration affirms right of Northern Ireland to self-determination; Maastricht Treaty comes into force.

Ciaran Carson, *First Language*; Gillian Clarke, *The King of Britain's Daughter*; Carol Ann Duffy, *Mean Time*; Paul Durcan, *A Snail in my Prime*; Lavinia Greenlaw, *Night Photograph*; Jackie Kay, *Other Lovers*; E. A. Markham, *Letter from Ulster and the Hugo Poems*; Don Paterson, *Nil Nil*; Denise Riley, *Mop Mop Georgette*

1994
(Ire.) Fine Gael coalition government: John Bruton, Taoiseach; IRA declares ceasefire; Nelson Mandela becomes President of South Africa; privatization of coal industry; opening of Channel Tunnel; Church of England begins ordination of women.

Eavan Boland, *In a Time of Violence*; Roy Fisher, *Birmingham River*; Kathleen Jamie, *The Queen of Sheba*; Medbh McGuckian, *Captain Lavender*; Derek Mahon, *The Yaddo Letter*; Paul Muldoon, *The Annals of Chile*

1995
David Trimble becomes leader of Ulster Unionist party.

Death of Donald Davie; Seamus Heaney wins Nobel Prize for Literature; James Berry, *Hot Earth, Cold Earth*; Michael Longley, *The Ghost Orchid*; Derek Mahon, *The Hudson Letter*; Sean O'Brien, *Ghost Train*

1996
IRA bomb destroys Arndale Centre, Manchester.

Death of George Mackay Brown; Seamus Heaney, *The Spirit Level*; Geoffrey Hill, *Canaan*; Grace Nichols, *Sunris*

1997
(UK) Labour government: Tony Blair, Prime Minister; (Ire.) Fianna Fáil government: Bertie Ahern, Taoiseach; Scotland, Wales referenda pass; control of Hong Kong transferred to China; death of Diana, Princess of Wales; Ireland permits divorce under certain circumstances.

Simon Armitage, *CloudCuckooLand*; Jean "Binta" Breeze, *On the Edge of an Island*; Lavinia Greenlaw, *A World Where News Travelled*; Ted Hughes, *Tales from Ovid*; Derek Mahon, *The Yellow Book*; Andrew Motion, *Salt Water*

1998
Belfast (Good Friday) Agreement; establishment of Northern Ireland Assembly (First Minister: David Trimble).

Death of Ted Hughes; appointment of Andrew Motion, Poet Laureate; Seamus Heaney, *Beowulf*; Geoffrey Hill, *The Triumph of Love*; Ted Hughes, *Birthday Letters*; Jackie Kay, *Off Colour*; Glyn Maxwell, *The Breakage*; Medbh McGuckian, *Shelmalier*; Paul Muldoon, *Hay*

1999
Scottish Parliament opens (Scottish Labour government: Donald Dewar, First Minister); Welsh Assembly established.

Carol Ann Duffy, *The World's Wife*; Kathleen Jamie, *Jizzen*; Don Paterson, *The Eyes*; J. H. Prynne, *Poems*

2000
(Scot.) Death of Dewar: Henry McLeish, First Minister; last prisoners leave Maze Prisoner under Northern Ireland Peace Process.

Death of R. S. Thomas; Thom Gunn, *Boss Cupid*; Jo Shapcott, *Her Book*

2001
(Scot.) MacLeish resigns: Jack McConnell, First Minister; attacks on New York, Washington; US and UK attack Afghanistan; race riots in Burnley, Bradford.

Death of Elizabeth Jennings; Ciaran Carson, *The Twelfth of Never*; Lavinia Greenlaw, *Mary George of Allnorthover*; Seamus Heaney, *Electric Light*; Selima Hill, *Bunny*; Trevor Joyce, *with the first dream of fire they hunt the cold*; Sean O'Brien, *Downriver*; Benjamin Zephaniah, *Too Black, Too Strong*

2002
(Ire.) Fianna Fáil–Progressive Democrats government; euro introduced in Ireland; Irish voters accept Nice Treaty in second referendum; suspension of Northern Ireland Assembly following "Stormontgate"; Golden Jubilee.

Glyn Maxwell, *The Nerve*; Paul Muldoon, *Moy Sand and Gravel*; Alice Oswald, *Dart*

2003
United States and Britain attack Iraq.

Ciaran Carson, *Breaking News*; Lavinia Greenlaw, *Minsk*

2004
Ireland votes to reform citizenship law.

Death of Thom Gunn; Kathleen Jamie, *The Tree House*; Michael Longley, *Snow Water*; Tom Paulin, *The Road to Inver*

2005
London transport bombings; Irish recognized as a working language by the European Union.

Carol Ann Duffy, *Rapture*; Jackie Kay, *Life Mask*; Derek Mahon, *Harbour Lights*; Alice Oswald, *Woods, etc.*

2006
Government of Wales Act gives Welsh Assembly enhanced legislative powers; St Andrews Agreement restores Northern Ireland Parliament.

Seamus Heaney, *District and Circle*; W. N. Herbert, *Bad Shaman Blues*; Paul Muldoon, *Horse Latitudes*; Robin Robertson, *Swithering*

2007
(UK) Blair resigns: Gordon Brown, Prime Minister; (Scot.) minority government: Alex Salmond (National), First Minister; Northern Ireland Assembly reconvenes: Ian Paisley, First Minister; Martin McGuinness, Deputy First Minister.

Edwin Morgan, *A Book of Lives*; Sean O'Brien, *The Drowned Book*

2008
(N. Ire.) Paisley resigns: Peter Robinson, First Minister; global financial crisis.

Introduction

Nigel Alderman and C. D. Blanton

The concise title of this collection is perhaps best taken quite literally. Both the volume and the dozen essays it contains are relatively brief, especially when weighed against the ever-thickening mass of British and Irish poetry written and published since World War II. Each piece proposes one possible angle of entry to that field, exploring a context of particular importance to poetry written over the past half-century and more, not to chart it exhaustively, still less to anthologize and account all the works and figures that define it, but rather to suggest ways in which the field might productively be encountered, by those beginning to read and teach this material, or merely hoping to re-read it critically. Accordingly, each essay is designed to offer not a definitive set of readings or canonical judgments, but rather a survey and analysis of the tendencies, habits, and patterns that distinguish poetic production in Britain and Ireland over the past several decades. Together, they are offered as a rough, necessarily provisional, guide to a period that is perhaps still too close to view in a single historical glance, but one that is simultaneously receding from the recollections of simple memory into those of literary history.

What is certain is that the years between 1945 and now have witnessed a radical transformation in the cultures of the British archipelago and the larger global system in which they negotiate an often uneasy place. From the rise of the welfare state in the 1940s to its fall in the 1980s, from the proclamation of the Irish Republic in 1949 to the Good Friday Accords in 1998, from the dismantling of the

British Empire after the war to the devolution of British power onto the Scottish Parliament and the Welsh National Assembly at the century's end, the literal meanings of political terms such as "British" and "Irish," of the "English" language that reaches across them and beyond, have fundamentally changed over the past half century and more. With those changes, sometimes slow and sometimes abrupt, the idea of an English literature has necessarily changed as well, entailing an interrogation of what poetry is or does that continues into the new century. In large measure, these redefinitions constitute shifting borders, blurred lines of demarcation not only between political entities but also among the various practices of language that circulate within and among them. As even the casual reader of recent verse will quickly note, the idea of poetry has often been contested and uneasy over the past six decades or so, spinning a literary history capacious enough to include the Movement lyric and dub beats, and spawning inevitable controversies in the process. Simple definitions have often proven elusive, either too indistinct or too partial. What seems clearer is that the question itself has remained charged, that an ever-expanding field of poetic writing has engaged and incorporated every shift of recent times. We have therefore attempted less to define what poetry is or what it means than to describe what it has been and what it has meant at crucial moments in a still developing literary history. To that end, each essay in this volume surveys one important corner of a larger map, gathering some of the figures and poems that have made it significant and summarizing the critical questions that have arisen in the process.

Accounts of postwar literature often adopt an apologetic or even elegiac tone, as if the historical loss of the triumphal certainties of earlier moments necessarily implied an aesthetic diminution. When coupled with the perceived marginalization of poetry more generally, such accounts can reduce the writing of recent decades to a rather melancholic affair. But historical melancholia need not imply simple poetic mourning. To the contrary, the very intensity and speed of recent historical shifts have often prompted striking reconsiderations of form and spawned larger questions that poetry is uniquely equipped to answer. Writing of the history of postwar Europe more generally, Tony Judt has recently observed that the years after 1945 have "now come to be seen not as the threshold of a new epoch but rather as an interim age: a post-war parenthesis, the unfinished business of a conflict that ended in 1945 but whose epilogue had lasted for another half century" (2005: 2). Much the same can be said of the poetry that sought to define a new sense of place and a new set of relations – political certainly, but also social and formal, sexual and economic, historical and existential – proper to the twentieth century's latter half. Mindful then (in Judt's phrase again) "that 1945 was never quite the fresh start that it sometimes appears" (2005: 6), this volume therefore takes the "post" in its title seriously. The turmoil and social upheaval that defined the twentieth century's first half, between 1914 and 1945 especially, spared little in the realm of culture, imprinting traces across all the arts. But poetry in particular has proven an extraordinarily sensitive instrument to that history, whether recording the horrors of soldiers fighting on the Western Front, in the work of Wilfred Owen or Siegfried Sassoon, or registering the enchantments and disenchantments of those left, like W. B. Yeats and T. S. Eliot, at home. The consolidation of new political orders after 1945 may have qualified some anxieties and introduced others, but it also left newer generations of poets to struggle with and re-adapt some of the same insoluble questions and forms that had vexed their predecessors.

The mere fact that we have no better term than "postwar" for a historical interlude already over half a century long, then, should already suggest the inevitability of a backward glance, toward those revolutions, disasters, and new beginnings that brought the postwar order (and its various disorders) into being. It should also suggest a fact discovered in different ways by many of the essays included here: that much of the energy generated by postwar poetry has been sparked by the need to sort out, break with, exorcise, criticize, escape, or reconfirm a host of contradictory legacies – or at least to make some sense of the immediate past. In all probability, every age is an age of criticism. What often seems to distinguish recent decades, however, is the degree to which the work of criticism – assessing formal debts, arguing over historical precedents, disputing the ways in which poems accrete meaning – has guided not only the ways in which poems are read, but also the ways in which they are written. The need to take stock of everything that the postwar follows, whether lying in the archaic past or in living memory, has often left the period to define itself by defining the larger history to which it forms an epilogue. (It is perhaps worth noting, in this regard, that the first such companion to postwar poetry was offered by Stephen Spender in a small pamphlet entitled *Poetry since 1939*. The year was 1946.)

But the other half of Judt's parenthesis is equally important. If the postwar marks "an interim age," then it also gestures forward, to our own contemporary moment certainly, but also to futures in the process of taking shape. In both present and future, that plural usage remains inevitable. The current *Oxford English Literary History*, for example, segments the twentieth century alone into no fewer than five volumes, the postwar into three (dividing period boundaries alternately at 1940, 1948, 1960, 1970, and 2000), and traces the transformation of English literature into a complicated international fact. Major anthologies overlap similarly. The recent Oxford *Anthology of Twentieth-Century British and Irish Poetry* spans the entire century (Tuma 2001), while the *Norton Anthology of Modern and Contemporary Poetry*, published two years later, divides the century in half, imposing no national borders within English (Ramazani et al. 2003). Other important collections have chosen other organizing frames. Edna Longley's *Bloodaxe Book of 20th Century Poetry from Britain and Ireland* (2000b), for example, concentrates attention on the continuity and development of the lyric, while Simon Armitage and Robert Crawford's *Penguin Book of Poetry from Britain and Ireland since 1945* locates the underlying story of postwar poetry, as of postwar society in general, in the gradual but implacable movement of democratization and the corollary achievement of a "contemporary culture of pluralism" (1998: xxii). For Armitage and Crawford, the postwar is largely defined by the transformation of England from "the widely acknowledged fount and centre of English language culture" to a tributary "anglophone culture within an English-speaking world" (xxiii), a world in which "apparent genealogies become disrupted" (xxvi).

All of these constitute so many provisional descriptions of a field not yet finished, signs that, as Armitage and Crawford put it, "a sense of belatedness grows, mixed with a sense of anticipation" (1998: xxxii). Inevitably, different accounts will attempt to impose coherent narratives on any such span of time. More often, they will be forced to acknowledge several. Against the largely optimistic story offered by Armitage and Crawford, then, might be placed Andrew Duncan's more polemical account of the systemic "failure" of twentieth-century British poetry (2003: 2), measured largely in its apparent devotion to older styles and familiar subjects. What Duncan terms "conservatism" might as easily be characterized as a certain constriction of voice. Somewhat paradoxically, the persistence of a healthier public market for poetry in Britain and Ireland, less bound to the university system than elsewhere, has occasionally tended to stratify the poetic field, even as the proliferation of new technologies and the formation of new sub-cultures generate new poetic practices on all sides. A recent Arts Council study diplomatically notes what it terms "a high degree of concentration" (Bridgwood & Hampson 2000: i) in the book market, with a single imprint (Faber) responsible for over 80 percent of contemporary poetry sales (2000: 16) and two poets (Ted Hughes and Seamus Heaney) accounting for the vast share of titles sold. Such a situation can be praised or deplored, but it forms an important underlying fact in either case, suggesting that postwar poetry is defined not only by its range of styles, but also by even larger disparities between large houses and small presses, popular and professional readers, mainstream and experimental sensibilities, continuous and discontinuous traditions. This is a pluralism of a different kind, one that underscores a larger critical question about what poetry does or can be expected to do in the early years of the twenty-first century: whether it looks forward or back, and whether it should.

What is more certain is that any attempt to characterize the postwar period in general will have to acknowledge all of these tendencies at once, taking occasionally discordant and often contentious critical discussions as historical symptoms in their own right. Where possible, this volume seeks to discern points of connection across competing camps, in order to isolate the larger critical concepts and basic cognitive equipment that organize the period at large. Similarly, it seeks to engage the broadest possible historical frame, noting the emergence of many pitches and tones that reverberate not only across the British archipelago but globally as well. Throughout the postwar period, it has become increasingly clear that poetry in English – even British and Irish poetry in English – arises from multiple tributaries and geographies, often originating well beyond the traditional centers of English literature. It is not possible, if it ever was, strictly to divide British poetry from Irish, or to separate either from the poetries of America and the former Empire, any more than it is possible to evade the differences. (It should be noted, too, though such traditions largely fall beyond the scope of this volume, that the British and Irish poetry of the era remains by no means exclusively Anglophone, that it exists vibrantly in the older languages of Ireland, Scotland, and Wales, as well as in more recent arrivals to a polyglot social order.) What is most important in the context of this companion is the fact that all of these histories quickly become part of the field they narrate from different points of view, indispensable components of the critical apparatus needed to read postwar poetry. It is thus more than mere millennial curiosity that requires a critical accounting of recent decades; such an accounting is also part of what the poetry of recent decades has done most compulsively. The contexts sketched here comprise a historical backdrop against which individual poems and the work of individual poets can be seen, to be sure. But they also constitute parts of a larger history of the period that poets have already begun to draft in real time, imagining pasts and futures still in formation.

Given the density of those pasts and the multiplicity of those futures, we have chosen to impose no single narrative arc on what follows. Instead, we have attempted to account for some of the movements, moments, and tendencies that have shaped postwar poetry across Britain and Ireland. Some chapters therefore concentrate on significant generations or chronological turning points, moments that either proposed or challenged significant orthodoxies. Others move geographically, considering sites and particular histories that have intersected or even redirected the larger course of recent work. Still others examine guiding concepts that have made themselves felt across larger sweeps of time and space, organizing or inflecting the work of more diverse groups of poets. We have sought to avoid segmenting the field too strictly, hoping instead that individual essays may recombine and reorder themselves in useful and even surprising ways. Canonical names like Eliot, Auden, Larkin, and Heaney have thus been left to recur in a variety of contexts, on the assumption that it is precisely their relevance within and across an array of frameworks that has guaranteed their lasting influence. But other names, often less familiar, have emerged regularly as well. Needless to say, the accounts offered and the suggestions made here are far from exhaustive, and much work of importance will remain untouched, even unmentioned, in these pages. For that reason, references to fuller accounts and suggestions for further reading have been included at the end of each essay, in the references, and in the accompanying chronology.

The volume's first three essays move chronologically, tracing the sequence of generations that forms the central line of the century's middle decades. Vincent Sherry's "Poetic Modernism and the Century's Wars" considers the two terms that shape the early years of the period most decisively: war and modernism. In retrospect, the pressure that gave rise to a modernist style in poetry seems inseparable from the larger tectonic forces that also produced the cataclysm of two world conflicts, ended European global hegemony, and unsettled the British Empire. Modernism, in this sense, was not merely a taste for aesthetic experimentation or an explosion of avant-garde energies, but also a cumulative response to a much larger set of social shifts, an ending as much as a beginning. Conceived as a kind of war poetry in its own right, in a war spanning several decades, modernism refracts the same underlying crisis that produced the war itself: the historical end of the progressive ideological certitude of Liberalism, with its attendant moral confidence in the structures of rationality. But in so doing, it also establishes the social and aesthetic terms with which succeeding decades will struggle, in an often desperate attempt to restore the breach.

Although resolutely skeptical of modernism's occasionally apocalyptic strains and suspicious of its larger historical claims, a younger group of English writers acknowledge such a rupture differently. Stephen Burt's "The Movement and the Mainstream" concentrates on the first major generation of poets to emerge after the war's end, tracking the development of the precisely ironic lyric mode with which "The Movement" claimed canonical centrality and established itself as the predominant voice of a shrinking English culture. Shaped by the new circumstances of the Cold War and a diminished postwar state, the poets grouped around Philip Larkin sought continuity where their modernist predecessors had found none, more reconciled to the loss of ideological certainties. In the process, Burt demonstrates, the Movement not only formulated a new consensus in reverse – defined by everything it is not – but also provided a polemical target against which every succeeding counter-movement in English poetry would react. Nigel Alderman's "Myth, History, and *The New Poetry*" traces the first such reaction, perhaps the most successful attempt to enact a workable compromise between modernism's mythical methods and the Movement's more orthodox meters. Alderman argues that the poets of the 1960s – figures like Ted Hughes, Geoffrey Hill, and Seamus Heaney – take myth as the ground of historiographical method, re-adapting poetry both to imagine and to control the contingencies of an altered political world. These three essays, then, follow the pendulum swings of reaction and counter-reaction that form so crucial a part of our current poetic vocabulary, delineating the most durable touchstones of later decades.

They also register an ongoing redefinition of the national social order. The slow collapse of that political consensus against which so many of the modernists strained, which the Movement wistfully sought to reclaim in diminished form, and which the poets of the 1960s attempted to reinvent as a new set of historical mythologies, left an abundance of poetic traditions rather than the vacuum that so many had feared: not one order but many possible ones. In large measure, the most striking tendency of recent years lies in a movement outward from the historical center and a perpetual rediscovery of heterogeneous poetic elements that a lost consensus had previously held in place. The next cluster of pieces accordingly turns from chronology to geography. Michael Thurston's "Region and Nation in Britain and Ireland" examines the re-emergence of national and regional modes at the traditional periphery of the United Kingdom, exploring the flourishing poetic cultures of Northern Ireland, Wales, Scotland, and the north of England. For Thurston, nationalist and regional desires reveal themselves as a series of "structures of feeling" that enable a complex variety of poetries, each committed to a previously marginal and subordinate tradition marked also by an inescapably ironic self-awareness. This oscillation between commitment and irony finds its correlative in wide-ranging topographies of places that must be continuously overwritten and renamed. John Waters' "Form and Identity in Northern Irish Poetry" builds on Thurston's account by concentrating on the remarkable but perhaps inevitably controversial renaissance of poetry in postwar Northern Ireland. Suspended for most of a century between the contrary national imperatives of Ireland and the British state, Northern Ireland has produced several generations of remarkable poetic work, at a prolific rate perhaps unmatched anywhere else in the English-speaking world, by poets both Protestant and Catholic, nationalist and unionist. It is here that poetry has most forcefully arisen as a privileged domain: where the informing categories, both aesthetic and political, of a broader culture can be considered and argued; where questions of identity can be either posed or evaded; and where, Waters argues, the question of identity itself becomes a central symptom of historical circumstances.

The seemingly entropic tendency of the British state toward a gradual dissolution or partial devolution at home is of course only the latest phase of a much longer trend, one that originates at a much greater distance. The logic that impels the cultural re-emergence of the smaller nations of the United Kingdom (including England itself) follows almost inexorably from the more systematic decolonization of the former British Empire. Jahan Ramazani's "Poetry and Decolonization" continues the emphasis on naming and renaming, exploring the ways in which postcolonial poetries reoccupy the space of the sublime to unleash an enormous catalog of names, languages, traditions, and temporalities previously occluded and suppressed by imperial control. But the centrality of nomenclature also joins newly independent states to a newly post-imperial British state, increasingly redefined by its former colonies as a multicultural and hybridized society. The meaning of such naming, Ramazani suggests, always relates to difference, to both the difficulty and the promise of a poetic subjectivity that fluctuates in the interstices between solidarity and alienation, between community and isolation.

The following two essays, by C. D. Blanton and Drew Milne, continue to resituate the idea of a national literature within a larger frame. Both show how the various canonical and anti-canonical claims and counter-claims (most clearly revealed by the various polemical anthologies that litter the period) are in fact mutually constitutive. Blanton's "Transatlantic Currents" focuses on the complex interrelations between the United States and Britain and on the inevitable political division of the English language and poetic tradition between them. Anglo-American poetry thus exists as a practice of translation within English, one that slowly shapes the work of poets constantly overhearing the charged static of American speech on global airwaves. Milne's "Neo-Modernism and Avant-Garde Orientations" argues that the possibilities of late modernism and contemporary avant-garde work in British and Irish poetry need to be understood not as paradigms or fixed categories, but rather as what Alan Sinfield (1992) calls "faultlines" that reveal the system of differences across schools, traditions, groups, genres, forms, poets, and poems. Rather than fracturing the poetic field, experimental poetic practices thus constitute a mode of orientation toward the whole.

The volume's final cluster of essays approaches the changes wrought by the postwar era through three of the most venerable *topoi* in English poetry: the lyric self, place, and religion. In "Contemporary British Women Poets and the Lyric Subject," Linda Kinnahan analyzes the reoccupation of the lyric "I" by groups to whom it has traditionally been denied, at least in the canons of high culture. Noting the ways in which the lyric and its attendant self have been reframed and refashioned by the representational strain of newly visible identities (constituted through gender, nation, race, ethnicity, and sexuality), Kinnahan explores the ability of the "I" to offer both cultural authority and the opportunity for social intervention. In "Place, Space, and Landscape," Eric Falci traces the obsessive return to the idea of place by poets seeking to unearth a deeper stratigraphy of sedimented historical and poetic counter-traditions. Falci links this spatial turn, with its twin excavatory and scopic drives, to a larger dialectical relation, one that paradoxically encrypts the global even within the sensory experience and reconstruction of the local. In "Poetry and Religion," Romana Huk argues that seemingly anachronistic questions

9

of theology have remained central to the poetry of the period, especially as it has wrestled ever more pointedly with the ethical questions raised by an increasingly various social world. By soliciting the otherness of the sacred and straining to maintain it as a function of language, she demonstrates, poets have recovered a religious logic that often survives religion as such, finding a means to represent difference in the capacity of religious thought to evade the snares of representation itself.

The last essay in the companion, Peter Middleton's "Institutions of Poetry in Postwar Britain," concludes by exploring the material contexts of poetic production – and the ways in which those contexts condition and alter the significance of a poem. In a crucial and defining historical shift, poems in the postwar period have been transmitted by a qualitatively different array of media (in performance, journals, books, small press pamphlets, anthologies, text books, or broadsheets; on radio, television, records, tapes, discs, or online, even on the tube). Middleton underlines what all of these essays stress: that larger historical claims need to emerge from attentiveness to the particularity of poetic form itself. Too frequently, surveys and assessments of postwar British and Irish poetry have repeated received opinion and perpetuated polemical categories; this companion seeks by contrast to demonstrate the fitful and often tense negotiations between old contents and new forms, old forms and new contents, that have arisen to gauge the historical pressures of the moment.

Chapter 1

Poetic Modernism and the Century's Wars

Vincent Sherry

I

Writing from an internment camp at Pisa in 1945, where he was imprisoned for treason to the United States government, Ezra Pound turned his attention to another, better time. In the Cantos he composed during this moment his mind shifted insistently from the indignities the sixty-year-old was suffering at Pisa to the promises the young adult had cultivated in London – from the end of World War II, that is, to the period just before the start of World War I. This was the beginning, these the sap years of the movement for which he had been designated, at least by himself, as leader and agent provocateur. His recollection of artists gathering before that earlier war in the Wiener Café in the British Museum district (Canto LXXX), for example, locates a center of reference for the energy he shared with his companion talents; here, in effect, was the vortex and origin-point for the extraordinary force field that would become literary modernism in English. This group included those British and Irish and American writers Pound knew by first (and nick-) names – Wyndham Lewis and T. S. Eliot, Ford Madox Ford and T. E. Hulme, William Butler Yeats and James Joyce. "[T]hese the companions," goes the invocation in the ritual memory of his first Pisan Canto (LXXIV), which is now, however, a wholly elegiac commemoration:

> Lordly men are to earth o'ergiven
>   these the companions:
> Fordie that wrote of giants
> And William who dreamed of nobility
>   and Jim the comedian singing . . .
> are to earth o'ergiven.
>
> (Pound 1998: 452–3)

As Pound turns this opening line by repetition into a refrain and lament, does he concede the fading of the movement as well as the passing of the protagonists? Recognizing this fact but also resisting its truth, Pound inscribes the powerful counter-rhythm of this moment in his life as a poet – and in the history of literary modernism.

Writing from a London now besieged in the aerial campaign of World War II, in the fourth of his *Four Quartets*, Eliot also gives himself over to retrospection on the earlier period. In the verse story of a night walk (drawing on his experience as a fire watcher), his character-in-voice encounters "a familiar compound ghost" – some imaginative amalgam of Yeats and Pound, a com*pound* indeed. This personage reviews the principles of a recognizably modernist program, representing its literary sensibility in mottoes like this:

> . . . our concern was speech, and speech impelled us
> To purify the dialect of the tribe.
>
> (Eliot 1991: 203–4)

Like Pound's, Eliot's memories are shadowed by feelings of mortality – as their generation ages, and "body and soul begin to fall asunder," the attribution of "the gifts reserved for age" features the indignity of "the cold friction of expiring sense" – but this meditation on human mutability moves to apprehensions that cut closer to the literary quick – to the core of a particularly, identifiably modernist poetics:

> Last season's fruit is eaten
> And the fullfed beast shall kick the empty pail.
> For last year's words belong to last year's language
> And next year's words await another voice . . .
>
> (Eliot 1991: 204)

If, in the special emphasis of its suffix, modern*ism* denotes not just a condition of chronological modernity but a self-consciousness about living in a specific time ("modern" derives from *hodie*, "today," so that modernism, in a radical but rooted sense, means *today-ism*), Eliot is grounding the verbal consciousness of modernism in its proper time. Yet one must observe in the formulations he poses that, in the tripartite division that includes Past and Future on either side, the central, crucial phase of the Present has gone missing. There is no word for Now – no mean absence in the literary history of modernism, as recorded by its now most venerable representative.

Eliot elaborates this absence in the second of the *Four Quartets*, in "East Coker" (1939). Here, in the opening year of World War II, he frames the period defined by the two wars as the interval of significance in his career – the years which, for the literary historian, comprise the long moment of modernism. In this characterization, however, it is a period without a speech:

> So here I am, in the middle way, having had twenty years—
> Twenty years largely wasted, the years of *l'entre deux guerres*—
> Trying to learn to use words, and every attempt
> Is a wholly new start, and a different kind of failure
> Because one has only learnt to get the better of words
> For the thing one no longer has to say, or the way in which
> One is no longer disposed to say it.
>
> (Eliot 1991: 188–9)

Dismissing the possibility of poems spoken out of their most immediate moment, settling for a poetics of retrospect and secondary intensity, Eliot is drafting a sort of ante-post-modernist program, for verse that is always already too late – one that decisively preempts the signal condition of a modern*ist* verse. The somewhat stylized humility in this self-deprecation, however, may be assigned to the not-too-reliable pieties of Eliot's later, adopted identity as Anglo-Catholic. And the need to make the disclaimer may itself serve to claim the relevance and validity of the issue being addressed. It is in its radical timeliness that modernist poetry will have found its word, its rhythm, its written signature and living speech – or not.

Pound also attests to this condition of the timely, as the establishing category of power and value in the poetics that matter, in his retrospect from Pisa on the London he shared with Eliot and others. In the extraordinarily moving Canto LXXXI, he is interrogating the excesses that have led him to his current state. "Pull down thy vanity, / I say pull down," goes this liturgy of self-recrimination, scorching in its intensities and apparently unforgiving in its reach: "Rathe to destroy, niggard in charity, / Pull down thy vanity, / I say pull down"

13

(Pound 1998: 541). But when he directs his questions to the energies he spent in the defining and identifying work of modernism, that is, to the task of making new poetry and making poetry new, of reviving the literary legacy in a present condition and idiom, well, this is different. "But to have done instead of not doing," he gestures to open this alternative consideration, suggesting through the antithetical conjunction that there is some better dimension to the energy he is questioning. "To have gathered from the air a live tradition," he proposes specifically, where this image of tradition as a wavelength energy living in the electric air of the moment identifies the mission specific to a recognizably modernist literature. And so the last, forgiving judgment comes: "This is not vanity" (1998: 541–2).

"To have done . . . *to have* gathered": the past perfect tense of the infinitive moves the action represented into a completed present, in effect, an already accomplished past. Here is Pound's version of Eliot's disclaimer: his poetics owned the moment, at least *in illo tempore*, even if that time is now gone. His version is tenser with the resistance that underscores the point that this category of the timely actually matters. And the two poets would also concur in specifying the period of the timely as the years comprised by the two World Wars – explicitly defined as such by Eliot, effectively framed by Pound as he speaks from the end of World War II of a time from before World War I as the interval of a now completed work.

Seeing the two poetic careers from these two respective points helps to mark the historical moment of modernist poetry, and it also suggests that the experience of war, in defining the times, also provides the historical content and timely import of their verse. Perhaps the most vivid and impending lesson any sentient imagination could draw from the events of the twentieth century at its mid-point was that war was no longer a particular or limited and finite event but a general, continuous condition of existence – a presentiment to be extended over much of the second half of the century in the experience of Cold War. The novelties introduced by World War I include most notably perhaps an impression of endless conflict – in mass war, which is also total war, the aim of military action has not to do with specific strategic goals, say, the acquisition of territory by a professional or mercenary army, but rather the gradual, protracted, seemingly interminable task of wearing out the enemy's capacity to make war: all resources of military and cultural and economic capital must be exhausted. (Think of the final days of World War II in Europe, where Germany maintained resistance to the last city block of Berlin, or in the Pacific, where an already decimated Japan held on until the apoc-alyptic horror of atomic bombing was *repeated*, that is, until total destruc-tion became redundant.) While a number of factors need to be considered in accounting for these conditions in twentieth-century warfare, the experiential truth of the circumstances is witnessed in the shorthand formulation of these poets. For Eliot, the historical experi-ence of the twentieth century, which provides the timely content (yes, it does) of his own verse, is defined as the continuum of the two major wars of the century. For Pound, looking back from Pisa in 1945 to the foregathering of London modernism in the cenacle of the Wiener Café, the century shapes as the significant instant beginning just before "the world was given over to wars . . . in those days (pre-1914)," that is, just before "that first so enormous war" (1998: 526, 521).

One way of understanding the experience as an ongoing war is to see the two conflicts in terms of repeated themes. Indeed, the same set of values and attitudes reappears – as an ever more heavily embat-tled protagonist. This protagonist may be cast, in the character of a single word, as Liberalism – the ideology that dominated the previ-ous century. Its master narrative of history offered a story that was plotted to the establishing value of Progress and paced to the cadence of rational gradualism. As a step-by-step process, where each phase is scaled in measurable advance from the last (*ratio*nality means first of all ratio, scale, measure), history was moving like a grand syllogism, as reasonably as a sequenced and progressive thought, to a conclu-sion that was always better, a conclusion that involved an ongoing improvement of human circumstance. Empirical reason designed the chief vehicle for this process as it worked in the sphere of material science, in technology. Here is the sensibility that would be discredited so heavily in the experience of war, and of history as war, in the twentieth century, when time arrives at its dystopic end. Scientific inven-tion and technological application have now resulted in the armaments of the two World Wars, those engines of destruction whose intensity and range would be unimaginable before 1914, or again, in the series of shocks that constitute the new history, before 1945, when the instruments of genocide are revealed as the intimate expression of the colossal atrocity of atomic war. The rationality of *Liberal*ism, where human reason *frees* the species increasingly through the measures of progressive thought, plays the part of an epic hero in a history that is no longer believable.

This process provides one framework for understanding the emo-tional range in Auden's elegy for Freud, who died at 80 in September

1939. Freud appears here as a late nineteenth-century Liberal rationalist. He has applied his science to the work of freeing the spirits of perfectible humankind; he has led the creaturely person out of "the night" (this darkness is both a residue of the species' biological past and the shadow of the moralist's false understanding) into and through "the bright circle of his recognition" to a better legacy, this improved and enlarged capacity:

> . . . he would have us remember most of all
> to be enthusiastic over the night,
>   not only for the sense of wonder
>   it alone has to offer, but also
>
> because it needs our love. With large sad eyes
> its delectable creatures look up and beg
>   us dumbly to follow:
>   they are exiles who long for the future
>
> that lies in our power, they too would rejoice
>   if allowed to serve enlightenment like him . . .
>   (Auden 1958: 169)

The "bright circle" of Freud's "enlightenment" depicts the same framework of values and attitudes that is passing into history, into this particular moment of history, so that, in this historically informed elegy, Auden's representation of Freud's principles in the present tense adds to the expressive pathos: the sadness of one man's passing is expanded, clarified, intensified as his death registers the failure of these ideals on a historical scale. And so, in the last stanza of the poem, the poet presents the prospect of a Europe fallen into the ruins of that high dream of millennial Reason:

> One rational voice is dumb. Over his grave
> the household of Impulse mourns one dearly loved:
>   sad is Eros, builder of cities,
>   and weeping anarchic Aphrodite.
>   (Auden 1958: 170)

The legacy of World War II appears in advance of the actual conflagration, since, in a real sense, what will be lost in the process of its conflicts has been undermined as a possibility already and beforehand in World War I. The future memory of a history that has already happened provides the imaginative tense of this finale.

If the public convulsions of Liberalism in the twentieth century extend from 1914 to 1945, this lengthened moment may be synchronized as the interval of modernism, which achieves its signal intensity as the expression of the climax and climacteric of that failing intellectual and political institution. Not that modernism is pro- or anti-Liberal. Rather, the energy that we represent under this heading of "modernism" finds the timeliest crisis of its period as the defining experience of living in its surcharged present, and so represents the extended trials of Liberalism as its intensifying condition. Whereas World War II can be taken as a confirmation of the worst possibilities already augured by World War I, there is not a secondhand but at least a preconceived or anticipated feeling even to the apocalyptic horrors of this latter day. It is in the modernist poetry of World War I that the watershed event of the new age, the shock of the modern in the twentieth century, is felt with an original energy and represented with an equivalent intensity. This is also the historical moment – roughly, 1914–1922 – in which the body of literary work that would constitute the canon of modernist poetry was composed, at least in England. Certainly, for many poets writing in Britain and Ireland in the second half of the century, it is the verse coming out of the years just before and after that Great War of 1914–1918 that defines the effective legacy of poetic modernism. This bibliography remains the literature of modernist record, I suggest, because the original, large-scale crisis of the mainstream values of nineteenth-century Liberalism provides its establishing circumstance. To restore its original context and timely voice is to recover some of the historical content and imaginative depth of this legacy for the rest of the century, and this necessary work of historical excavation may be undertaken first.

II

In August 1914, circumstances shaped the political situation in London as one of the liveliest sites in the global picture of this first World War. The governing party was racked at this moment by internal divisions. English Liberals had to maintain support for a war that, by precedent and convention, by partisan tradition and policy principle, they ought to have opposed. This contradiction, which undermined some of the major values of the Liberal party and so located a true watershed in the traditions of liberal modernity, provides the formative ground for the most important modernist verse of the occasion.

The lines of opposition in the 1914 crisis may be drawn from the major division within the Liberal party on the question of war, in general. To one side, the memory of the great Victorian Prime Minister W. E. Gladstone preserved the ethic and method of moral rationalism. This liberal tradition of public reason maintained that armed force required an informed act of logical conscience, a choice reasoned freely and in public and in accord with the loftiest moral values (see Rawls 1996 for the best representation of this salient value and its comprehensive practice in Western political tradition: especially xxiv, xxvi–xxviii, xxx, 47–59, 212–27). To the other side, Liberal imperialists proceeded under the operative standards of realpolitik. In this way of thinking, the British military served as an instrument of security: its power could be parleyed through agreements with other European nations. These alliances might require involvement in hostilities, but these engagements might hardly be appealed to the codes of Gladstonian probity – the imperialists tended to negotiate English interests within a frame of global reference that put practical or local advantage and commercial concerns first (see Hobhouse 1910: 104, 221). Since 1906, the most powerful positions within the majority government were held by Liberal imperialists – Prime Minister H. H. Asquith and his Foreign Secretary Sir Edward Grey – but the logic of foreign policy was still controlled in its public discussions by Gladstonian protocols. In this situation, Asquith and Grey needed to keep private their alliance building with France and Russia. Officially, they continued to deny the existence of these "secret agreements" (so dubbed by an already suspicious public), at least until early August 1914, when the network of European connections was activated (Morel 1916: 35–41, 273–300). At this moment, as Britain paused before the awful prospect of a Continental war, these rival traditions within Liberalism were evidenced in tensions that anticipated, in substantial detail, the major crisis this developing event would present to partisan – and national – life.

The Foreign Secretary's speech before Parliament on August 3 provided the loftiest expression of the Liberal rationale for war, arguing the moral cause of a righteous defense of France in view of the imminent German incursion into neutral Belgium (Grey 1914; 7–8). But other pressures – the commitments hidden in the "secret agreements" – were also coming to bear on the Liberal government. The tension between these rival frames of partisan reference is reflected in the editorial reports on Grey's address in the two leading Liberal dailies on August 4.

The *Manchester Guardian* holds true to the standard of reason at liberty, which, in this instance, the writer depicts as a compromised principle. This report protests that citizens and Parliament have not been given information sufficient to "form a reasoned judgment on the current of our policy." In Grey's conclusion that Britain must go to France's aid, even when Germany has vowed not to move on any undefended areas, the writer accurately intuits that the Secretary is being compelled by forces that exceed those of the moral rationale he has claimed. "His reasons are extraordinary," the editorial demurs. "Is it rational? Can it be deduced, we will not say from the terms of the Entente, but from the account of secret conversations which was given yesterday? Can it be reconciled with any reasonable view of British policy? It cannot" (*Manchester Guardian* 1914: 6).

The especially strenuous effort of "reconcil[ing]" these eventualities with a "reasonable view of British policy" may be evidenced in the language of the news leader in the *Westminster Gazette*, which offers this narrative – and argumentative – paraphrase of Grey's speech:

> Sir Edward Grey passed to the consideration of the present position of the French fleet in the Mediterranean which *evidently* sprang out of the plans for co-operation. The French fleet was in the Mediterranean *because of the feeling of confidence* between the two countries. *Hence it followed* that if a foreign fleet came down the channel we could not stand aside and see it attack the defenceless coast of France. *The House was brought to the conclusion* that we had a definite obligation to defend the coast of France from attack, and, generally speaking, it showed that it was prepared to support the government in taking action. France was *therefore* entitled to know and know at once that she could depend on British support. (*Westminster Gazette* 1914: 10 [emphases added])

Tellingly, this report of "The House and Sir Edward Grey's statement" bears the subtitle: "Logic of events." Complying entirely with Grey's own rationalistic stratagems, the report pays special attention to insert those conjunctions that establish cause and reasoned transition in the argument. This language of analytical and ethical reasoning, however, is obviously imposed on a resistant circumstance. The second-thought, secondhand, overlaid nature of this rhetoric of ethical reasoning is the one conclusion that may be safely drawn from this passage.

"Reason in all things" is a poetics, ethically addressed but aesthetically prepared, and the fact that it springs into service already and immediately reveals its established, well-endowed power. But if Anglo-American modernists write their English, as Hugh Kenner has

19

quipped, like a foreign language, handling it with the care of relative aliens, the outsider status that Pound and Eliot share in wartime London helps to account for their ability to reiterate the Liberal idiom, with a difference. It is the difference that takes the measure of that profound contradiction in the language of high partisan culture, which, all in all, witnesses the discrediting of the great tradition of moral rationalism within Liberalism. This dissonance provides as it were the tuning fork for the major modernist poetry of the moment.

III

Pound conducted a review of literary and political journalism in wartime Britain in "Studies in Contemporary Mentality," a twenty-part series published through 1917 in the *New Age*. An indomitable "reasonableness" appears as the dominant quality in this verbal culture but, in its service to the current war effort, this quality is under heavy stress. Pound pronounces this consolidating insight when he defines British political idiom through the exemplary standard of the leading literary weekly, the *New Statesman*:

> I knew that if I searched long enough I should come upon some clue to this mystery. *The magnetism of this stupendous vacuity! The sweet reasonableness, the measured tone, the really utter undeniability of so much that one might read in this paper!* . . .
> . . . The "New Statesman" is a prime exemplar of the species, leading the sheltered life behind a phalanx of immobile ideas; leading the sheltered thought behind a phalanx of immobile phrases. This sort of thing cannot fail. Such a mass of printed statements in every issue to which no "normal, right-minded" man could possibly take exception! (Pound 1917: 407 [emphases added])

A "reasonableness" that consists of "measured tone" only, and so coalesces into the merest feeling of rationality; a logic as hollow as it is polished in presentation, well-managed indeed in all its impressive "vacuity," its "stupendous" emptiness: these are the sounds of contemporary Liberalism at war, a linkage Pound clinches with the metaphors of mobilization and images of military formation. This sensibility stands exposed at the extremity of his ridicule in its vapid sagacity and absurd sententiousness. "That is really all there is to it," he summarizes, but tauntingly: "One might really learn to do it oneself" (1917: 407).

How might Pound do it himself? How to parley the rational inanities of official war discourse into new words, in verse? Pound's boast locates the main project and major dare of his emergent enterprise. But his mimic initiative proves a good deal more difficult – and so, potentially, more significant – than his vaunt might concede. The extent and strength of the majority power's ownership of the common language may be witnessed by the fact that to engage it substantially Pound had first to travel far outside the home domain, to imperial Rome, where the task of rendering ancient Latin poetry opens up the possibility of an alternate voice within his own literary English. This opportunity locates the motive for the otherwise idiosyncratic labor of *Homage to Sextus Propertius* (1919), the (highly) creative translation Pound undertook as his main poetic endeavor through the second half of the war (see Pound 1971: 90; also Carpenter 1988: 324).

This Roman poet was chosen also for reasons beyond Pound's imaginative interests in linguistic difference. In his *Elegiae*, Propertius presents himself as a poet desiring to write of love when conventional expectation pressures him to proclaim a martial-minded verse. A poet of this moment is supposed to celebrate the imperial aims and military campaigns of the Augustan dynasty. His crafty engagement with those rules shows his persona making his evident requests for permission to sing about "Cynthia" but addressing instead, more interestingly and slyly, quietly and indeed devastatingly, the attitudes and practices of an imperial poetics (see Sullivan 1964: 58–64, 75–6). The mock-heroic diction of his *Elegiae*, his parodic Virgilisms, the hollow triumphalism and empty finishes of those all too heavily labored martial cadences, which turn Augustan verse convention into august inanities: Propertius provides Pound a model for echoing the times against the times. This is a pattern the modern poet adapts to the syntax and vocabulary of his own political present.

The opening verse paragraph of Pound's poem recasts its Latin original in an extensive interpolation, which, in the guise of a poet's invocation of his Roman muse, acknowledges the deity reigning over the discourses of the current war:

> Out-weariers of Apollo will, as we know, continue their Martian
>   generalities,
> We have kept our erasers in order.
>
> (Pound 1990: 205)

Liberal divinity, god of logic as well as music and poetry, Apollo has been suborned to the work of current verse, worn out not by generals but by the "generalities" of war, by political abstraction, by ideological argument. How, Propertius-like, might Pound play along with and pull against this existing linguistic condition?

The verbal art special to *Propertius* features an interplay between an archly rationalist syntax and a wittily impenetrable vocabulary. On one side, the persona of the classics translator demonstrates a declarative knowiness about the *materia poetica*, here the site of ancient history and myth. Moving easily through this range of reference, Pound's speaker builds a progression of apparently factual statements as logical, common-sensible propositions of obvious knowledge. On the other side, however, Pound's reader frequently experiences allusions to chronicle legend and literary fable that are fetched from the depths of Mediterranean antiquity and featured, it seems, for their very unfathomability. Consider, in this representative catalog, the inter-action between the local knowiness of Pound's persona and the distant incomprehensibility of these citations, which, one by one, and with the help of a classics manual, might be identified, but which, as substantial parts of a single imaginative narrative, challenge almost any reader's grasp of what the story is, of what is actually going on here:

> For Orpheus tamed the wild beasts—
>   and held up the Threician river;
> And Cithaeron shook up the rocks by Thebes
>   and danced them into a bulwark at his pleasure,
> And you, O Polyphemus? Did harsh Galatea almost
> Turn to your dripping horses, because of a tune, under Aetna?
> We must look into the matter.
>
>   (Pound 1990: 206)

Who, most of us must ask, was Galatea? And how close did she get when she *almost* turned to the horses of Polyphemus? That specify-ing adverb is Pound's interpolation, whose blank space in the Latin original reveals the hollowness of his own (carefully) concocted know-ledgeability (Ruthven 1969: 89). There is a particularly *pseudo*logical quality to this tone, as indicated by another interpolated word, the first: "For." This conjunction establishes the expectation of cause-and-effect sequence, the impression that some logical proposition is in process. It builds some presentiment of common-sense meanings, one that Pound complements with those reassuring words of common speech. He steadily undercuts this promise, however, by enforcing the awareness that we do not know these mythological personages very well, if at all. "We must," the next interpolation goes, "look into the matter," but when we do we see through the easy loquacity, the familiarizing fiction of inserted words like these, and find reason-seemingness as the aim and intended effect.

Pound's new conceit echoes to the background sound of these times. It also opens in his own further work in a newly studious freedom of statement, a quasi-logical prosody, which helps him in the rhetorical work of negotiating an ever-burgeoning matter-of-documentary-fact in the Cantos. As a model of poetic innovation in the twentieth century, Pound's life-long project lives the initiatives of 1917 forward into the major literary history of the second half of the century. This longevity measures the pressure and intensity of those earlier working conditions. And these are the same conditions that are shared by his co-national and modernist accomplice.

IV

Eliot's arrival in London in early August 1914 (a fugitive of the European war, whose outbreak found him summering in Germany in anticipation of a year's study at Marburg) coincides with the beginning of an identifiably dry time in his poetic life. The heavy pressure being exerted on an imaginative language by the verbal culture of the political war may be taken to account in some part for this strained silence.[1] And it is revealing that the way out of this condition led through the same exercises Pound was conducting, concurrently, in his engagements with the other tongue of literary Latin. For Eliot, it is French.

Consider "Petit Epître," the first of the spring 1917 efforts:

> Ce n'est pas pour quo'on se dégoute
> Ou gout d'égout de mon Ego
> Qu'ai fait des vers de faits divers
> Qui sentent un peu trop la choucroute.
> Mais qu'est ce que j'ai fait, nom d'un nom,
> Pour faire ressortir les chacals?
>
> (Eliot 1996: 86)

---

[1] Eliot's antipathy to the premises and methods of modern Liberalism, the majority power in literary and political London in 1914, may be thought of as one source of his shutting down poetically when he arrives in Britain in August 1914. His complex interaction with the cultural infrastructures of Liberalism, and the strongly negative attitude he expresses toward the premises of pan-European liberalism, are surveyed by Sherry (2003: especially 157, 162–3, 171, 351 n.13).

Eliot encloses echoes of whole words within others – "gout" in "dégoute," "d'égout," – and reiterates similar phonetic formations across differing phrases – "fait des vers" in "faits divers" – to emphasize and consolidate the material sound of these words. He arranges the physical body of the language, however, inside a highly elaborate apparatus of syntactical ratiocination – that very French array of rhetorical negatives, antithetical conjunctions, subordinate and relative clauses. The discriminating thinking that this rationalistic syntax fosters in standard French, however, has turned into a sheer mouthful of Gallic bread and cheese. And the sauerkraut – "choucroute" – to which Eliot's speaker refers worriedly gestures toward the local prompt for this new conceit of reason-seeming nonsense in the civilian culture of the war, which proscribed this stereotypically German food and overwrote his own poetic response – until now. The freeing effect of writing in French does not represent escape but, like humor, works through a sort of transforming exaggeration, which amplifies the bizarre capacities that the language of the English political moment is demonstrating. Here a native sense has become a stranger indeed to its own verbal reason. Eliot's poetic language reads as English, just in French.

This initiative extends into English literary idiom for Eliot in a poetic form for which his French interlude has also refreshed his attention: the quatrain stanza, modeled for him (as for Pound) by Théophile Gautier. In late spring 1917, Eliot composed at least five poems in this new measure (Eliot 1988: 178). This rush of productivity displays the release of energies pent up for several years, but it also registers the stimulus of his discovering a shape most particularly cadenced to the instigations of the current political day. Within its tightly maintained structure of alternately rhyming lines, a regimen that translates into a stiffly disciplined metric, Eliot's quatrain stanza develops a rationalistic syntax and semi-discursive vocabulary to convey an impression of well-regulated thought that dissolves constantly, however, into preposterousness. It is a rhythm that quickens to presentiments that have been forming in his verbal imagination over several years of this ongoing war.

The familiar instances of this literary wit include the rationalistic opacities of "Mr. Eliot's Sunday Morning Service." Incorporating Pound's revisions, the liturgy opens thus:

> Polyphiloprogenetive
> The sapient sutlers of the Lord

> Drift across the window-panes.
> In the beginning was the Word.
>
> In the beginning was the Word.
> Superfetation of τὸ ἕν,
> And at the mensual turn of time
> Produced enervate Origen.
> (Eliot 1996: 377)

As Huck Finn remarked, in escaping a similar verbal service, "The statements was interesting, but tough" – and toughened here by the archly declarative, apparently reasonable syntax, which consorts and contrasts magnificently with the wholly fugitive sense of the Latin and Greek formations. This logically pompous nonsense carries the deeper meaning of the discourses it has raised into this heckling echo.

This historical origin may be recovered through the archaeology of one of Eliot's earliest efforts in the quatrain prosody. Not a very good poem at all, "Airs of Palestine, No. 2" offers nonetheless direct evidence of the incentive this new quatrain measure takes from current political lingo. It takes as its target and point of critical mimicry Sir John Spender, editor of the Liberal *Westminster Gazette*. "God from a Cloud to Spender spoke," the poem opens joco-seriously,

> And breathed command: "Take thou this Rod,
> And smite therewith the living Rock";
> And Spender hearkened unto God. . . .
>
> And such as have the skill to swim
> Attain at length the farther shore
> Cleansed and rejoiced in every limb,
> And hate the Germans more and more.
>
> They are redeemed from heresies
> And all their frowardness forget;
> And scales are fallen from their eyes
> Thanks to the Westminster Gazette.
> (Eliot 1996: 84–5)

Where scriptural references and religious diction mingle with the rhythm of a barracks-room ballad, the odd tonality serves at once to replicate and characterize the moral rationales for the war, that doggerel logic, which Spender's paper and its partisan likes have tirelessly offered. This tone also offers a rough-but-ready replica of the mock-sententiousness and pseudo-reasonableness that the later, more polished quatrains will smooth out.

The conceit of Eliot's quatrain art finds its signature piece in "Sweeney among the Nightingales," the poem whose dramatic location lies in a seedy London bistro of the war years. In keeping with the counter-rhythm of his new poetics, the stanzas work equally to invite and defy an impression of consistent significance, a promise at once centered and compromised in the figure of Sweeney himself.

The "zebra stripes along his jaw" reflect the creases cut into the fat of Sweeney's neck by the stiff collar of the dress uniform worn by military personnel in the Great War – Sweeney is the soldier, returned to London from the front. Just so, the poem opens onto another level of potential significance, which its imaginative apparatus makes every effort of rhetoric and gesture to claim. The majestic cadenza of the final quatrains –

> The host with someone indistinct
> Converses at the door apart,
> The nightingales are singing near
> The convent of the Sacred Heart,
>
> And sang within the bloody wood
> When Agamemnon cried aloud
> And let their liquid siftings fall
> To stain the stiff dishonoured shroud
> (1996: 380–1)

– includes, in the reference to Agamemnon, a closural event Eliot has prepared in advance by the epigraph, which spells out (in Greek) the death-cry of the tragic protagonist in Aeschylus's *Agamemnon*. The heroic soldier returning from the Trojan War has been stabbed by his scheming wife Clytemnestra – a feminine menace Eliot also reflects in his poem in the threat these various "nightingales" (the word, in French, is slang for prostitutes) present to the male protagonist. Could Agamemnon really be the heroic prototype of Sweeney?[2] The modern soldier's "apeneck" might equip him with a gift for simian mimicry, but it hardly enables him to resemble the Hellenic hero credibly.

---

[2] The late addition of the Greek epigraph – it is not included in the penultimate draft of the poem – suggests that the heroic parallel comes to Eliot as a second thought, which he includes to complicate the hermeneutic of Sweeney; see the summary of the manuscript evidence by Ricks (Eliot 1996: 381).

Why devise this parallel *manqué*? The meaning of Eliot's framing action may lie not in the content it organizes but in the gesture it represents – specifically, in the empty gesture it presents, where the epigraph and last stanza join to promise a formal logic that is not embodied in the poem's content, its central mise-en-scène. This absence is amplified through the rhythm particular to the quatrain, which appears driven, inexorably as ever, but by a premise as contradictory as Sweeney's claim to heroic fame. It is an imaginative rationale as blank as the logic of the policy that sent Sweeney and his likes to war to begin with.

The formal conclusion to hostilities, the "peace" treaty signed at Versailles in July 1919, provides the occasion – circumstantial as well as imagined – for Eliot's richest poetic deliberation on the war. "Gerontion" takes shape through July 1919, and the poem makes several references to these contemporary events (Eliot 1988: 312).

Eliot's speaker represents the substance of his monologue-disquisition in its conclusion as "small deliberations" – *small*, presumably, because *Gerontion* means, specifically, a *little* old man. Where he expands these "small deliberations," in his mind's eye, to "multiply variety / In a wilderness of mirrors" (Eliot 1996: 350–1), however, the poet is conveying a larger circumstance as the framing occasion of the poem's event. He is imaging the scene in which the "deliberations" of (supposedly) "great men" have recently taken place – in the Great Hall of Mirrors of the Trianon Palace at Versailles. If the "wilderness of *mirrors*" secures this allusion, an irony special to the history being inscribed at Versailles lies in that otherwise unlikely figure of "*wilderness.*" This royal estate stood originally as a monument to Enlightenment *civilization* – its reflecting halls and formal gardens mapped a scheme of metered and reasoned degree to the rationalist plan of the universe. The emblematic edifice of this first Age of Reason is overshadowed now by the consummation of the second, in the rituals of savage, retributive justice just conducted at Versailles. Reason in All Things is the sensibility under whose signature the war will have been authorized and prosecuted in Eliot's England, too, and he puts this specifically English sensibility on the rhetorical line in the poem's character-in-voice.

Eliot's aged speaker belongs to the senescence of contemporary British Liberalism, a generation that has authored in words a war its old men have not fought in body. Making this admission in the opening lines, Gerontion complements it with an expressively mangled syntax and grammar:

> I was neither at the hot gates
> Nor fought in the warm rain
> Nor knee deep in the salt marsh, heaving a cutlass,
> Bitten by flies, fought.
>
> (Eliot 1996: 349)

The clausal construction projects the progressive discriminations of verbal reason – "neither / Nor / Nor" – as its stipulative spirit, its motivating action, but the ambitious plan of a thrice suspended period turns into the wreckage its phrasal sequence actually makes of it. Behind this verbal rite, so badly performed (but well rehearsed), echoes the wreckage of the policy logic Liberals like this authored to prosecute the war.

Eliot extends the sensibility of his speaking character to its revealing extreme in the central meditation on "History." "Think now," his speaker proposes to open this deliberation, and repeats the injunction several times, several ways:

> Think now
> [History] gives when our attention is distracted,
> And what she gives, gives with such supple confusions
> That the giving famishes the craving. . . .
>
> Think
> Neither fear nor courage saves us. Unnatural vices
> Are fathered by our heroism. Virtues
> Are forced upon us by our impudent crimes . . .
>
> Think at last
> We have not reached conclusion, when I
> Stiffen in a rented house. Think at last
>   I have not made this show purposelessly . . .
>
> (Eliot 1996: 350)

Verging compulsively on some deliberated significance – "Think now," "Think now," "Think neither," "Think at last," "Think at last" – the speaker proceeds to a "conclusion," however, which is "not reached." The logic is promissory at best, really only hortative. Eliot seizes this conceit of meaning-seemingness as a poetics, as witnessed especially near the end of the main passage, where he turns the words of progressive and logical proposition into a composite of contradictions. How is it, after all, that an "*unnatural* vice" can be biologically "*fathered*," and a vile unreal thing begotten from a natural good? Whose "impudent *crimes*" are capable of generating "*virtues*"? The speaker talks through these disparities with every pretence of reasonable and coherent meaning. The inverse ratio and particular power of this verse show in its capacity to outsize its own rationalist measures, reaching down through the sense it feigns to the illogic it really means, where the emotion that is released grows in ratio to its overwhelming of an older Reason. This complex effect is the meaning recent "History" has revealed to the critical imagination of the modernist, who, like Pound, distinguishes his art by the special faculty he manifests for tapping this awareness and providing the extraordinary moment of history the answering echo of a new imaginative language.

Coda

The poem most closely associated with the cultural experience of the modernist war is surely Eliot's *The Waste Land* (1922). The mood of exhaustion in this work is usually attributed to the conditions of post-war ennui, but this emotional affect may not in every respect derive from the actual lived experience that the poem represents. In fact, a number of lines and images in the poem antedate the Great War, reaching back to Eliot's years as a doctoral student at Harvard (an archaeology of the working drafts of the sequence, provisionally titled "He Do the Police in Different Voices," shows the considerable proportion of this earlier material and suggests that the completed work turns on several conceits of imaginative feeling that are at least a decade old). What may account for the poem's assignably postwar location, its identifiably contemporary stress, its most notably modernist accent, is perhaps its legendary fragmentariness, its splendidly expressive discontinuity. This quality of fragmentariness was not a sharply marked feature in much of the material Eliot drafted into the initial sequence, but it was assisted considerably in 1921 through the editorial interventions of Pound (Eliot 1971: *passim*). A "break" with the past is of course the establishing condition of the special present of modernism, of its radical Now, and the section-by-section, even line-by-line experience of discontinuity in *The Waste Land* can be taken as the signature expression of this founding circumstance – close equivalent of the immense watershed that the war itself defined.

Allowing for the mild irony that this hallmark work of poetic modernism infers rather than contains the determining event of the Great War, Eliot's sequence has assumed that place in literary history. And so it is fitting to follow its legacy as a testamentary witness of that historical instigation: "I think the day by day in the Waste Land, the sudden violences and long stillnesses, the sharp contours and unformed voids of that mysterious existence, profoundly affected the imaginations of those who suffered it. It was a place of enchantment. It is perhaps best described in Malory, book iv, chapter 15 – that landscape spoke 'with a grimly voice'" (Jones 1937/1963: x–xi).[3] So David Jones invokes the landscape he witnessed on the Western Front, where he served as an infantryman in the Royal Welch Fusiliers from 1915 to 1918. Here, in the Preface to his book-length poem *In Parenthesis* (1937), he turns the terrain of his combat experience into a rich crypt of literary history, using Eliot's poem as a touchstone for the poetic traditions that inform *The Waste Land* and provide the affective register for his own representations of the war.

It is not surprising, then, to find in Jones's poem a kind of history-in-miniature of the literary modernism that was put into exemplary practice in *The Waste Land*. The strategies and attitudes of that now accomplished literary tradition – discontinuous or episodic narratives, verbal textures that mix idiomatic concision with dense allusive references, a cast of dramatic characters-in-voice that matches the range of speakers in Eliot's vocal collage – do exemplary service in Jones's representation of his experience. Most particularly, Jones's poem (really a verse-with-prose experiment, an initiative this painter-writer could indulge in some part because his education in art school spared him the restrictions of the standard literary curriculum) turns a good deal of its imaginative action around this typically modernist challenge of "making it new." Most obviously, he adapts Joyce's hallmark instance of the technique Eliot named "the mythical method" (Eliot 1975: 178). For each of his narrative's seven parts he provides an epigraph from the early medieval Welsh bardic epic *Y Goddodin*. The older poet's account of the mustering, march, preparation, and consummation of the Battle of Catraeth, fought between local Britons (under the leadership of a figure who is the conjectured original of the legendary Arthur) and invading Saxons, affords one of the available analogues for this modern Welsh regiment meeting the new German army in 1916. These technical incentives join a great depth of legendary memory to the felt intensities of Jones's lived experience in the war.

[3]   The introductory note by Eliot to the 1963 edition, recalling his major part in soliciting the work for publication by Faber in 1937, supplies context and literary history for the continuities he perceives between Jones's work and his own as well as Pound's and Joyce's.

This technical regimen generates an imaginative record that represents the marking event of cultural modernism in one consummate instance of modernist prosodies.

In the last sentence of his Preface, Jones offers an explanation for the title of his book:

> This writing is called "In Parenthesis" because I have written it in a kind of space between – I don't know between quite what – but as you turn aside to do something; and because for us amateur soldiers (and especially for the writer, who was not only amateur, but grotesquely incompetent, a knocker-over of piles, a parade's despair) the war itself was a parenthesis – how glad we thought we were to step outside its brackets at the end of '18 – and also because our curious type of existence here is altogether in parenthesis. (1937/1963: xv)

The omen encoded here is glossed best perhaps by the dates Jones inscribes just below this last sentence: "1st March 1937." No great prescience was necessary at this moment to feel the next war coming. The image of the parenthetical bracket thus situates the composition of the book already but certainly in an interwar period. This figure encloses the same moment of historical experience, and it defines the same feeling about historical time, that we have seen on the far side of that second war, in the formulations of Eliot and Pound. Indeed, Jones is suggesting that the time of the modern – here modernist – century is defined by repeated, in effect, ongoing war. These are the conditions of a literary sensibility that takes the fracture of existing codes as provocation, and the challenge to precedent ideologies as warrant, for the inventions that would be preserved through the rest of the century as the record and legacy of the most important – newest, most timely – poetry of modern experience.

Further Reading

Hobhouse, L. T. (1910). *Liberalism*. London: Williams & Norgate.
Morel, E. D. (1916). *Truth and the War*. London: National Labour Press.
Rawls, John (1996). *Political Liberalism*. New York: Columbia University Press.
Richards, I. A. (1926). *Science and Poetry*. New York: Norton.
Sherry, Vincent (2003). *The Great War and the Language of Modernism*. New York: Oxford University Press.

Chapter 2

The Movement and the Mainstream

Stephen Burt

Who were the true "Poets of the Fifties"? In an article of that title
in the August 27, 1954 *Spectator*, assistant literary editor Anthony
Hartley declared that he had found them. Thom Gunn's *Fighting
Terms*, George MacBeth's *A Form of Words*, and an untitled pamphlet
by Donald Davie (all from Oxfordshire's Fantasy Press) displayed,
Hartley, wrote, "common influences and circumstances," evidence
of "a not too vague *zeitgeist*" (Hartley 1954: 260). He found that
zeitgeist in their tone: " 'non-conformist, cool, scientific and analytical,"
"critical and destructive of myth," "egalitarian and anti-aristocratic,"
"opposed to fashion in the metropolitan sense of this word," "the poetic
equivalent of liberal, dissenting England" (Hartley 1954: 260). In the
October 1, 1954 *Spectator*, J. D. Scott expanded on Hartley's claims,
detecting a trend in Gunn's and Davie's verse, and in first novels by
Kingsley Amis, John Wain, and Iris Murdoch: for lack of a better
name, he called it the Movement. "The Movement, as well as being
anti-phony, is anti-wet: sceptical, robust, ironic, prepared to be as
comfortable as possible in a wicked, commercial, threatened world"
(Scott 1954: 400).

In poetry, at least, the label endured. In 1956 Robert Conquest assembled an anthology called *New Lines*, including poems by Amis, Davie,
Gunn, Wain, and Conquest himself, as well as by D. J. Enright, John
Holloway, Elizabeth Jennings, and Philip Larkin. "*New Lines* represents,"
as Robert Hewison writes, "the moment of the Movement" (Hewison
1981: 99). All these poets attended either Oxford (Amis, Holloway,

Jennings, Larkin, Wain) or Cambridge (Gunn, Davie, Enright) during the 1940s. Their early works appeared from a variety of small presses, among them Fortune, Marvell, and especially Fantasy, whose pamphlet series began in 1952 (Bradley 1993: 88). Eric Homberger notes that the Fantasy pamphlets owed their contents in part to the tastes of American graduate students at Oxford, among them Donald Hall and the young Adrienne Rich (Homberger 1977: 94–5). Most of the poets had spoken on John Wain's BBC Third Programme radio series "First Reading" during 1953; all but Gunn had already appeared in Enright's *Poets of the 1950s* (1955), printed in Japan and much less widely circulated, but likely an influence on Conquest's choice.

From 1956 on, the term "The Movement" would describe Conquest's assembly of English poets (some of whom were novelists and critics as well), or else the aesthetic they supposedly shared. Despite their "considerable agreement and interaction," most of them denied that they shared very much: "we ridiculed and depreciated 'the Movement,'" Davie recalled, "even as we kept it going" (Morrison 1980: 6; Hewison 1981: 125). Larkin said that "the only other writer I felt I had much in common with was Kingsley Amis" (Larkin 2001: 20). "The Movement didn't exist," Gunn later averred, adding, "what we had in common was a period style" (Gunn 1993: 219). Hartley, Scott, Enright, and Conquest had indeed identified a period style, a phase in the history of English (not necessarily British) poetry: their term both described a moment in cultural history, and launched several original poets' careers. The Movement as a set of poets, of poems, or of ideas, has been described, attacked, belittled, and occasionally admired ever since.

*   *   *

New Lines presented poets who prized clarity and technical facility, and who in some ways aimed low: they evidenced, Conquest wrote in his polemical introduction, "refusal to abandon a rational structure and comprehensible language" (Conquest 1956: xv). Neil Corcoran calls the Movement "characteristically empiricist, wry, discursive-argumentative, emotionally restrained, much given to aphorism, marked by the use of reader-aware asides" (Corcoran 1993: 82). Conquest's selection from Larkin began with "Maiden Name," whose first stanza reads, in part, "Marrying left your maiden name disused. / Its five light sounds no longer mean your face, / . . . you cannot be / Semantically the same as that young beauty" (Conquest 1956: 19). The focus on

33

the lost past is in part Larkin's own, but the logic of argument, the attention to widely shared experiences, and the unambiguous (but intricate) syntax exemplify shared goals; Movement poets in general stood for formal deftness, and "common sense."

It was easier, often, to say what they stood against. Hartley called Davie's and Gunn's poetics "a reaction to the loose romanticism current during the war years" (Hartley 1954: 261). Gary Day writes that "Movement poetry was a reaction to . . . modernism and to the visions, mangled syntax and runaway rhetoric of 1940s verse," as exemplified by the so-called New Apocalypse of Vernon Watkins, Henry Treece, and Dylan Thomas; Blake Morrison finds "antipathy toward Thomas" (whom Amis called "a pernicious figure") throughout Movement prose (Morrison 1980: 146; Amis 1991: 132; Day & Docherty 1997: 1). "What poets like Larkin, Davie, Elizabeth Jennings and I had in common," Gunn remembered, "was that we were deliberately eschewing Modernism" (Gunn 1982: 174). Modernism – understood narrowly as the techniques brought into English-language poetry by Eliot, Pound, and the later Yeats – viewed poetry as individual, writerly expression, thus allowing writers to disregard their readers, whom Movement poets instead kept always in mind. "[U]p to this century," Larkin contended, "literature used language in the way we all use it," just as "painting represented what anyone with normal vision sees"; "'modernism' in the arts consisted of doing the opposite" (Larkin 1982: 72).

The intellectual program of anti-modernism and anti-Romanticism had emotional implications as well as intellectual ones: the poems praised and tried to embody a plainspoken determination to see things exactly as they are. Conquest's "Classical Poets," in his poem by that name, "could energize only by angers / Their clear illustrations of aspects of truth which were well / Understood" (Conquest 1955: 32). When struck by their own Romantic or vatic "urges,"

> With descriptions of reason or nymphs or military glory
> They corrected the impulse. And, for the whole of their lives,
> Like the mermaid on land in the Hans Andersen story
> Pretending to notice nothing, they walked upon knives.
> (Conquest 1955: 32)

Movement poets' self-reproach, their restrictions *on* emotion, became in their best poems a subject, self-restriction *as* emotion: this topic suited, in different ways, Davie's and Conquest's insistence on ethical clarity,

Jennings' tentative understatements, Gunn's early muscular existentialism, and Larkin's self-diminishments and regrets. "In metrical verse," Gunn wrote, "it is the nature of the control being exercised that becomes part of the life being spoken about" (Gunn 1982: 179); though intended more broadly, his claim surely fits Movement verse.

Movement attitudes had political meanings too. We can see the Movement as a postwar, or Cold War, formation: Corcoran adds that, "syntax, measure and a logic of statement were, in the Movement poem, almost an act of post-war reconstruction" (Corcoran 1993: 83). "If one had briefly to distinguish this poetry of the fifties from its predecessors," Conquest wrote in introducing *New Lines*, "the most important general point would be that it submits to no great systems of theoretical constructs nor agglomerations of unconscious commands" (xiv–xv). In other words, none of the poets put much faith in psychoanalysis, none saw visions, and none were doctrinaire Marxists: most expressed a chastened postwar skepticism about grand visions in literature as outside it.

Amis and others later became men of the Right. Conquest's journalism and historical research did much to expose Stalin's crimes; his first three books on the topic appeared in 1960, *The Great Terror* (still the best-known) in 1968. Amis described his own early-1960s conversion from Labour to Tory, and his opposition to the mid-1960s expansion of higher education, in several essays, among them "Why Lucky Jim Turned Right" (1967). Always a grumpy reactionary in his politics, Larkin became more outspokenly so in the 1960s. All three poets supported American involvement in the Vietnam War. Viewing the 1950s through the lens of the 1960s, hostile critics such as Andrew Duncan understandably view the Movement as a Tory attack on all things ambitious or new.

It makes more sense, however, to see the Movement in its own time, in the context of an internationally salient liberal anti-communist empiricism, a postwar suspicion that ambitious programs for the rapid transformation of anything – whether a text, a state, or a single human being – do more harm than good. Davie later saw it in just that way, arguing that "the scientific humanism to which [T. H.] Huxley and [Thomas] Hardy gave their allegiance survive[d] as a working ethic" for literary writers after "the Second World War . . . discredited the reactionary or religious alternatives" (Davie 1972: 5). Anti-Romanticism, empiricism, and postwar caution were thus of a piece. Amis's "Against Romanticism" warned readers not to seek "grand meaning," nor to "discard real time and place" (Conquest 1956: 67); Davie's poem

"Rejoinder to a Critic" linked strong feeling in literature to mass casualties, as if modernism or Romanticism had provoked the decision to drop the A-bomb: "How dare we now be anything but numb!" (Conquest 1956: 45). Davie described his own later critical work as "making the case for the political Centre" (Davie 1973: 56).

The Movement also reflects demographic changes in postwar Britain: its poets, and many of its readers, were the sons and daughters (mostly sons) of the middle classes, who received the elite education their parents had not, but had no particular use for elite tastes. This view links the poets to the Angry Young Men, novelists and dramatists who took their subjects from Northern or working-class life, and their nickname from John Osborne's 1956 play *Look Back in Anger*. Robert Hewison contends that the Movement's "poetic revolt can be treated as a dress rehearsal" for "the better-known *coup d'état* in theatre," since in both cases a "Mandarin [i.e. elite] tradition was challenged by a group of younger writers who were the first to benefit from the post-war Welfare State" (Hewison 1981: 85). Amis's widely lauded first novel, *Lucky Jim* (1954), placed him among the Angry Young Men himself.

This anti-Mandarin feeling could produce a defensive insularity. Amis's narrator in *I Like It Here* (1958) "fancied that he had a long history of lower-middle-class envy"; his wife "accused him . . . of pretending to like beer because he thought it was working-class, British, lower-middle-class, Welsh, anti-foreign, anti-upper-class, anti-London, anti-intellectual" (Amis 1958: 23, 79). "You have decided for your part," Davie wrote in a poem addressed to Amis, "That poems on foreign cities and their art / Are the privileged classes' shorthand' (Davie 1990: 65). Larkin when young translated Baudelaire, but boasted later that he ignored the Continent: "Foreign poetry? No!" (Larkin 2001: 25, 2002: 246). Davie, Jennings, and Conquest, however, wrote travel poems on European subjects; Enright's verse and fiction described locales farther afield, such as Japan and Egypt (and, later, Singapore), in whose universities he taught.

"Members of the Movement," Hewison writes, shared "an interest in art forms without any appeal to Mandarin taste" (Hewison 1981: 114). Larkin and Amis met at Oxford through their shared collector's interest in jazz; during the 1960s Larkin penned a jazz column for the conservative *Daily Telegraph*, collecting his pieces later as *All What Jazz*. Gunn's most famous (and some of his best) 1950s poems described leather-clad motorcyclists; one praised Elvis Presley. Conquest and Amis edited the *Spectrum* series of science fiction anthologies; Conquest's novel

A World of Difference (1956) "featured a verse-writing computer, with profuse specimens given, and of course a 'Poet' class of space cruisers that included the *Jennings, Larkin, Enright, Amis, Gunn* and *Holloway*" (Amis 1991: 146). The Movement men also shared less savory tastes: Amis remembered that "all" his early 1950s acquaintances "were . . . devotee[s] of girlie mags," and Robert Conquest "led the field" (Amis 1991: 145). The young Larkin made serious study of girls' school fiction, and wrote (partly pornographic) school fiction himself (published posthumously in 2002 as *Trouble at Willow Gables*).

Critics have seen these shared interests, not wrongly, as evidence of a "provincial lower-middle-class" revolt against self-conscious sophistication – a revolt sometimes indistinguishable from the Philistine (Morrison 1980: 178). Jazz and science fiction were also (then more than now) adolescent tastes: some Movement writers preferred the unpretentious immediacy of these entertainments to whatever the culture had on offer for grown-ups. In one of Larkin's early poems "interest passes / Always towards the young and more insistent"; in another, "Smiles are for youth" (Larkin 1988: 22, 194). A resistance to adulthood links Larkin's jazz collecting not only to Amis's and Conquest's science-fiction fandom but also to Gunn's interest in bikers, young toughs, and rock and roll.

The Movement in retrospect seems defined by what it resisted or attacked: Communism, modernism, Romanticism, mysticism, elitism, maturity. Robert Conquest wrote later that the poets shared "no more than a wish to avoid certain bad principles" (Conquest 1982: 33). It may be objected that the Movement writers, as a group, saw no distinctive value in poetry as such: Davie would ask whether "Hardy's engaging modesty and his decent liberalism represent a crucial selling short of the poetic vocation, for himself and his successors" (Davie 1972: 40). "The Wondering Scholar" in Enright's poem by that name nearly stops writing: "It was the emotions of people that surprised him vastly, not of poets— / Those were his task at school, these were a job for life. / His poems grew shorter and shorter" (Conquest 1956: 63).

And yet these poets had common admirations, even attempted to construct a common project: they imagined a community which linked present-day poets to present-day readers and to poets long dead, a continuity of verbal enterprise in which no one could start from scratch, and no one would want to. Larkin sometimes described "an underground tradition" of English non-modernist verse, running through Thomas Hardy and Wilfred Owen to John Betjeman, "then nobody really"; he tried to limn that tradition, with mixed success, as editor of the controversial *Oxford Book of Twentieth-Century English Verse* (1972) (Larkin 2001: 29, 26). Another model was Auden, whose 1930s poetry the earliest writings of Larkin and Amis imitate. Larkin would praise the early, and deprecate the later, Auden, in his 1960 essay "What's Become of Wystan?"; Davie offered measured praise for the so-called Auden generation in his poem "Remembering the Thirties" (Conquest 1956: 70; Larkin 1982: 123).

Movement poets aimed for a level, civil, unpretentiously amicable, if sometimes stern, speech, setting the poets beside (rather than above) imagined readers. Despite their "anti-academic impulse," Morrison argues that Movement poems – so conscious of their own goals, and of an English tradition – "derive from, and cater for, an academic elite" (Morrison 1980: 129, 117). One might connect the Movement writers' desire to reach an audience to the actual diminishment, as measured by sales figures, of that audience: Homberger notes that the readership for serious literature of all kinds declined sharply in England during the 1950s, as austerity receded and citizens could afford other pleasures (such as the movies). He adds that perhaps in consequence, the "predominant note" in 1950s English poetry "is one of sadness and nostalgia, a positively hangdog tone of regret at a dimly perceived alteration in the social base of art itself" (Homberger 1977: 70).

* * *

The clearest drive toward communication, entertainment, even verse journalism, among these poets comes in the verse (and prose) of Kingsley Amis. Amis's unpublished Oxford thesis of 1948 considered Victorian poets and their imagined readers: Paul Fussell writes that Amis even then regarded all literature as "a responsible social transaction with readers" (Fussell 1994: 28). He imagines readers very much like him: well read but suspicious of sophistication, more or less "hearty," hard to fool, English, and male. Perhaps Amis's best-known poem, "A Bookshop Idyll" (called, in *New Lines*, "Something Nasty in the Bookshop") presents him both as literary critic and as sociable cynic. The poem asks:

> Should poets bicycle-pump the human heart
>   Or squash it flat?
> Man's love is of man's life a thing apart;
>   Girls aren't like that.
>
> (Amis 1980: 56)

Amis becomes less flip by the end of the poem, concluding first that "Women are really much nicer than men," and then resolving to "forget those times / We sat up half the night / Chockfull of love, crammed with bright thoughts, names, rhymes / And couldn't write" (Amis 1980: 56–7). The poem indicts women on behalf of men, and then indicts men for sharing in women's faults . . . or does it indict men for their lack of self-knowledge? Though Fussell admires its "natural, demotic diction," it stands out also for what it assumes of its audience: they will expect poems as sociable communications, they will distrust claims of vatic originality, they will enjoy and identify with complaints (especially if the complainer includes himself), and they will expect their poets to draw upon a shared experience both of present-day England and of the literary past (Fussell 1994: 174). (The quatrain would have far less comic impact for readers who did not know that the third line quotes Byron.)

By far the most assiduous interest in literary history, and the most original critical accomplishment, among these poets comes in the verse and prose of Donald Davie. Davie's *Purity of Diction in English Verse* (1952) – for much of its length a study of eighteenth-century writing – recommended "a speech of civilized urbanity" as opposed to Romantic and modernist "private wilderness" (Davie 1952: 117, 107). Davie later called *Purity of Diction* "a thinly disguised manifesto" (Davie 1955: ix). His 1955 follow-up, *Articulate Energy*, argued against any separation of poetic language (and especially poetic syntax) from other ways in which language is used: "syntax articulates not just itself, not only its own world, but the world of common experience" (Davie 1955: 165).

Davie's 1950s poetry often versifies his critical stance, praising "the strong though cramped and cramping tone / Of mutual respect": he maintained that tone even as his range of subjects widened (Davie 1990: 15). (Davie would later puzzle early admirers by writing sympathetically about Pound and a Poundian tradition.) In explaining, justifying, or diagnosing his own goals and faults as a poet – tasks his poems take on again and again – Davie is less likely to credit a *zeitgeist* than to bring up his own Northern, dissenting, heritage, described in his memoir *These the Companions* (1982) and in many a poem:

> How else explain this bloody-minded bent
> To kick against the prickings of the norm;
> When to conform is easy, to dissent
> And when it is most difficult, conform?
> (Davie 1990: 73)

His best poems often foreground his self-reproach, taking a guilty pride in his own limits, or in his stern commitment to limits. The pentameters and quatrains of his early work bespeak his hopes to revive eighteenth-century norms, while the trimeters and halting lines of his later styles convey frustration or self-restraint. Davie's "Life Encompassed" begins:

> How often I have said,
> "This will never do,"
> Of ways of feeling that now
> I trust in, and pursue!
>
> (Davie 1990: 103)

The guarded admission, the palinode, are characteristic, as is the quatrain form.

Despite his later fascination with modernism in the arts, Davie remained a small-c conservative in many ways: "corruption / in every detail / (notably, of language)"; "teen-age newsmen," and "Brutal manners, brutal / simplifications" populate Davie's mid-1960s poem called, simply, "England" (Davie 1990: 177–9). In 1965 he left Cambridge University for the new University of Essex, which he would abandon in disgust after the student revolts of 1968–9. He then taught in America, first at Stanford and then at Vanderbilt: late in life he joined the Anglican Church. Davie's poetry of the 1980s and 1990s is insistently religious, but otherwise of a piece with the rest of his work. "Standings" presents itself as a defense of orthodoxies by a man temperamentally suspicious of them:

> We need to know where we stand.
>
> Happy the man or the brute
> who stands correct,
> stands like that, helped like that to stand,
> enabled to,
>
> hungry for judgement always.
>
> (Davie 1990: 389)

Thom Gunn embraced the social trends of the 1960s with as much energy as Davie denounced them: Gunn would eventually admire San Francisco nudists, the Jefferson Airplane, a teenage drug dealer in "dirty denim and dark glasses," and "outlaws" whose "throng / bursts from street to / street . . . in orgy" (Gunn 2000: 195, 211, 207, 265). Yet both poets preserve Movement qualities, and try to embody them, throughout their careers. Gunn's "Flying Above California," for example, lauds the "limiting candour" of "a cold hard light without break // that reveals merely what is" (Gunn 2000: 116).

Gunn's early poetry is a procession of self-tormenting, strenuously self-regulating, or ostentatiously tough alter egos (soldiers, prisoners, ascetics, a werewolf), who re-create themselves in response to physical agony, emotional repression, or existential angst. "Over the ankles in snow and numb past pain," an early poem begins, "I stared up at my window three stories high" (Gunn 2000: 13). One of Gunn's best early lyrics presents him as both "Tamer and Hawk":

> I thought I was so tough,
> But gentled at your hands,
> Cannot be quick enough
> To fly for you and show
> That when I go I go
> At your commands.
> (Gunn 2000: 29)

The stanza described both the relation of lovers, and the relation a poet might have to his language.

Gunn thought well enough of the Movement (or minded the connection little enough) to call his second collection (1957) *The Sense of Movement*, and to open it with the poem "On the Move." In this poem about a motorcycle gang, "gleaming jackets trophied with the dust," Gunn declares a hip and careful existentialism: "Much that is natural to the will must yield," as the bikers demonstrate, "self-defined, astride the created will" (Gunn 2000: 39–40). Exemplars of self-control, and control over language, which began as rejections of Romantic self-indulgence, gradually became in Gunn's poetry symbols for individuating heroic – and homoerotic – strength. One transitional figure is the young man in "Market at Turk" (a street intersection in San Francisco):

> It is military, almost,
> how he buckles himself in,
> with bootstraps and Marine belt,
> reminders of the will.
> (Gunn 2000: 58)

Alan Bold writes that late-1950s Britons sometimes conflated Gunn with Ted Hughes, since both were "young and tough and vigorous and

41

aggressively masculine" (Bold 1976: 1). In 1963, Faber scored a popular hit with a two-in-one Gunn-and-Hughes *Selected Poems*. Yet the two men exhibit almost exactly opposed ways of viewing physical conflict: for Hughes it is instinctive, natural, animal (one might add, Romantic); in Gunn both actual violence, and its admirable tropes in physical exaltation, are conscious choices, forms of human communication. Every gesture in Gunn, even sex, involves a choice: this idea, as much as his insistence on clear syntax, extends Movement views.

Gunn moved to the United States in 1954, following his American life partner: he lived in California and Arizona in the late 1950s, settled in San Francisco thereafter, and during the 1970s began to write unmistakably about his sexual life as a gay man. Like Davie, Gunn admired the strict, anti-Romantic California-based critic Yvor Winters; like Davie, Gunn adopted a careful free verse (drawn indirectly from William Carlos Williams) for many later poems, while retaining inherited meters for others. By the 1970s he had created a confident, even celebratory poetry, albeit one still focused on strong bodies, masculine heroes, and clear syntax: *The Passages of Joy* (1981) praised eighteenth-century virtues such as friendship and intellectual honesty even as it found them in discotheques. His next book, *The Man with Night Sweats* (1995), achieved wide recognition for its elegies and depictions of men with HIV and AIDS.

Few poems by any poet so perfectly make Movement characteristics into virtues as those Gunn wrote in his last two decades. One such poem is "The Beautician," whose title character finds herself in a morgue:

> In their familiarity with the dead
> It was as if the men had not been kind
> With her old friend, whose hair she was assigned
> To fix and shape. She did not speak; instead
> She gave her task a concentrated mind.
>
> She did find in it some thin satisfaction
> That she could use her tenderness as skill
> To make her poor dead friend's hair beautiful
> —As if she shaped an epitaph by her action,
> She thought – being a beautician after all.
> (Gunn 2000: 455)

Movement poets who remained in England took fewer chances to expand their poetic range: some devoted their energies to criticism and editing (Holloway, Wain), novel writing (Amis), or historical and political work (Conquest). Others simply continued. The only woman in the Movement, and the only pious Christian among its poets (at that time), Elizabeth Jennings pursued clarity and accessibility throughout her long career. Her poems, like those of her peers, take the shape of arguments, with evidence, abstractions, and examples; sound more like considered speech than like song; meet readers' expectations before (or rather than) trying to alter those expectations; and deny that her verse techniques give her special powers.

If these qualities make Jennings a Movement writer, others set her apart: she avoids both ironies and outright attacks, and regularly tries to console both herself and her readers. She seeks systems of transcendental belief, and uncomplicated kinds of worldly beauty, as stays against a vertiginous solipsism: "We have retreated inward to our minds / Too much," one early poem warns, "have lost the power that made us lose ourselves" (Jennings 2002: 9). A poem set in Rome finds Jennings explaining, "My mind / Needs the large echoing churches and the roar / Of streets outside its own calm place" (Jennings 2002: 30). Her verse presented itself, as surely as Conquest's or Davie's did, as a mode of resistance to the omnivorous ego, though for Jennings this resistance comes in different tones. In her crisply stanzaic "Poem in Winter," "children press / Their image on the drifts the snow has laid / Upon a winter they think they have made," and Jennings praises their "wise illusion": it is, she adds, "Better to / Believe the near world is created by / A wish, a shaping hand, a certain eye" than to believe, as "we" modern adults might do, that the external world as we know it comes from our own minds (Jennings 1967: 4). Children in that poem become artists' of Jennings' ilk, making lyric impressions of themselves from pre-existing materials whose nature they acknowledge; the adults are less fortunate late-Romantics, who cannot bring themselves to venture outside.

Jennings' religious poems discover evidence of God's presence in this world, outside the poet herself, but in created things; in a church interior, she meditates on "the way / The light refuses to be called abstract" (Jennings 1967: 74). She finds Christ-like forbearance in a circus clown, a figure for the restrained and empirical, and yet pious, author: the sad clown's "helplessness, / His lack of tragic gesture, tragic mood, / Remind me of the abject beast we press / Our own despairs on, Christ nailed to the wood" (Jennings 1967: 110). Besides her faith, Jennings' recurring subjects include pre-modern paintings and painters, especially those from early modern Italy, and mental illness, especially her own, for which she entered hospital in 1961: the verse of *The Mind Has Mountains* (1966) portrayed her psychiatric treatment. Despite her non-academic popularity, she never attracted the critical attention some of her peers gained; her editor and publisher, Michael Schmidt, calls her "the most unconditionally loved writer" of her generation (Jennings 2002: xix).

By far the most widely *admired* Movement poet, today as at any time in the past four decades, is Philip Larkin. Larkin's biographer called "the invention of the Movement . . . one of the most important moments in his career" (Motion 1993: 244). Larkin's best critics note his tentative reachings-out toward transcendence: "while Larkin is exemplary in the way he sifts the conditions of contemporary life," Seamus Heaney explains, "there survives in him a repining for a more crystalline reality to which he might give allegiance" (Heaney 2002: 159). Such comments acknowledge Larkin's dependence on Movement norms even as they show how his poetry challenges them. Indeed, Larkin's poems bring into relief the limits and contradiction in any theory of poetry as communication or community: "even the most triumphant of Larkin's poems are about failure," Andrew Swarbrick concludes, and "ultimately prefer silence to words" (Swarbrick 1995: 153).

During the 1940s an imitator of Yeats, Larkin switched his declared allegiance to Hardy before writing the poems of *The Less Deceived* (1955), which (along with *New Lines*) made his name. These poems stand out not only for their Hardyesque pathos and craft, but for their more-than-Hardyesque resignation: Larkin seems convinced that nothing, neither social life nor art, can relieve his loneliness or abate his concentration on his own death. That conviction informs at once his wry humor, his careful observations of youth, middle age, and old age in postwar England, and his gestures away from social and sexual life, towards a negative sublime. Larkin's collected poems now exist in two versions, an earlier compilation that includes verse unpublished during his lifetime, and a later volume with only the poems Larkin himself chose to publish (and which retains the arrangements of Larkin's individual books). The broader, earlier *Collected Poems* drew attention to the unfinished "The Dance," by far the longest poem Larkin ever attempted, in which his yearnings for contact with a particular woman struggle against an embittered dread of social life as such: her "eyes greet me over commonplaces," her "arms are bare, / And I wish desperately for qualities // Moments like this demand, and which I lack" (Larkin 1988: 155).

Larkin owed some of his popularity to his bitter sociological eye: Davie wrote of "the widest possible agreement . . . that Philip Larkin is for good or ill the effective unofficial laureate of post-1945 England," mirroring many citizens' post-imperial "lowered sights and patiently diminished expectations" (Davie 1972: 64, 71). The poems bring in novelistic, or journalistic, observations about the pleasures and travails of the postwar working and middle classes, who in poems such as "The Large Cool Store" and "Here" window-shop for "Cheap suits, red kitchen-ware, sharp shoes, iced lollies, / Electric mixers, toasters, washers, driers" (Larkin 2003: 79). Yet Larkin's poems also challenge their commitment to the present-day, the specific, and the real. "Maiden Name" (its first stanza quoted above) calls its bride's former appellation "a phrase, applicable to no one"; "it means you. Or, since you're past and gone, // It means what we feel now about you then" (Conquest 1956: 19). "Lines on a Young Lady's Photograph Album" (also in *New Lines*) asks whether the poet finds the photographs so affecting because "this is a real girl in a real place, // In every sense empirically true! / Or is it just *the past?*" (Conquest 1956: 29).

A poetry of journalistic argument could be a poetry of sociability, but a poetry of insistent nostalgia, of "the past," is perforce a poetry of solitude, of being and doing without. "Deprivation is to me what daffodils were to Wordsworth," Larkin quipped (Larkin 1982: 47). "Wants" presented the poet as self-defeating, asocial, and grim, repeating two of its ten lines: "Beyond all this, the wish to be alone," "Beneath it all, desire of oblivion runs" (Larkin 2003: 52). In "Dockery and Son," "Life is first boredom, then fear" (Larkin 2003: 109). A tension between isolation, loneliness, and existential dread as subjects, on the one hand, and socially welcomed and welcoming forms and tones, on the other, provides Larkin's poetry with much of its power.

Barbara Everett writes that Larkin's "subject is the terms on which the isolated individual may become socially available": she intends a particular poem ("Vers de Societé") but she might well have been describing his oeuvre (Everett 1991: 232). His mixed feelings about social life of all sorts – his poems' sense that any community might do for others, but would never quite include *him* – emerged fully in *High Windows* (1974), whose title poem began, perhaps not sarcastically:

> Whenever I see a couple of kids
> And guess he's fucking her and she's
> Taking pills or wearing a diaphragm
> I know this is paradise.
> (Larkin 2003: 129)

This sexual community or communion offers a false (or is it a true?) freedom in which the lonely, middle-aged Larkin takes no part. The half-rhyme of that first stanza, *paradise/her and she's*, evolves, quatrain by quatrain, toward full rhymes as the poem backs away from social observation, toward imagined church windows whose sky "shows / Nothing, and is nowhere, and is endless" (Larkin 2003: 129). Larkin's popularity – given his grimness – has seemed to some to require explanation; for other readers, his emotional powers, his verse technique, his lack of surface difficulty, or his attention to the condition of postwar England, "where nothing's made / As new or washed quite clean," furnish explanation enough (Larkin 2003: 113).

*   *   *

As early as 1957, Morrison contends, the Movement "was seen to represent the values against which future writers would have to react" (Morrison 1980: 243). Conquest's *New Lines II* (1963) dropped Holloway and added sixteen poets, Hughes among them (Bradley 1993: 69). By then several anthologies had positioned themselves as responses or rejoinders to Conquest's initial gathering, among them *Mavericks* (1957) and A. Alvarez's *The New Poetry* (1962). Movement writers and tastes (especially as identified with Larkin) have since the 1960s become identified with a "mainstream" in British poetry, affiliated with London-based trade publishers, more comfortable with premodern forms than with modernism, and accessible in intention, if not always in practice, to a public as large as that for the serious novel.

In consequence, every attempt save one to change British taste in verse over the past fifty years has cast itself as an attack on the Movement. "Discussion of the new poetry after 1960," writes Duncan, "rightly starts with Larkin, as the thing which [many] poets hated, execrated and rebelled against" (Duncan 2003: 67). Even Morrison and Andrew Motion, whose 1982 anthology *Contemporary British Poetry* attracted censure for its supposed conservatism (as well as for calling Seamus Heaney "British"), "claimed that their choice of poets signaled an imaginative freedom and linguistic daring wholly absent from Movement verse" (Day & Docherty 1997: 2).

At the same time we can see elements of the Movement in many subsequent groups and trends: the Liverpool Poets (opposition to elites), "the Group" around Philip Hobsbawn in the early 1960s (self-conscious attention to craft), the formally conventional, journalistic recordings of working-class life in Douglas Dunn (whom Larkin "supported . . . and recommended") and, slightly later, in Tony Harrison (whom he did not) (Motion 1993: 380); the attention to community and communication, and to non-London subjects and audiences, in the operations of Neil Astley's Bloodaxe Press; the interest in news, in recording and renewing the everyday, that characterized both the Oxford and London "Martians" of the early 1980s and the Scottish "Informationists" of recent mint; most of all, the interest in argument, statement, and a non-modernist English tradition, and the aversion to programmatic leftism, in C. B. Cox and Michael Schmidt's *Poetry Nation* (now *PN Review*), which sought a "reassertion of standards of form, of a sense of potential in the integrity of received language" (Schmidt 1973).

The exception mentioned above is the New Generation Poets promotion spearheaded by Peter Forbes and *Poetry Review* in the early 1990s, whose most prominent faces were Simon Armitage, Glyn Maxwell, and Don Paterson. The so-called NewGen took its populist anti-modernism and its "much more professional approach to the marketing of poetry" partly from Movement rhetoric, partly from the participatory, performance-oriented Liverpool Poets, and it made reaching ordinary or amateur readers (especially those outside London, Oxford, and Cambridge) its stated goal (Paterson 2001). Armitage in his first years as a publishing poet worked as a probation officer; his early verse arguably shows a Movement inheritance in its understated reportage. Many of his poems are compressed narratives: one that is not, "Don't Blink," serves as a reportorial manifesto, skimming pathos, irony, and oddity from

> things we can take
> or leave: the ambulance that stubs its shock absorbers
> on the sleeping policeman; the incensed batsman walking
> back towards the bowler, saying if he does that again
> he'll ram this steel-spring Duncan Fearnely down his throat
>
> or through the windscreen of his Ford Fiesta.
> Not that this match could be close or anything;
> the home team only have nine man and one of those
> is the scorer's friend, who at a sensitive age looks
> ridiculous in blue shorts and his sister's jumper.
>
> (Armitage 1989: 25)

The caution, the humility, and the self-control recommended by the Movement ethos have some part in Armitage's effects, but dominate the verse (and the moving prose fiction) of Lavinia Greenlaw, herself one of the 20 NewGen poets (though not often part of the NewGen hype). The urbane observation of Greenlaw's "What's Going On," its clipped dealings with recent loss, typify her strengths, while the subject and last line respond to Larkin's "High Windows":

> The demolition crew are petulant.
> Swinging the ball, they could lay bets and lose.
> We cannot help but stand in the street,
> smile up at the light where half the roof
> has fallen away and the sky comes at us
> from all three sides through a couple of windows,
> surprisingly large and somehow intact.
>
> (Greenlaw 1997: 27)

Neither Armitage nor Greenlaw supports autarkic ideas of English tradition: Greenlaw's poetry could not exist without Elizabeth Bishop, nor Armitage's without Paul Muldoon. Both poets also illustrate an unremarked change in "mainstream" English poetry between the mid-1960s and the mid-1980s: abstract terms and arguments are much less common, replaced by description and unglossed anecdote. The most self-aware "mainstream" poets, Greenlaw among them, query that hypertrophied empiricism: is description now all we can trust? "Why is it I can get no further than the weather?" (Greenlaw 1997: 38).

Davie's essay "Remembering the Movement" (1959) noted "the way" its supposed members "spoke of it among ourselves inside invisible quotation marks" (Davie 1977: 72). He found in this self-belittling tendency both the core motives of the Movement – solicitousness toward a public, humility about poetic vocation – and its chief fault, "the unforgivable literary sin of going much further than halfway to meet our readers, forestalling their objections, trying to keep in their good books" (Davie 1977: 72). "The common touch / Though it warms, coarsens," Davie warned (in the persona of a stonemason): "Never care so much / For leaves or people, but you care for stone / A little more" (Davie 1990: 83). By these lights the NewGen's Maxwell and Armitage (though not Greenlaw) might be called not only the Movement's heirs, but heirs to the Movement's faults – to its documentarian chattiness, for example, or to its oversolicitousness for inexperienced or impatient readers.

Such a verdict might instead see the Movement's virtues in another range of less-publicized writers – in Peter Scupham, for example, or in Alison Brackenbury. Both Brackenbury and Scupham can trace their influences farther back than the 1950s, to Edward Thomas, Robert Frost, and ultimately Wordsworth for Brackenbury, and to Walter de la Mare, Walter Pater, and even Tennyson for Scupham. But to say this is to say that both poets attempt to articulate a tradition whereby contemporary English poetry may be continuous with non-elite experience and with the poetry of the past, just as syntax and reference in verse may be continuous with syntax and reference in discursive prose. And to say this is to say that something of the Movement endures. Here is Brackenbery's poem "Agenda":

> It is said, we tell our truths in private,
> on crumpled pillows, over the stained cup.
> It is in public. At the yawning meeting
> the thin man straightened up
> spoke, as the gilded china rattled round,
> one sentence of an absolute despair—
> the biscuits snapped to dust—but not to us;
> to one he loved, who lived, and was not there.
> (Brackenbury 1995: 33)

Brackenbury makes an ironized social occasion reflect an intimate, isolating absence, as Larkin had done, without copying Larkin's tones. As for the more ornate poetry of Scupham, "A Borderland" serves as his *faute de mieux* manifesto, and it recommends (as Movement poets would) a saddened, careful alertness both to present facts, and to the shape of the past:

> Here childhood and the trees make their last stand
> About the half-bricks and the foundered sheds,
> Play out their let's-pretends and might-have-beens.
>
> Thick-set beyond Tom Tiddler's Ground, the wood
> Is run by dogs – there it might start to snow,
> Old Shaky-fingers pass his poisoned sweet:
> The place where mother said you never should.
> Its otherness might sweep them off their feet;
> The wood itself has nowhere else to go.
> (Scupham 1990: 75)

Further Reading

Davie, Donald (1952). *Purity of Diction in English Verse*. London: Chatto & Windus.
Davie, Donald (1972). *Thomas Hardy and British Poetry*. Oxford: Oxford University Press.

Gunn, Thom (1982). *The Occasions of Poetry*. London: Faber & Faber.

Hewison, Robert (1981). *In Anger: British Culture in the Cold War, 1945–1960*. New York: Oxford University Press.

Larkin, Philip (1982). *Required Writing*. London: Faber & Faber.

Morrison, Blake (1980). *The Movement: English Poetry and Fiction of the 1950s*. Oxford: Oxford University Press.

Swarbrick, Andrew (1995). *Out of Reach: The Poetry of Philip Larkin*. Basingstoke: Macmillan.

Chapter 3

Myth, History, and
The New Poetry

Nigel Alderman

Poetry is always historical in nature, in part because any poem always and necessarily takes its stand in relation to other previously written poems. Such remains the case even with works that declare their originality since their apparent newness and evident modernity always emerge from either an explicit or implicit critique of previous modes and forms. What could be regarded as the foundational poem of modern twentieth-century poetry in English, Ezra Pound's "In a Station of the Metro," exemplifies this process as it dismantles the dominant lyric modes of late nineteenth- and early twentieth-century poetic enterprises. Pound refuses the structuring principle of the lyric "I," rejects any form of narrative development (however attenuated), and removes any clear subjective affect:

> In a Station of the Metro
>
> The apparition of these faces in the crowd;
> Petals on a wet, black bough.
>
> (1990: 111)

As has been noted, the poem immediately raises the question of how to read a moment of seeming epiphanic intensity without the first person singular to provide orientation. Moreover, the poem contains no main verb or grammatical connection between phrases and, therefore, withholds clear causality and connection. Consequently, the initial interpretive gesture has to be concerned with structure rather than psychology. The poem displays three distinct levels: the man-made yet inhuman, mechanical upper stratum of the title; the human yet ghostly stratum of the first line; and the natural, organic stratum of the final line. The poem implies, then, the co-existence of incommensurate layers of worldly experience.

The poem positions itself in a longer line of familiar epic similes, stretching (as John Hollander has noted) from Homer and Virgil through Dante and Milton, each comparing the shades of the underworld to falling leaves blown by the wind (Hollander 1981: 120–2). Rather than simply seeking to add yet one more identical simile-alluding-simile, Pound strives to bring this tradition to its end by disclosing the difference between his poem and its forbears. Whereas the earlier writers urge a metaphoric linking that carries a relationship across the supernatural, human, and natural realms, here the poem's lack of grammatical comparison constructs metonymic blankness – empty space – between them. In addition, the translation from the supernatural underworld to a mechanical one through the medium of the foreign word "Metro" suggests that the earlier mythic world no longer exists and that the underworld remains no longer outside the present of human existence and productivity. It implies an absolute break between that past and both the present of the poem and the future that the poem initiates.

In this relationship to the past, present, and future, the poem thematizes what Fredric Jameson has called the "dilemma of any 'historicism'" – historicism here understood as "our relationship to the past, and of our possibility of understanding the latter's monuments, artifacts, and traces." This dilemma, he argues, "can . . . be dramatized by the peculiar, unavoidable, yet seemingly unresolvable alternation between Identity and Difference" (1988: 150):

> if we choose to affirm the Identity of the alien object with ourselves . . . then we have presupposed what was to have been demonstrated, and our apparent 'comprehension' of these alien texts must be haunted by the nagging suspicion that we have all the while remained locked in our own present, . . . that our feeling of *Verstehen* is little better than mere psychological projection, that we have somehow failed to touch the strangeness and the resistance of a reality genuinely different from our own. . . . Yet if . . . we decide to reverse this initial stance, and to affirm, instead . . . the radical Difference of the alien object from ourselves, then at once . . . we find ourselves separated by the whole density of our own culture from objects or cultures thus initially defined as Other from ourselves and thus as irremediably inaccessible. (Jameson 1988: 150–1)

"In a Station of the Metro" alternates between these two poles, simultaneously tracing its similarity and identification with the epic similes of the past, while separating itself as being absolutely different and alienated from that tradition.

I want to suggest that this opposition can be initially remapped in poetic terms as an opposition between myth and contingency. Myth is here understood in relation to John Milton's *Paradise Lost*, in which the structuring frame of Christian belief and ideology enables the construction of an epic that remains located in communal ritual and belief as it narrates and explains the past, present, and future history both of the collective and of the individual in relation to that collective. Romantic and Victorian poetry and poetics ceaselessly sought to reimagine and reproduce such a mythic structure. Throughout *The Prelude*, for example, William Wordsworth claims that the poet and his imagination performs the privileged role of uniting the individual with the social world through the mythic and yet historical growth of his archetypal mind. However, *The Prelude* remained unpublished and the greater *Recluse* project of which it was a part was left unfinished; as such, they reveal the tentative and unsuccessful nature of his attempt.

This epic ambition continued throughout the nineteenth century, from the failure of John Keats's two *Hyperions*, which seek to imagine a relevant pre-Christian myth that originates in historical defeat, violence, and trauma, to Alfred Tennyson's *Idylls of the King*, which maps notions of chivalric knightly honor upon the idea of the bourgeois gentleman, and on to Robert Browning's dramatic monologues, which focus on a moment when a new world is emerging, at the edge of earshot, within the last outpourings of the old. Such epic ambitions remain central to the most influential poets in Britain and Ireland in the first half of the twentieth century, as T. S. Eliot, D. H. Lawrence, Pound, and W. B. Yeats all attempt some form of confrontation with history in a polemical and systematic manner.

It was these attempts or, to be more precise, the ways in which these attempts were read that found the poetic response not only to them, but also to the interpretation and representation of history in post-1945 British and Irish poetry. I will, therefore, begin by delineating this literary response to modernist poetic myth-making, before adapting Jameson's terms for the four "traditional 'solutions' to the dilemma of historicism" centered on the question of identity or difference. Jameson calls them "antiquarianism, existential historicism, structural typology, and Nietzschean antihistoricism" (1988: 152); by renaming them as empirical, existential, typological, and textual his-toricopoetics I will use them heuristically in sequence to chart a series of contrasting poetic responses to the problem of historical represen-tation since 1945, particularly those of the 1960s and early 1970s. This heuristic enables a theoretical and historical map on which, first, to position the hegemonic poetic anthologies of the first two decades (Robert Conquest's *New Lines* published in 1956 and A. Alvarez's *The New Poetry* published first in 1962, and then in a revised edition in 1966); second, to situate three symptomatic central slim volumes of the 1970s (Geoffrey Hill's *Mercian Hymns*, Ted Hughes's *Crow*, and Seamus Heaney's *North*); and third, to examine Paul Muldoon's exemplary response to these earlier formal and thematic solutions by way of a conclusion.

Modernist Myth-Making

In the British context, as Stan Smith points out, the two most influential statements of modernist poetics in relation to myth and history were Eliot's 1919 essay "Tradition and the Individual Talent" published in *The Egoist* and his 1923 review of James Joyce's *Ulysses* published in *The Dial*, entitled *"Ulysses,* Order and Myth." Smith argues that the former essay raises the question of the difference between the past and the present, but in the end uses the concept of "tradition" to dissolve them into being identical. "'Tradition' in fact," Smith contends, "is a substitute for the concept of 'history,' for the interpenetration of past and present of which Eliot speaks takes place in a *timeless* moment, in a cerebral, *aesthetic* space which is ultimately not answerable to history at all" (1982: 6). In the latter essay, Eliot replaces the concept of tradition with that of myth as he asserts that *Ulysses* is "the most important expression which the present age has found" because of its ability to wrestle order out of the chaos of modern life through the pattern provided by *The Odyssey* (1975: 175). Eliot asserts that Joyce's patterning of the novel on Homer "has the importance of a scientific discovery" because "using the myth, . . . mani-pulating a continuous parallel between contemporaneity and antiquity . . . is . . . a way of controlling, of ordering, of giving a shape and a significance to the immense panorama of futility and anarchy which is contemporary history" (1975: 177). Eliot then links Joyce not only with Yeats, but equally significantly with "psychology . . . ethnology and *The Golden Bough,*" the combination of which provides the replacement of "a narrative method" with that of a "mythical method" (1975: 178). This connection between modernist poetry and poetics and concomitant work on myth in anthropology and psychology, especially Freudian psychoanalysis, came to be emphasized in the modernists themselves and in their critics.

In *The Modern Construction of Myth*, Andrew Von Hendy reveals how for Eliot, Yeats, and Lawrence anthropological work on myth seemed to "demonstrat[e] . . . the permanent and intimate structural relation between the 'savage' mind and the civilized" (2002: 135) and, therefore, to suggest that "the distance" between the archaic past and the modern present "can be annihilated" and that "in myth we experience the racial past immediately" (2002: 135). In contrast to Eliot's idea of a static mythic organizing principle, Yeats developed the idea of spiraling historical repetition which enables him to privilege the lyric, since he came to believe that the lyric simultaneously contains within it not only the matter of epic (the building of cities and dynasties), but also that of tragedy (the apocalyptic fall of cities and dynasties). The lyric poet becomes the apocalyptic bard whose moment of prophetic vision reveals itself as both intensely creative and intensely destructive. In poems such as "No Second Troy," "The Second Coming," and "Leda and the Swan," the fall of a culture originates in its very beginnings as the oracular founding of a new order always foretells its own destruction. Von Hendy also points out that in works such as *Etruscan Places* and especially *The Plumed Serpent*, Lawrence similarly emphasizes what he terms "blood consciousness" and the necessity of sacrificial and apocalyptic violence (2002: 141–5). Symptomatically, Yeats in his late lyrics celebrates the possibility of violent destruction and, indeed, in "Under Ben Bulben" praises "Mitchel's prayer" to "'[s]end war in our time, O Lord!'" (1989: 326).

Such statements and beliefs are, to put it mildly, a problem in 1938 when Yeats had been in the Irish Senate, Eliot is the foremost cultural critic in Britain, Pound is about to broadcast from Mussolini's Rome, and, of course, Hitler and Stalin loom and threaten. It becomes an even greater problem after the accumulated killings of World War II, especially those of the Holocaust. W. H. Auden suggests one influential solution in his 1939 elegy "In Memory of W. B. Yeats" where he removes poetry from the political realm, famously declaring, "poetry makes nothing happen" (1977: 243). When he revised the poem after 1945, however, Auden felt the necessity of excising the stanzas which suggest not only that "Time" "Worships language and forgives / Everyone by whom it lives," but also that it "[p]ardons [writers] for writing well" irrespective of their political views (1977: 242–3). Auden's editorial decision displays the deeply fraught relationship that the immediate postwar British poets had with their modernist predecessors as the imbrication of modernist aesthetics and totalitarian poetics became increasingly accepted.

Probably the most powerful and influential linkage of modernism, fascism, and mythic versions of history in the first two decades after 1945 in Britain occurs in the writing of Frank Kermode, especially in his 1967 book *The Sense of an Ending*, where he explicitly seeks to explain both the "correlation between early modernist literature and authoritarian politics" and how "totalitarian theories of form [are] matched or reflected by totalitarian politics" (1967: 108). He does so by setting up a distinction between myths and fictions: the former "operat[e] within the diagrams of ritual, which presupposes total and adequate explanations of things as they are and were," and "call for absolute" assent, whereas the latter "are for finding things out and they change as the needs of sense-making change" and "call for . . . conditional assent" (Kermode 1967: 39). In a passage worth quoting at length, Kermode argues that, for the modernist writers, all too often fictions became myths and, hence, for him, become inextricably linked to Nazism:

> [M]odernist radicalism in art . . . involves the creation of fictions which may be dangerous in the dispositions they breed towards the world. There is, for instance, the fantasy of an elect which will end the hegemony of bourgeois or of *Massenmensch*, which will end democracy and all the 'Bergsonian' attitudes to time or human psychology, all the mess which makes up a commonplace modern view of reality. Instead of these there is to be order as the modernist artist understands it: rigid, out of flux, the spatial order of the modern critic or the closed authoritarian society; such a society we were told in 1940, as would persist, all inferior races, all *Untermenschen*, excluded for a thousand years. (1967: 110–11)

In some sense, Kermode codifies the dominant climate of opinion since 1945. In his 1952 *Purity of Diction in English Verse* (often seen as the Movement's manifesto) Donald Davie simply declares as a fact that "the development from imagism in poetry to fascism in politics is clear and unbroken" (1952: 99). This climate of opinion provides the horizon that helps explain the Movement's relationship to historical representation and it is to their empirical historicopoetics that I will now turn.

Empirical Historicopoetics

The 1955 and 1956 publications of D. J. Enright's and Robert Conquest's anthologies, *Poets of the 1950s* and *New Lines*, respectively, have traditionally been viewed as the beginning of post-1945 British poetry, introducing the Movement to a larger audience and ushering in a series of "programmatic and polemical anthologies" that Randall Stevenson (quoting Anthony Thwaite) uses to structure his narrative of the poetry of the period in his volume of the new Oxford English Literary History, *The Last of England?* (2004: 166). Andrew Crozier, among others, has argued that such a beginning actually marks the hegemonic power of Movement poetics, rather than being historically accurate (see Crozier 1983, 2000). Be that as it may, for the purpose of this essay the crucial point about the work in these two anthologies is the dominant and continuing emphasis on what Crozier calls "the enunciation . . . of an empirical subject" and an insistent depiction of an empirical world (2000: 193). Conquest himself famously asserts this in his preface to *New Lines*:

> If one had briefly to distinguish this poetry of the fifties from its predecessors, I believe the most important general point would be that it submits to no great systems of theoretical constructs nor agglomerations of unconscious commands. It is free from both mystical and logical compulsions and – like modern philosophy – is empirical in its attitude to all that comes. (1956: xiv–xv)

Jameson suggests that this type of "empiricist position is essentially a second-degree, reactive . . . one . . . and . . . presupposes for its own vitality as a stance the existence of those other visions of history which its mission lies in subverting" (1988: 153). It is, of course, the mythic visions of the modernists that are the frequent targets of the poems in Enright's and Conquest's anthologies.

Philip Larkin became and remains the dominant and representative figure of the Movement and its poetics. In his prefatory "Statement" to his selection of poems in *Poets of the 1950s*, for example, he argues that a poem should be a separate, empirical fact:

> As a guiding principle I believe that every poem must have its own sole freshly created universe, and therefore have no belief in "tradition" or a common myth-kitty or casual allusions in poems to other poems or poets which last I find unpleasantly like the talk of literary understrappers letting you see they know the right people. (Enright 1955: 78)

With his own casual allusions, Larkin mocks Eliot and intimates that the intertextuality and universal mythic systems of Eliot's modernist poetics reveal the class anxiety of a social climber. In this "Statement," Larkin circumscribes the individual poem, declaring that it should focus solely on representing in contemporary vernacular language the poet's individual experience as it occurs in a present moment of time: "I write poems to preserve things I have seen/thought/felt . . . both for myself and for others, though I feel that my prime responsibility is to the experience itself, which I am trying to keep from oblivion for its own sake" (1955: 78). Jameson argues that this type of "empiricist position" is in fact a "demystifying one, a form of what Deleuze and Guattari conveniently term the 'decoding' of persistent, conventionally received interpretive codes" (1988: 153). It is no accident, then, that Movement poetry and poetics perpetually set themselves up in opposition to modernism and what are seen as its mystifying, authoritarian master codes, as Corcoran observes when he quotes Davie's words, "At Dachau Yeats and Rilke died" (1993: 83).

Larkin usually reveals the incommensurable distance from the past to the present and his poetry performs an encounter not with the past, but rather with a present moment in all its irreducible difference from the past (see Alderman 2004: 174–5). In his set-piece autobiographical poem "I Remember, I Remember" (published in *The Less Deceived* in 1955 and anthologized in *New Lines*), Larkin mocks portraits of artists as young men – whether Wordsworthian, Joycean, or Lawrentian – that locate later artistic achievement in the seeds of the past and show how events in childhood analogically prefigure the future lifework. In spite of its mockery of ostentatious claims of artistic importance, the poem is itself a bravura piece of formal control: it divides on the page into seven five-line stanzas and a single concluding line, but it also divides in terms of its complex and idiosyncratic rhyme scheme (ABCCBAABC) into four nine-line stanzas. "Coming up England by a different line," the speaker is surprised when the train stops at Coventry and "exclaim(s) . . . 'I was born here!'" (Larkin, of course, was in fact born there.) A friend asks him if that was "where you 'have your roots'?" The quotation marks show the ironic and clichéd nature of such ideas in Larkin's poetic universe. Larkin then represents his past purely in negations: he did "not invent / Blinding theologies of flowers and fruit," he "never ran" to a "splendid family" when he got "depressed," he never found the farm "where I could be / 'really myself'," he "never . . . [sat] . . . trembling" in "bracken," and his teenage "doggerel" was never published. The concluding line bluntly refuses and blankly renounces any meaningful encounter with the past, "Nothing . . . happens anywhere" (1988: 81–2).

This ironic tone strikes the dominant note of Larkin and his descendents – and probably of British, certainly English, poetry since 1945. The structure of poem after poem after poem during this period turns upon the dismantling of seemingly idealistic and metaphysical beliefs or visions as they are brought down to empirical earth by the speaker's encounter with quotidian reality. In 1999 the dramatic monologues of Carol Ann Duffy's *The World's Wife*, for example, hinge on the disjunction between the speaker's contemporary voice and her mythic or historical male surname. "Mrs Sisyphus" ends:

> But I lie alone in the dark
> feeling like Noah's wife did
> when he hammered away at the Ark;
> like Frau Sebastian Bach.
> My voice reduced to a squawk,
> My smile to a twisted smirk;
> While, up on the deepening murk of the hill,
> He is giving one hundred per cent and more to his work.
> (1999: 22)

Sisyphus, Noah, and Bach become contemporary workaholic husbands and the ironic collapse of historical difference produces the larger political claim concerning the universal and timeless oppression of women.

As Jameson suggests, this form of empirical historicopoetics tends to banish any form of relationship between the past and present (1988: 152). The past is either seen as so absolutely different from the present that either no connection can be made or any such connection becomes folded into the present of the speaker. In both cases, the past effectively ceases to exist. Larkin's "Reference Back" exemplifies this mode of poetic thought and lyric strategy. Here, the speaker has returned home to visit his mother and is "play[ing] record after record" when he suddenly hears his mother call out to him *That was a pretty one.* The second stanza initially suggests that their mutual listening to the jazz music of "Oliver's *Riverside Blues*" recorded "the year after" he "was born" will enable some form of "bridge" between themselves and their various pasts. In fact, however, the music actually bridges only the present moment of his mother's "unsatisfactory age" and his own "unsatisfactory prime" (Larkin 1988: 106).

The final stanza, however, reveals how even though such a poetics is predicated upon the abolition of the past and upon the circumscription of the immediate present, its emphasis upon the empirical subject has a tendency to transform it into a poetics that records instead a historical subject as it seeks to encounter the past:

> Truly, though our element is time,
> We are not suited to the long perspectives
> Open at each instant of our lives.
> They link us to our losses: worse,
> They show us what we have as it once was,
> Blindingly undiminished, just as though
> By acting different we could have kept it so.
> (Larkin 1988: 106)

And it is this distinction between the atemporal experience of an empirical subject and the temporal experience of a historical subject that motivates Alvarez's 1962 attack on Larkin and the Movement in his "Introduction" to *The New Poetry*.

Existential Historicopoetics

Although "Reference Back" suggests a tentative link between the past and the present, this linkage is made up of losses. The past, then, has no genuine content but rather empties itself into the present moment, making all time identical in the end. For Jameson, "existential historicism," in contrast, "designates something like a transhistorical event: the experience, rather, by which *historicity* as such is manifested, by means of the contact between the historian's mind in the present and a given synchronic cultural complex from the past" (1988: 157). In other words, an existential historicopoetics will attempt to represent not so much the past as the subject's experience of attempting to encounter and represent the past. James Longenbach summarizes the idea when he writes, "history is not produced from a collection of facts but is manifested by the historicity of the very experience of investigating the past" (1987: 14). Such a method measures the difference between the past and the present, and historicity emerges in encountering the experience of this difference.

Neil Corcoran emphasizes the enormous influence of both the 1962 and 1966 editions of Alvarez's anthology, *The New Poetry*, and he does not exaggerate when he says, "[t]hat anthology, with its introductory essay 'The New Poetry or, Beyond the Gentility Principle,' remains one of the central documents for an understanding of the evolution of poetry" in the 1960s (1993: 132). At the heart of Alvarez's polemical essay lies the belief that English poetry has failed to develop historically. Instead he argues that "the machinery of modern English poetry seems to have been controlled by a series of negative feedbacks designed to produce precisely the effect Hardy wanted" when he "remarked to Robert Graves that *vers libre* could come to nothing in England. 'All we can do is to write on the old themes in the old styles, but try to do a little better than those who went before us'" (1966: 21). For Alvarez, English poetry has become fixed and preserved in the antiquated, irrelevant, and historically inaccurate view of the world that he calls "the concept of gentility": "gentility is a belief that life is always more or less orderly, people always more or less polite, their emotions and habits more or less decent and more or less controllable; that God, in short, is more or less good" (1966: 25). In contrast, Alvarez argues that the twentieth century has made it clear "that all our lives . . . are influenced profoundly by forces which have nothing to do with gentility, decency, or politeness" but instead are "forces of disintegration . . . [and] . . . their public faces are those of two world wars, of the concentration camps, of genocide, and the threat of nuclear war" (1966: 26). As a consequence, English poetry has become unable to represent whole "new areas of experience" that have opened up historically in the twentieth century. More specifically, Alvarez believes two crucial changes mark his era's difference from all previous ones: "First, mass evil . . . has been magnified to match the scale of mass society" (1966: 26) and "second, . . . the forceable recognition of a mass evil outside us has developed precisely parallel with psychoanalysis" (1966: 27). Alvarez argues that an investigation of either the subjective or the objective pole, an analysis of either the individual or the empirical world, will inevitably lead to an examination of the other pole since both are historically situated and are produced by the difference that is the twentieth century.

As Stevenson points out, for Alvarez it was Sylvia Plath's work written after 1962 that "fulfilled the demands" of his introduction and in the 1966 edition he added Plath to the anthology by selecting seven poems to represent her, including "Lady Lazarus," "Daddy," "The Swarm," and "Mary's Song" (2004: 192). (Although an American, Plath's influence on British poetry, especially for the two decades after her death is, as Corcoran notes, pervasive "on an entire generation of women poets," but it can also be "sensed more unexpectedly elsewhere"

(1993: 133). Corcoran mentions Heaney and Douglas Dunn, but the supposedly original "Martian" techniques of Craig Raine are fully formed in Plath's "You're.") In "Lady Lazarus" Plath sets up an extraordinary oscillation between identification and difference as she moves through a series of analogies between the contemporary speaker's suicide attempts, Jewish deaths in the concentration camps, a striptease to "the peanut-crunching crowd," being bandaged and unbandaged by a doctor, a theatrical performance, Lazarus being raised from the dead, being visited in hospital, an examination by a psychiatrist, and a phoenix arising like a fury to "eat men like air" (1981: 244–5).

Unlike the stable irony in Larkin and other Movement poets, Plath's irony is radically unstable, especially since in later Plath metaphor tends to generate metaphor with the vehicle of one becoming the tenor of the next in a dizzying sequence of accretion. (Often, as in "Mary's Song," a poem ends in the collapsing of tenor and vehicle to produce an image redolent with signification but without referent.) In "Lady Lazarus," as critics have often noted, it seems impossible to assess how seriously we are supposed to take such comparisons between the female speaker and Jewish Holocaust victims: the tone suggests an absolute intensity of seriousness to the analogies and yet, paradoxically, this very intensity also intimates a preposterousness to them.

"Daddy" makes this unstable ironic structure even clearer since the nursery rhyme rhythms, repetitions, and rhymes jut against the violence of the content. The poem also makes even more explicit the comparison between the speaker's psychological state or case history and the Final Solution. The unease that these later poems of Plath have (and should) evince in critics results from the way in which this unstable ironic structure alternates between identification and difference: the absolute difference between the deaths of the collective victims of the Holocaust and the pain of the contemporary speaker can only be measured through the gauge of absolute identification.

Geoffrey Hill is another poet introduced to a larger audience by *The New Poetry* who also consistently addresses the Holocaust and uses a similar unstable irony. Hill's irony, however, functions generally through the use of dense ambiguities produced by puns, wordplay, connotations (indeed the whole panoply of paronomasia), syntax, and grammar, including, as Christopher Ricks has exhaustively shown, punctuation (1984: 319–55). In poems such as "Two Formal Elegies," "Ovid in the Third Reich," and "September Song," Hill emphasizes the distance between his present representation of the past and the past's violent materiality. In fact, he often explicitly addresses the questions that Plath's poems raise. Jon Silkin points out, for example, that the pained parenthesis in Hill's "September Song" – "(I have made / an elegy for myself it / is true)" – means both that the events it describes are true (they really happened), and that the poem is self-pitying (it is true that it is really about the poet himself) (1972: 146).

Hill's poetry perpetually takes as its motivation the violence of the past and the poet's relationship to representing such violence. Indeed, Hill's career can be seen as a concerted engagement not only with Walter Benjamin's oft-quoted sentence, "There is no document of culture which is not at the same time a document of barbarism" but also the sentence that follows, "And just as such a document is never free of barbarism, so barbarism taints the manner in which it was transmitted from one hand to another" (2003: 392). Hill's most ambitious attempt to chart the process by which history is transmitted is the pocket epic, *Mercian Hymns*, published in 1971. The poem has the double focus intrinsic to existential historicopoetics, moving between the Anglo-Saxon King Offa who ruled Mercia from AD 757 to 796 and Hill's childhood in the same area. In terms of their suggested titles the sequence of thirty prose poems charts Offa's life from his naming, to his crowning, to his ruling practices, and finally to his death and funeral, but it also traces Hill's own childhood and family background. Hill himself has suggested the complex relationship between the tyrannical egocentrism of such a king and that of an imaginative child: "The murderous brutality of Offa as a political animal seems again an objective correlative for the ambiguities of English history in general, as a means of trying to encompass and accommodate the early humiliations and fears of one's own childhood and also one's discovery of the tyrannical streak in oneself as a child" (Haffenden 1981: 94).

In Hymn X, for example, there is an explicit "exchange with the Muse of History" for the poem describes not only Offa as a child learning Latin and as a ruler using that language to make laws and deliver authoritative commands, but also the mid-twentieth-century grammar school boy doing his Latin homework: "He wept, attempting to mas- / ter *ancilla* and *servus*" (2000: 102). This final line exemplifies how Hill's poetic practice displays the transmission of civilization and barbarism, learning and violence. The "[h]e" refers to Offa and Hill, creating identity, but the difference between the two remains equally stark. Offa was a master, an owner of people, and so *ancilla* and *servus* have a contemporary social referent for him. For the twentieth-century child, such personal ownership is unknown and, therefore, the mastery becomes only an educational one. However, the reason for the belief that mastery of Latin was necessary remains identical: it provides access to a history of power, to a tradition of imperial rule, and to the heritage of a dominant and masterful culture. The poem then speaks both of the continuous history of the victors – with their narrative of ordered development – and the discontinuous history of the defeated – with their instants of catastrophic destruction. The sequence highlights the rulers of the land, but also brings to light what both Michael North and C. D. Blanton have called the anonymous laborers who worked on and in the land (North 1987; Blanton 2000). In Hymn XXV, for example, Hill remembers his grandmother who was disfigured by "the searing wire" of an industrial machine (2000: 117) and links her to all the unnamed workers who built the great cultural monuments of the state – the "Opus Anglicanum," the cathedrals, castles, and palaces (2000: 115) – and to all the unknown "swathed bodies in the long ditch" who suffered the "anger" of kings (2000: 103).

The larger historical structure of the sequence's investigation of Englishness is both genealogical and teleological. Chronologically, it begins with what it figures as the emergence of England as England out of the separate regions and kingdoms of the island. As Hill's notes direct us, Offa was the first Anglo-Saxon king to inscribe "*Rex / Totius Anglorum Patriae*" on his coins, and the complex provenance of the title *Mercian Hymns* brings together Hebrew, Greek, Latin, and Anglo-Saxon (2000: 105). Indeed, one of the sequence's conceits is that these poems perform the moment when England and the English language are about to coalesce and form themselves out of all their attendant cultures and traditions. These, in turn, become seen as England's various tributaries once such unification occurs. And it ends chronologically with England's dissolution into its various regional and devolutionary constituencies of which Mercia or rather the West Midlands is simply one of many. It could be said that *Mercian Hymns* begins as marginal interlinear glosses of Latin Christian passages, foretelling the emergence of England as a Christian nation, and ends as marginal footnotes of that English Christian tradition, telling of the emergence of a post-Christian devolved federation. Consequently, the sequence suggests the mutually exclusive propositions that the meaning of all its myriad histories (personal, social, aesthetic, legal, numismatic, religious, archaeological, architectural, horticultural, geological, and so on) can be located in the origins of Offa's Mercia and that, simultaneously, this meaning can be found in the representational culmination of the present of the sequence itself.

What in the end holds the poem together are these various oscillations between past and present as they become centered, as Harold Bloom's introduction notes, in "Hill's own complex subjectivity, and so the poem is 'about' himself, which turns out to be his exchange of gifts with the Muse of History" (Bloom 1975b: xxii). As such, then, Hill's poem reveals that an existential historicopoetics with its emphasis on the "contact between an individual subject in the present and a cultural object in the past" tends to open itself up, as Jameson argues, to "complete relativization" since "an infinity of possible histories is possible" (1988: 159). Hill's poem, indeed, is only one of a whole host of regional poetic histories during this period and such poems always claim centrality for their own marginal regions, which, in turn, guarantees the poet's own vocational impulse. In what can be seen as a response to this emphasis on the subjectivity of the poet-historian and the problem of its consequent relativization of historical representation, other poets, in what Jameson terms a "dialectical counterposition," begin to emphasize "the historical object" (1988: 165). In the early 1970s both Ted Hughes and Seamus Heaney, for example, move in *Crow* and *North*, respectively, toward a typological historicopoetics in which events in the present are seen to prefigure or allegorically represent deep structures of universal historical patterns.

Typological Historicopoetics

If Hill perceives every and any word's etymological accretion of denotation and connotation as a means to access complex historical contextures that locate contemporary users and usages of language in a mutual and changing relationship with all past and future users and usages, then Hughes regards words as recapitulating endlessly the same recurring fable of humanity's fall into scientific rationality and into an alienated abstraction from the organic world of fauna, flora, and minerals. More specifically, Hughes locates this fall in the West and in Protestantism:

> The fundamental guiding ideas of our Western Civilization . . . derive from Reformed Christianity and from Old Testament Puritanism. . . . They are based on the assumption that the earth is a heap of raw materials given to man by God for his exclusive profit and use. (1994: 129)

Instead Hughes imagines, prior to the construction of the "iron arteries of Calvin" (2003: 167), a sacred world of myth and ritual at whose center is "the idea of nature as a single organism":

65

> It was man's first great thought, the basic intuition of most primitive theologies. Since Christianity hardened into Protestantism, we can follow the underground heretical life, leagued with everything occult, spiritualistic, devilish, over-emotional, bestial, mystical, feminine, crazy, revolutionary, and poetic. (1994: 132)

Hughes consistently asserts that such belief has continued and continues its subterranean life both in British culture as a whole and in the lives of those he views as its most significant artists. Indeed, he maps his longer readings of Shakespeare, Blake, Coleridge, and Eliot onto a pattern of conflict and resistance between the "young Puritan Jehovah" and the "goddess of natural law and of love, . . . of all sensation and organic life" (1994: 110).

For Hughes, words in this prior world function as symbolic tokens that carry with them "complete communication" (1994: 310) and contain the universal meaning of a sacred language. His poetry and poetics, as Paul Giles notes, long for this type of performative language in which signified, signifier, and referent become one in the ritualistic act of speaking the words in sacred, communal space (1996: 153–4). Accordingly, in his nature and animal poems Hughes strives to unify ontology and activity so that within a single instantaneous moment the creature and outside world become one. More often than not Hughes figures these moments of suddenness either as an act of killing or being killed, or as an aspect of mating, whether ritual display or copulation.

Crow, or to give it its full title, *Crow: From the Life and Songs of the Crow*, was first published in 1970 and for the rest of his life Hughes continued to add poems to the sequence. He regarded the sequence as akin to the selection of songs and tales anthropologists collected from oral cultures, and in readings, letters, and essays Hughes sketches out the larger myth of which the poems were a part (Hughes 1994: 239–43; Sagar 2000: 170–80). In his 1985 essay "Crow on the Beach," Hughes calls it a "song-legend" composed in "the thick of contemporary literatures," and the poems are dense with allusions to the contemporary world of mass media and mass violence (1994: 242). The sequence centers on the adventures of a trickster figure, Crow, who, like all such figures, consistently transgresses all order and all boundaries. He constantly shifts between a myriad of different planes: the metaphysical ones of natural, human, and supernatural; the temporal ones of past, present, and future; the ontological ones of human, fauna, flora, and mineral; and many others including the foundational taboos of incest and various forms of familicide. For Hughes, Crow becomes the Christian God's counterpart who enables the connecting of all realms not through origin, creation, and unification, but through endings, destruction, and separation.

The Crow poems tend to structure themselves around a series of encounters between Crow and a world of things outside of him. As each thing encounters Crow's rapacity, it consumes itself, usually ending up inside Crow, who, in turn, becomes a figure of empty hunger, blackness, and death. "Crowquill," for example, ends with a series of what Ricks terms self-infolded similes (1984: 56):

> The feather is falling and falling
>
> And people clasp each other close
> With their froglike hands, inside houses
> And look out of the windows at
>
> The emptiness through which the feather falls
>
> Like a wand
>
> That has swallowed its wizard.
> (Hughes 2003: 199)

As Margaret Dickie observes, frequently Crow's targets are words themselves which materialize as things, animals, representations, and abstractions and are consumed by the remorseless swallowing capacity of Crow (1983: 57–60). In "Crowego," for example, after "Ulysses," "Dejanira," "Hercules," and "Beowulf," have transformed into something else ("a worm," "Hercules' two puff-adders," "ashes," and "blood," respectively), Crow destroys them, seemingly leaving only himself, but then he too begins to translate:

> His wings are the stiff back of his only book,
> Himself the only page – of solid ink.
>
> So he gazes into the quag of the past
> Like a gypsy into the crystal of the future,
>
> Like a leopard into a fat land.
> (Hughes 2003: 240)

As usual, a part of himself ("his wings") becomes a single item ("his only book") that becomes "himself" that compresses even further (an "only page") that then coalesces into a black image both of fullness and emptiness, of meaningfulness and meaninglessness (a single page of "solid ink"). This image of total compressed blackness figuratively turns into an eye that looks into the past and into the future, and, with a final simile, regenerates itself as a predator ready to kill.

In miniature, then, "Crowego" repeats and foretells the universal pattern that Hughes sees structuring the history of the world from its beginning to its end and that each Crow poem recapitulates in turn. This mode of typological historicopoetics solves, then, the problem of relativization that a greater focus on the subject produces in its existential version, but by so doing it creates the problem of collapsing all history into one eternal and never-ending identity. The danger of flattening complex historical situations into eternal archetypes becomes ever more pronounced the more poems directly refer to present events. This helps explain why, although Seamus Heaney's *North* was published in 1974 to great acclaim in England, Irish reviewers were more critical. Like Hughes, Heaney maps history onto a typological structure organized around the central opposition of male and female, writing that "the enmity [in Northern Ireland] can be viewed as a struggle between the cults and devotees of a god and a goddess" (2002: 24). For Heaney, the masculine principle stands for England, the English language, iambic pentameter, Protestantism, rationality, and wood made into longships, and the feminine represents Ireland, the Gaelic language, oral meters, Roman Catholicism, physicality, and wood dissolved into peat bogs.

The volume's individual poems often veer between an existential and a typological poetics, between a pained analysis of the observing poetic subjectivity's own guilty relationship with the violent historical events it seeks to represent, and a powerful portrayal of archaic and archetypal ritual practices, between what Ciaran Carson calls "the need to be precise, and the desire to abstract, to create a superstructure of myth and symbol" (1975: 183). Indeed, Carson's review of *North* criticizes Heaney for attempting to "emulate Eliot, or Yeats, or both," imitating the modernists with "a kind of Golden Bough activity, in which the real differences between our society and that of Jutland in some vague past are glossed over for the sake of the parallels of ritual" (1975: 184). The most sustained poetic engagements with Heaney's work and this sort of typological historicopoetics, however, has probably come from Paul Muldoon, whose poetry exemplifies a textual historicopoetics where the past is approached through the obliquity of its textual representations.

Textual Historicopoetics

Muldoon's poetry since the publication of *New Weather* in 1973 is representative in British and Irish poetry of a turn to a textual historicopoetics that emphasizes, in Barry Windass and Paul Hirst's words, "the object of history is whatever is *represented* as having hitherto existed. The essence of this representation is preserved records and documents" (quoted by Jameson 1988: 170). Accordingly, two central formal devices of Muldoon's poetry are *mise en abyme* and meta-narrative. As Corcoran points out, he repeatedly sets up Chinese box or Russian doll structures in which narrative, event, character, image, and word refer to other narratives, events, characters, images, and words to such an extent that it becomes impossible to decide which version has priority (1993: 211–12). Akin to Michael Riffaterre's notion of the "hypogram" or "semantic nucleus," Muldoon's poems often deliberately proffer a word or a phrase which seems to offer up a summary or explanation, but whose reference in the end remains the poem itself and some always still opaque private experience (1983: 76). "Cuba," published in *Mules* in 1977, suggests some form of relationship between the Cuban missile crisis and the sexual crisis of his sister staying out all night. Symptomatically, the poem lends itself to an array of possible sexual innuendos and ironic parallels whose relevance and appropriateness remain difficult, if not impossible, to gauge. (In both cases, for example, full engagement was averted.) The first part of "Lunch with Pancho Villa," from the same volume, sets up a description of an encounter with an Irish Republican who urges the poet to write more political poems but its second part reveals this encounter to be purely fictional. It is impossible to decide how ironically and critically the allusion and suggested parallel with Pancho Villa should be read. "Why Brownlee Left," from the 1980 volume of the same name, is the title of the poem, its first line, and a question never answered in the poem. "Quoof" is also the title of a poem, the title of his 1983 volume, and the Muldoons' private "family word" for a "hot water bottle" (2001: 112).

Setting up such series of self-referential and intertextual parallels enables Muldoon to describe the violence of both past and present history without any transcendental claim for his own poem's representational truth. The title poem of his 1987 volume, "Meeting the British," for example, describes the meeting between General Jeffrey Amherst and the Ottawans when he handed over blankets impregnated with the smallpox virus. The poem weaves its way through a dizzying suggestion of linguistic, national, ethnic, cultural, and viral disseminations. It is written in English by an Irishman, while the speaker of the poem is an Ottawan, who speaks in French to the British, among whom is Colonel Henry Bouquet, a Swiss, who speaks the French sentence in the middle of the poem. In addition, this meeting with the British is, in fact, a meeting between the Ottawans and the British who both become those new things, "Americans," after such encounters. In other words, the term, "Americans," absent from the poem, emerges after this moment of germ warfare that functions as a synecdoche for imperial conquest and the founding of states. As such, this moment simultaneously makes the British invaders, "Americans," and makes the indigenous inhabitants of the continent enter a historical process that eventually names them "Native Americans."

Translation ironically parallels the transmission of smallpox since Bouquet's French comment, beginning "C'est la lavande," answers the speaker's presumed question about "the unusual" smell coming from Bouquet's "hand- / kerchief" (2001: 160). Within the context of the narrative, this answer provides the words for the initial image that begins the poem, concerning the lavender color of sky and snow. The speaker has acquired the word, lavender, and its metaphoric, descriptive power, but the reason behind this acquisition lies in the other transmission with which the poem ends: "They gave us six fishhooks / and two blankets embroidered with smallpox" (2001: 160). (As well as hiding the smell, lavender was also thought to ward off infection.) The shock of history emerges in the opposition between the richness of the poem's language and the horror of its content, between "a document of culture" and "a document of barbarism" (Benjamin 2003: 392). The poem's semantic nucleus turns out to be the appalling historical accident of the chilling appropriateness of Bouquet's name. His name couples the imperial and conquering languages of French and English as do the rhymes of "Hand- / lavande" and "unusual / ciel," with their phonetic contiguity. However, the poem also redemptively connects the lost Gaelic and Ottowan languages, discloses those lost forms of life, through the "secret index" of their non-existence upon which the poem depends (Benjamin 2003: 390).

As such the poem contains the sort of negated utopian moment that Theodor Adorno argues is symptomatic of lyric poetry written in the epoch of capitalism, especially after World War II. Such moments unite empirical, existentialist, typological, and textual historicopoetics and they are ubiquitous in post-1945 British and Irish poetry: Larkin's negative prefixes, Plath's collapsing of tenor and vehicle, Hill's etymological contextures, Hughes's regenerating self-infolding similes, Heaney's necroptic personifications, and Muldoon's disseminative phonetics, all figure "a hidden 'it should be otherwise'" (Adorno 1977: 194). As Hill's poem "Respublica" emblematically ends:

Respublica
brokenly recalled
its archaic laws
and hymnody;

and destroyed hope
that so many times
is brought with triumph
back from the dead.
(2000: 190)

By recalling archaic laws and destroyed hope, poetry bears witness to other possibilities, other stories; it is perhaps not too much to claim that the task of poetry since 1945 has been (adapting a phrase of William Blake's), to keep the utopian vision in time of trouble. And it is through these visions of "destroyed hope" that such poetry seeks to arrest, if only in its formal space, the destructive triumph of progress.

Further Reading

Hewison, Robert (1986). *Too Much: Art and Society in the Sixties, 1960–75.* London: Methuen.

Jameson, Fredric (1988). Marxism and Historicism. In *The Ideologies of Theory: Essays 1971–1986,* vol. 2: *Syntax of History.* Minneapolis, MN: University of Minnesota Press, pp. 148–77.

Kermode, Frank (1967). *The Sense of an Ending: Studies in the Theory of Fiction.* Oxford: Oxford University Press.

Marwick, Arthur (1998). *The Sixties: Cultural Revolution in Britain, France, Italy, and the United States, c. 1958–c. 1974.* Oxford: Oxford University Press.

Smith, Stan (1982). *Inviolable Voice: History and 20th-century Poetry.* Dublin: Gill & Macmillan.

Waugh, Patricia (1989). *The Harvest of the Sixties: English Literature and its Background, 1960–1990.* Oxford: Oxford University Press.

Chapter 4

Region and Nation in Britain and Ireland

Michael Thurston

In "Welsh Landscape," one of his best-known poems, R. S. Thomas writes that "To live in Wales is to be conscious / At dusk of the spilled blood / . . . / Dyeing the immaculate rivers." To this interweaving of history (the English imperial conquest of Wales) and landscape, Thomas adds, a few lines later, the strand of language: "The soft consonants / Strange to the ear" (1986: 16). The rope woven of these strands, by the end of the poem, is shown to bind the people of Wales at once to land, language, and history. Their identity derives from these and locates them as constituents of a nation at once in and apart from the British Empire. In this (if not in the ambivalent note on which the poem concludes), "Welsh Landscape" participates in a widespread poetic grammar of nationalist motives, one that generates Seamus Heaney's "Anahorish," William Neill's "Mapmakers," Ted Hughes's *Remains of Elmet*, and numerous other poems and volumes in the postwar decades.

Tom Nairn's *The Break-Up of Britain* (1977) describes the nationalist desires that are spoken in this poetry and that exerted enormous centrifugal force within British culture halfway between the end of World War II and the close of the twentieth century. Those desires manifested in forms ranging from the violence of paramilitaries in Northern Ireland to the 1979 St David's Day referendum in Wales to the proliferation of nationalist literature in Scotland, Wales, and Ireland. While the middle and late 1970s mark just one of several nationalist high-tide points in the postwar decades, Nairn argues that the "break-up of Britain" to which they contribute accelerates during that period. He analyzes these rises of "peripheral nationalism" as displacements of class rebellion and as mechanisms for the management of tensions wrought by historic economic shifts, writing that they suggest the "extremely long-delayed crisis of *the* original bourgeois state form," which was England (1977: 14). While others might attribute the emergent nationalist movements in Scotland and Wales to cultural factors, Nairn writes that, "politically speaking, the key to these neo-nationalist renaissances lies in the slow foundering of the British state, not in the Celtic bloodstream" (1977: 14).

Poets from these regions/nations, and from the north of England, an area both economically and culturally distinct from London's metropole, do not, as a rule, include such analyses in their work. Nationalist desire, for them, is what Raymond Williams terms a "structure of feeling" rather than an object of Marxist analysis (1977: 128–35). This is not to suggest, however, that all Northern Irish, Welsh, Scottish, or northern English poets sing full-throated hymns to the emergent or imagined nations or to "the Celtic bloodstream." Rather, they tend to explore the costs and rewards of that structure as these are experienced in the lives and emotions of individuals (often by focusing on how those lives are lived in the tangle of landscape, language, and history so clearly traced in Thomas's poem). Most work to focus what Terry Eagleton (1990) has called the difficult "double optic" that enables a simultaneous vision of the desired nation and national identity and of the impossibility of that desire's fulfillment. In this, they register the complexity of national and regional identities even as they attempt to articulate them. The poets treated in the pages below, that is, work within nationalist or regionalist structures of feeling but, at the same time, seek, in Eagleton's words, "to prefigure . . . styles of being and identity for which we have as yet no proper names" (1990: 24). Each poet's peculiar focus differs, of course, from those of other poets. It is useful, therefore, to situate their work at various points along a continuum we might imagine within the range of this double optic, a continuum with a national identity at one pole and an ironic distance from such an identity at the other.

Northern Ireland

Perhaps no part of the United Kingdom has produced such a wealth of powerful poetry since 1950 as has Northern Ireland. It is impossible to survey this rich and varied terrain in a fairly brief discussion, and I will not pretend to do so here. Rather, I will locate along the continuum suggested in Eagleton's work four of the major poetic voices in Northern Irish poetry: John Montague, Seamus Heaney, Ciaran Carson, and Paul Muldoon. I will suggest that where Montague and Heaney are situated nearer the commitment end of the continuum, Carson and Muldoon hover at the ironic end (not least by ironizing the commitment of their elders).

In his preface to *The Rough Field* (1972), John Montague recalls his compulsion to record and understand his native Northern Ireland and "the unhappiness of its historical destiny" (1972: 7). While he acknowledges the region's similarity to Brittany or the Scottish Highlands in almost Nairnean terms, as "remote areas where the presence of the past was compounded with a bleak economic future," he sets out to explore the complex terrain of Garvaghey, his local "rough field," and he does so in the form that Fredric Jameson has named the "pocket epic" (2007: 17). The multivocality, the openness to extra-literary documents, the intrication of language and history on the ground of a specific regional landscape that characterize the regional epics of late modernist poets shape what MacDiarmid called the "wonderful achievement" of *The Rough Field*.

Montague's sequence juxtaposes fragments of historical documents, letters, sectarian tracts, riddles, and other texts to re-create the rough discursive field of Northern Ireland in the 1960s. In "The Bread God," the third of the sequence's ten sections, for example, he juxtaposes lyrical descriptions of local Catholics at Mass with italicized prose recollections by Montague's uncle, a priest who left Northern Ireland for Australia in the 1960s, and with excerpts from a Loyalist Protestant pamphlet (titled "The Bread God") that recall historical "massacres" of and attempts to "exterminate" Irish Protestants. Montague's lyric moments limn the quiet faith of rural Catholics patiently and prayerfully waiting "For the advent of the flesh-graced Word" during the Christmas season when "red berried holly shines against gold / In the door of the tabernacle" (1972: 28). The juxtaposition of these moments with passages like "ROME'S CENTRAL ACT OF WORSHIP IS THE EUCHARISTIC WAFER! / IDOLATRY: THE WORST IDOL UNDER HEAVEN" and "ECUMENISM *is* THE NEW NAME *of the* WHORE OF BABYLON! / SHE *who* SHITS *on the* SEVEN HILLS" explicitly criticizes a colonial remnant anxiously seeking to retain political and cultural power. I do not want to overstate the poet's commitment, since Montague complicates this picture by framing the section with a letter in which the Belfast County Orange Lodge expresses to the British Prime Minister its concerns that the United Kingdom's entry into the European Common Market will amount to submission to (Catholic) Rome and an "Ulster Prophecy" that imagines a United Ireland in which British troops fire on the (Protestant) Shankill Road area of Belfast (1972: 30).

The next generation's Belfast poet most clearly following Montague's model is Ciaran Carson, whose 1989 *Belfast Confetti* similarly brings to bear several quite different forms (long poems and shorter lyrics, both in Carson's characteristic long lines, alongside prose essays and translations of haiku) in its attempt to read the titular city's geography, history, language, and culture. Each piece explores the city through its specific conjunctions of land and language; "Farset," for example, offers a set of etymologies for Belfast, each of which isolates and interprets some feature of its geological substrate, so that the city's name might derive from *"Beala Fearsad, which signifies a town at the mouth of a river"* or from *"'farset', or sandbank . . . i.e. Bel-feirste, the 'bel' or 'ford' of the 'farset'"* (1989: 47). Alongside this linguistically archaeological analysis of the city, Carson sets moments of sectarian violence in the city's present. These, too, are conceived in terms of language. "Punctuation" figures gunfire as ellipsis points ("another shadow steps out from behind the hedge, going, dot, dot, dot, dot, dot . . ." (ellipsis in original), while the speaker of "Barfly" offers gunmen who "punctuate the lunchtime menu" and a speaker who imagines himself as "a hyphen, flitting here and there" between one pub and another. Ultimately, the text of the city – its history and its geography – becomes so overwritten and partially erased that it is "indecipherable"; it suffers a "frottage effect" so that "the pencil-lead snaps off, in a valley of the broken alphabet // And the streets are a bad Photostat grey" (1989: 55). Finally, "whole segments of the map have fallen off" and the chief characteristic of Carson's nation torn by nationalisms is its illegibility, perhaps even its meaninglessness, as he writes, in "Snow," "I broke open the husk so many times / And always found it empty; the pith was a wordless bubble" (1989: 20).

A similar contrast is apparent in the work of Seamus Heaney and Paul Muldoon. While poems like "Anahorish" and "Mossbawn" show Heaney's intense awareness of the way language shapes and is shaped by the specific character of local geographies, he has been more preoccupied with recording the warping of society by sectarian division. Like Montague, he has reckoned the costs and consequences of internecine violence in Northern Ireland, but Heaney seems keenly interested not only in those suffered by its agents and victims but also in the difficulties endured by the poet who must work out a responsible relationship to his historical moment. His returns to this problem throughout the 1970s and 1980s suggest that Heaney found successive resolutions unsatisfactory. Heaney first deals at length with the "Troubles" in post-1968 Northern Ireland in his 1975 volume, *North*, worrying in "Punishment" about his unwilling complicity in the conflict and in "Singing School" about his ethical responsibility to address it. That volume's most certain-sounding resolution comes in the title poem, in which the speaker accepts the wisdom spoken by the tongue of the Viking longboat and recognizes that the tangle of hatred and betrayal that has ensnared contemporary Northern Ireland is but the latest manifestation of an ineradicable human tendency toward violence. The poet must be content to burrow in the word-hoard so as to name the perceptions and pleasures of the body and offer these as a stay against destruction, a consolation in the face of unavoidable conflict. In *Field Work* (1979), Heaney is provoked by the sectarian murder of a relative (his second-cousin Colum McCartney) to revisit the question of the poet's proper role. In "The Strand at Lough Beg," he imagines cleaning his cousin's corpse not only with the reeds that grow alongside the lake but also with the aestheticizing and meaning-making capacities of poetry (metonymically present in the poem's allusion to Dante's *Purgatorio* and Virgil's preparation of the poet as he ascends from Hell). By 1984, this resolution too seems untenable, and in a climactic passage in "Station Island," Heaney stages a scene in which McCartney's ghost, still covered with the mud and blood the earlier poem had imagined washing away, accuses Heaney of indirectly participating in his murder by veiling it in comforting allusion, sweetening it with literary "saccharine," and confusing "evasion with artistic tact" so that the reality of violence is made invisible and acceptable (1984: 3). While his earlier work sought to disavow responsibility, to remain neutral, or to dissolve sectarian violence in the long view of human history or the redemptive promises of nature, Heaney sets out in "Station Island" to acknowledge and reckon the specific gravity and cost of contemporary violence as he "translates" it through aesthetic attention.

Paul Muldoon's approach to the questions that so provoke Heaney is characterized by the trickster's irony, an acidic acknowledgment of the claims pressed by national history, culture, literature, and identity that seeks at the same time to dissolve them. A number of poems from his early books (*New Weather*, *Mules*, *Quoof*) limn the divisions wrought by national or cultural identity (legacies of what he calls, in "The Mixed Marriage," "factions of the faction-fights" [1977: 61]) in the private spaces of a marriage, a family, a bed. The title poem of *Quoof* (1983) posits the speaker's local language, comforting within its familiar (and familial) place of origin, as a weapon or divider in other contexts. The same volume's "Aisling" nods to the traditional Irish dream-vision poem in which the speaker encounters a female figure for the nation but replaces Eire with "Anorexia," a goddess who refers to the grounding of national identity in a history of starvation (the famine of the 1840s, the IRA hunger strikes of the 1980s). His union with this goddess leaves the speaker diseased and linked through the imagery of bodily fluids not only to this tainted national ideal but also to the failed rebellion of "the latest hunger-striker / to have called off his fast" and to the colonial institutions ("Belfast's Royal Victoria Hospital") that contain it (1983: 127). Where Heaney, in "Punishment," worries over his inescapable collusion with his co-religionists as they tar and feather young women who fraternize with British troops, Muldoon, in "The More a Man Has the More a Man Wants" (also in *Quoof*) imagines a similar scene in an insistent hail of puns and allusive wordplay:

> Someone on their way to early Mass
> will find her hog-tied
> to the chapel gates –
> O Child of Prague –
> big-eyed, anorexic.
> The lesson for today
> is pinned to her bomber jacket.
> It seems to read *Keep off the Grass*.
> Her lovely head has been chopped
> and changed.
> > (1983: 130)

The "undernourished" bog-preserved girl in Heaney's poem has become an "anorexic" echo of "Aisling," her sin against the community spelled out in the slang reference to an informant ("grass"). The violence is as graphic here as it is in Heaney's poem (a line-break momentarily decapitates the girl, strengthening her resemblance to Heaney's addressee), but no speaker here sympathizes with her or struggles with the ethics of representation and silence. As Clair Wills has written, "Muldoon seems, perversely, to be purely interested in effects: the distorted effects of paramilitary justice, which far outweigh their cause, and his own, poetic, effects" (1998: 95). The scene is dissolved in the fatally playful narrative of the poem's protagonist, Gallogly, a nationalist terrorist whose name evokes the "gallowglass" class of soldiers who once fought for Irish chieftains. His acts (various larcenies, liaisons, and assaults) and his ultimate fate (blown up by another terrorist group's homemade bomb) suggest Muldoon's corrosive critique of national identity; everyone suffers for no discernible purpose. The poem's final stanza quotes bystanders on the character of Gallogly's remains – " 'They foun' this hairy / han' wi' a drowneded man's grip" – so as to recall the legend in which a chieftain claims Ulster by touching it first, cutting off his hand and throwing it ashore to do so. No redeeming *sparagmos*, Gallogly's death, like his life, is simple, destructive dissolution. Muldoon's relation to the nationalist desire embodied in this Republican anti-hero is corrosively ironic.

Wales

Contemporary English-language poetry in Wales (or Welsh poetry in English) offers a range of attempts to think through what David Lloyd has called "the urgency of identity" (1994). These strategies, too, map onto Eagleton's continuum between a confident nationalism with little anxiety and an almost entirely ironic engagement with a culturally specific nation. Tony Conran and Nigel Jenkins write nearer the first extreme. Each expresses a forceful anti-imperialist critique of England and both position Wales as a natural, though threatened, nation. Each emphasizes the marginalization Welsh identity entails. Conran's "Elegy for the Welsh Dead, in the Falkland Islands, 1982" (1988: 14–15), like the "Gwales" variation in his 1993 book-length poem *Castles*, finds only death in the Welsh soldier's service to the English monarch, and implies that such service grows out of forgetting one's true Welsh identity. The "Note" to *Castles* suggests that this identity grows not only out of history but also out of the landscape itself – "trees, communities, the flow of the world" (1993: 6). Conran's poetry wears the residue of this process, whether in the bardic boasting for the soldiers named in the "Elegy" or the attenuated *cynghanedd* (a traditional Welsh form of versification) in his long poem "Blodeuwedd." Jenkins takes a more nuanced but no less committed approach to Welsh national identity in his work. In "How to get lynched in a bourgeois democracy," he locates "be Welsh" in second place on a list of putatively lynchworthy identities, just after "Be black" and just before "Be a woman"

(1990: 88). Welshness thus takes its essential place between race and gender, and Jenkins adopts an unproblematic assumption of marginal and victimized identity. "Never Forget Your Welsh," on the other hand, turns its critical rhetoric on contemporary Welsh citizens as well as their English colonizers. The criticism of the Welsh, though, is leveled at their failure of nationalist nerve: "bland bitter brewed with Wales in mind / mad March hares even the gogs / 2 to 1 against" (1990: 90). This scathing reference to the St David's Day Referendum of 1979 sets off a series of comparisons in which Jenkins finds the present-day Welsh wanting against the horizon of historic Welsh heroes.

Nearer the other end of the continuum, Robert Minhinnick conducts his own search for the heroic past in poems like "Looking for Arthur," but he finds only junk. In "a valley stranger than most / In the legends," a place through which the mythic King of the Britons (with roots in the Welsh *Mabinogion*) might have ridden, Minhinnick encounters "A heap of rusted cars." In place of castles or cathedrals, the junkyard boasts an engine house, "Its gorgeous brickwork prickly with red moss" (1989: 76). Here the speaker's children find a single relic: "This one horseshoe, whose rusting leaves / As yew wood does, a regal dust." No Excalibur lying pristine in the lake, the mundane artifact rusts amid refuse and pollution ("the pool of green / Nitrogen simmered between the rocks"). Minhinnick's careful adjective – "regal" – pulls Arthur's chivalric culture down to a ruined earth. This, and not legend, is the ground on which the nation must be built.

Oliver Reynolds' search for foundations to support a Welsh national identity runs into similar difficulties. "Daearyddiaeth" asserts a traditional identification of land and language (the title is Welsh for "geography" or "world-writing"), but questions the power of this connection in the context of the contemporary city. While in the country, the speaker reads national-cultural meanings in natural signs, expressing them in Welsh: "*hiraeth*" or "longing (for one's country)," "*Gwlad*" or "country" (1985: 64). Walking in Cardiff at dawn, though, he encounters only English place-names: Jonkers Terrace, Thornbury Close, Thornhill. *Daearyddiaeth* becomes "geography." The poem concludes with a discovery, a bit of Welsh "avowal" stamped into a lamppost's iron base: "D. Evans Eagle Foundry / Llandaff 1911" (1985: 66). The inscription suggests a Welsh ground for the English-speaking city, an engagement with the earth that, after mining and refinement, yields illumination. But the "bulb is lit but pale," an artificial light, weak against the burgeoning day.

Gillian Clarke's poems scatter across this continuum, but continually address the problems posed by nationalist desire. Her well-known
1984 lyric, "Fires on Llyn," addresses the arson campaign of the 1970s
and 1980s, in which militant Welsh nationalists (members of Meibion
Glyndwr) burned English-owned holiday cottages in Wales. Clarke's
image of English boys throwing stones suggests a cultural violence that
infects her vision generally so that when she sees the sun reflecting
in distant cottage windows she assumes the light is flames, a Welsh
violence answering the English provocation. More often, though,
Clarke sets out to complicate Welsh identity (or the desire for such
an identity) by showing how the local landscape is inextricable from
a larger world. "Neighbours" enacts just such a recognition when a
lamb "sips caesium on a Welsh hill" or a child lifting her face to the
rain "takes into her blood the poisoned arrow" of fallout from the
Chernobyl nuclear reactor disaster (1997: 85). The prevailing winds
that carry radioactive isotopes across vast distances bring home the fact
that we all live under the same sky, that the Welsh water, the "dwr"
divined in Clarke's early lyric "The Water-Diviner," is all too easily
contaminated by a cloud generated far away.

In her 1989 sequence *Cofiant*, Clarke goes farther, not complicating
so much as evacuating national identity of any real or legible substance
(see Thurston 2003). The poem derives its title and its form from a
traditional Welsh biographical miscellany, typically composed for local
clergymen and comprising a selection of the subject's sermons as well
as an account of his life and a concluding tribute or elegy. Clarke's
cofiant, though, testifies to absence rather than the continuing presence suggested by a minister's writings. Several sections of the poem
recall the poet's ancestors only to acknowledge their inaccessibility.
While Clarke's father, who died when she was a young woman, lingers
somehow in "the margins of books . . . // lists; old letters; diaries; notebooks," these traces are fragile (many are in "washable Quink" [1997:
125]). The traces left by more distant ancestors have already faded to
illegibility; Clarke stages one after another attempt to read these traces
only to be frustrated. Seeking an eighteenth-century couple, she "can't
find their grave / lost to the rampant daneberry" (1997: 132) and the
next step back marks the end of the trail: "His grave, his stone, / his
parts of speech all gone / under the city's monotone" (134). If one's
familial identity depends upon a knowable continuity, and if that
continuity depends upon a knowable foundation in the past, then
Clarke's frustrated searches reveal the ultimate emptiness of that
identity. Its foundations are eroded, its traces illegible, its continuity

at once unfounded and ruptured. A series of interpolations from medieval chronicle histories of Wales suggests that Clarke's evacuation of family identity's foundations is a figure for the evacuation of national identity's foundations as well. In place of both, Clarke offers, in several of the sequence's lyrics, a transnational and cosmopolitan identity figured by the sea, which

> drafts and re-drafts the coast
> and is never done
> writing at the edge
>
> its doodle of scum,
> driftwood, rope and bottles
> and skulls of birds.
>   (1997: 135)

While the sea swallows the past – Clarke's father, the villages and farms of more distant ancestors, a crumbling pre-Norman hill-fort – and cleanses memory with the wash of salt, while it erodes those signs in which one might read the specific and distinctive history on which a specific and distinctive national identity might be based, it is, at the same time, a maternal and eternal maker of new texts. Clarke writes that all humans are born of it, composed of and by it, and so are united in their descent from it. With its vast scale and its corrosive effect on the edifices of national history, the sea is a quite different water from either Minhinnick's polluted "pool of green / Nitrogen" or the contaminated Welsh puddle of Clarke's "Neighbours." It is the global environment *as* global environment, without the parochial hook of the local.

Scotland

The sixth of W. S. Graham's "Seven Letters" figures the speaker's relationship to the pastoral Scottish landscape through the metonym of a beloved linked by her breath to "the crushed smell of the moor." In the absence of speech between the lovers when they wordlessly part, the moor curls "its cries far / Across the still loch" and the sea responds with its "great verbs" (2004: 135). Such natural noises provide the poet with what the second letter calls his "musing love." This consociation of language and landscape characterizes a great deal of postwar Scottish poetry, whether the landscape at issue is the blighted city of Glasgow, the abandoned fields and crofts of the Highlands, or the Norse-graffitied stones of Orkney. The specific gravity of this relationship, though, varies in the hands of poets with quite different aesthetic and political agendas. At the same time, the explicit attention many Scottish poets pay to class reveals the ways much of the desire for a Scottish national identity in this poetry is, in Nairn's terms, a displacement of class-based anxieties.

From opposite ends of the country, George Mackay Brown and Iain Crichton Smith offer readings of the landscape that find traces of often violent history, traces echoed in the language that arises from the same locations. Mackay Brown's Orkney Islands left Norwegian hands to become part of Scotland only in the seventeenth century. Like his novel *Magnus*, his poems register the lingering cultural and linguistic influence of Viking Scandinavia. "The Five Voyages of Arnor" recounts the life of a Viking *skald* breathing out his last in the Orkney town of Hamnavoe and makes this linguistic legacy explicit by pointing out the Norse derivation of Scottish and Irish place-names, while "Runes from a Holy Island" wryly translates marks left on the islands by their history. It is the short lyric "The Kirkyard," though, that most powerfully condenses Mackay Brown's concerns. The poem's three stanzas offer three readings of the "island dead" in the cemetery, three interpretations of the marks their lives have left in gravestones. First figured as a "silent conquering army," the dead in the cemetery become a "green wave full of fish" and, finally, a honeycomb (1971: 68). The island's history thus embodied is transformed in the poem from threat to nourishment; even when imagined as "waxen pain," its fragrance is sought by the poet. Where "The Kirkyard" reads the preserved traces of historic lives, Crichton Smith's "The Clearances" first registers and then resists the landscape's reclamation of such evidence. Thistles overtake the thatch of forcibly abandoned Highland crofts and stars dance to rhythms far removed from earthly history, but Crichton Smith's speaker resolves to "remember" and, on the basis of this remembering, to hate (even as he acknowledges the evil of hatred) those who perpetrated the clearance of peasants from the countryside.

In a similar way, Crichton Smith's "The White Air of March" represents the Isle of Skye's Cuillin mountains standing tall, their streams screaming, their hollows filled with "Gaelic bluebells," a geological figure for memory set against a culture insistent upon forgetting the history for which the defeat of Stuart-supporting Highlanders at Culloden stands as metonym. In "Shall Gaelic Die?" he makes clear that these losses result from the loss of the language in which history was experienced by the nation's natives: "He who loses his language loses his world.

The / Highlander who loses his language loses his world" (1981: 66). The linguistic loss is itself a consequence of history and not nature. In the poem's concluding section, Crichton Smith writes:

I came with a "sobhrach" in my mouth. He came with a "primrose."
"A primrose by the river's brim". Between the two languages, the
word "sobhrach" turned to "primrose."
Behind the two words, a Roman said "prima rosa."

(1981: 66)

Like the Highland clearances, this linguistic colonialism threatens to leach meaning from the landscape. Against such forces, Crichton Smith offers only his poems' insistence on remembering, on reading and so rendering legible the land's marks, and on suggesting the national metonymy of individual lives like his own. He develops that metonymic sense of the individual poetic self at greatest length and with greatest effect in *A Life*, which follows the contours of his own biography from a childhood on the Hebridean island of Lewis ("a boyhood among glens and bens") through young adulthood in the western town of Oban. In his recollections of the latter, Crichton Smith offers his model of an ideal identity in the form of a "Roman rector" whose grounding in the classics enables a cosmopolitan complication or expression of the Scottishness suggested by nearby Mull and Iona. "'Transposing Greek to Gaelic,'" the rector easily "chats to the crafting man" and is able with equal facility to scan "vast hexameters or the pibroch" (1989: 39–40).

Douglas Dunn recalls similar figures in "Dominies," apologizing for his sonnet's "gauche lines" and commemorating the cosmopolitan voices of his youth, voices that urged him to continue his translations (his citizenship in the world) even as they asked whether he would "stand for [his] country" against the Caesars. Dunn's work is central to any narrative of postwar Scottish poetry since he contributes to that poetry not only in such books as *Barbarians* (1979) and *St Kilda's Parliament* (1981) but also as editor of the Faber Book of Scottish Poetry and as frequent writer about contemporary Scottish poets. In *St Kilda's Parliament*, he explores the specific shape taken by links between language, history, and landscape in Scotland. "The Harp of Renfrewshire" echoes a poem like Heaney's "Anahorish" in its embodiment of local pronunciation in local landmarks: "Annals of the trilled R, gently stroked L, / Lamenting O of local literature, / . . . / Land-language chattered in the river's burr" (1986: 160). "Galloway

Motor Farm" resembles poems by Tony Curtis or Gillian Clarke in the way it registers colonizers' marks on the landscape. The core modes of Dunn's poetic contribution, though, are to be found in two of the book's longer poems. In "St Kilda's Parliament" and "Green Breeks," Dunn takes on and takes seriously the role of the writer and artist in the preservation of national culture and memory. The artist figure in "St Kilda's Parliament" is a photographer who has snapped the last picture of the titular island's leadership. A century later, the island abandoned and its society extinct, he meditates upon the picture's limited ability to keep present these men, its failure to capture "the groans / And sighings of a tongue [he] cannot speak" (1986: 145). Even given these limitations, though, the photographer suggests the necessity of remembering. "Green Breeks" implies through its castigation of a bad example the proper way for a Scottish writer to remember and preserve the land's people. Responding to a passage in Sir Walter Scott's memoirs, Dunn castigates his predecessor for both his fawning devotion to the Sutherland nobles who will go on to "clear" their "kinsmen from the land" and for his self-serving representation of a working-class boy against whom the young Scott had fought in the streets of Edinburgh's New Town. In throwing in his lot with the nobility, Dunn argues, Scott lost "what was old, and fierce, and true" of Scotland. Dunn himself sets out, and suggests by example that his fellow Scottish writers should set out, to let the youth, Green Breeks, "*be*" as "light, conspirator, and spy" (1986: 180).

In the work of many contemporary Scottish poets, language itself, especially literary language and the relative literary value of Scots dialect, becomes at once a primary preoccupation and a salient formal feature. Raymond Vettese, for example, equates Scottish national independence with the revival of Scots in a Scots-inflected idiom: "I hae a vision o Scotland set free / and freedom and language tae me is ane." He wonders, though, whether his linguistic and literary efforts have any chance at success, perhaps not coincidentally in the passage most difficult for a reader unfamiliar with this idiom to parse:

> Ay, and sae it micht be
> wi mysel, and my footrin' phraisie style:
> snashgab, nocht mair, a silly dashelt screed,
> bummlin aboot, barmy on words, skinkin orra bree –
> ach, the thocht o the waste is whit I maist dreid,
> waste o span hundin a deein cause,
> my thick bluid dreepin clause by clause.
>
> (Dunn 1992: 361)

The city outside is quiet as the speaker works through his anxiety, its silence an apparent signal of its indifference to both linguistic reclamation and literary imagination. The poem closes with the speaker's resolve to continue his efforts, regardless of where they might lead.

Tom Leonard is less doubtful and more aggressive in his treatment of the relationship between Scots and poetry. His poems assume skepticism about or downright denial of his language's suitability for poetry (in "Ghostie Men," for example, he begins: "right inuff / ma language is disgraceful" (1984: 103) and he opens "Unrelated Incidents" by quoting an antagonist saying "its thi lang- / wij a thi / guhtr" ("it's the language of the gutter") (1984: 86). Against such attitudes, Leonard marshals a compelling variety of poetic weapons. In "Just ti Let Yi No," he writes a variation on William Carlos Williams's "This is Just to Say":

> ahv drank
> thi speshlz
> that wurrin
> this frij
> n thit
> yiwurr probbli
> hodn back
> furthi pahrti.
> (Dunn: 1992: 334)

Leonard suggests an analogy between the American modernist's incorporation of everyday language into poetry and his own programmatic use of Scots; if Williams's much-anthologized poem, with its colloquial language and mimicry of a mundane speech act, is accepted, Leonard implies, then his own similarly colloquial poem merits acceptance. Elsewhere, he takes on the "BBC accent" more directly. After listing various authorities, from "ma maw" to "po-faced literati," who have "tellt" him that his language is disgraceful, Leonard responds:

> ach well
> all livin language is sacred
> fuck thi lohta thim.

"Good Style," the sixth of "Six Glasgow Poems," threatens those who "canny unnirston" Leonard's poems with a kick ("stick thi bootnyi good style / so ah wull" [1984: 14]), and "Unrelated Incidents" imagines one interlocutor falling down an elevator shaft, but Leonard does not restrict himself to simple (if funny) tellings off. The second section of "Unrelated Incidents" offers a theory of language to justify the difficulty an English reader might have with Leonard's orthography, pointing out the difference between sound and object and symbol, while "Fathers and Sons," in straightforward English, deploys pathos, the speaker recalling his shame at his father's tenuous literacy when he is asked whether he finds his "phonetic urban dialect" "constrictive" (1984: 140).

More recent Scottish poets have tended toward the ironic end of the commitment continuum, imaging their Scottishness largely in terms of cosmopolitan citizenship (though often with an almost elegiac tone). Kathleen Jamie, for example, in "Skeins o Geese," maintains a ghost of something like Leonard's dialect – "I'm as empty as stane, as fields / ploo'd but not sown" – and finds history's text written on the landscape – "Wire twists lik archaic script / roon a gate" – but the words the geese write on the dusk, the word the wind whispers through the wire's rusted barbs, is not "like the past which lies / strewn aroun" (2002: 159). The speaker turns away from that past and imagines instead that the natural and extra-national world utters a "word niver spoken," a word that denotes commitments larger than those demanded by the nation. The wind's "dumb moan" is a sound "maybe human," as opposed to Scottish, and "bereft," as if it has witnessed or experienced the universal human condition of loss.

Northern England and the Midlands

While nationalist desires and discontents shape the work of these poets of Northern Ireland, Scotland, and Wales, it is a sense of regional heritage and identity that manifest in the work of some northern English poets since the 1960s. This work bears little of the centrifugal cultural force that we might see as one element in the broad array that includes agitation for political devolution of power from the metropole to the margins or the development of national institutions. It does, though, at once draw on and advance the historical and cultural specificity of the north and the industrial midlands. The poetry of northern England (or the poetry of northern Englishness) deploys many of the same poetic resources evinced in the nationalist poetry I have surveyed so far. Like Tom Leonard, for example, Tony Harrison engages the tension between metropolitan expectations and marginal language to explore his native region's constitutive conflicts and peculiar ways of being. In "Them and [uz]," he lays claim to poetry in terms quite similar to Leonard's: "So right, yer buggers, then! We'll occupy / your lousy leasehold Poetry. // I chewed up Litterchewer and spat the bones. . . ." Harrison's region is the industrial north of England, especially Leeds and Newcastle; his poems both mine and demonstrate the worth of that region's cultural wealth. "Them and [uz]" goes on to argue for the poetic centrality of northern dialect, pointing out that "Wordsworth's *matter/water* are full rhymes." Much of his work derives its energy precisely from the marginality of Leeds and its language (1987: 123).

Harrison titled his 1972 volume *The Loiners*, for the nickname given Leeds' citizens. That book's "Newcastle is Peru" sketches the atmosphere of Leeds and the folkways of its working-class population. The interweaving of Leeds dialect, family drama, and the dynamics of local history becomes Harrison's central poetic project in the ongoing sonnet sequence *The School of Eloquence* and the 1985 long poem, *v*. In the sequence's individual poems, Harrison dramatizes conflicts between dialects, classes, and generations. Many of the poems focus on the poet's relationship with his father, a baker with little understanding and less patience for his son's poetic calling. Others weave conflicts from the city's past (Luddite uprisings and the military suppression of them) and present (older working-class residents' fear of new immigrant neighbors) into the family, vocational, and aesthetic strands. The long poem, *v*, a rewriting of Gray's "Elegy Written in a Country Churchyard" set in Leeds' Beeston Hill Cemetery, tightens this braid. The poem finally condenses all the poet's primary concerns in the multivalent image of coal, the substrate upon which Leeds and its culture are built. This substrate is rendered unstable by the geological effects of mining, Thatcherite pit closings, and the miners' strike of 1984; Harrison writes that he walks "with weary tread" over subsidence in the cemetery's terrain and that

> Further underneath's the cavernous hollow
> that makes the gravestones lean towards the town.
> A matter of mere time and it will swallow
> this place of rest and all the resters down.
>
> (1991: 14)

A synecdoche for the industrial north of England, Leeds is, for Harrison, a landscape pitted by its past, a city whose life is "supported by the dead," but whose very existence is threatened by "the great worked-out black hollow." This existential instability manifests in the poem not only in this geological register but also in various ways throughout the poem, down to Harrison's memory of his aging father walking "wobbly on his pins," and it, as much as (because it is produced by) dialect, history, and culture, seems to define northern English regional identity for Harrison.

While they, too, evoke northern atmospheres, Ted Hughes and Jon Silkin ground these atmospheres more fully in the history of human interaction with the northern landscapes they describe. Hughes's *Remains of Elmet* (1979) repeatedly reads walls, ruins, and football pitches as signs of human labor and conflict. In "Walls," the stones are "syllables" that speak long-ago lives and "the labour // Buried in them" (2003: 462). Erosion, a natural occurrence legible in simply atmospheric terms, Hughes reads as an erasure of the "bodies and names" of those who have worked the Yorkshire land, but the re-maining wall continues to mark the historical fact of enclosure that altered those lives. Similarly, "Mill Ruins" record in fragmentary form the rising of workers and smashing of looms, while poems like "Heather" and "Wadsworth Moor" figure the natural forces that grind the landscape in terms of human industry (the "upper millstone of heaven," the "millstone of the sky" [2003: 474]). Silkin's historical references are more specific. In "Astringencies" (1961), he begins with a description of York in familiar, if not cliché, terms, emphasiz-ing the juxtaposition of industry and religion, the river and the cold. He goes on, though, to link these aspects of atmosphere to the city's history; the cold is York's punishment for the 12th-century suicide of the city's 800 Jews, who "Took each other's lives / To escape chris-tian death / by christian hand" (1980: 34). In "The Killhope Wheel" (1974), Silkin also moves quickly from a description of Durham that emphasizes its industrial present to a multivocal account of miners' lives there during an 1860 strike. Just as York's cold derives from its history, Durham's "clagged" soil, its "bituminous / and rank" essence, is an inexorable consequence of the suffering of the city' s miners, who are crushed by the state like the ore they mine is crushed by the wheel (1980: 125–6).

The two great contemporary poetic works of the midlands – Geoffrey Hill's *Mercian Hymns* and Roy Fisher's *City* – synthesize the atmospheric, autobiographical, and historical impulses of Harrison, Hughes, and Silkin. More than this, each of these marks a formal achievement that trans-forms its location into a matrix of thought and imagination. Fisher has written that his native Birmingham is what he thinks with; the same might be said for Hill's West Midlands.

Hill's sequence blends a speaker's recollections of childhood with language and images that hearken back to early English history. The lived experience of present-day middle-England and the mythos of the distant British past merge on the grounds of landscape, language, and labor. Hymn VII in the sequence describes

> Gasholders, russet among fields. Milldams, marlpools
> that lay unstirring. Eel-swarms. Coagulations of
> frogs.
>
> (1984: 99)

It goes on to narrate a childhood episode played out on this terrain – Offa's punishment of his friend Ceolred for the latter's loss of a precious toy. The toy is a biplane, "already obsolete and irreplaceable," a signifier for British military exploits in the twentieth century. After flogging Ceolred, Offa roams in "his private derelict sandlorry / named *Albion*." The contemporary (toy, school, sandlorry) and the mytho-historic past (Offa, Ceolred) are laminated on this landscape and the whole sweep of human habitation and conflict suggested in these compact signifiers is offered as essential Englishness. In the thirty *Mercian Hymns*, Hill works in a similar way, shuttling between past and present, mining landscape and language and refining what he finds in order to forge, temper, and sharpen this regional sense of English identity.

Fisher has written that *City* (1961) sets out not to posit or define a regionally specific identity or atmosphere but to limn instead "a city which has already turned into a city of the mind" (1975: 12). While the city Fisher represents is "not meant to be an historical / spatial city entailed to an empirical reality," however, it is no less a recognizable Birmingham. The poem traces what Fisher calls "the EFFECTS of topography," but the topography is that of a Midlands city formerly an industrial capital and now fallen upon hard times and, in places at least, fallen into rubble and ruin. The "Introduction" to *City* notes that in an area near "the centre of the city all of the buildings have been destroyed within the past year: a whole district of the tall narrow houses that spilled around what were a hundred years ago outlying factories has gone" (1961: 21). The city's historically identifiable heart is now a "waste," just as the district "that fills the hollow" beneath it is "impenetrably black." Only a factory, "stretching across three or four whole blocks just below the edge of the waste," is alight and clearly visible. The city of *City* might be a "city of the mind" and might not be "entailed to an empirical reality," but the terrain Fisher explores in the project is both regionally and historically specific. Both the poems and the prose interludes of *City* marshal images of the industrial midlands – dye-works, pithead gears, prefabricated workshops jutting into allotments, brick dust. Even a pseudo-pastoral scene like the one sketched in "By the Pond" is shot through with regionally specific bitterness; the first stanza's "pallid water" is offset by the "staring wire fences" around a pit-mound in the second, and the yellow rushes by a fisherman's shack crowd under an "ashen sky" (1961: 27). The images thus juxtaposed, like the moments of lyrical intensity in the volume's poems when framed by prose passages about the city's appearance and inhabitants, "serve as conscience."

If the Birmingham of *City* must be interpreted by the reader, the Birmingham of Fisher's 1986 volume *A Furnace* is both explicitly named and readily recognizable. The book's title and organizing image are drawn from the city's industrial past and identity, but Fisher is interested here, as in his earlier work, in understanding the material text written by that history and the subjects who embody that identity in the present. The projects are connected by an emphasis on that text's revision as the city's economic base shifts. Where the old neighborhoods were being cleared in *City*, they have been replaced in *A Furnace* by the glass towers of finance. The contemporary age has, Fisher writes, "a cold blackness of hell" that manifests in all "cities at night," from Chicago to London to the various districts of Birmingham. The atmosphere recalls the bitter cold of Silkin's "Astringencies," but where Silkin grounds York's cold in the sins of history, Fisher locates it precisely in the fact of economic/historic change, the transformation of the means of production:

> Puritan materialism dissolves its matter,
> its curdled massy acquisition; dissolves
> the old gravity of ponderous fires
> that bewildered the senses,
>   and for this
> glassy metaphysical void.
>   (1986: 35)

While his way of understanding contemporary Birmingham might suggest a loss of regional specificity, Fisher's poem continually imagines the city's people as formed by the city's history so that there remain such phenomena as the "Birmingham voice" and "the sunlight / of a Sunday morning on / Saltley Viaduct."

Fisher's work, characterized by its restless commitment to the topography of the imagined city and by its "superimposition of landscape upon landscape instead of rhythm upon rhythm," might offer the most powerful model for a new poetic exploration of regional and national identity in the Britain that continues, long after Nairn's prediction, slowly to break up.

Further Reading

Eagleton, Terry (1990). Nationalism: Irony and Commitment. In Terry Eagleton, Frederic Jameson, & Edward Said, *Nationalism, Colonialism, and Literature*. Minneapolis. MN: University of Minnesota Press, pp. 23–42.

Kerrigan, John (2000). Divided Kingdoms and the Local Epic: *Mercian Hymns* to *The King of Britain's Daughter*. In Nigel Alderman & C. D. Blanton (eds), *Pocket Epics: British Poetry After Modernism*. *Yale Journal of Criticism*, 13(1) (special issue), 23–42.

Lloyd, David (1993). *Anomalous States: Irish Writing and the Post-Colonial Moment*. Durham, NC: Duke University Press.

Lloyd, David T. (1994). *The Urgency of Identity: Contemporary English-Language Poetry from Wales*. Evanston, IL: Triquarterly.

Nairn, Tom (1977). *The Break-Up of Britain: Crisis and Neo-Nationalism*. London: New Left Books.

Peach, Linden (1992). *Ancestral Lines: Culture and Identity in the Work of Six Contemporary Poets*. Brigend: Seren.

Ryan, Ray (2002). *Ireland and Scotland: Literature and Culture, State and Nation, 1966–2000*. Oxford: Clarendon Press.

Williams, Raymond (1977). *Marxism and Literature*. New York: Oxford University Press.

Chapter 5

Form and Identity in Northern Irish Poetry

John P. Waters

I

The rubric of Britishness describes only partially and contentiously the poetic field of Northern Irish culture. For the entirety of the historical period surveyed in this volume, Northern Ireland has remained a part of the constitutional government of the United Kingdom of Great Britain and Northern Ireland; this is the political entity created by the Government of Ireland Act in 1920, and is thus a remnant of the Act of Union of 1800. The provisional solution to the centuries-old Irish problem through the expediency of partition continues to stir the pots of British and Irish politics; the welcome changes introduced by the peace process begun in 1994, especially the dramatic reduction in military and paramilitary violence following the Good Friday Agreement of 1998, have not yet solved the problem of the state. Consequently the terminology used to name the poetic field itself is implicated in the political crisis, as even a brief survey of the terms in play makes clear. There is, to begin with, an appreciable difference between describing a "Northern Ireland" poetry and a "Northern Irish" poetry; the former describes a political State that has never enjoyed unchallenged legitimacy, and the latter denominates a subset of an ethnicity and another State with which many residents of Northern Ireland vehemently do not wish to associate. Other names have proven yet more unpalatable. "Ulster," for example, the traditional name for the northernmost of the four provinces of the island of Ireland, has become the by-word of regional identification among the Unionist community, those residents of Northern Ireland principally drawn from Protestant denominations, who favor maintaining the British connection. "Loyalists," a name generally given to the more strident element of the Unionist community, would also employ Ulster as a designation of regional identification, though their sense of Britishness is yet more firmly held and expressed. The political use of the term Ulster, however, to refer to the six-county state of Northern Ireland removes three of the nine counties traditionally part of the province that were excluded at partition to secure Protestant dominance in Northern Ireland. Donegal is every bit as much a part of Ulster as County Down, though it is in the Republic of Ireland and is overwhelmingly Catholic. Cathal Ó Searcaigh, for example, might be called an Ulster poet, though in no very usable sense a British one; born and still living in northern Donegal, a short distance from the border of Northern Ireland, he writes in the Irish language and principally mines the traditions of Irish rather than English poetry.

The use of "British" within the poetic field of Northern Ireland has been especially contentious, provoking a famous response from Seamus Heaney. After a substantial selection of his poetry was chosen by Blake Morrison and Andrew Motion to appear in *The Penguin Book of Contemporary British Poetry* (1982), Heaney replied with "An Open Letter," first published in 1983 as a pamphlet by the Field Day Theatre Company, where he sought with characteristic diplomatic sensitivity to reject, "As Empire rings its curtain down / This 'British' word" (Heaney 1985: 23). Although he addresses directly his own imbrication within the institutions of British/English poetry since his "audience is, / Via Faber, / A British one," he goes on to declare his Irish citizenship as a matter of both positive law and cultural preference: "but be advised, / My passport's green. / No glass of ours was ever raised / To toast The Queen" (1985: 25). "An Open Letter" ends with a fable of Miroslav Holub's that inscribes the moral imperative of precise naming, and concludes by declaring "British, no, the name's not right" (1985: 29).

The "British problem" in the context of Northern Irish poetry lies in its connection to British imperial power, Irish colonial history, and the contemporary crisis of civil society. And yet if "British" is "not right," "Irish" can also require clarification. The challenge posed by the macro-political narratives of British and Irish politics to this poetry resides in the problem of taking national identity and associated cultural and linguistic traditions to be the essential determinants of how "identity" enters into a given poet's language or chosen forms. The civil crisis during the period necessarily provoked an aesthetic crisis since educational and cultural institutions have been by no means innocent of the social and political inequity that characterized society under the Unionist statelet, and the problems of audience and of the demands on artists for engagement have been especially acute in the divided polity of Northern Ireland. As Clair Wills argues in *Improprieties* (1993), it is in the development of poetic forms that we can grasp the full implications of the revisions both to poetic traditions and to political identities by Northern Irish poets.

Indeed, issues of identity and aesthetic politics inform the criticism of Northern Irish writing at every turn, and two opposing positions have tended to dominant the critical field. The first has been an aesthetic-formalist position most influentially advanced by Edna Longley, a gifted and argumentative critic whose political and cultural commitments might elsewhere be considered liberal and humanist. Longley has battled fiercely against what she regards as the politicization of poetry, a politicization that, tellingly, she most often associates with Catholicism or nationalism. Peter McDonald has taken this position a step further, arguing in *Mistaken Identities* (1997) that all "identity discourse" is by its nature partial, from a given and therefore limited perspective, and thus radically inimical to good poetry. The second position has robustly critiqued this perspective, as critics such as Robert Garratt in *Modern Irish Poetry* (1989), Dillon Johnston's *Irish Poetry after Joyce* (1985/1998), and more recently Stan Smith in *Irish Poetry and the Construction of Modern Identity* (2005) have read poetry from Northern Ireland within an island-wide tradition. Therein the issue of identity is recognized for what it is, an inescapable feature of modern life. As with much of modern life, the desire to wish it away is a reaction to what cannot, or will not, be controlled.

Following some brief consideration of three important precursor poets active in the 1950s, Louis MacNeice, John Hewitt, and Patrick Kavanagh, this essay first focuses on the crucial decade from the mid-1960s to the mid-1970s, when Seamus Heaney, John Montague, Derek Mahon, and Michael Longley began careers as poets, the first two by complicating the prevailing poetics of post-Romantic lyric sensibility via explorations of landscape, identity, and myth, the latter two by a different elaboration of lyric forms within an urbane skepticism (Mahon) and a conservative naturalism (Longley). The essay then considers three poets, Paul Muldoon, Ciaran Carson, and Medbh

McGuckian, who came of age as poets during the full-blown crisis of sectarian civil war of the 1970s. All three have fashioned a poetics of formal innovation that dissolves the political and cultural determinations of poetic forms.

II

Within criticism of postwar Northern Irish poetry, the models of poetic practice and patrimony are contested, for the most part unhelpfully, along a sectarian and national divide. This typically has on one side Louis MacNeice and John Hewitt (urban, Protestant, British/Northern Irish), and on the other Patrick Kavanagh (rural, Catholic, Free State Irish). Although all three poets began publishing in the 1930s, their continued publications after 1945 provided crucial local models for poets coming out of university in the 1950s and early 1960s, and helped authorize the possibility of writing poetry in the seemingly unpromising and provincial circumstances of Ireland, North and South, in the immediate postwar period.

MacNeice's complex attitudes toward Ireland tend to be simplified through "Section XVI" of his 1939 *Autumn Journal,* where he disparagingly says "the land of scholars and saints my eye" (1966: 132) and offers a litany of eloquent complaint. Critics frequently employ this section to represent fixed beliefs, forgetting MacNeice's own caveat in his preface that "it is the nature of this poem to be neither final nor balanced" and that there were "over-statements" in the passages dealing with Ireland (1966: 101). Indeed in the poem itself, although MacNeice recognizes a partitioned country, he gives to the nation a discrete identity in the form of personalized address: "Why should I want to go back / To you, Ireland, my Ireland?" (1966: 133). In other words, when MacNeice addresses the question of his own identity and background he cannot avoid the singular name of "Ireland." This recalls MacNeice's earlier "Valediction" where he similarly seems to bid farewell to Irish antiquarianism and to any visionary poetics based on an idealized view of the Irish people:

> I can say Ireland is hooey, Ireland is
> A gallery of fake tapestries,
> But I cannot deny my past to which my self is wed,
> The woven figure cannot undo its thread.
>   (1966: 52–3)

As the poem progresses MacNeice rejects not only the cult of the past in Irish politics and literature, but also the modernization of Ireland as tourist fantasy founded upon this past. At the poem's conclusion, however, even as he turns away, he is unable to resist the seductive and irresolvable attraction of the landscape of the island itself: "I must go east and stay, not looking behind, / Not knowing on which day the mist is blanket thick / Nor when sun quilts the valley and quick / Winging shadows of white clouds pass / Over the long hills like a fiddle's phrase" (1966: 53–4).

MacNeice's contemporary John Hewitt was for a time a fellow exile in England, but returned to Belfast, where for the last 15 years of his life he was an active presence on the cultural scene. Hewitt has been closely identified with a cultural politics of "Ulster Regionalism," an attempt to address the divisions between Protestant and Catholic, Planter and Gael, through a concerted and devoted attention to the local region. As Mary Burgess has argued, this effort, especially in historical and geographical studies, sought to naturalize the partition of Ireland (Burgess 2005). In many of Hewitt's more frequently anthologized poems, such as "Ireland," "The Colony," "Once Alien Here," and "An Irishman in Coventry," he confronts the colonial history of plantation and conflict in Ireland with ambivalence, writing poetry out of the examination of conscience. If, in a poem such as "An Ulsterman in England Remembers," written during violent conflict in 1969, he could offer testimony of discrimination and violence against Catholics during the Belfast riots of 1932 and 1935, Hewitt could also offer images of enduring defiance of a kind that would rhyme with the political discourse of power in Ulster Protestantism, as in "Rite, Lubitavish, Glenaan" from 1952:

> Above my door the rushy cross,
> the turf upon my hearth,
> for I am of the Irishry
> by nurture and by birth.
>
> So let no patriot decry
> or Kelt dispute my claim,
> for I have found the faith was here
> before St Patrick came.
> (Hewitt 2007: 44)

Hewitt's struggle with the inveterate political complications of identity in Northern Ireland has a poignancy of honest effort and good faith wagered against an uncompromising historical legacy sown into the landscape and the visions it inspired.

In exploring the ambivalent and unhappy inheritance of his native place he was joined by his very different contemporary from Country Monaghan in the Republic of Ireland, Patrick Kavanagh. No one did more to reclaim the poetry of Kavanagh from critical condescension and neglect than Heaney. Heaney's first volume of prose, *Pre-occupations* (1980b), heralded the example Kavanagh gave to someone of his background. Rural, unpolished, shaped by hard physical labor and the intimate proximity of nature, Kavanagh modeled a fierce commitment to poetry as well as the necessity of giving oneself permission to write about the world one knows. For Kavanagh, this meant first an unsuccessful period of exile in London, followed by a retreat to Dublin where he fought, often quite literally, for a claim on the dignity of being called poet. It also meant both a rejection of the Revivalism still dominant in Ireland of the 1930s (Kavanagh was from the peasant stock viewed from an Olympian and distorting distance by Yeats), as well as a suspicion of the modernist cosmopolitanism championed by Pound. In their place he championed the idea of parochialism as a way of rendering the universal in the concrete particular. Kavanagh's poetry fashioned an anthropology of rural Ireland in which the poet becomes a native participant with a gift for observation. Like MacNeice and Hewitt, Kavanagh's attention to a historically inscribed landscape leads to both alienation and love. Despite their differences of temperament and of cultural identity, the joint example of all three gave confidence to poets from both sides of the sectarian divide in Northern Ireland.

III

Among the many critical descriptions of the formal distinction of recent Northern Irish poetry, Terence Brown's concentration on the "well-made poem" is especially useful. In a discussion of the concept of a "Northern Renaissance" of Irish poetry, Brown identifies the "well-made poem" within a specifically English poetic. But this unnecessarily limits his argument, for surely the governing concepts and available examples of formal exaction and precision of speech have multiple cultural sources. Furthermore, as Brown acknowledges in a brief conclusion to his essay, the debate on a poetic Northern Renaissance rests as much on experimental narrative poetry as on formal lyric poems, especially in the works of Carson and Muldoon (1988: 218–21).

Seamus Heaney has, of course, dominated the field in terms of critical attention and international fame. Emerging within a poetic culture that held the restraints of the formal lyric poem in the center of its aesthetic value system, Heaney's early career successes and subsequent critical acclaim resulted from a disciplined apprenticeship as lyricist and Romantic naturalist, with both his first two books deriving from a central metaphor of Romantic poetry. *Death of a Naturalist* (1966) performs a Wordsworthian poetic maturation that moves from naïve absorption within Nature to the crisis of subjectivity. *Door into the Dark* (1969) announces an investigation of the unconscious in terms laid out by John Keats in his famous letter of May 3, 1818 where he compares the poetic achievements of Milton and of Wordsworth in the exploration of the mind as a "Mansion of Many Apartments" (1958: 1.280). In these books Heaney established a reputation for finely tuned lyric poems that evoke for his predominantly urban readership the rural world of Mossbawn, the Derry farm on which he was raised as the eldest of ten children. Both books embody the most widely recognized characteristic of Heaney's imagination: his exploration of worlds beneath surfaces. Metaphors of digging and uncovering, of sounding wells and gazing into their depths, become (and remain) his central metaphors for the poetic process. Allied to this figurative claim are the many poems devoted to farm, artisanal, or craft labor whose final metaphoric movement elides this physical work with poetic craft. Indeed, the identification between poetic and other forms of labor constitutes a principal ground for David Lloyd's influential critique of Heaney's poetics (Lloyd 1993: 13–40).

In his third volume, *Wintering Out* (1972), Heaney's preoccupation with what lay buried underground broadens out to include history and politics more explicitly, especially in relation to violence. In poems such as "A Northern Hoard" and "The Tollund Man" Heaney explores the metaphoric resonances of Neolithic and Iron Age bodies buried and preserved in peat bogs. P. V. Glob's suggestion in *The Bog People* that these bodies had been sacrificed in the service of a matriarchal religion and had then been mummified by the preservative properties of peat bogs provided Heaney with a powerful conceit to figure the historical violence of Ireland. This became the controlling conceit of his next book, *North* (1975). This volume launched Heaney's entry into public fame and began sustained critical attention to his writing. It also marked not only the beginning of the critical resistance to

Heaney's governing metaphors, but also the emerging sense that subsequent poets would have to confront Heaney's poetry, poetics, and public persona in order to find their own creative spaces. Almost immediately Ciaran Carson, in a review in *The Honest Ulsterman*, argued *North* worryingly obfuscated contemporary reality: its cloak of aboriginal Scandinavian and Danish violence being offered as an explanation for a modern urban guerilla war.

"Punishment" has been the crucial poem around which the debate on *North*'s poetics and politics has been organized. The poem's potent mixture of sexual voyeurism and conflicted self-examination links a sacrificial victim of Bronze Age tribal violence with women brutalized for crossing the sectarian divide of twentieth-century Ulster by fraternizing with British soldiers. The sexual subject matter, however, is framed by the poem's emphasis on writerly conscience, literary-formal discipline, and an economy of meaning that grounds the present in a history susceptible of metaphor. To assert metaphor as a mode of reconceptualizing reality and making possible what had been prohibited led Heaney to weigh the ethical sufficiency of writing as a form of social action. Heaney closed the volume with "Singing School," an extended, autobiographical reflection on the political crisis in Northern Ireland and the challenges it posed to the ethics of writing. The epigraph from Book I of Wordsworth's *Prelude* ("Fair seed-time had my soul, and I grew up / Fostered alike by beauty and by fear; / Much favoured in my birthplace" [1980a: 217]) embraces both an earnest celebration of his early life in Nature, and, via irony, an indictment of the police state that he encountered on his visits home from school. It should be apparent that if Heaney embraced the concept of Wordsworthian organic becoming of the English Romantic tradition, he did so by embedding it within his own social-historical context. In their examination of Seamus Deane's handwriting at a checkpoint, the Unionist state made such cultural appropriation by a rural Catholic an act of defiance against the status quo. As he announces memorably in the poem "Singing School" (addressed to fellow St Columbs graduate Deane), "Ulster was British, but with no rights on / The English lyric" (1980a: 220).

Heaney's concern with conscience and the ethics of writing moves to the center of his poetry during the late 1970s and 1980s when the violence and political stalemate in Northern Ireland seemed utterly intractable. During this period Heaney increasingly faced the issue of his own poetic craft necessarily drawing him into political controversy. Once again, in *Field Work* (1979), the volume's title announced a sustained metaphor, albeit one less conceptually abstract than *North*. Some critics found the volume to mark a retreat to an identity politics that compromised aesthetic value, especially in poems such as "Toome Road," where the poet asks of a British Army patrol of armored personnel vehicles: "How long had they been coming down my road?" (Heaney 1979: 15). McDonald objects to the assertion of ownership in such lines, and calls the poem's concluding return to the "enduring, invisible Omphalos" a kind of "navel-gazing" (McDonald 1997: 58). Revealingly, McDonald transforms Heaney's explicit political claim of ownership to the land based upon his identity as an Irish Roman Catholic into a form of solipsistic, immature egocentrism. An assertion of collective belonging is seen as a revelation of subjective isolation. Such poems, however, make it clear that political questions are intrinsic to any poetry from this place with any claims on reality; they also argue that Britishness, whatever it is, could neither shelter nor coexist with Irishness, whatever that is. "Toome Road" shares the conceptual formulation that Heaney's friend Deane advanced in essays, lectures, and interviews: by the early years of the 1970s, Catholics in Northern Ireland experienced in their everyday movements through the security apparatus of the state the failure of Britishness to adequately incorporate or embrace Irishness. Internment, the imprisonment, for up to six months, without charge, of those Catholics suspected of subversive actions or affiliations, destroyed whatever possibility might have existed for British state institutions to overcome those local forms of discrimination that had been guaranteed by partition and subsequent one-party, majoritarian rule.

Heaney's abiding concentration on identity grounded in place and the cultural traditions specific to the Ulster countryside are shared by John Montague, though with the crucial distinction that Montague's search for a sense of stable belonging ends in the contemplation of historical alienation, "Our finally lost dream of man at home / In a rural setting!" (1972: 82). Of the poets to emerge in the 1960s, Montague most frequently has been linked with Hewitt because of their poetry's shared address to the historical dimensions of the Ulster landscape. Montague's poetry begins from perception and meditation on landscape and opens from there to encompass a wide range of experience, including most notably the colonial history of Ulster, especially of County Tyrone, Montague's home county and ancestral land of the O'Neils. It is the volume *The Rough Field*, published in 1972, that will secure Montague's intellectual importance within poetry in English. In a series of ten lyric sections, some previously published, *The Rough*

Field addresses the deteriorating crisis in Northern Ireland through the multiple lenses of local and national history, personal and familial memoir, and a collage of contemporary and historical quotations. It has become the iconic volume of poetry about the Troubles.

The Rough Field, like its successor volume, *The Dead Kingdom* (1984), embodies the modern poetic-formal crisis wherein the epic poem – the attempt to express the totality of the social order – has had to yield to social complexity and social fragmentation that can only be expressed through the long poem as lyric sequence. *The Rough Field* takes the fullest advantage of sequential form since it allows Montague to employ sonnets, quatrains, and tercets, as well as more complex and distinctive verse forms, such as the short, restrained, or broken lines of "A New Siege," his poem on Derry dedicated to Bernadette Devlin. Dedicating a poem to Devlin, radical civil rights leader and imprisoned MP, in 1972, the year of Bloody Sunday, when British paratroopers killed 13 unarmed Catholic demonstrators, constituted a political commitment too far for many of Montague's critics, who objected especially to this section of the poem.

Montague's most recent volumes have demonstrated in new ways his distinctive gift for infusing thought with rhythm; *Drunken Sailor* (1998) and *Smashing the Piano* (2003) gather lyric poems that draw on familial memory, Montague's most consistent source of inspiration and focus, but also poems such as "The Family Piano" that mix the inexplicable and surprising in human behavior with elegy and remembrance (Montague 2003: 70–1). These poems are consistent with the poetics of identity elaborated throughout Montague's career, in that they seek a ground for identity in a gapped or discontinuous history. Montague has been committed to a kind of realism and self-examination that resist more explicitly the comforts of myth or of genre that Heaney explores. Both poets have found themselves in the position of having to carefully respond to demands on their public voice; both have given us a poetry in which the ethical question and the social fact of violence have been confronted and engaged rather than condemned without effort. Montague's careful attention to form, then, should be considered in ethical terms as a necessary feature of his art, at the level of the individual poem and at the level of the book itself. All of Montague's volumes demonstrate something all the poets under discussion here share, a trait they can be said to have learned from each other, as much as from Yeats, the model for modern poets generally: the internal composition and arrangement of poems within an individual volume must be a work of art in its own right.

If to many readers of his poetry Heaney emerged as a poetic singularity, the one contemporary poet, let alone Irish poet, they buy and read, the striking achievements of his contemporaries and friends Michael Longley and Derek Mahon provide a strong challenge to such assumptions. Both Mahon and Longley had attended the Royal Belfast Academical Institution, a solidly Protestant institution that nonetheless sheltered a number of left-wing teachers critical of Unionist political hegemony. They both attended Trinity College, Dublin, in the early 1960s when the long Protestant Ascendancy dominance within Trinity had begun to wane; Trinity was no longer a sectarian institution, as the career of their contemporary, the Kerry poet and Catholic Brendan Kennelly, a Fellow at Trinity and later Professor of Poetry, attests.

As early as his first volume, *Night Crossing*, published by Oxford University Press in 1968, Mahon had declared his intellectual dissent from the legacy of sectarian politics threaded through Northern Protestant rhetoric. Mahon is a native of the north Belfast suburbs, a place he consistently rendered from a disillusioned distance as offering only, as he writes in "In Belfast," "the unwieldy images of the squinting heart" under "The cold gaze of a sanctimonious God" (Mahon 1968: 6). The poem "Ecclesiastes," for example, clearly had a follower of the Reverend Ian Paisley's thundering voice in mind when it ironically addressed a "God-fearing, God- / chosen purist little puritan" who could "shelter your cold heart from the heat / of the world, from woman-inquisition, from the / bright eyes of children" (Mahon 1999: 35). Mahon's early poems express not a specific political philosophy but rather the conscience of a hesitantly public intellectual whose critical obligations are internal to the operation of a descriptive and meditative art.

In keeping with a skeptical but resolutely cosmopolitan intellectual stance, Mahon has been drawn to ekphrasis, the verbal description of visual art. A characteristic example is the title poem of *Courtyards in Delft* (1981); there the contrary vision of the final stanza, where the pent energy of rigorously cleansed domestic order, the private sphere of a Protestant ethic, incubates dreams of imperial war, theologically justified but psychologically haunted. His most frequently anthologized poem is the masterful catalog of neglected life, "A Disused Shed in County Wexford," a poem that in its formal perfection and slowly gathering energy shows us what a poem by Philip Larkin would be if he had become a sympathetic humanist. Like Larkin's, Mahon's verse often has a witty edge sharpened by profanity, but unlike Larkin, he positions his disenchantment with the banalities of idealistic poetics within a concrete, historical, and political situation. In "Afterlives," for example, living in London is framed by returning to Belfast:

> What middle-class shits we are
> To imagine for one second
> That our privileged ideals
> Are divine wisdom, and the dim
> Forms that kneel at noon
> In the city not ourselves.
>
> (1999: 58)

Although, like Heaney and Longley, Mahon is a disciple of the well-made poem, a lyricist adept at a wide range of stanzaic forms and varying line lengths, he has found his distinctive voice within verse letters. In Mahon's poems the poised irony of the lyric generated a conversational and accretive irony whose natural form became the verse letter. Epistolary form, especially when devoted to a consistent authorial voice committed to clarity of communication, suits Mahon's rejection of the atavisms and manipulated privileges of Northern Irish society. It allows him to reflect on the shifts in location and the turns in fortune that have defined his career as a writer. Self-deprecation and a skeptical survey of his own talents and achievements are consistent features of these poems, from the closing lines of "The Sea in Winter" (1999: 115–17) through the forthright cultural aliena-tion and personal crises of "The Yaddo Letter" (1999: 182–5) and "The Hudson Letter" (1999: 186–222), to his recent self-portrait in "Harbour Lights" (Mahon 2005). Mahon's voice of literate disillusion marks another affinity with Larkin, though Larkin had postwar bour-geois liberal Britain to lash rather than the concentrated vulgarity of Celtic Tiger Ireland:

> Magic survives only where blind profit,
> so quick on the uptake, takes no notice of it,
> for ours is a crude culture dazed with money,
> a flighty future that would ditch its granny.
>
> (Mahon 2005: 63)

There is, of course, a consistent if predictable future in writing poetry that catalogs, in however clear a voice, the disappointment and amused alienation occasioned by capitalist hyper-modernity. What solace would such a voice find in a return to nature, to a poetics of observation? An answer is to be found not in Mahon, the inveterate if detached social observer, but in Michael Longley, the poet of nature.

Longley is exceptional among the poets under consideration here in that his family was not long resident in Northern Ireland before he was born. His parents emigrated to Belfast from London in 1927; his father served in the British army in World War I, where he was gassed and wounded with shrapnel and where he was decorated for both bravery and leadership. Married to the critic Edna Longley, a gifted advocate for Leavisite formalism and an acerbic critic of any political contamination of the higher pleasures of the aesthetic, he would thus seem to be an ideal candidate for upholding the category of a Protestant Imagination, a concept advanced in the 1980s by Edna Longley and Gerald Dawe, the poet/critic from Belfast. Longley's poetry is indeed shaped by humanist imperatives and assumptions, in that it forgoes experiment, mystery, allusiveness, and formal irregularity in favor of measured regularity, continuity of tone, and formality of address. Unlike Mahon, however, whose profound alienation has been balanced by wit and acerbic skepticism and vented in long poems of personal reflection, Longley has sought steady poise and descriptive accuracy that found expression over the course of his career in nature poetry. Beginning with his 1991 collection *Gorse Fires*, however, the predominant themes of his poetry shift. Early poems integrated quotidian detail with atrocity as a way to image the senseless and irrational (such as "Wounds" and "Wreaths"), yet Longley has devoted relatively few of his poems to the Troubles despite being one of only two of the poets under consideration here never to have moved away from Belfast. Poems devoted to World War I, especially "The War Graves," approach, in ways characteristic of Longley's aesthetic, the immensity of slaughter and loss through a resigned, tentative enumeration. If botanical subjects and metaphors were always present in his work, with *Gorse Fires* (1981) they move to the center of his poetic output, and indeed by giving himself the freedom to concentrate his energies on the inexhaustible intricacies of the microcosmic, he has enjoyed a flourishing productivity and a willingness to write poems that make the smallest possible rhetorical gestures. In such poems as "War and Peace" and "Interview" in *Snow Water* (2004), the Homeric subject matter that served in earlier poems such as "Laertes" as a way of addressing violence and inhumanity could be slimmed down and stripped of narrative. If Longley's humanist sensibility is often cited as a counterpoint to the irrationality of the Troubles, his capacity to embody the figure of the poet in a divided culture is not without risks. The public voice of the poet can be enlisted not only by sectarian politics, but also by corporate capitalism; Longley provided a poem celebrating, in uncharacteristically imprecise phrasing, the commercial culture of Belfast for a huge upscale shopping center called The Egg. The demotic wit of Belfast has been hard at work deconstructing the poem since it was etched in the glass high atop The Egg.

IV

One of the many complex questions presented to poetry critics by the success of the first generation of poets from Northern Ireland is the wealth of talent quickly demonstrated by their successors. For the poets who came to prominence in the 1970s and 1980s, there were more than a few available models within the small world of Belfast where they went to university. Of these poets, Paul Muldoon, Ciaran Carson, and Medbh McGuckian are the most challenging and the most rewarding, each having developed highly distinct careers that befit the poetics they each have fashioned. Muldoon, the first to be published, presents students of his poetry with the problem of how to respond to the immense variety of styles, forms, subject matters, genres, and fields of reference in his writing. No easy summary can capture the many features of his distinctiveness, though exquisite mimicry and an abiding exactitude with etymological implication underlie much of his writing. Early criticism emphasized the postmodernist elements of pastiche and radical decontextualization, while the absence of an explicit embrace of the Republicanism expected from some quarters of an Armagh Catholic seemed to combine with this abstract allusiveness to constitute the kind of retreat from political engagement characteristic of the most glib examples of postmodern art. Muldoon's poems, however, have a more sophisticated relation to the politics of reading and writing than many critics have been willing to grant.

Muldoon was raised in a small village in County Armagh, the southernmost of the Ulster counties incorporated within the Northern Ireland state after partition. The son of a schoolteacher mother and agricultural laborer/market gardener father, Muldoon had two worlds in his sights growing up, his mother's imaginative and culturally open world of books, and his father's world of agricultural labor, which valued patience, quiet skill, and persistence. In his approach to the political crisis of Northern Ireland and the colonial and anti-colonial elements of Irish history, Muldoon carefully resisted the seduction of political currency that an Armagh Catholic background might have afforded. This is not to say that he has not explored those questions; on the contrary, a poem such as "Gathering Mushrooms," from *Quoof*, might well constitute the most sensitive, albeit oblique, literary treatment yet written of the strange reality of the "Dirty Protest" in the Maze prison, where Irish Republicans, refused the designation of political prisoners, turned their bodies, even their excrement, into weapons.

If some critics emphasize the rejection in his poems of Republican ideology and the ideas that have sustained it, from the questionable authority given a former schoolmate in "Anseo" to the dangerous ideological seductions displaced by the lyric poem "Aisling" or within the verse play *Six Honest Serving Men* (1995), others emphasize the critique of Protestant paramilitarism and British colonialism, in its imperial and genocidal forms in "Meeting the British" or its utopian literary forms in *Madoc: A Mystery*. His unwillingness to be enrolled in a cause that would set limits on thought or his ways of imagining defines Muldoon's relation to literary as to political traditions, and especially any effort to link the former to the latter. Consequently, the problems of determinacy and indeterminacy lie at the center of Muldoon's poetry, and articulate a rich meditation on the formal qualities of political, literary, and linguistic authority. From his earliest lyrics, in *New Weather* (1973) and *Mules* (1977), to his most recent volume, *Horse Latitudes* (2006), Muldoon's poetry has figured indeterminacy and balanced indecision. "The Boundary Commission" redacts this to the problem of partition and the rigid oppositional politics of Northern Ireland, but the state of indeterminacy portrayed in that poem extends to every element of Muldoon's poetic, particularly the allusiveness that signifies Muldoon's postmodern proclivities. Muldoon constantly elides and reorganizes his source texts. In "The More a Man Has the More a Man Wants," for example, Muldoon combines passages several pages apart from Aldous Huxley's *The Doors of Perception* and Lewis Carroll's *Alice in Wonderland* in such a way that they seem to come from the same single source. This allusive practice forces readers to consider how one thing actually relates to another and whether any such relation is determined or contingent.

This embrace of indeterminacy links thematically in Muldoon with metamorphosis, particular of a violent nature. His 1983 volume *Quoof*, for example, mixed oblique personal poems, such as "The Unicorn Defends Himself," "Gathering Mushrooms," and "Quoof," with poems on animals and on Native American, Scandinavian, and Irish myths. All the poems in *Quoof* are preoccupied with the problem that violence presents to consciousness, specifically the sudden rupture in time and the difficulty of representation that violence presents. John Goodby argues persuasively that they do not begin from the idea that violence is abnormal and aberrational, but rather from the idea that violence is an integral feature of psychic and civic life (Goodby 2000: 258). For Muldoon, indeterminacy, allusiveness, metamorphosis, and violence connect the literary myths and history of Ireland and Anglo-America with the video games and films of contemporary society against which they are often set.

Ciaran Carson has been linked with Muldoon for biographical as well as conceptual and literary reasons; like Muldoon, Carson in his poetry conducts a restless, critical, improvisational, and irreverent reinvention of literary forms. They met at Queens University, where both studied English and began writing and reading their poems. Carson was native to Belfast, having grown up in the Catholic Falls Road and Andersonstown communities, the son of two language enthusiasts who decided to raise their children in Irish. If the Irish language gave Carson access to the riches of the Irish language literary tradition, then Irish music has also opened a world and time of great complexity and richness to his poetry. Carson devoted much of his twenties and early thirties to roaming over every part of Ireland to learn from and play with the carriers of traditional music. Whether seen as cultural inheritance or acquisition, or some measure of both, Irish music and the cultural artifacts of travel formed the subject for Carson's first books, *The New Estate* (1976) and the chapbook *The Lost Explorer* (1978). *The New Estate* was fashioned within the prevailing formalist weather of Queens in the 1970s, bearing the chisel marks of revision in the line breaks, in the measured rhythms and symmetry, and in the poetic voicing of observations that most often end in irony. The thematic concerns and formal disciplines forecast yet another promising career for an Irish lyric poet, one whose shifting narrative perspectives aligned him with Muldoon's more elusive work.

The decade between *The New Estate* and *The Irish For No* (1987), however, allowed a very different poet to emerge, one every bit as engaged with literary form but free from the minimalist anti-discursive aesthetic that is one end point of the well-made lyric poem. Critics have concentrated on the inspiration of American poet C. K. Williams for the long, 14-syllable line that Carson adopted in *The Irish For No*, but have rarely mentioned the musical inspiration of ballads and of *Sean-Nos* or old-style singing in Irish, which depend upon exquisite modulation of breath and syllabic shape. Carson's use of the long line to craft narrative poems of great internal complexity derives less from any specific literary tradition than from the social voice of the Irish storyteller, the spinner of yarns, the talker whose digressive moments define the art form because they call attention to the here and now, in its infinite recursive relation to the past. This narrative style, an experiment in *The Irish For No*, was brilliantly elaborated in the mixed mode of poetry and autobiographical prose poems in his next volume *Belfast Confetti* (1989). Fragments of a then-unfinished prose book about Belfast were interspersed with discursive, semi-autobiographical poems that made up a collective historical portrait of a city transformed not only by the Troubles but also by the history of capitalism and industry. A key to the conceptual architecture of the book is given by its epigraph from Walter Benjamin; Carson's model of the poet-as-flâneur has kinship with Benjamin's never-finished poetic historiography of Paris. The mixed form proved especially suitable for capturing the shifting psychological landscape of surveillance and conflict that made Belfast the exemplary test space for the assertion of state power through technology. Many of the poems in this volume explore the existential indeterminacy, the neither this nor that, A balanced against B, that Muldoon has also favored throughout his career.

Carson continued to employ the longer line in *First Language* (1993), but the grim humor of many of the poems of *Belfast Confetti* had modulated into quirky jokes and playful literary games, especially in the contorted off-rhymes that forced the reader to endure the pleasurable expanse of the long lines. "58," for example, plays off the "57 varieties" of Heinz against bomb-making materials, with rhymes on "flex," "flicks," and "flux" (Heraclitean flux, of course), followed by "caff," "kiff," and "cuff" in stanza two, and "truck," "track," and "trick" in stanza three.

The prose poems of *Belfast Confetti* and the translations (from Ovid and Rimbaud) in *First Language* point to two distinctive aspects of Carson's writing. A series of volumes of poetry in the mid-1990s were constructed within and against artificial formal constraints, allowing Carson to play against conventions that seemed whimsical and arbitrary but expressed a formal and historical logic particular to the circumstances of poetry in Northern Ireland. *Opera et Cetera* (1996) continued to explore and exploit the long line and witty rhymes of *First Language*, but hewed to a ten-line, five-couplet form in four distinct sections, the first an A to Z "Alphabet," the second a series of

Latin quotations, the third a translation of the Romanian poet Stefan Augustin Doinas, and the fourth, Opera, the A to Z of radio operators' code, picked up while Carson listened to British military chatter in Belfast. If there was lyric formalism in the 77 sonnets of *The Twelfth of Never* (2001), and in the translations of Baudelaire, Mallarmé, and Rimbaud in *The Alexandrine Plan* (1998), it was of a kind distinguished by Carson's inventive, often hilarious, rhymes. Indeed, the centrality of the sonnet within English literary traditions has been pushed off-kilter by Irish contortions of the form beginning in the 1980s with Muldoon's *Quoof* and Brendan Kennelly's *Cromwell* (1983). Carson's play with the alexandrine line within the sonnet form in these two books opened the poems into one another, linking the book-length sequence in *The Twelfth of Never* via an ingenious series of playful riffs on Irish folklore, Irish poetry, and Irish music, Japanese history and Japanese culture, and a variety of experiences unclassifiable but by dreams or drugs or the way they feed each other. The relation between narrative and metamorphosis within the chosen form creates for Carson's reader an experience of pleasure that is itself of historical interest, in that it allows him to inhabit the cultural space of the entertainer, the trickster, the wise but wily artist whose subversive gift keeps meaning mobile and in play.

Those readers who have found Muldoon and Carson frustratingly elusive and allusive have found Medbh McGuckian baffling and inscrutable. She takes seriously T. S. Eliot's injunction that modern poetry must be difficult, and the demands she makes on her readers are integral to her poetry. Her poems consistently tease out the relations between public and private spheres and as they move fluidly between both they focus on the figuration of the epistemology of being, particularly gendered and sexual being that emerges from within the specific antinomies of the Irish poetic tradition and the Irish national question. Central to her distinctive poetics of difficulty is the relationship between the first-person speaker, the given set of other figures within her poems, and some greater authorial context. "A Conversation Set to Flowers," for example, in *On Ballycastle Beach* (1989) might be about the loss of an unsuccessful pregnancy, but this content becomes displaced into a meditation on indirection and displaced emotion within relationships and the acts of making relations more generally. McGuckian consistently links birth with the difficulty of becoming within time, and both are often figured either as the process of moving away from the mother, or the mother's difficulty in recognizing the essential need of the child/other for differentiation and independence.

Such figurations are then refracted to enable McGuckian to address the problematic displacement of becoming to which Catholics in Northern Ireland have been subjected since the Ulster Plantation. The hermetic address to emotions via descriptions of rooms and the metamorphic shift of body into conjunctive or approximate relation to spaces or objects that characterize McGuckian's early volumes have given way in *Shelmalier* (1998), *The Soldiers of Year II* (2002), and *Had I a Thousand Lives* (2003) to a more direct address not only to the problem of the public and national space of Ireland, but also to the various manifestations of the desire for an Irish republic. *Shelmalier* draws on the failed 1798 rebellion to conceptualize the difficulty of achieving a proper relation between individual and community; and *Had I a Thousand Lives* meditates on the layered meanings given to the Irish national martyr Robert Emmet in the bi-centenary of his rebellion and execution. The volume in between, *The Soldiers of Year II*, mediates, as Guinn Batten observes, the relation between history and representation via images that blend uneasily the otherwise separate temporalities of present and past. The poems in all three volumes work to retrieve a national culture of Republican commitment from the sanctifying piety of nationalist historiography and the demonizing fear of contemporary politics, but they do so in McGuckian's oblique, quiet, radical way. The turn to controversial historical subjects with the technical skills developed in her radical investigation of the contradictions within modern self-identity has allowed a truly original poetics to emerge, one in which the specific dilemmas of being that are attached to being Irish are given an appropriately complex poetic form.

Further Reading

Garratt, Robert F. (1989). *Modern Irish Poetry: Tradition and Continuity from Yeats to Heaney*. Berkeley, CA: University of California Press.
Johnston, Dillon (1998). *Irish Poetry after Joyce*, 2nd edn. Syracuse, NY: Syracuse University Press.
Lloyd, David (1993). *Anomalous States: Irish Writing and the Post-Colonial Moment*. Durham, NC: Duke University Press.
McDonald, Peter (1997). *Mistaken Identities: Poetry and Northern Ireland*. New York: Oxford University Press.
Smith, Stan (2005). *Irish Poetry and the Construction of Modern Identity: Ireland between Fantasy and History*. Dublin: Irish Academic Press.
Wills, Clair (1993). *Improprieties: Politics and Sexuality in Northern Irish Poetry*. Oxford: Clarendon Press.

Chapter 6

Poetry and Decolonization

Jahan Ramazani

In the postwar period, the decolonization of the British Empire profoundly reshaped the geography and aesthetics of English-language poetry. As in fiction, drama, and other literary genres, Anglophone poetry was no longer the preserve of the British Isles and the white settler colonies, but also flourished in new nations emerging from British colonial rule in Asia (e.g. India and Pakistan), Africa (e.g. Nigeria and Uganda), the Caribbean (e.g. Jamaica and Saint Lucia), and other parts of the so-called Third World. Earlier in the twentieth century, before and during the decolonization of Britain's oldest colony, writers of the Irish literary renaissance such as W. B. Yeats had reclaimed and reimagined Irish identities, topographies, and traditions. Now, writers from new Asian, African, and Caribbean nations – whether writing within these regions or as migrants to the British Isles, North America, or elsewhere – reimagined colonial and postcolonial spaces, reconceived their emergent society's identities, and hybridized indigenous cultural resources with metropolitan literary traditions (Ramazani 2001).

This chapter explores the poetry and poetics of decolonization in the postwar period. To do so, it builds on Edward Said's analysis of postcolonial writers' efforts "to reclaim, rename, and reinhabit the land" as part of the broader struggle of "decolonizing cultural resistance" (Said 1993: 226, 215), and it draws on the insights of Kwame Anthony Appiah, Homi Bhabha, and Gayatri Spivak into the vexed interstitiality of postcolonial writers straddling native and imperial worlds, colonial and ex-colonial temporalities (Appiah 1992; Bhabha 1994; Spivak 1999). Informed by postcolonial studies, it also makes use of the analytic tools of poetry studies to investigate how poems verbally and formally fashion postcolonial histories, selves, and collectivities. Why poetry? Alert to what Derek Walcott calls "Adam's task of giving things their names" (Walcott 1973: 152), poetry helps illuminate the colonizing and potentially decolonizing force of naming and renaming in the (post)colonial context. And because of its compressed tessellation, its articulation of multiple and often contending affiliations, poetry also helps reveal the self-divisions and ambiguities of emergent social identities in the wake of decolonization. Hence this chapter pursues two sets of questions about postwar Anglophone poetry. First, how do poets from new postcolonial nations and from the imperial center imagine, articulate, and name decolonization? How do they represent its sublimity, yet also its unfulfilled promise? By what strategies do poets enact, announce, describe, and even satirize decolonization? Second, what is the implied audience for poetry from decolonizing nations? How do Anglophone poets conceive their relation to their emerging national communities? Do they represent themselves as citizen-spokespersons, fully immersed in and writing from within their communities of origin, or as marginal outsiders, writing in estrangement from them? What can we learn about poetry from decolonization and about decolonization from poetry?

Imagining Decolonization

Few political processes were more central to twentieth-century history than what Said calls "the great movement of decolonization all across the Third World" (Said 1993: xii) and the resultant withdrawal of Western imperial powers – Great Britain, France, Belgium, Portugal, Italy, Spain, etc. – from their former colonies. In 1914, 85 percent of the earth's surface was under European control (Said 1993: 8). At the end of World War II, a third of the world's population still lived in non-self-governing territories. Fewer than two million do today (United Nations 2000–2008a). This momentous shift from colonial to postcolonial status, though far from complete, is reflected in the emergence of an English word: while the term "colonization" goes back to Edmund Burke's use of it in the imperial eighteenth century, "decolonization" was coined in the 1930s and gained wide currency in the 1960s, when many African, Caribbean, and Asian nations were winning independence. Most of the eighty new nations counted by the United Nations – the world body overseeing formal decolonization – had been colonies of Great Britain – "in an imperial class by itself," as Said remarks, "bigger, grander, more imposing than any other" modern empire (Said 1993: xxii).

To evoke the magnitude of decolonization, Resolution 1514 of the UN's General Assembly, the Declaration on the Granting of Independence to Colonial Countries and Peoples, occasionally reaches toward "the poetic": it conveys its meaning in part by its rhetorical elevation and its syntactic patterning, its vast scope (*"Recognizing* that the peoples of the world ardently desire the end of colonialism in all its manifestations"), and its identification with "the passionate yearning for freedom in all dependent peoples," its idealistic assertion "that the process of liberation is irresistible and irreversible" (United Nations 1960). Adopted in 1960, the year of Nigeria's and Cyprus's independence and coming just after the decolonization of Ghana, Malaysia, and Sri Lanka, and just before that of numerous African, Caribbean, and Asian nations, the Declaration on Decolonization summons a verbal power and urgency that seem meant both to reflect and advance the eruption of many states out of a few, the thunderous collapse of a political system built on "alien subjugation, domination and exploitation" (United Nations 1960).

Evoking the *postcolonial sublime*, the immense historical spectacle of imperial disintegration and resurgent indigenous multiplicity, other documents on decolonization share these and other "poetic" qualities. Even the UN's blandly matter-of-fact list of decolonized nations ironically resembles one of the most ancient forms of poetry: the list poem or catalog verse. In the West, the topos is familiar from Homer's list of ships, the genealogies of the Bible, catalogs in Chaucer, Shakespeare, Milton, and Whitman, up to Marianne Moore and Kenneth Koch, but it is also widespread in the non-European world – in lists of place-names, for example, in Polynesian and Abyssinian verse (Hornsby & Brogan 1993: 174), or more recently, in the poetic songs of the Ugandan Okot p'Bitek. In its roster of decolonized nations, the UN lists under the United Kingdom names that are no longer subordinate possessions but, at least formally, sovereign equals:

Aden Colony and Protectorate	Independence as South Yemen	1967
Bahamas	Independence	1973
Barbados	Independence	1966
Basutoland	Independence as Lesotho	1966
Bechuanaland Protectorate	Independence as Botswana	1966
British Guiana	Independence as Guyana	1966
British Honduras	Independence as Belize	1981
British Somaliland	Independence as Somalia (joined with Italian Somaliland)	1960
Brunei	Independence Now Brunei Darussalam	1984
Cyprus	Independence	1960

The ABCs of British decolonization extend on and on, to the Zs of Zambia, Zanzibar, and Zimbabwe (United Nations 2000–2008b). The catalog structurally imputes commonality to these names, which nevertheless display a stunning geographic and linguistic variety. Kant's concept of "the mathematical sublime" helps theorize the poetic effect of such lists and of the history they signify. The on and on repetitive series, as in Kant's examples of the storied heights of an Egyptian pyramid or the vastness of St Peter's Cathedral, defies comprehension by its amplitude (Kant 1951: 90–1). So too, the postcolonial sublime is evoked by the awesome incremental series in the history of decolonization – first India and Pakistan, then Ghana, Malaysia, and Sri Lanka, then Cyprus and Nigeria, then the unstoppable flood of Sierra Leone, Tanzania, Jamaica, Trinidad and Tobago, Uganda, Kenya, Malawi, Zambia, Singapore, and so forth. Yet the UN's heading of its list of former British colonies by the name of the "administering state," or empire, circumscribes the catalog's potential sublimity, raising the perennial question in postcolonial studies of whether, after formal decolonization, the postcolonies remain in the grips of an officially absent yet persistent neocolonialism.

Poems of the decolonizing world also often list the names of liberated nations and dependent territories. Empires colonize territories not only through bullets and battleships but also, as Brian Friel's play *Translations* (1980) memorably demonstrates and Said's *Culture and Imperialism* argues, through the verbal process of renaming and remapping the land. Consequently, imaginative writers often make use of the decolonizing list to invert this process, repossessing their countries and regions through toponym-studded poems. Derek Walcott's "A Sea-Chantey," in his 1962 volume *In a Green Night*, twins the repetitive structure of prayer with the secular incantations of a work song at sea, as if by the verbal magic and labor of nomination to reclaim the islands of the Lesser Antilles in a north-to-south arc:

> The litany of islands,
> The rosary of archipelagoes,
> Anguilla, Antigua,
> Virgin of Guadeloupe,
> And stone-white Grenada
> Of sunlight and pigeons.
>
> (Walcott 1986: 46)

Similarly, Kamau Brathwaite's "Calypso," a poem from *Rights of Passage* (1967), begins with a creation myth in which Caribbean islands are formed by a rock-skipping game:

> The stone had skidded arc'd and bloomed into islands:
> Cuba and San Domingo
> Jamaica and Puerto Rico
> Grenada Guadeloupe Bonaire.
>
> (Brathwaite 1973: 48)

In a collapse of temporalities, the original emergence of geologically discrete islands in the Caribbean is made to foretell their political self-definition millions of years later. Here again, the equalizing syntactic structure of the list is counterbalanced by the diversifying effect of toponymic heterogeneity. These and other postcolonial lists transvalue names that Europeans once invoked to demonstrate the boundless reach and might of empires on which the sun would never set. By their number, range, and geographic diversity, such catalogs of place-names assert a sublime heterogeneity that can no longer be contained in an imperial treasure box.

The multiplicity of emerging national and regional identities, central to these poems of the 1960s, is occasionally internalized in later poems, which revel in the toponymic variety to be found even within a single decolonizing nation. Lorna Goodison's "To Us, All Flowers Are Roses" plays on postcolonial Jamaica's multifarious place-names as the linguistic deposits left by colonization, the slave trade, and indigenous peoples:

115

> There is everywhere here.
> There is Alps and Lapland and Berlin.
> Armagh, Carrick Fergus, Malvern
> Rhine and Calabar, Askenish
> where freed slaves went to claim
> what was left of the Africa within,
> staging secret woodland ceremonies.
>   (Goodison 1992: 1)

Rejecting the colonial image of the West Indies as a peripheral backwater, with "no people there in the true sense of the word," according to an infamous remark of the British historian James Anthony Froude (1887/1897: 347), Goodison uncovers in Jamaica's toponyms a vibrant cosmopolitanism, spanning Europe and Africa, Northern and Southern hemispheres. Highlighting African survivals, such as the Nigerian place-name Calabar, Goodison etymologically links Accompong to the history of Jamaica's ex-slave rebels, or maroons:

> Accompong is Ashanti, root, Nyamekopon
> appropriate name Accompong, meaning
> warrior or lone one.
>   (Goodison 1992: 1)

The linguistic deposits in a place-name bespeak a buried history of transcontinental slave transport and rebellion, a history largely suppressed under British colonialism and now made visible by topographic and linguistic decolonization.

Poets thus marshal toponymic sprawl, whether concentrated within a single nation or distributed across islands and regions, to signify the sublimity of decolonization – the unleashing of a cultural and national multiplicity once squelched by the homogenizing force of empire. In Kant's philosophical model, the "dynamical sublime" is the aesthetic experience of "immensity" or "might," as evoked by phenomena such as volcanoes, hurricanes, thundering clouds, and a tumultuous ocean. Postcolonial writers also find something like the dynamical sublime in the newly uncovered "immensity" or freshly unleashed "might" of decolonization, which produces awe, yet is sublime precisely because "without any dominion over us" (Kant 1951: 99–101), unlike the immense and mighty empire that once ruled the waves.

If poetic lists are one kind of literary gathering meant to evoke the global ungathering of decolonization, an anthology of poems, plays, and stories is another kind – etymologically a flower gathering (*anthos* + *logia*) – and it often accompanies decolonization on the assumption that a literature of one's own helps prove a people's right to a country of their own. *The Independence Anthology of Jamaican Literature* (1962), published in the year of that country's official decolonization, instances this attempt at national self-legitimization by virtue of a distinctive literature (Hendriks & Lindo 1962). Dedicated to "THE FREE PEOPLE OF JAMAICA" and published by Jamaica's Arts Celebration Committee of the Ministry of Development and Welfare, the volume includes poems meant to justify political self-sufficiency through poetic self-representation and self-nomination: "Jamaica Market," "Jamaica Symphony," "Jamaica Fisherman," and simply "Jamaica" establish the nation's self-identity by locating a corresponding self-identity in the sphere of culture.

Just as postcolonial poets rename and reclaim their formerly colonized lands in lists, litanies, and anthologies, so too black British poets, such as Linton Kwesi Johnson, Grace Nichols, and Bernardine Evaristo, re-chart the space of the imperial center, undoing the image of a supremely civilized "motherland." Born in Jamaica, Linton Kwesi Johnson arrived in London at the age of eleven in 1963, and, as John McLeod writes, his work, often centered in the African Caribbean community of Brixton, "offers an alternative inventory of place-names wholly devoid of mythical charm and rewrites the map of London to reflect a sombre geography of the city's realities that is grounded in the experiences of British-born or -raised black youth" (McLeod 2004: 132). To help decolonize metropolitan space, Johnson represents it as a site not of monumental beauty and civilization but of systemic oppression and determined resistance. In his verse, "Landan toun" in particular and England in general are seen as having re-imported and internalized the colonial divide – between black and white, colonizer and colonized. In the refrain of one of his most famous poems, he declares:

> Inglan is a bitch
> dere's no escapin it
> Inglan is a bitch
> dere's no runin whe fram it
> (Johnson 2002: 39)

There is no escaping it in a double sense. There is no escaping the truth of England's exploitation of people such as the West Indian migrant to London, described as shuttled from one demeaning job to another – underground worker to dish washer, ditch digger to factory worker, and finally the dole. And there is no "escapin" or "runin" away from England, a prison that lures and then confines peoples from lands it once colonized. Immigrants find themselves worked hard for meager pay and then repeatedly fired, and yet their countries of origin, still in the grip of the ravaging and impoverishing aftermath of colonialism and now economic neocolonialism, can offer few alternatives.

If, as Johnson suggests, colonialism persists in new guises both within Britain and in the ex-colonies, then what happened to the exalted expectations of formal decolonization? Already at the time of independence, postcolonial poets such as the wily Jamaican Creole poet Louise Bennett, a key influence on Johnson, were raising questions about the promise of decolonization, in poems such as Bennett's "Independence Dignity," "Jamaica Elevate," and "Independance." Bennett's verse sometimes seems to greet decolonization as heroic accession, as in "Independence Dignity":

> It was a sight fi cure sore yeye,
> A time fi live fi see:[1]
> Jamaica Independence
> Celebration dignity.
> (Bennett 1983: 117)

Yet this bundling of Jamaica with a list of three seemingly triumphal nouns comes at the end of a poem that has earlier mocked the commodification of the nation's birth in a listing of souvenirs:

> Independence pen an pencil,
> Cup an saucer, glass an tray;
> Down to Independence baby bawn
> Pon Independence Day.
> (Bennett 1983: 116)

Abruptly shifting from commodities to a baby, Bennett's poem deploys the list not to celebrate a new multiplicity unleashed by decolonization but to poke fun at the homogenizing use of the new nation's identity to brand everything, from pens and pencils to babies. While

---

[1] "It was a sight to cure sore eyes, a time to live to see."

celebrating and even attempting to enact decolonization through rites of naming, postcolonial poets such as Bennett also playfully satirize representations of the nation-state as the sole arbiter of worth.

Writing in the heyday of African independence movements, Okot p'Bitek more sternly questions the sufficiency of political decolonization, even as he supports an African cultural revolution. Although his long poem *Song of Lawino* (1966) affirms indigenous cultural values, it cannot be reduced to a literary cheer for decolonization without ignoring its critique of the viciously feuding political parties that supposedly fight for Uhuru in Uganda and elsewhere in Africa. For these groups, self-interest is in fact paramount:

> Someone said
> Independence falls like a bull buffalo
> And the hunters
> Rush to it with drawn knives,
> Sharp shining knives
> For carving the carcass.
> And if your chest
> Is small, bony and weak
> They push you off,
> And if your knife is blunt
> You get the dung on your elbow,
> You come home empty-handed
> And the dogs bark at you!
> . . .
> And the other men
> Carry large pieces of fatty beef,
> You hear their horns loud and proud!
> (Okot p'Bitek 1984: 107)

Like the native bourgeoisie that Frantz Fanon feared would protect its entrenched interests after the revolution (1963: 148–205), these party leaders and their families seize on independence as an opportunity for gorging themselves, as sonically emphasized here by the assonance of "loud" and "proud." Instead of imagining decolonization as the triumph of the weak over the strong, the rising up of a newly empowered collectivity, Okot p'Bitek's Lawino says "Independence falls," as if an animal felled by the strong for the strong.

Political decolonization, moreover, seems to bring little change to the lives of the dispossessed:

> . . . the hip bones of the voters
> Grow painful
> Sleeping on the same earth
> They slept
> Before Uhuru!
> And they cover the ulcers
> On their legs
> With animal skins.
>   (Okot p'Bitek 1984: 110)

Formal decolonization may be a desirable aim, but if it brings about no material alteration to the lives of the dispossessed, it can have scant meaning and may even deepen despair. Being able to vote – from the Latin *votum*, "vow" or "wish" – can turn into a cruelly ironic betrayal of vows and wishes. A "bullfrog bellowing for the vote" is Derek Walcott's satiric epithet for the postcolonial politician in "The Sea Is History" (Walcott 1986: 367). Toward the end of Walcott's poem, the political decolonization of the West Indies – "each rock broke into its own nation" – fails to meet hopes for genuine rebirth. In the form of a beast fable, Walcott mocks the frog-like politicians, fly-like clerics, bat-like ambassadors, and bug-like police and judges who assume control in postcolonial societies, betraying the promise of a sublime eruption of a new "History," a fresh "beginning," after centuries of colonial subjugation (367). In brief, while postcolonial poets often celebrate the creation of new nations – multiple, sublimely hetero-geneous, freed from the grip of imperial domination – they also question and even ridicule expectations that political independence will fundamentally transform the economic, social, or geopolitical order. Nationality can become a deceptive fetish with little genuine meaning, if neither the formerly colonized nor their colonizers fundament-ally alter economic and political structures of exploitation. Even so, disillusioned independence poetry – Bennett's ebullient self-mockery, Okot p'Bitek's angry accusations, Walcott's fabulistic satire, even Johnson's militant critique – does not extinguish all hope for "History, really beginning," as Walcott puts it in the last words of his poem (367). Indeed, these witty and acerbic responses to the failures of decolon-ization can be seen as caustic poetic efforts to help spur emancipatory alternatives to the failed promises and despair, the misplaced priorities and entrenched interests of the status quo.

* * *

How does the decolonization of British territories look to poets on the other side of the colonial divide? As we might expect, decolonization is not always a cheering, amusing, or sublime spectacle. After the Suez Crisis of 1956, Britain's confidence in the imperial project dwindled, and by the 1960s, after the decolonization of much of the empire, the British government decided to draw down troops east of Suez. Philip Larkin's "Homage to a Government" (1969) laments the diminishment of the British Empire and satirizes its shrinkage for the sake of monetary savings:

> The places are a long way off, not here,
> Which is all right, and from what we hear
> The soldiers there only made trouble happen.
> (Larkin 1988: 171)

Larkin's coupling of the homonyms "here" and "hear" suggests, as does his restriction of rhyme to three repeated words in each six-line stanza (*home/home*, *right/right*, *orderly/orderly*, etc.), the claustrophobia of an empire that is folding in upon itself. His poem contrasts sharply with the rhetoric of the postcolonial sublime, whether in poems or UN documents, and while its deflative tone has more in common with satiric poems on decolonization, those postcolonial poems retain, in contrast to Larkin's post-imperial bleakness, a sense of emergent possibility. The sonic and tonal detumescence of Larkin's lament for "Little England" bespeaks an anxious somnolence, a bored disquiet, about the sameness (and indeed "same" is one of the repeated rhyme words in the last stanza) of a "country" (another repeated word) without overseas possessions and with little expectation of reversing the decline in its world status. The anti-sublimity of a poem with a narrowly limited verbal, tonal, and sonic palette becomes emblematic of a nation deprived of the reach and resources of the *imperium*.

But just as the response to decolonization was mixed among poets of the decolonizing world, not all white British poets greeted decolonization with sour melancholy. In the empire's waning years, one Englishman, for example, turns on its head the triumphant roll call of British territories on which the sun would never set. In his song "Mad Dogs and Englishmen" (1932), Noël Coward ranges from Burma to Hong Kong, Bangkok to Bengal, invoking geographic and cultural variety to satirize Britain's attempt to force a rigid uniformity on the world:

> In the Malay states
> There are hats like plates
> Which the Britishers won't wear.
> At twelve noon
> The natives swoon
> And no further work is done.
> But mad dogs and Englishmen
> Go out in the midday sun.
>   (Coward 1983: 122)

Although Coward's verse is shot through with British imperial attitudes, this song wryly compiles a list of colonial sites that refuse conformity with an inflexible British custom. As in the toponymic lists of postcolonial poetry, the names themselves indicate an ungovernable heterogeneity. But whereas postcolonial lists often evoke the uncontainable sublimity of decolonization, Coward's rigidly boundary-setting versification and jauntily insistent rhyme risk echoing the imperial limits that the toponyms and varied cultural attitudes are meant to unsettle.

Some British poets go further in their identification with the resistance to empire. Tony Harrison, from a working class family in the economically depressed, coal-mining city of Leeds, dedicated his poem "On Not Being Milton" to two members of Frelimo, Mozambique's independence party. Bringing into poetry the unheard Yorkshire voices and north-of-England accents of the dispossessed – their "lumpen" rage, their despised "glottals" – Harrison in this lyric identifies his struggle as an educated man to "go back to my roots" with that of Martinican poet Aimé Césaire's *"Cahier d'un retour au pays natal, /* my growing black enough to fit my boots" – that is, the poet's recovery of his coal-blackened origins (Harrison 1987: 112). Like the Negritude poet who twisted the poetic forms of the colonizer to assert the experience and identity of the colonized, Harrison seeks in the sixteen-line poems in "The School of Eloquence" series to push the regional, sonic, and stanzaic boundaries of the sonnet: he would stretch the form and load its riffs with non-standard oral urgency and resistant anger. The poet's Yorkshire stress pattern "clangs a forged music on the frames of Art, / the looms of owned language smashed apart!" (Harrison 1987: 112). Even a poet of the "motherland" draws sustenance from parallels between his resistance to the imperial center and that of other decolonizing peoples around the world.

In brief, poets both of decolonizing nations and from the heart of empire seek verbal and formal correlatives for the sudden unraveling of empire and the volcanic emergence of new nations. The postcolonial poetry of Walcott, Brathwaite, Goodison, and Okot p'Bitek both rejoices in the sublime global unbinding that is decolonization and skeptically asks whether political independence affords a true break with the past or more of the same under new national labels. When politically disillusioned, their poems vigorously rename and reclaim, satirize and chastise, in ways that suggest fresh possibilities beyond the stale entrenchment and internalized colonialism of the native bourgeoisie. Louise Bennett's trickster aesthetic is thus jubilant, energetically celebrating yet mocking her new nation. By contrast, Larkin, Bennett's near contemporary in England, exemplifies a wry, shrunken, deflated poetics of post-imperial boredom. His language suggests an exhausted sense of being at the end of an era, a political order, a literary tradition, Bennett's the vital possibilities of being at the start. Even so, the temper of the poetic response to decolonization cannot always be predicted by race or nationality: Tony Harrison's transnationally affiliated poetics of resistance may defy our expectations of "British" poets, the self-satirizing poetry of Bennett, Okot p'Bitek, and Walcott our expectations of the once colonized.

Alienation and Community

The prefix "de-" in "decolonization" reminds us that the umbrella term for the postwar creation of new nation-states is a negative construct, defining the new political reality by its outward push away from empire. But during and after this struggle for freedom *from*, poets must find ways of representing their relation *to* the internal communities they help will into being. How do postcolonial poets of Africa, Asia, and the Caribbean imagine their relation to their audiences, their societies, their new nations? Do they see their poetry as marginal or central to the process of decolonization? Do they represent themselves as alienated from, or integral to, the emergent, postcolonized collectivity?

One way to gauge the relative "alienation" or "solidarity" of postcolonial poets is to draw them into a triangulated comparison with two groups of earlier twentieth-century poets – the Euromodernists and the poets of the Harlem Renaissance – a comparison across periods, races, and hemispheres that can help specify the dynamics of postcolonial poetry's social imaginary. In definitions of modernism, "alienation" is one of the most frequently invoked categories of experience, understood as the marginalized writer's predicament in a bustling, commercially driven, late capitalist modernity that has little use for bards or shamans. As Raymond Williams sees it, alienated modernists turn to a preoccupation with their formal materials, in the absence of meaningful social bonds: they "found the only community available to them: a community of the medium; of their own practices" (Williams 1989: 45).

Among the most famous modernist personifications of this social alienation are T. S. Eliot's painfully self-conscious Prufrock, who feels in company as if his nerves have been projected on a screen, and the protagonist of Ezra Pound's *Hugh Selwyn Mauberley*, who, repulsed by mass-produced art and writing, looks within himself for authentic feeling and creativity. By contrast, an iconic poem of the Harlem Renaissance, Langston Hughes's "The Negro Speaks of Rivers," purports to speak from within a transhistorical and translocational black and "human" experience (Hughes 1995: 23). Many Harlem Renaissance poets look to "folk" or oral forms for inspiration, implicitly joining their expressive capacity to that of African American common people – whether absorbing the rhetorical structures and narrative style of the sermon, like James Weldon Johnson, or the structure and imagery of the blues, spirituals, and tall tales, like Langston Hughes and Sterling Brown. Spurning and being spurned by what Yeats calls "the noisy set / Of bankers, schoolmasters, and clergymen" (Yeats 1989: 80), Euromodernist poets develop an art that – in its arcane mythologies, scholarly allusions, learned polyglossia, and private references – both reproduces and reinforces the very estrangement it mourns. Sometimes this social alienation turns rhetorically violent, as when Pound in his "Hell Cantos" unleashes a torrent of invective – "slow rot, fœtid combustion" – toward politicians, bankers, clergymen, and other pillars of modern society (Pound 1998: 63).

This schema needs, however, to be qualified. As an Anglo-Irishman bestriding the divide between colonizer and colonized, Yeats also tries to reclaim indigenous resources for a nation-shaping poetry, and Eliot and Pound betray a fascination with the mass culture seemingly scorned in their often elitist references to advertising, consumerism, and popular ditties (North 1994; Chinitz 2003). For the purposes of this chapter, a still more important qualification pertains to Harlem Renaissance poets, whose nonalienation, like that of postcolonial poets, should not be overstated, despite their eschewal in most cases of the public-estranging ferocity of high modernist diction, rhetoric, and reference. In its janus-faced form, diction, and persona, Hughes's "The Weary Blues" probes the dividing line between the poet, writing for a literary audience, and the blues singer, more closely affiliated with the poor masses (Ramazani 1994: 144–7; Hughes 1995: 50). When in his manifesto "The Negro Artist and the Racial Mountain" Hughes embraces the common folk as the rightful source of forms and materials for the black artist, his exoticizing idealization of "the low-down folks" betrays at least some difference: "Their joy runs, bang! into ecstasy. Their religion soars to a shout. Work maybe a little today, rest a little tomorrow. Play awhile. Sing awhile. O, let's dance!" (Hughes 1926: 693). As poets articulating emergent cultural and social identities and straddling dominant and historically oppressed social collectivities, Harlem Renaissance writers resemble poets of decolonizing nations as poets of in-betweenness – between middle-class black audiences and the poor creators of the blues, between white patrons and the African American "folk" experience.

"Postcoloniality," writes Kwame Anthony Appiah, "is the condition of what we might ungenerously call a comprador intelligentsia: of a relatively small, Western-style, Western-trained, group of writers and thinkers," mediating between the Third World and the West through cultural goods (Appiah 1992: 149). The interstitiality of postcolonial writers, like that of Harlem Renaissance poets, necessarily involves some distance between them and their communities of origin, even as postcolonial poets attempt to epitomize and speak for the nation or region, to engage their home audience as members of the same social world. Sometimes the sense of apartness becomes so intense that poets of the global South more nearly resemble the Euromodernist example of diffident withdrawal from, and hostility toward, the larger social world, however exaggerated that sense of apartness may be; sometimes, it recalls instead Harlem Renaissance examples of greater identification with, and participation in, a communal identity, however troubled and complex that solidarity may be; and at other times, postcolonial poetry shuttles productively between these poles.

That the social distance most evident in the attitudes and forms of white modernist poetry could bear comparison with the work of postcolonial poets may be surprising. Yet some postcolonial poets represent themselves as no less alienated from their societies than do the Euromodernists from theirs. The Nigerian poet Christopher Okigbo clearly recalls Euromodernist inwardness and estrangement, especially in his early poetry, if not in the manner of his death – fighting among Igbo secessionists for an independent Biafra during the Nigerian civil war. Dying in a blaze of public solidarity, Okigbo had, nevertheless, grown up a member of the tiny stream of students who attended elite secondary and higher educational institutions under British colonialism, his father a Catholic mission teacher in Igboland. His poetry does not disguise his distance and difference from Nigerian society at large, or "the people" (Okigbo 1971: 29). Despite the antiphonal structure of some poems, the persona of Okigbo's poetry is characteristically solitary, speaking for and often to himself, exploring a penumbral state of consciousness between dream and waking. Even when he purports to return to and reclaim his African roots, his language evokes intense isolation and perpetual "exile" (17): "I was the sole witness of my homecoming" (53). Poetry arises not from collectivism but from an inward, agonized quest: "out of the depths my cry" (3). Only through communion with his or her innermost self, Okigbo's verse seems to suggest, can the poet discover lasting truths and reveal mythopoeic visions. Like the high modernists, Okigbo mythologizes the quest within and dons a depersonalizing mask, though as an African, Okigbo needs to explain his mask in contradistinction to the ritual object: "Mask over my face – // my own mask, not ancestral – I sign" (17). To inscribe this mask, as emphasized by the syntactic inversion ("Mask . . . I sign"), is to make his own a cultural inheritance with a dual pedigree in both high modernist and Igbo mythologies. In the African context, he remakes a ritual object saturated with social significance into a tool of paradoxically depersonalized personal expression.

The dreamy inwardness of Okigbo's poetry sometimes coincides with bitterly satiric attacks on society at large, to the effect of abrupt tonal swings between inward brooding and outward assaults. Okigbo denounces many of the same social groups decried by the Euro-modernists: "fanatics and priests and popes, / organizing secretaries and / party managers," all of whom exploit the society they pretend to serve, keeping in place colonialism's structures of domination (7). Put together an inward-questing poet and a society corrupted by "vendors princes negritude / politicians" (56), and the result is an image of the poet, as in much high modernist verse, as martyr or even scapegoat. At times Okigbo compares himself to Orpheus, Tammuz, and other dying gods. Elsewhere, he identifies with historical victims, such as the assassinated Congolese leader Patrice Lumumba, who is part Shakespeare's betrayed Caesar, part Eliot's drowned Phlebas: "They struck him in the ear they struck him in the eye; / They picked his bones for scavenging" (40). Okigbo worries that his poetry likewise puts him at risk: "If I don't learn to shut my mouth I'll soon go to hell" (67). Even without the many allusions scattered through his verse to Eliot, Pound, and Yeats, Okigbo's poetry can be said to bring into expression specifically postcolonial estrangement by adapting and indigenizing the alienated social structure and language of modernist verse.

At the other end of the postcolonial social spectrum are poets who more nearly resemble Harlem Renaissance writers in their efforts to summon the voices, forms, and language of the people, however troubled may be their acts of poetic identification. Kofi Anyidoho of Ghana seems to have poets like Okigbo in mind when he disavows the merely "private dreams of poets" and "pampered dreams of poets" (Anyidoho 1998: 130). For Syl Cheney-Coker of Sierra Leone, it is not enough to be read in English honors class – "my country I do not want that!" – but rather "to be the breakfast of the peasants who read" and "to help the fishermen bring in their catch" (Cheney-Coker 1998: 339). Seldom, if ever, has this ideal fusion been realized, but it is especially alluring in "developing" societies where material and collective needs are pressing and massive, often making poets feel guilty about their individualist and apparently useless aesthetic pursuits. Still, such a synthesis may not be altogether impossible; a few postcolonial poets can at least claim to have garnered a national or regional audience, including Okot p'Bitek of Uganda, whose *Song of Lawino* enjoyed widespread popular, as well as critical, esteem, and Louise Bennett, whose multimedia dissemination of her Creole poetry through the newspapers, radio, and television helped valorize the use of Jamaican English. Often performed to musical accompaniment, Linton Kwesi Johnson's "dub" or "reggae poetry" represents a determined effort to write from within and to the specifically defined community of "black Britn" (Johnson 2002: 55). In "New Craas Massakah," Johnson grounds his relation to this collectivity in a shared experience of racial victimization: "wi did know seh it couda happn / yu know – anytime, anywhe / far dont it happn to wi / an di Asians dem aready?" (Johnson 2002: 54–5). This poem attempts to merge "wi" and "yu," speaker and audience, poet and micro-society, delimiting a separate sphere of collectivity in opposition to violent racists, an indifferent police, and a white British public at large.

Most postcolonial poets move between these poles, recognizing their status as members of a small, highly educated, literary elite, like the Euromodernists, yet aspiring, like the Harlem Renaissance poets, to announce, define, and participate in an emergent cultural identity. Even the individualist dreamer Okigbo sees himself as a "town-crier" (Okigbo 1971: 67), and even the collectivist Johnson mourns personal losses and writes to his "own sense a time" (Johnson 2002: 95–7).

This in-betweenness both vitalizes and vexes postcolonial poetry. Poetry's function in the postcolonial imaginary has often been, at least in part, to mediate between the antinomies of introspective alienation and communal solidarity. The overdetermined slide of pronouns between first person singular and plural in a poem such as the Nigerian Ben Okri's "On Edge of Time Future" is illustrative: "I remember the history well," begins this poem, referring one strophe later to "our history" as Africans, only to shift again from "I remember" to "We emerged from our rubbish mounds" (Okri 1998: 302). By the poem's end, the speaker is referring "To us // Who remember the history well," claiming his writing of poetry for the collective, national project of restoration and healing: "We shall spin silk from rubbish / And frame time with our resolve" (304). Poetry is thus affirmed as playing a vital role in decolonization, helping to imagine a new future forged out of the detritus of the past. But the pronominal instabilities of the poem hint at the difficulty of fusing the individuated poetic self to the larger national aspiration of spinning silk from the rubbish of colonial and postcolonial history.

Derek Walcott's high diction and rhetoric, his use of Western literary forms, his self-identification with Western poets – all would seem to place him squarely on the side of alienated, introspective, modernist elitism. And, indeed, the hero of "The Schooner *Flight*" declares, after abandoning and being abandoned by both whites and blacks in the Caribbean, "I had no nation now but the imagination" (Walcott 1986: 350). Yet in this same work, poetry is figured as saturated by its environment, much as the poet's verb forms are inflected by West Indian Creole: "when I write / this poem, each phrase go be soaked in salt; / I go draw and knot every line as tight / as ropes in this rigging" (Walcott 1986: 347). The formal interstitiality of metaphor (the poem *as* and *as not* a wave, a boat, rigging) and of linguistic register (somewhere between Creole and standard English) instantiates the poem's social ambiguity, its mixture of communal longing and melancholy separation. The stinging recognition that his poetry is not at one with the Caribbean common people recurs in Walcott's poetry. In "The Light of the World," he writes of taking a public minibus or "transport" to his hotel, and of a beautiful local woman humming to a Bob Marley song on the van's stereo: "I had abandoned them," he reflects, feeling the painful contrast between Marley's songs' assimilation into everyday Caribbean life and his apartness, as an elite poet frequently living abroad, with nothing to offer the common folk except a poem such as "The Light of the World," which they will likely never read or hear (Walcott 1987: 48, 50). The hope of Walcott's poetry is that even with this gulf between poet and the people, he can help summon into literary existence the dignity and promise of Caribbean identity – mongrelized, polyglot, burdened with multiple inheritances, yet born afresh out of the imperial and post-imperial violence, racism, and rot of the past.

The tension between estrangement from postcolonial community and the longing to serve and give expression to emerging national and social collectivities was discomfiting but generative for poets like Walcott and Okigbo who came of age during the post-World War II decolonization of the British Empire. It continues to animate the work of postcolonial writers born twenty years later, such as Agha Shahid Ali and Lorna Goodison, as the multifaceted process of decolonization continues, leaving these and many other poets uncertain in their relation to this often delayed, sometimes violent, process. For these poets, migration to the metropole has exacerbated issues of communal affiliation and identity. The sense of the privileged intellectual's social isolation, already evident in Okigbo's and (even the pre-émigré) Walcott's verse, is only intensified by the geographic displacement of poets in the postcolonial diaspora. The fraught imagery of connection yet disconnection in Ali's poems, such as the title poem of his 1997 collection *The Country without a Post Office*, exemplifies the struggle to honor one's birthplace (for him, Kashmir) and community of origin (South Asian Muslims), while frankly conceding the solitary condition of the postcolonial expatriate. Having learned about the conflagration that destroyed the Kashmiri town and shrine of Chrar-e-Sharif while he was living in the US, Ali vividly imagines the ruin – a minaret is entombed, houses burn and are buried, a wall of fire caves in – but at the same time signals his geographical and social distance from his traumatized homeland in images of writing that redounds on itself: seemingly unreadable messages are "scratched on planets"; stamps are canceled but "blank," with no nation; addresses are written but "doomed"; there is a strange "card lying on the street"; envelopes have "vanished"; the speaker's cries are "like dead letters." "My words go out in huge packages of rain," laments the poet, "go there, to addresses, across the oceans," but never seem to arrive at their destination (Ali 1997: 48–51). "'These words may never reach you,'" plaintively cries a prisoner's letter. Undelivered or unreadable, misfired or self-canceling, the letters in Ali's poem suggest the frustration of writing to and for a community from which the poet knows he stands apart. This sense of exilic isolation in an expatriated conscience is formally embodied in the poem's mirror-like rhyme scheme, each stanza structured in an *abcddcba* pattern. Pronouns in the poem also suggest both a desire to reach the poet's community of origin and an elegiac admission of inevitable failure. "Again I've returned to this country," begins the poem, and this "I" soon morphs into a hopeful "us," "our," and "we," eventually splitting into self-address ("Phantom heart") and into self-accusing address to a Kashmiri other: "Then be pitiless you whom I could not save." The ambiguity and instability of Ali's address – now to himself, now to an imagined Kashmiri interlocutor – and of tone – now frantically yearning, now skeptically mournful – embodies the postcolonial expatriate's fragile sense of poetic identity as alienated from, yet longing to reconnect with, a community of origin – in this case, one still struggling to define its political destiny.

The poems of Lorna Goodison's collection *Controlling the Silver* (2005), largely set in Jamaica but written after years of living in North America, also make frequent use of second-person address in ways that similarly encapsulate the interstitiality of the postcolonial expatriate. "Island Aubade" begins by describing in the third person a morning in Jamaica, but soon the voice has shifted to insistent second-person address: "Come drink this cup of Blue Mountain coffee / stirred with a brown suede stick of cinnamon" (Goodison 2005: 2). Deploying the second person to ground herself in her recuperated homeland, the poet seems continually to be inviting the reader in, as a host introducing outsiders to her (former) social world: "Don't shake hands with the wicked, eat greens, abase / and abound" (3). In "Ode to the Watchman," the desire to form imaginative community is poignantly evident in the gracious shift from third-person description of an exhausted night watchman who has kept even ghosts, or "rolling calves," at bay ("evidence of his vigilance against nocturnal / furies red in his eyeballs") to second-person address: "All praise to you O beneficent watchman // for keeping guard over us while we slept." The watchman becomes a more intimate "watchie," at the height of the poem's willed communion, before he is surrendered to the more formal "kind" and finally "good watchman," as blessing turns to imagined camaraderie and then to decathectic farewell (Goodison 2005: 8–9). The speaker would turn her connection with the watchman into a dialogic, "I-Thou" relation, but her use of apostrophe also records the absence and unavailability of the relation it conjures into being. Goodison's poetry represents itself as extending ever outward, ever desirous, into a world that may or may not receive it. Its continual apostrophic gestures embody both ferocious hope and elegiac melancholy over the possibilities of communion, with both her imagined international reader and with her community of origin. The grammar of address and the mercurial pronouns, the shifts in register between Creole and Standard English and in tone between melancholy and blessing, form the tissue of a longingly inclusive yet inevitably incomplete identity-in-community.

"Triple exile" is Ali's self-description, as "exile" from Kashmir to India to the United States. A fundamental source of creativity for the displaced Euromodernists, "exile" is no less so for doubly or sometimes triply "exilic" poets such as Walcott, Ali, and Goodison. Indeed, the complexities of their geo-social affiliations may even exceed those of the expatriate modernists, since the geographic and cultural distances crossed are still greater, and since, to the extent that they belong to a "comprador intelligentsia," postcolonial poets write out of divided allegiances to local or "native" community and to the culture and language of colonization, even without migrating abroad. We might assume comfortable and tightly knit relations between poets and the decolonizing societies for and to which they (partly) speak, as if they were the rousing loudspeakers of their emergent nations, at least by comparison with First World poets, whose "alienation" from modern capitalist societies is more readily presupposed. And, indeed, many postcolonial poets, like poets of the Harlem Renaissance, aspire intensely to reconnect with and help shape the national or regional community of origin from which they are "exiled" – social and political collectivities that remain fluid after the withdrawal of imperial armies and governments. Yet whether they are nativists or cosmopolitans, postcolonial poets are set apart by their education, literary inheritances, class status, geographic mobility, and their cultural function as intermediaries between First and Third Worlds. This is true even of the most "native" poets, such as the Creole-performing Jamaican localist Louise Bennett, who attended the Royal Academy of Dramatic Art in London on a British Council scholarship, the proverb-wielding Acoli poet Okot p'Bitek, who was trained in anthropology at Oxford, and the "dub" poet Linton Kwesi Johnson, who studied sociology at Goldsmiths College, University of London, and half-mockingly concedes his professional aspiration to be counted a "tap-natch poet / like Chris Okigbo / Derek Walcot / ar T. S. Eliot" (Johnson 2002: 94). Still more clearly for postcolonial poets such as Goodison, Ali, Walcott, and Okri, poetry plays, shuttles, distends across the fractures between experiential and remembered, colonial and postcolonial, solitary and communal worlds.

* * *

While enormously promising at mid-century, decolonization is far from being a finished process. As indicated by poets such as Bennett, Okot p'Bitek, and Walcott, native regimes have perpetuated a held-over colonialism within many Third World nations. For poets such as Linton Kwesi Johnson, an internal colonization of immigrant communities persists within Britain, where non-European peoples often face a version of the economic and racial barriers that divided European colonial territories. And global corporate neocolonialism has held in place enormous economic imbalances between "developed" nations and much of the "developing" world. Yet while decolonization has fallen short of the changes resonantly proclaimed by the UN – the end of colonial "subjugation, domination and exploitation" – the significance of the end of direct European rule in many parts of the world, the withdrawal of armies and district commissioners, and the reclamation of lands once occupied and cultural resources once denigrated and suppressed under colonialism should not be cynically dismissed. Decolonization is incomplete, but it began with resistance to direct foreign domination, the transfer of sovereignty from European powers, and the sublime eruption of multiple nationalities, cultures, and identities. Keenly aware of the limitations of nationalism as a salvific response to colonialism, poets have nevertheless vigorously participated in the momentous process of decolonization. They have renamed and re-charted both native spaces and centers of metropolitan power; they have satirically wrestled with pseudo-decolonization that perpetuates the imperial status quo; and they have articulated emergent postcolonized identities and their own vexed relations to these collective formations. This is not to say that literary decolonization has been able to lift forever the yoke of European influences and attitudes, as advocated by the authors of *Toward the Decolonization of African Literature* (Chinweizu, Jemie & Madubuike 1983: 1); indeed, the complex web of continuing interrelations between colonizer and once colonized – both cultural and material – complicates the teleological trajectory embedded in the very concept of decolonization and renders improbable any final decolonization of the mind (Ngũgĩ 1986). Yet poetry helps remind us that decolonization is not only a political and military process but also an imaginative one – an enunciation of new possibilities and collectivities, new names and identities, new structures of thought and feeling. Just as the imposition of British poems and novels on subaltern peoples played a role in colonization, both at home and abroad, so too the imaginative labor of articulating an experience and a world after independence – in its sameness and its difference from what came before – continues to play a part in decolonization. If decolonization seems a diminished thing, it would be all the more so without the rich self-divisions and split affiliations, the imaginative exuberance and bracing skepticism of postcolonial poetry.

Further Reading

Appiah, Kwame Anthony (1992). *In My Father's House: Africa in the Philosophy of Culture*. New York: Oxford University Press.

Bhabha, Homi K. (1994). *The Location of Culture*. London: Routledge.

Fanon, Frantz (1963). *The Wretched of the Earth*, trans. Constance Farrington. New York: Grove.

Le Sueur, James D. (ed.) (2003). *The Decolonization Reader*. New York: Routledge.

McLeod, John (2004). *Postcolonial London: Rewriting the Metropolis*. London: Routledge.

Ngũgĩ wa Thiong'o (1986). *Decolonising the Mind: The Politics of Language in African Literature*. Portsmouth, NH: Heinemann.

North, Michael (1994). *The Dialect of Modernism: Race, Language, and Twentieth-Century Literature*. New York: Oxford University Press.

Ramazani, Jahan (2001). *The Hybrid Muse: Postcolonial Poetry in English*. Chicago, IL: University of Chicago Press.

Ramazani, Jahan (2009). *A Transnational Poetics*. Chicago, IL: University of Chicago Press.

Said, Edward W. (1993). *Culture and Imperialism*. New York: Knopf.

Spivak, Gayatri Chakravorty (1999). *A Critique of Postcolonial Reason*. Cambridge, MA: Harvard University Press.

Chapter 7

Transatlantic Currents

C. D. Blanton

In 1967 the American poet Edward Dorn published a thin volume of poems with London's Fulcrum Press under the title *The North Atlantic Turbine*. Like Dorn's *Geography*, published by Fulcrum two years earlier, the volume is preoccupied with vectors of movement, with the use of poetry as a mode of cartography. But *The North Atlantic Turbine* has moved beyond the spaces of Dorn's American West, turning from the terrestrial art of geography to "the fluxes of those oceans" and the vast currents that attune "the poet's senses" to "the multiple world" (1967: 9). The American poet has begun to travel and to colonize in another direction, crossing the Atlantic to rediscover English, only to find the language in a state of transatlantic drift.

The map that forms the volume's cover makes the point explicitly. The British archipelago appears prominently, but off center, placed to the top and right of the front cover. It is thus a peripheral detail, occupying a space roughly equivalent to that of Iceland (to the top), a cropped portion of the Iberian Peninsula (to the right), or the Moroccan coast (bottom right). Nearer the map's center is a different set of details, lines following the respective motions of the North Atlantic drift current (along the jet-stream), the northeast drift current (veering at Ireland past the Orkney and Shetland Islands, toward Norway), the southeast drift current (circulating clockwise along the Portuguese coast toward Africa), and the trade winds (returning from West Africa toward the Caribbean). Noting a set of earlier transatlantic voyages in passing (the Carthagenians to the Azores, Pytheas to the British Isles, attempts to map the Atlantic from Eratosthenes to St Brendan), Dorn's geography thus moves outward into the ocean itself, into the deep fact of circulation that relates far-flung lands as mere outposts and scattered ports of call along an endless circulating loop.

Dorn's suggestion is as polemical as it is inevitable. For the American poet writing abroad, the figure who (aware of his own country's Cold War projection as a bumptious global hegemon, from Europe to southeast Asia) comes to England as "a stranger on this continent / and more a stranger on this detached fragment of it" (1967: 31), the experience of Britain is both quaint and familiar. "Ghosts complete our present" (1967: 15), he observes, taking momentary comfort in the limestone blocks of Oxford and the chalky soils of Cambridge, in the calculations of British latitudes, in a train ride to Croydon. Under Dorn's theory, however, such places are "endlessly transferrable" (1967: 13), simple phases of "the atlantic turgidity" that "defines still our small era" (1967: 19), points from which the circulation of money and transfer of force from continent to continent become visible. It is thus the back cover of Dorn's volume that completes the observation, juxtaposing verso against recto by opening the map to include other such places on the opposite Atlantic edge: to the Bahamas (in the lower left corner), along the North American coast (on the left) to the tip of Greenland (at the top). At its mildest, the full map would seem to portend a certain universalism, at the very least a transatlantic internationalism of the sort slyly promised by the presence of the word "FULCRUM" along the book's spine.

But Dorn's point is also considerably more ominous, caught in an underlying refrain that is less parochial than resigned: "*America / is the world*" (1967: 42). Under this theory, America is to be distinguished from the simpler cartographic fact of the United States, itself merely another isolated part (albeit a large one) of the rotating turbine, historically in debt to Africa for its labor and to England for its language, as Dorn insists. In this larger sense, "America" is a global fact, formed on "the cliff of 1945" (1967: 37) and discernible everywhere in the operation of the world system formed in the years that followed, something that takes over everywhere and adapts all histories to its own. This "America" travels along the same currents, lagging behind exchangeable goods, but imposing its own culture with just as much force. Standing at Hadrian's wall, then, as photographers for *Life* magazine arrive "a symbiosis for to seek / of America and Rome," one empire standing metaphorically for another, Dorn meets an English scene with an unmistakably American idiom, frustrated "to find the

motherfucker covered / a 'natural' occurrence of winter / with *snow*"
(1967: 15). In an emblematic moment, the iconic gesture that would
equate American influence with Roman territorial conquest is fore-
stalled, interrupted by a demotic American voice – and by the weather.
Moving from west to east, the weather of Dorn's turbine fuses
history and nature into a single allegorical figure. But the easy figurative slide from oceanographic to literary currents on one hand and
to political ones on the other has a longer history of its own. Since
Ezra Pound's arrival in London in 1908 at least, the fitfully confluent
histories of British and American writing have slowly altered the very
notion of English, reattaching the adjective not merely to a nation but
also to a state of linguistic circulation, multi-accented and grounded
in two hemispheres. Of course, the vast circuits that once guaranteed
British hegemony have long since scattered English more broadly even
than that: even Stephen Dedalus recalls that "[a]ll Ireland is washed
by the gulfstream" (Joyce 1961: 16). The century between Stephen's
return to Dublin and now has witnessed a profusion of proprietary
claims on English as a literary language from across the globe, from
Asia to Africa to the Caribbean. But inevitably, it is the United States
that has usurped the language most freely and projected it back from
a position of worldwide authority, concretizing in political terms a
system of cultural exchange much longer in development and renat-
uralizing English as its own idiom in the process.

In the first number of *BLAST*, the 1914 manifesto with which they
announced the arrival of a new modernist approach to the arts,
Pound and Canadian-born Wyndham Lewis simultaneously excoriated
and excused England for its currents, bemoaning "A 1000 MILE
LONG, 2 KILOMETER Deep BODY OF WATER even, . . . pushed
against us from the Floridas, TO MAKE US MILD" (Lewis 2002: 11),
even while blessing "the vast planetary abstraction of the OCEAN" (22).
The summer that brought both *BLAST* and the first stirrings of world
war to Britain would also bring another young American to London,
one who had "actually trained himself *and* modernized himself *on his
own*" (as Pound put it to Harriett Monroe [Pound 1971: 40]). Within
a decade, T. S. Eliot had inherited Pound's place as cultural arbiter
and poetic figurehead, all but definitively institutionalizing this new
poetic internationalism (with its own vast planetary abstractions) in
The Waste Land. In 1915, Pound included two of Eliot's poems alongside his own in the second *BLAST* and arranged the publication of Eliot's
first volume, having already shepherded Joyce's work to press in London
(Lewis 2000: 48–51). Taken together, such works would begin to

compose the early canon of an equivocally internationalist modernism. But the canon of Pound's often transient enthusiasms included not only such figures as Joyce, Lewis, and Eliot, alongside a range of European artists; it also incorporated such momentary expatriates as Amy Lowell and Robert Frost. The swirling energy of the early London avant-garde, it would seem, was designed at least partially to solve a national problem. In 1912, even while militating for a distinctively American national art, Pound had admitted that the United States "is almost a continent and hardly yet a nation, for no nation can be considered historically as such until it has achieved within itself a city to which all roads lead, and from which there goes out an authority" (1973: 101). His solution lay in a temporary compromise. Lacking such a city within, he would find it without, in London, a place to which all currents might lead and from which a displaced aesthetic authority might subsequently emanate. The lack of a serious artist in the United States did not preclude the production of a serious art by Americans. It would simply have to be produced elsewhere.

To a considerable degree, then, the center of American poetic production in the early decades of the twentieth century was not in the United States at all, but rather in Europe, in what Raymond Williams calls "the new metropolitan cities, the centres of the also new imperialism, which offered themselves as transnational capitals of an art without frontiers" (1989: 34). Trained in the younger universities of the new world (and spared the obligations of military service by American neutrality), figures like Pound and Eliot gravitated to older centers of cultural power, trading the promise of academic certification (romance philology in Pound's case; philosophy in Eliot's) for a less certain existence among Europe's developing avant-gardes. As Williams suggests, such emigration patterns provide the crucial underlying element of modernism's experimental styles, creating a class of figures "[l]iberated or breaking from their national or provincial cultures, placed in quite new relations to those other native languages or native visual traditions, encountering meanwhile a novel and dynamic common environment from which the older forms were obviously distant" (1989: 45). Almost unique in this case, however, for a generation of Americans dispersed across Europe, is the simple fact of a shared dominant language, the paradoxical way in which migration simultaneously requires translation (as a cultural negotiation) and precludes it (as a linguistic practice), bridging disparate cultural orders within a language rather than across languages, and opening the possibility of an eventual process of naturalization.

Writing in 1932, two decades after Pound's plaint about America and a decade after Eliot's publication of *The Waste Land*, F. R. Leavis would locate in their work (along with that of Hopkins) "a decisive re-ordering of the tradition of English poetry" (1932: 195), effectively validating both the destruction of the pentameter and the American expropriation of English verse. Implicitly at least, any "new bearing" in English poetry would retain the trace of a distinctively non-English accent. Writing at about the same time in retrospect, Pound summed up the situation more polemically: "the language is now in the keeping of the Irish (Yeats and Joyce); apart from Yeats, since the death of Hardy, poetry is being written by Americans. All the developments in English verse since 1910 are due almost wholly to Americans. In fact, there is no longer any reason to call it English verse, and there is no present reason to think of England at all" (1968: 34). Apparent in both declarations is a shift in both the touchstones of a tradition and the notion of tradition as such. Leavis's new bearings lead outward, away from the recognizable continuities of English (both national and linguistic) verse to a more capacious field of often discontinuous references. Eliot's modernism had boldly substituted "the mind of Europe" for the concept of a national literature, while Pound's ever-amassing *Cantos* had begun to range well beyond even that continental limit for material. But in that process, modernism had also left tradition behind as a problem to be sorted out and argued over, something more than a tacit assumption. In the "English writing" at which originally modernism took aim, "we seldom speak of tradition," Eliot had observed in 1919, as if only an American could note the difficulty that the term implied (1975: 37). But in the wake of an internationalized modernism – "the durable writing no national tradition can plausibly claim," as Hugh Kenner defined it (1988: 4) – it would often prove difficult to speak of anything else. For British poets of later decades, however, such grand claims would often do little more than reconfirm a version of Dorn's fear: America is the world.

It is hardly surprising that Pound's curt dismissals and Leavis's stark proclamations would provoke a series of quick rejoinders. The poets gathered in the 1932 *New Signatures* anthology – W. H. Auden, Cecil Day Lewis, Stephen Spender, and William Empson among them – would uniformly react against both the formal radicalism and the authoritarian political drift of an institutionalized high modernism, proffering more regular meters and progressive political inclinations in their place: "a clear reaction against esoteric poetry in which it is necessary to catch each recondite allusion," as Michael Roberts explained in his preface (1932: 12). What is perhaps more notable, however, is that even such a reaction against modernism would quickly produce the need to provide an account of the tradition that authorizes it. The *New Signatures* poets, Roberts argues, "have discovered rhythms not alien to the normal movement of English speech, yet definite enough to make perceptible these subtle variations similar to those which formed the pattern of eighteenth-century verse and of Shakespearean and Miltonic blank verse" (1932: 16). Roberts' deliberate understatement fixes a middle range, an accentual zone neither fully foreign nor fully domestic, variable enough to accommodate some of the breakages and stops of free verse but comfortable still in the longer run of English prosody. The rejection of one tradition, in other words, requires the substitution of another, or at least the more explicit articulation of a tradition that had been there all along. But in either case, the modernist recalibration of the notion of a tradition that merely passes through or around an English center has the peculiar effect of provoking a need to think of England, of making the tradition of English verse a point of explicit contention and argument.

By the early postwar period, Eliot had declared a break from the modernist revolution as well, suggesting to the British Academy in 1947 that "the poetry of the rest of this century" should "discover new and more elaborate patterns of a diction now established" (1975: 273), committing himself to an ever more insular Englishness. Meanwhile, the Auden generation had paradoxically completed the transatlantic circuit of modern English verse by moving in the other direction, most definitively with Auden's own immigration to New York in 1939. Having retraced the migration of his elders in reverse, Auden recorded European catastrophe from an American vantage point, witnessing the end of "a low dishonest decade" from "one of the dives / On Fifty-Second Street" (1977: 245). What Spender called "the great, inevitable, everpredictable shift in wealth, power and civilization from the eastern to the western side of the Atlantic" (1974: 3) would, over the century's second half, deposit British and Irish poets on American shores (and in American universities) as inexorably as an earlier moment had led an older generation eastward. It would also give rise to a new form of literate anxiety, fears over language and identity that Spender referred to the figure of America itself:

> In English, an Americanism is not an ideal goal for Americans but an American usage threatening the integrity of the English language. Americanization, the process of Americanizing, is the shadow of a

future in which the world becomes America. For Europeans, the deepest fear is of the dissolution of European methods and ways of thinking, and of the European past, into the American present. (1974: 36)

If Spender was right to see in Americanization a force as irresistible as dialectics or the weather, then the real question of the postwar period lies not in the fact of a transatlantic current but rather in its shape. To a large degree, the situation of English poetry at the middle of the century – described by Neil Corcoran as a choice of "Eliot or Auden" (1993: 3) – has turned out to be no choice at all. In fact, either route has implied a larger movement beyond national boundaries, an often nervous awareness that the idea of "English" poetry attaches more easily to a language than a nation.

The decade following the war witnessed a decisive readjustment of Britain's place in the world. Even before American entry into hostilities, the 1941 Atlantic Charter had acknowledged a reconfiguration of Anglo-American relations under the pressure of a global international system. As a new Labour Government reassembled the domestic social infrastructure after 1945, nationalizing major industries and constructing the institutions of a welfare state (from National Health to National Assistance), it also engineered the effective end of empire, leaving emergent nations from Asia to Africa to the Caribbean to develop state structures of their own. The renegotiation of British power, however, severely strained and depleted by the exertions of war, left another series of vacuums as well. In 1947, weeks before the official independence of India and Pakistan, the British government announced the withdrawal of military aid from Greece and Turkey, citing the economic straits imposed by domestic reconstruction. Fearing the projection of Soviet power into Europe, the United States quickly moved to assert its own global reach, formulating in the Truman Doctrine a geopolitical commitment to "contain" Soviet expansion. That substitution of American for British influence in fact announced a much larger pattern. It was a former British Prime Minister who declared the descent of a Soviet-made "Iron Curtain," but the subsequent execution of a counter-strategy was left largely in American hands. The reason for deference was simple enough. Throughout the war, Britain had maintained its military commitments through a combination of American loans, transfers, and subventions. The consolidation of Allied power under American control by the end of the war thus reflected an economic as well as a military reality; indeed the collaborative effort that opened a western front in the summer of 1944 found its economic counterpart in the negotiations among Allied powers convened at the same time, at Bretton Woods, talks that decisively reorganized the world economic system by placing it firmly under the sign of the American dollar.

Under the agreements reached at Bretton Woods, world currencies were correlated and exchanged against the reserve currency of the dollar – and by implication against the political guarantee of American might. Though partners in the design of such a system, the British would progressively find themselves submitted to the inexorable logic of American hegemony. The suspension of lend-lease payments at the end of the war accordingly required the negotiation of massive loans from both the United States and Canada in 1945, negotiated by John Maynard Keynes. Such partial measures could not forestall the progressive devaluation of the pound, however, or its slow erosion against a dollar that functioned not only as a national currency in the United States but also (and more importantly) as the expression of a notionally universal category of value, a legally chartered proxy for gold. What Bretton Woods left implicit was articulated more directly in 1949 with the formation of NATO. Spurred by the Berlin blockade and the emergence of the Soviet Union as a countervailing nuclear threat, NATO joined most of Western Europe with the United States and Canada under the aegis of a single military and diplomatic bloc, anchored by the same projection of American power into Europe that had shortened two world wars. In one sense, then, postwar arrangements merely ratified the more provisional measures of the war years, redeploying ideological forces against the alternative economic and political models of the Eastern bloc. But in another, they also marked the eclipse of an older claim to imperial sovereignty, the common-sense assumption of straightforward self-governance that had long underwritten (however contentiously) a British national identity. The debates of later decades, over British entry into Europe (first blocked by France, then deferred into the 1970s), over the settlement of Northern Ireland, or the possibility of devolution in Scotland and Wales, could only compound the sense that Britain itself had entered a semi-peripheral zone, surviving the larger shift from a European to a global system as a great state caught in an age of superpowers.

The rather sheepish provisional conclusion that might be drawn from such tendencies is an uncomfortable one at best. If British culture itself expresses the mildly anachronistic logic of a bygone era, then its persistence becomes a difficult matter. The years after the war, it would often seem, could only produce a halting manner, "conditioned by manifold contingencies," as Donald Davie puts it, contingencies that constrain the poet as fully as anyone else: "hence his qualifications, his hesitancies, his damaging concessions" (1972: 186). The "changed relationship of the English-speaking partners in other fields – in politics, in economics" becomes a poetic question too, as material power begins gravitationally to recast cultural production. In Davie's account, poetry thus becomes a space of contact, but non-communication:

> One is tempted to say that for many years now British poetry and American poetry haven't been on speaking terms. But the truth is rather that they haven't been on *hearing* terms – the American reader can't hear the British poet, neither his rhythms nor his tone of voice, and the British reader only pretends to hear the rhythms and tone of American poetry since William Carlos Williams. And so what we have had for some years now is a breakdown in communication between these two English-speaking poetries, though for civility's sake the appearance of a continuing dialogue between them is maintained. (1972: 184)

So long as the position of Oedipal authority remained unusurped, Davie suggests, the tonal disparity between American overstatement and British understatement permitted exchange, perhaps even (over the decades between Whitman's moment and Pound's) encouraged it. With the construction of a postwar world, however, guaranteed by American power and increasingly awash in American culture, only the frustrations of ongoing non-recognition are possible, with one side uncompelled to hear, the other unable to be heard. For a North American critic like Kenner, the aftermath of modernism thus lay in "a literature written out of English dictionaries that England either can't claim or doesn't know if it wants to" (1988: 3) and a language scattered among Anglophone former provinces: the United States, Ireland, and England, in order of priority (other nations of the empire, in Britain or elsewhere, remain unmentioned). But Kenner's paradox is instructive, not least for specifying the connection between international modernism and the cultural logic of the American postwar order. As Alan Sinfield notes, "[i]t was as a US construct – often recognized explicitly as such – that Modernism was recentred in Britain from the end of the 1950s. Cultural power normally follows economic, political and military power, and as with jazz, rock-'n'-roll, Coca-Cola and blue jeans, the 'American' way of doing things, of seeing things, seemed impossible to ignore" (2004: 218). Each new attempt to map the terrain of British poetry returns compulsively not only to the question of American

influence, rejecting or embracing it by turns, but also to those informing political categories through which cultural influence operates,
effectively passing through the terms of modernism even to resist it.

The landmark anthologies of succeeding decades all recapitulate
the basic gesture of *New Signatures*, delineating a separate but subordinate sphere of influence by constructing an authorizing poetic line
(both prosodic and genealogical). For the poets of *The New Apocalypse*
(1940), that enabling tradition is primarily bardic, concerned "with the
study of living, the collapse of social forms and the emergence of new
and more organic ones" (Hendry 1940: 9). For those gathered as
the Movement in Robert Conquest's *New Lines* (1956), it runs more
quietly through Hardy to (an English) Auden, clearing a lyrical space
unsullied by modernist sprawl, or sits modestly in Davie's earlier
substitution of "diction" for "poetry" as the surest tool for the maintenance of the "language of the tribe" (1952: 5–6, 29ff), exactly as
the older Eliot had suggested. Conversely, A. Alvarez's *The New Poetry*
(1962) launches a polemic, assailing the Movement's uniformity of tone
by gathering younger English figures behind the banner of American
confessional poets John Berryman and Robert Lowell (joined by
Sylvia Plath and Anne Sexton in subsequent editions).

Most notable in each case (along with the ironic invocation of
the "new" as a kind of patterned verbal tic) is the need to claim
legitimation by reinventing a tradition. As Davie suggests, however,
tradition seems to block communication in each case, interposing a
barrier to reading that preserves linguistic rights only at the price of
legibility. Indeed, for at least one line of postwar poets, this quiet refusal
of exchange will emerge as the privileged site of English poetry,
the last resource over which England can claim an unchallenged
proprietary hold. Refined as irony or understatement, this practice of
disarticulation maintains at the level of culture a possibility of distance
unavailable in political or economic terms. For Philip Larkin, most
famously, the incursions of American cultural products and the commodification they unleash will demand both an embrace and a
refusal, often at the same time. The rhythms of traditional American
jazz are accordingly welcomed as populist forms, while the more improvisational structures of bebop drive Larkin to deplore the modernist
tendencies evident even in music, linking Charlie Parker to Pound
and Picasso as mascots of aesthetic decadence. Lurking in Larkin's
argument is a deeper sense of incommensurability between accents.
For American poets working in modernism's aftermath, jazz experimentation has frequently suggested new compositional practices,

integrating multiple voices and refrains, even chipping at the boundary between the single poem and the longer sequence, the lyric and the serial poem. But to the degree that experimental jazz liberates the phrase from the underlying structure of the line, creating a variable and potentially multivocal metric, it also undermines the seemingly natural cadence of the Movement lyric. At stake is a deeper notion of musicality, a disparity in assumptions about composition. If, as Pound claimed in Canto LXXXI, free verse had broken the pentameter (1998: 538), the deeper modernist encroachment of the postwar years had begun to make of that rupture a more permanent state of affairs, eventuating in what Charles Olson would dub "COMPOSITION BY FIELD, as opposed to inherited line, stanza, over-all form" (1966: 16). From the perspective of Larkin and his contemporaries, however, the abandonment of such buried formal predicates might as easily amount to a disavowal of irony as such, and with it of any poetic persona capable of maintaining its minimal distance from the normalizing designs of a new global sameness.

Larkin's discernment of a modernist break in the history of jazz thus masks a deeper technical disagreement over the basic molecular unit of English verse, over the displacement of the metrical foot as a primary unit of composition and the corollary substitution of the phrase, the line, or the page in its place. It is not the American reference *per se*, however, that provokes; it is instead the implied loss of a matrix of sensibility, one of those older "ways of thinking" over which Spender worried. For the poets of the Movement especially, American influence often portends both the disruption and the quieter reinvestment of identity, as when Larkin's poem "For Sidney Bechet" loosens its iambic opening and falls into a ragged *terza rima*, composed largely in hendecasyllables. The extra cadences may threaten a moment of excess, even conjuring fantasies of identification ("On me your voice falls as they say love should, / Like an enormous yes. My Crescent City / Is where your speech alone is understood" [2003: 87]), but they fail to revoke the underlying idea of a regular signature. More importantly, if somewhat paradoxically, they situate the possibility of communication in an impossibly ironic gap, using the odd harmonies of an American vernacular to underscore the voice of an English poet. Similarly, Thom Gunn's early poem to Elvis Presley superimposes the common-time signature of American rock-and-roll over a matrix of iambic quatrains, as Presley's voice is overheard through a corner jukebox. The poem thus anchors its first stanza in two time signatures that travel together until the second stanza:

> The limitations where he found success
> Are ground on which he, panting, stretches out
> In turn, promiscuously, by every note.
> Our idiosyncrasy and our likeness.
>
> (2000: 57)

Suddenly, Gunn's line begins to lengthen and grind, distended on the vowel-heavy words "promiscuously" and "every" (ambiguous enough in accent to suspend the poem momentarily between pentameter and hexameter) and pushed beyond its measure with the nigh-unscannable "idiosyncrasy." In Gunn's paradox, Presley's exotic singularity offers a point of identification and even self-reflection, a momentary subversion that turns language to unexpectedly coded ends:

> We keep ourselves in touch with a mere dime:
> Distorting hackneyed words in hackneyed songs
> He turns revolt into a style, prolongs
> The impulse to a habit of the time.
>
> (1994: 57)

As the poem regathers itself into full rhymes and slowly effaces the distinction between substance and style, the English poet finds himself in league with (perhaps even defined by) Presley's song, distorting and prolonging the words and beats that ambiguously constitute "a habit of the time."

Gunn's appropriation of Presley is surely an exemplary instance of what Dick Hebdige describes as the work of style within sub-cultures: "gestures, movements towards a speech which . . . challenges the principle of unity and cohesion, which contradicts the myth of consensus" (1987: 18). Gunn's poem seeks to fracture the pace of language while leaving its organizing structures in place and thereby to maintain the possibility of an ongoing revolt, a sexual and political counter-identification against and across the culture at large. For Gunn as for Larkin and Davie, then, even the instinct of revolt requires the maintenance of a recognizably English cadence against which the poet can strain, even if that poet should find himself adopting the idiom of an American singer, overheard in an American bar. But the gesture requires a measure of collaboration, an investment and even complicity in the preservation of the new global culture against which it strains. In a sense, the lyric shaped in such measures derives its force from simple demurral, what Tony Lopez describes as "a kind of English 'cultural cringe'" (2006: 140–1) that consigns poetry to the realm of nostalgic sub-culture and incipiently private language, "the literary equivalent to the neo-Tudoresque, post-Georgian late glimmering village being built in Dorset on Duchy land by associates of the Prince of Wales" (Lopez 2006: 141). In this light, the Movement's passage into the contemporary mainstream, perhaps definitively codified in Blake Morrison and Andrew Motion's selection for *The Penguin Book of Contemporary British Poetry* (1982), testifies to a quiet entente, an agreement by which England endures as a self-preserving sub-cultural pose, reserving the right to claim its own tradition by the simultaneous incorporation and refusal of another one.

But the institutionalization of Movement irony as an orthodoxy securely ensconced in major presses and reviews has failed, in retrospect, to settle relations between English-speaking poetries. In 1962, Alvarez's *The New Poetry* had already questioned the adequacy of such a tradition, reaching back to a missed generation of Scottish and Welsh figures (Norman McCaig and R. S. Thomas, respectively), before reaching forward to a younger generation of poets both insistently English and open to the suggestion of a continuing modernism, with a trace of an American accent. Ted Hughes, Geoffrey Hill, and Charles Tomlinson, among others, would seek to reground the open forms of modernism on an English terrain, effectively performing an act of critical translation in the process. For Tomlinson especially, the figure who has perhaps theorized the question most relentlessly, the attempt to rechristen English poetry in so narrowly *English* a fashion, mistakes what it has always been: a poetry that – from Chaucer to Dryden to Pound – exists primarily by acts of translation and incorporation (Tomlinson 2003: 1). The simple need to hear figures like Pound, Williams, or Marianne Moore requires an ongoing expansion of the possibilities of English verse and a slow dislocation of the idea that it has ever had a center at all. Tomlinson thus opens his tribute to American poets in translation by recalling a line from the English poet George Barker, mockingly included by William Carlos Williams in *Paterson*: "*American poetry is a very easy subject to discuss for the simple reason that it does not exist*" (Tomlinson 2001: 1). At stake are the familiar images of American provincialism and British parochialism, along with Williams' peculiar fantasy of an autonomous American language. But the work of Tomlinson and others suggests a more subtle reading as well: what distinguishes American poetry most forcefully is the fact that no properly American *language* exists, but merely a capacity for, indeed an inescapable need for, practical forms of cultural translation. In a sense, this lack has proven an indispensable advantage, and in the postwar period, it is this condition that British poetry has begun to share again.

The easy critical shorthand that would use "American" as a shorthand for modernist excesses thus misses the deeper point. What American influence has signified more regularly is a structure of translation that emerges most fully at the moment when a shared but contested language enters global circulation and thus begins to detach itself from the narrower anchorage of an implicit national tradition on either side. If the cultural history of the United States is inevitably underwritten by reference to British models, then the distinctly American fact of an Atlantic turbine imposes a new predicate that has more recently reshaped Britain and the United States together, binding "two worlds" and "the many languages a' English" (as Dorn puts it) under the logic of a single system fully visible from neither perspective. In the modernist aftermath, what both sides of the Atlantic share is an inability to claim English as a fully native language and a corollary need to incorporate a practice of translation as the ground of a poetics. Thus understood, the idea of translation also changes. In the postwar period at least, translation becomes a method, neither British nor American exclusively, for rewriting (or inventing) traditions retrospectively and tweaking history after the fact, for moving within the histories of English. Significantly, perhaps, the transatlantic market for translations has never been more lucrative than at the century's end, with legions of Ovids, Beowulfs, and Dantes distributed globally in glossy trade paperback, inviting each new generation of poets to try its hand at a proven classic. As a formal mechanism with historical consequences, however, translation is a more serious business than the bestseller lists might suggest. For poets recoiling against the conceits of insularity, translation has more regularly offered a way to reimagine the abstract lines of connection that define a postwar historical order, a way to evade the weight of tradition at home even while constructing alternatives to it.

The North Atlantic Turbine opens with three dedications, each accompanied by an epigraph. The first lifts a line from J. H. Prynne's "Sketch for a Financial Theory of the Self," a close meditation on the tense relationship between financial and linguistic abstractions, while the second echoes and answers it with a moment from Davie's "From the New World." Together, the two passages compose a single syntactical thought, almost seamlessly turning on the phrase "what we are": "we give the name of / our selves to our needs. / We want what we are" (Prynne); "British is what we are. / Once an imperial nation,

/ Our hands are clean now, empty" (Davie, in Dorn 1967: 6). Read in sequence, the lines conspire to banish an older identity from the present altogether, relegating the thought of an identitarian imperial tongue to the realm of either desire or nostalgia. The cumulative effect of the passage, however, operates on both sides of a sustaining contradiction. In a literal sense, English has begun to reflect on itself, on its lapse as the medium of a singular tradition able to declare "what we are" with any persistent confidence. When spliced and quoted back in the montage of a New World poet, however, the lines also begin to suggest a new model of how English might work, lashed together from dispersed voices to describe a political entity that is no longer simply American or British, but is instead defined by the movements of English across space. Appropriately enough then, Dorn's final epigraph, from Tom Raworth's wry "Love Poem," turns sharply from such large economic and political assessments to the question of the weather: "(once i tried to let a smile be my umbrella. i got awful wet)" (Dorn 1967: 6). If the shifting first-person of the dedication underscores the movement of the volume itself, diagrammed across the cover and throughout the sequence, it also imagines a new and more genuinely transatlantic poet, composed about equally of American forms and British contents.

This confluence of styles and voices is more, however, than a thematic effect, as is the inscription of transatlantic passage at the volume's literal and figurative fulcrum. Throughout the late 1960s and early 1970s, Stuart Montgomery's aptly named Fulcrum Press regularly published titles by such poets as Roy Fisher, Ian Hamilton Finlay, Lee Harwood, and Jeff Nuttall, alongside Dorn and other American poets clustered in the tradition of Olson's Black Mountain. In so doing, Fulcrum followed the lead of Migrant Press, first established by Gael Turnbull and Michael Shayer in the late 1950s to propagate a range of native experimental styles – and to suggest a larger critical point in the process. By juxtaposing such figures as Fisher, Finlay, and Edwin Morgan against a work like Olson's *Maximus*, Migrant advanced two critical narratives at once, insisting on both the persistent relevance of a modernist style and the linguistic fact of a transatlantic connection. Practically, imprints such as Migrant and Fulcrum also recapitulated the founding gesture of a modernist avant-garde, chartering a series of alternative institutions outside the narrower boundaries of canonical taste. As Lawrence Rainey has noted, modernism's consolidation as a cultural orthodoxy half a century earlier had depended on the transformation of a scattered avant-garde program into an institutional reality, on the strategic construction of a system of production and distribution for works otherwise unlikely to circulate (Rainey 1998). By the 1960s, the very success of such brands as Eliot's Faber & Faber, long aged into respectability, had opened a space for a new network of small presses and little magazines to occupy. The only thing required was a catalyst.

Generations earlier, the appearance of *The Waste Land* had marked modernism's definitive arrival as a poetic fact. In 1966, it was Fulcrum's publication of a belated modernist masterpiece – Basil Bunting's *Briggflatts* – that consolidated what Randall Stevenson describes as a "counter-movement" (2004: 190). The resurgence of Bunting's distinct voice, with its Northumbrian tones and its Poundian rhythms, found an immediate answer in the work of a younger generation of poets like Tom Pickard and Barry MacSweeney, eager to exploit historical fissures in the language. Still more powerful than Bunting's regionalism was the implicit suggestion that the refraction of an American formal idiom might unbind other forces closer to hand, stirring what Clive Bush describes as "a very long tradition of British dissent which, somehow, the moment it has been declared dead, refuses to lie down" (1997: 549). From Migrant's Scottish-tinged list to the Irish accents gathered by Michael Smith and Trevor Joyce through the New Writers Press and its journal *The Lace Curtain*, an array of small imprints pushed beyond the national boundaries of Britain itself to imagine an altered set of national relations, remapping the identities of English as mechanisms of translation, "workings" (in Joyce's deliberately modest phrase) designed to provisionalize, perhaps even to provincialize, literary and political institutions at once (Joyce: 2001).

A few months before Bunting first read *Briggflatts* at Tom and Connie Pickard's Morden Tower, a rather different event had been staged at the Royal Albert Hall. With the "happening" of the International Poetry Incarnation (as its organizers dubbed it), Beat poets Allen Ginsberg, Gregory Corso, and Lawrence Ferlinghetti found their way on to London's newly sprawling cultural scene (an array of international Communist poets, including Pablo Neruda, had withdrawn from the program). Tacking between jazz and Blakean prophecy, the event announced an exuberantly visionary mode later codified in Penguin's *Children of Albion* anthology, edited by Michael Horovitz and designed to convey "the flexing of other (transatlantic) muscles at home" (1969: 318). Elsewhere, the 1966 appearance of *The English*

Intelligencer, edited by Andrew Crozier and Peter Riley, and the longer-lived *Grosseteste Review*, edited by Tim Longville and John Riley, suggested a rather different set of influences and began to define a style more academic and austere, ultimately centered on Prynne's Cambridge. Gathering such figures as Raworth, John James, Douglas Oliver, and Veronica Forrest-Thomson, the Cambridge group fused lyrical precision and speculative abstraction into a new objectivism, open simultaneously to the inherited patterns of the English line and a range of globally imported alternatives. With the formation of the Association of Little Presses in the same year, Fulcrum, Bob Cobbing's Writers Forum, and other small presses began to assemble themselves as a new avant-garde, linking a network of imprints, journals, readings, and happenings that would ultimately amount to an alternative (if occasionally ragged) system of poetic distribution (Griffiths & Cobbing 1988).

What the otherwise far-flung figures and sites of this counter-movement shared, beyond a fatigue with the fraught modesties of the Movement itself, was a sense that the formal imperatives of the post-war order entailed a more nuanced conception of the situation and sources of English. Taken together, the rough alliance of forces that Eric Mottram dubbed the "British poetry revival" (1993) unleashed a brief further wave of poetic deregulation, regarded alternately (in Mottram's phrases again) as "a treacherous assault on British poetry" or as a last chance to "resist limpet-clinging to past metrics, self-satisfied irony, the self-regarding ego and its iambic thuds" (Allnutt et al. 1988: 133, 131). In 1971, even such national institutions as the Poetry Society, with its house organ *Poetry Review*, would briefly succumb, "taking up the challenge," under Mottram's editorial leadership, "of a wide range of Twentieth Century poetics in Europe and America" (Allnutt et al. 1988: 131). As Peter Barry has exhaustively documented, the ensuing battle, waged throughout the decade, between shifting entrenchments of rear- and avant-garde, ended in a wave of public controversy. But if the Arts Council's 1977 dissolution of Mottram's editorial board marked a cessation of overt hostilities, it failed to realign the underlying terms of the conflict. Surveying the aftermath a decade later, Ken Edwards could credit the revival not only with an achieved revolution in the "mechanics of publishing and distribution" (1988: 266), but also with the recovery of "a range of poetries in these islands, largely ignored by or unknown to those who would hold the centre ground," emerging from "communities which may be united by discrete yet overlapping notions of culture, politics, gender identity and geographical locus" (1988: 269).

The resilient unknowing with which Edwards charges the mainstream was underscored in 1982, when Morrison and Motion pointedly bemoaned "a stretch, occupying much of the 1960s and 70s, when very little – in England at any rate – seemed to be happening, when achievements in British poetry were overshadowed by those in drama and fiction, and when, despite the presence of strong individual writers, there was a lack of overall shape and direction" (1982: 11). But the several qualifications in the otherwise sweeping claim – "in *England* at any rate," "*seemed* to be happening," "a lack of *overall* shape and direction" – perhaps sketch the situation of recent decades as accurately as the explicit sentiment. As much a symptom as an aesthetic insurgency, the rough contours of the revival delineated a series of gaps in the organizing critical categories of an established tradition. In its ability to negotiate the complex differences between England and English and to thrive in the disparity between styles shaped by large press runs and those adapted to a smaller scale, the revival insisted that the attempt to gauge a broader historical unity required other terms: an awareness that the conceit of insularity had itself outlived its former usefulness. As much as anything, the cumulative aftermath of such events lies in the difficulty of invoking any narrow singular description of English poetry itself, of relying unreflectively on the notion of a tradition that is merely inherited rather than made. For the poets represented more fully in such collections as *A Various Art* (Crozier & Longville 1987), *The New British Poetry* (Allnutt et al. 1988), and *Conductors of Chaos* (Sinclair 1996), and the more recent Oxford anthology (Tuma: 2001), any operative concept of a British tradition presumes an openness of influence as well as of form, reaching outward across (but also beyond) the Atlantic. Even Motion's more recent admission that "[f]or most of the last century, Britain marginalised the heirs of the great Modernists" (in Barry 2006: xii) acknowledges almost as much. But it is exactly the shifting of margins – at the edges of the poem or the nation – that lends the late century its overall shape and direction. In a world in which English returns globally, having traveled always across traditions that speak the language differently, it is the self-sufficiency not simply of a well-wrought English style that remains in question, but the self-sufficiency of any poem conceived in isolation.

If a belated British modernism has now overcome the communication breakdown that Davie felt decades ago, it has also introduced new modes of poetic abstraction, calculated to cast beyond the referential limits of the poem itself. The fundamental question that continues to be posed by those experimental poetries is whether a poem can, at century's end, be read according to the set of well-worn critical habits that have conventionally guided the appreciation of English verse. In large measure, the overhearing of American forms has offered twentieth-century British poets an instrument with which to gauge the occasionally invisible forms of recent historical experience, those gaps and nervous breaks where the Movement lyric falls silent. More crucial, then, than America itself is the other half of Dorn's equation, the abstract pressure of a larger world for which the United States can only stand in metonymically. From jazz to blue jeans, the detached emblems of American culture operate as reminders that traditions form dialectically, not only as native products but also as an archive of imported goods. Poetic translation stands as an ongoing sketch of the deeper patterns of world influence, an inevitable by-product of the fact that the postwar world admits no durable possibility of insularity.

This inevitability of translation assumes the status of a fully systematic logic in Caroline Bergvall's "Via: 48 Dante Variations," a piece that mentions America not at all, but depends entirely on the circulation of English's many languages. Noting that "translating Dante into English has become something of a cultural industry" (2005: 64), one that has produced over two hundred such translations in as many years, Bergvall collates the various English editions of the *Commedia* catalogued by the British Library before 2000, the 700th anniversary of Dante's vision. The result is a series of familiar renderings of the first tercet of the *Inferno*, culled from 47 discrete versions, ranging from Cary's 1805 edition ("In the midway of this our mortal life") to the two distinct interpretations offered by Seamus Heaney ("Halfway on our life's journey, in a wood"; "In the middle of the journey of our life"). But Bergvall does not arrange her selections along such a chronological arc. Following the archival logic of the library catalog, she instead orders them alphabetically, according to the first letter of each passage. The first two entries thus begin with the letter *a* ("Along the journey"; "At the midpoint"). The next seven, however, form an anaphoric cluster of their own, beginning in each case with a variant of "Half" or "Half-way." The next eleven begin with "In," followed by the largest cluster of entries, some nineteen lines beginning "Midway."

In one sense, Bergvall's order is entirely contingent, generated by the individual choices of translators working across two centuries and controlled only by the underlying order of the alphabet itself. But in another, the very act of editorial compilation begins to exert a different logic, an enumerative compulsion that returns always to some version of a midpoint, only to begin again in the next entry with another midpoint. That sense of mediality is confirmed in the piece's title, which takes the last word of Dante's first line (*vita*, "life") in foreshortened form, as *via*, "way" or "road." Bergvall's emendation thus catches a persistent slip of translation (lurking for example in Heaney's rendering of *cammin di nostra vita* as "our life's journey"), but in the process reconcentrates the entire idea of translation around an ongoing moment of passage. The architecture of Dante's text – its intricate theological design, its teleological progression through the stages of a Christian afterlife – is sacrificed, ultimately displaced by an arrested image of circulation: *half-way, in, midway*. In its place, Bergvall traces a profusion of English idioms, from the ornate to the colloquial, from incipiently prosaic or free verse rhythms to awkwardly stilted imitations of Dante's *terza rima*.

In a strict sense, Bergvall's poem provides an indexical representation not merely of Dante's text, but more systematically of the history by which that text finds its way into the center of English culture. What the poem grasps is therefore something larger than Dante, larger even than a modulation of poetic styles over the past two centuries. The poem's meaning lies elsewhere, in the entire system of mediations that lie between 1300 and 2000, radiating from all points of the globe but converging in the catalog of the British Library – a system that remains unrepresentable in itself but nonetheless conditions any attempt to describe what English poetry has been for two centuries and more. But precisely because the poem's object remains outside it, its form constitutes a historical map, marking the poetic trade routes across which traditions travel and insisting that it is exactly such an invisible system that a millennial poem must somehow render.

Further Reading

Davie, Donald (1972). *Thomas Hardy and British Poetry*. New York: Oxford University Press.

Kenner, Hugh (1988). *A Sinking Island: The Modern English Writers*. New York: Knopf.

Sinfield, Alan (2004). *Literature, Politics and Culture in Postwar Britain*. London: Continuum.

Spender, Stephen (1974). *Love–Hate Relations: English and American Sensibilities.* New York: Random House.

Stevenson, Randall (2004). *The Last of England?* Oxford English Literary History, vol. 12: *1960–2000.* Oxford: Oxford University Press.

Tuma, Keith (1998). *Fishing by Obstinate Isles: Modern and Postmodern British Poetry and American Readers.* Evanston, IL: Northwestern University Press.

Williams, Raymond (1989). *The Politics of Modernism: Against the New Conformists,* ed. Tony Pinkney. London: Verso.

Chapter 8

Neo-Modernism and Avant-Garde Orientations

Drew Milne

Amid the rubble left by World War II, the possibilities for avant-garde developments in Britain and Ireland were severely rationed. There are long-term continuities in poetic modernisms over the subsequent sixty years, but before trying to articulate the critical tendencies developed through these continuities, it is worth sketching the plurality of perspectives available in 1945 (Nicholls 1995; Kolocotroni et al. 1998; Tuma 1998, 2001; Rainey 2005). Geographical locations were secondary to the pervasive sense of historical catastrophe, but the social fragmentation of contexts out of which modernist resources might be developed had lasting consequences. Samuel Beckett, for example, chose to return from Ireland through Britain to France, working with the Red Cross amid the bombed ruins of Saint-Lô in what was then the largest hospital in Europe, experiences described in his broadcast "The Capital of the Ruins" (see Beckett 1990: 17–28). Although schooled in the many avant-garde possibilities of prewar Paris, Beckett's postwar writing developed a rigorously impoverished poetics, a poetics hardly recognizable as English poetry, even in translation, amid its many prosaic extinctions.

Beckett's return to France and to the French language remains a significant departure, part of a process of emigration that shaped the loss of continuities with pre-war modernism. W. H. Auden, another émigré, became a US citizen in 1946. His subsequent poetry erred towards eclectic variousness, a source for what became known as "New York school poetry," but scarcely registered by those working through the ruins of European modernism (Lehman 1998; Davies 2000; Ward 2000). Dylan Thomas's postwar collection *Deaths and Entrances* (1946) reflected experiences of war and the dissipation of the few surviving modernist and surrealist affiliations in his work. David Gascoyne returned to France, living there for the most part until the 1960s. His poetry bore traces of surrealism, albeit within a rather congealed and metaphysical romanticism, but few have preferred his later work to his prewar poems and translations (Gascoyne 1998). Surrealism continued to inform new work, but rather than looking to surrealist poetics from, say, Georges Bataille or Antonin Artaud, the more dominant French influence came from existential prose, and the writings of Jean-Paul Sartre and Albert Camus. A turn to existential reflection remains a key element in postwar poetry, both modernist and anti-modernist. Avant-garde orientations towards lived experience have nevertheless tended to fragment and disrupt assumptions about the authority of subjectivity. Indeed, a central dynamic in avant-garde poetics questions the ideology of existing subjectivities, and seeks to open up new political possibilities. Conservative anti-modernisms, by contrast, have preferred an empirically reduced, commonsensical poetic subjectivity, involving anecdotal epiphanies and minor transcendences of the everyday.

Among modernist poets who survived the war, T. S. Eliot's poetry and poetic paradigm were exhausted, producing nothing of substance after *Four Quartets* (1943). David Jones worked on in relative isolation. The historical and religious fragmentation of his long poem-book *The Anathemata* (1952) remains almost too explicitly programmatic in its modernism, too old-fashioned to seem anything other than belated. Basil Bunting, who worked for British military intelligence in the Middle East during the war and after, returned to Britain from Tehran in 1952. It was not, however, until the publication of his major poem, *Briggflatts* (1966), that the substance of his continuity with the work of Ezra Pound and the objectivists became apparent (Terrell 1981; DuPlessis & Quartermain 1999). Hugh MacDiarmid, having struggled with extreme poverty on the Shetland Islands and conscripted factory work in Glasgow, was granted a civil list pension in 1950, and thereby the possibility of a settled existence in Lanarkshire. With the possible exception of *In Memoriam James Joyce* (1955), a long poem combining a collage of found materials and synthesized linguistics, his ambitious postwar work never quite materialized until his almost posthumous collected poems (MacDiarmid 1978). The authority of his experiments in the 1930s is still to be assimilated, but by the early

1960s even MacDiarmid's admirers were looking around for new prospects. Although writers such as David Jones, Basil Bunting, and Hugh MacDiarmid are often mentioned as important influences on subsequent poets, the reception of such writers is patchy, secondary to enthusiasms for American poets. Indeed, they are more often honored in the breach opened up by parochial resistances to modernism in Britain, than they are evident as active influences.

It could be argued, then, despite the various productions of some of these major poets, that modernism in Britain never made it out of the bunkers of the war. Writers who might have become the focus for new avant-garde groupings were scattered amid scarce resources, with few institutions on which to lean. Numerous European modernists in flight from Nazi Germany passed through Britain – Bertolt Brecht, Theodor Adorno, and László Moholy-Nagy, for example – before ending up in America or returning to Continental Europe. Amid Britain's retreat from its former imperial and colonial powers, and up against various anti-modernist entrenchments among little Englanders, the continuity and development of modernist poetry in English seemed exhausted or in exile. The poetries produced out of Ireland's divisions have sometimes been read as postcolonial developments, rather than through British hostilities to modernist poetics, but hostility to modernism has perhaps been greater in Ireland than in Britain, despite the exemplary status of James Joyce and Beckett. The poetics of recent Irish modernists – such as Randolph Healy, Trevor Joyce, Maurice Scully, and Catherine Walsh – can be traced back through an earlier generation of neglected Irish modernists, such as Thomas MacGreevy, Brian Coffey, and Denis Devlin (Coughlan & Davis 1995; Davis 2003). These different poets nevertheless have more in common with British and North American modernism than with the paradigms of poetry associated with Philip Larkin and Seamus Heaney.

The burial of modernism in Britain is encapsulated by the fate of Kurt Schwitters, a fellow-traveller of Dada, and pioneer of the one-person avant-garde he called *Merz*. Having fled Germany and then Norway, Schwitters ended up in England, enduring internment on the Isle of Man before moving to Cumbria. His *Merzbarn* project, begun in 1947, developed his earlier principles of collage and assemblage, working various found materials into the architecture of an old stone barn. After Schwitters' death in 1948, it was not until 1966, in part through the efforts of Richard Hamilton, that some of the structure was "preserved," having been transported and resituated in the University of Newcastle's Hatton Gallery. Schwitters learned from Dada to produce a range of avant-garde techniques, from sound and concrete poetry to the use of found materials and collage, and from proto-"pop" recontextualization strategies to the building of environments and installations (Schwitters 1993; see Young 1981). Both as an artist and a poet, Schwitters exemplified the avant-gardist at work across different media, democratizing and radicalizing the forms and processes of artistic construction. Anyone looking to reconfigure modernist legacies in British poetry could begin with Schwitters and his work's subsequent accommodation within a university, but such connections, like so many other possible genealogies, seem only to have been possible retrospectively and then belatedly.

Bob Cobbing, a key early figure in British sound, visual, and concrete poetry, developed avant-garde practices analogous to those of Schwitters, largely out of his own understanding of art and music, rather than through direct connections with earlier avant-gardes. Cobbing set up Writers Forum in the early 1950s, providing a context for poetry and performance, which grew into a long-running counter-cultural publishing project (Mayer 1974; Cobbing & Griffiths 1992). He remained a focus for avant-garde formations through to his death in 2002, but despite many collaborations and overlaps, his work and performance also remained singular and home-grown, a very British modernism. Cobbing's one-person mode of production bears comparison with William Blake's poetics of production, a model also significant for poets as different as J. H. Prynne and Allen Fisher. J. H. Prynne's early collections, *Kitchen Poems* (1968) and *The White Stones* (1969), show some affinities with the poetry of Charles Olson and Ed Dorn (Prynne 2005). Sketchy attempts have been made to construe a "Cambridge school" around Prynne's work and the many poets with Cambridge associations, such as Tom Raworth, John James, Andrew Crozier, Veronica Forrest-Thomson, Rod Mengham, and John Wilkinson (see, for example, Stevenson 2004). Even the looseness of "school" hardly grasps the variousness of such writers and their respective differences. Prynne's teaching and example have provided a remarkable nexus for poetic networks, but his own poetic works remain singular and resistant to modernist or avant-garde contextualization. Allen Fisher's remarkable output is no less singular and difficult to contextualize. Sometimes anachronistically compared with North American "language" poetry, his poetic projects blend conceptions drawn from Fluxus, Charles Olson, and visual art practices into a process of poetic production that remains in flux, developing unusually suggestive layers across many different sequences and projects. More evidently avant-garde in orientation than Prynne's, Fisher's work has been widely recognized as a key point of reference, while nevertheless eluding anything resembling canonization. The internal articulations of the poetry of Prynne and Fisher have a depth and range which defeat the attempts of their admirers to imitate their work, suggesting horizons for poetic practice rather than paradigms that could be institutionalized through "schools" or coteries.

The Institute of Contemporary Arts (ICA) in London provided some context for avant-garde artistic connections in the 1950s (Aldred 2000). The more characteristic pattern, however, involves poets who came to some prominence in the 1950s and early 1960s – such as Ian Hamilton Finlay, Charles Tomlinson, Gael Turnbull, Christopher Middleton, and Edwin Morgan – making independent connections with international avant-garde currents, often through translations. Despite the prominent reception of modernism in architecture, visual arts, and music, Britain remained inhospitable for modernist poets. The range of recent modernist poetic practices continues to be various and resistant to synoptic characterization. This suggests flaws in the critical models associated with modernism. Even among those most sympathetic to earlier avant-gardes, many resourceful individuals have been sceptical of avant-gardism, while remaining aware of avant-garde tendencies. The opposition so often set up between modernist experiments and "mainstream" anti-modernism has nevertheless given rise to various emphases on tradition, difficulty, formal innovation, and hermeticism, rather than focusing on the singularity of individual poets and poems. Discussion of what might matter in British poetry has also been beset by the need to make analogies with European and North American modernisms. In 1971, for example, introducing an anthology surveying modernist trends, John Matthias suggested that:

> Too often "British" means *old* or *tired* in America, "contemporary" rather than "modern", Philip Larkin rather than Tom Raworth. In fact, the best British poets are refining and extending the work of the modernist revolution in the same way their American contemporaries are. (Matthias 1971: ix)

Raworth's work has affinities with contemporary American poetry, but also distinct sensibilities, interests, and experiences (Dorward, 2003). There can be no tidy model of what might count as the "same way." For American critics bemoaning the lack of contemporary British poetry in American modes, Raworth's work is often the exception used to labor a rule. He is one of the very few recent British poets regularly cited in Marjorie Perloff's many discussions of twentieth-century avant-garde poetry (see, for example, Perloff 1985: 234–7). While American models of the "traditions" of new and modernist poetry have played a significant part in the development of modernism in other English-language contexts, the forms and strategies of non-American poetries reflect different political contexts, different relations to the history of poetry in English, and different understandings of what might be "radical." While American poetry perhaps offers more explicitly liberal models of formal radicalism, the political radicalism of European avant-garde currents is often more closely related to socialist agendas. Alternative models need to be found through which to read the peculiarities of modernism in the British Isles.

Structural oppositions between modernist and anti-modernist, and between modern and postmodern, along with terms such as "experimental" and "avant-garde," allow for initial critical negotiations. The oppositions usually work, however, to contain problems, preserving traditional and restrictive reading protocols. Such oppositions tend, moreover, to position postwar modernism in Britain as an embattled minority or underground position, prejudging arguments for modernism as the dominant tradition in twentieth century English-language poetry, rather than a peripheral alternative. Any account of recent radical poetry and poetics needs to clear the burden of contextual categories and to rethink the processes by which modernism and avant-gardism are reconfigured.

Introducing the recent anthology *Vanishing Points: New Modernist Poems*, Rod Mengham offers some formulations germane to this process:

> Our subtitle proposes elements of continuity with an historically identifiable form of international writing that sets at a premium experiments with form and language. One thing our selection does is to reflect the extent to which the community of experimental poets is now, at the beginning of the twenty first century, genuinely international in its scope and in the directness of its interactions. Since the mid-1960s, the poetic avant-gardes of several English language-speaking countries have depended on communication with like-minded groups in other countries far more than with the mainstream writers they are geographically lumped together with. (Mengham 2004: xviii)

Modernism's historical legacy amounts to more than experiments with form and language, but this is nevertheless a helpful way of orientating new readings. *Vanishing Points* includes many British poets, along with Canadians, Australians, and Americans, but the volume's internationalism assigns such national categories to the margins, clues amid the notes on contributors. Although a historical category, "modernism" is also dissociated here from particular metropolitan locations, and understood as an experimental orientation developed through cosmopolitan networks. International interactions give poets new contexts, and a sense of the English language as the fundamentally shared horizon. Parallels cut across the agendas of traditionalists within nation-states and their respective literary nationalisms. Traditionalists might claim continuities with premodernist poetic forms, such as the subtleties of lyric form articulated by Thomas Hardy or W. B. Yeats (Garratt 1989; Davie 1998). Most modernist poets recognize continuity less with modernism as a whole, or with particular forms, than with the projects of particular writers. Where modernists might once have sought to break with preceding traditions, above all with Romanticism, postwar continuations of modernism involve renewals. As Mengham puts it: "the writers in this volume represent a strand in recent poetry that has stayed in touch with the agendas of modernism; they are not postmodernist, but late modernist writers" (Mengham 2004: xviii). The labels are secondary to the claim that shared continuities among these writers constitute a historically informed renewal of modernism, rather than a paradigm shift, but there remains a sense of historical belatedness, perhaps even nostalgia.

Faced with the fluidity of "modernism" as a historical category, the stress on reinventions of earlier models discourages the tendency to define a shared agenda in chronological or formal terms. Modernist poems look different. Various shared formal features can be identified, such as a new instability of the verse "line" length; an absence of conventional metrical schemes and rhymes; and new schemes of punctuation and page layout. Similar formal features can nevertheless be used for very different purposes. A genealogy of the functions of white space in twentieth-century poetry in English would reveal curious lacunae in any formalist approach to reading. A randomly associative, non-referential poem generated through chance procedures can look similar, superficially, to a poem written through a powerfully referential scheme, predetermined by some analytic or speculative methodology. One traceable form of rewriting is evident in explicit dedications and allusions, part of a more general process of intertextual double-coding established through dialogues with earlier poems. Edwin Morgan, for example, in "Unfinished Poems:

161

a sequence for Veronica Forrest-Thomson," writes through a tribute to Forrest-Thomson (Morgan 1990: 373–80); while Redell Olsen reworks Charles Olson's *Maximus Poems* among the materials of her sequence *The Minimaus Poems* (Olsen 2004: 75–108). Many poems can be read both as critical interventions and as forward-looking renewals, renewals that reorient perceptions of what remains contemporary. Degrees of familiarity among different writers, readers, and networks establish fluid orientations, a process of searching through the second-hand materials of modernism for what remains renewable. This suggests various avant-garde orientations informing production and reception, but no obvious paradigm shifts of the kind associated with postmodernism. Charles Jencks argues that postmodernism is "the eclectic mixture of any tradition with that of the immediate past: it is both the continuation of Modernism and its transcendence" (Jencks 1989: 7). The double-coding characteristic of recent poetry informed by modernism is less eclectic, however, less concerned with transcendence than with critical renewal. The resulting strategies of double-coding are pluralistic: less purist than those associated with earlier modernisms, and less ironic than the playful historicism characteristic of postmodernist paradigms.

The underlying agenda of renewal is not, then, experiment for experiment's sake – as if "experimental" poetry were the working umbrella – nor the formalism of form for form's sake, nor even innovation for innovation's sake. Emphasis on radical "innovation" or "radical" artifice often puts too much stress on formal methods, rather than recognizing the dialogue between poetic forms and the residual contents of language and experience. The history of poetic forms comes into conflict with the political mediation of such forms. The micropolitics of "radical" poetics generate interpretative decisions at the level of detail that are never simply formal, unconditioned, or new. Exploration into poetry's conditions of possibility combined with inquiries into the possibility of meaning, reveal the extent to which innovative formalism is often no more self-legitimating than the conservation of traditional poetic forms for tradition's sake. Modernist poetic "rigor" works towards a deeper informality or sense of play: its critical seriousness is double-coded by forces of wit, artifice, satire, and ingenuity. Mengham nevertheless asserts a shared project:

> What binds together their various kinds of innovative practice is a strong insistence on findings ways of continuing and renewing the lyric impulse in poetry in English. What is equally important is a

commitment to work that examines the political scope of poetry. (Mengham 2004: xix)

Political conceptions of poetry developed out of earlier, historical avant-gardes cannot be boiled down to a loose evocation of the avant-garde as such. Claims for continuity through the category of "late" modernism seek differentiation from what Mengham calls the "postmodernist ideology" associated with "Language" writing (Mengham 2004: xviii). A prejudice against postmodern tendencies is widely shared by recent poets seeking to renew modernism, with, for example, deep-seated hostilities to poststructuralist conceptions of the arbitrariness of the signifier. Such hostilities provide some context for the sharp differentiations suggested by engagement with what Mengham calls "lyric impulse." Many of those included in *Vanishing Points* would not, however, describe their work in such terms. Adapting Alan Sinfield's model of "faultlines," such terms reveal cracks amid a loose ideological consensus (Sinfield 1992). Rather than seeking to define or clarify the key terms continually thrown up by arguments in poetics, it is more important to trace the potential cracks which key terms plaster over, cracks which can indicate structural movements amid otherwise shared positions. Faultlines indicate more than mere mistakes in terminology. A new vocabulary would not end the difficulties over what might characterize the modernist, experimental, or innovative dynamics of "radical" poetry. The consequence of questioning the way key terms indicate faultlines is not to dispose of the terms or the problems, but to trace the animating conflicts and concerns. A significant faultline emerges, accordingly, for those whose poetry questions the political priority given to "lyric" as opposed to "text" or "writing," and for whom a condition of poetic innovation is the need to break with the authority of lyric voices and structures. The commitment to renew lyric traditions inevitably comes into conflict with the renewal of modernist poetics already sceptical of lyric forms.

Even allowing for the position-taking required of introductions and anthologies, there is a curious sense in which discussions of tendencies in recent British poetry inevitably stumble into sinking sands. The need to put a disproportionate emphasis on a shared tendency or mode of radical formalism tends to obscure the way shared avant-garde orientations involve as many disagreements. The ongoing differentiation of intertextual dialogue generates layers of interaction, familiarity, and political argument that disable the formation of manifestos or

avant-garde programs. Binary oppositions nevertheless appear structural in different attempts to account for continuities among diffuse,
diverse, and variously contentious positions and practices. From
within versions of "mainstream" orthodoxy, alternatives are pejorat-
ively positioned as "experimental," "underground," "elitist," "obscure,"
"difficult," "inaccessible," and so forth. From within avant-garde positions, mainstream orthodoxy is provincial, parochial, pseudo-populist,
unknowingly ideological, or historically naive. As Peter Middleton puts
it: "The great bulk of the poetry that is published by the main commercial publishers, reviewed in the newspapers, and distributed to ordinary bookstores, maintains a poetics that belongs to a premodernist
era" (Middleton 2003: 128). Variously dismissed, ignored, or ascribed
a false coherence, summary characterizations of "orthodox" British poetic
currents are more often assumed than argued, scarcely more subtle
than anti-modernist attacks on modernist currents. Compare another
anthology's formula:

> "mainstream" in this context may be said to include the narrow lineage
> of contemporary poets from Philip Larkin to Craig Raine and Simon
> Armitage, and encompassing their attendant "collectives" (Movement,
> Martians, New Generation). Generalisation about such (often nebulous)
> groups is fraught with difficulties, but it nevertheless holds that in each
> case the typical poem is a closed, monolineal utterance, demanding
> little of the reader but passive consumption. (Caddel & Quartermain
> 1999: xv)

Reductive constructions of a "bad" mainstream rarely offer a critique
of the poems dismissed (for an exception, see Crozier 1983).
Qualitative differentiations of good from bad poetry, active as
opposed to passive modes of reading, effectively map modernist and
anti-modernist poetry onto a more traditional difference between
verse and poetry, or onto an even simpler contrast between poetry
and hermetic nonsense. Evocations of a "bad" mainstream recur as a
straw target, lending the marginality of avant-garde alternatives a degree
of radicalism. A suspicion emerges that the structures of reciprocal ignor-
ance and hostility are mutually fulfilling, a constitutive negativity that
helps generate boundaries and taboos within diverse practices. Such
structural oppositions are more productive than the opposing forces
recognize, a constitutive dynamic in the publication and teaching of
poetry in schools and universities.

Within avant-garde poetics, a more interesting cluster of problems
concerns differences between British and North American avant-garde

paradigms. Mengham positions "late" modernism between modernism and postmodernism, but while "late" highlights the belated publication or delayed reception of aspects of modernism, the term shares the indeterminacy of "post" as a temporal qualification of modernism (cf. Miller 1999). Given attempts to renew modernism through resistances to postmodern paradigms, "neo-modernism" more accurately describes the underlying tendencies. "Modernism" itself is already an overburdened term, and hardly a stable point of reference, but recognition of its historical importance as more than a mere period in literary history encourages substantive attention to dynamics still relevant for the possibilities of poetry. Critical analysis of "modernism" developed by contemporary poets informed by modernism parallels new emphases in contemporary critical accounts of the historical phenomena associated with modernism. Even revisionist accounts of modernism offered by critics seeking to historicize or limit the historical significance of modernism could be understood as forms of critical neo-modernism. Critics more sympathetic to the achievements of modernism could be said to be engaged in neo-modernist poetics by other means. Marjorie Perloff suggests, for example, that: "at the beginning of the twenty-first century the term 'post-modernism' seems to have largely lost its momentum" (Perloff 2002: 2). With reference to Donald Allen's revised edition of *The New American Poetry*, entitled *The Postmoderns*, she suggests:

> With their "open-form," "authentic," process-oriented, improvisatory, colloquial, vernacular poetry, the New American Poets positioned themselves against the conservatism, formalism and suspect politics of modernism. . . . But from the hindsight of the twenty-first century, their fabled "opening of the field" was less revolution than restoration: a carrying-on, in somewhat diluted form, of the avant-garde project that had been at the very heart of early modernism. (Perloff 2002: 2–3)

"Avant-garde" works here to mark a critical difference within modernism, as if avant-gardism were the radical tendency within modernism's variousness. American resistances to modernism overlap with the overtly reactionary anti-modernisms developed in Britain, but amid different types of modernist reception, there is a shared hostility among different avant-garde orientations to the model of modernism as it was construed and institutionalized in the 1950s, the modernism associated with Clement Greenberg, New Criticism, and T. S. Eliot. As Perloff's formulation also hints, there is a tension between the critique of modernist formalism and the new formalisms offered to disguise often superficial paradigm shifts. The underlying continuity of shared problems and longer historical perspectives persists. Any concept of modernism's periodicity alive to such continuities needs to be non-linear, discerning cyclical renewal and uneven development rather than the march of "progress."

The will to open up form can be understood as an awkwardly historical dialectic, rather than as a series of paradigmatic innovations. The working through of this dialectic can continue to be understood as one of openness only for so long as it is not governed by some teleology of progress or the "new." Given that the "new" figures as a suspiciously repetitive and now ancient strategy of legitimation, modernism might better be recognized from the perspectives of neo-modernism as a negative dialectic, the working through of innovation fatigue (cf. Adorno 2002: 181–202). Insofar as strategic claims for innovation invite comparison with the variousness of earlier modernisms, repeated claims for "innovation" invite scepticism as to the viability of novelty as a strategy for legitimation or publicity. By implication, just as attempts to offer formulations of orthodoxy within poetic practice are easily refuted by contrasting the diversity of work produced, so the underlying tendencies are not reducible to formalist or technical accounts. Different types of poetics and criticism seem necessary to account for the aging of modernist paradigms within the cyclical developments of neo-modernism. Curiously, there is a parallel critical vacuum in which neither formally conservative poems nor the more radical formal innovations of neo-modernism have generated readings of the quality familiar in criticism of modernism. The respective formal strategies are either so self-evident as to make interpretation redundant, or so radical as to be too indeterminate or too daunting for existing models of criticism to discuss adequately.

Even if individual poets and critics are forced to ally themselves to terms such as "experimental," "linguistically" or "formally" "innovative," the tendency to reduce processual or procedural poetics to such terms is reductive, overly formalist. The sophisticated poetry and poetics of formal artifice developed by Veronica Forrest-Thomson tends towards formalism, but her reassertion of formal process as artifice has its own necessity (Forrest-Thomson 1978). A decisive quality of Forrest-Thomson's poetic works, however, is the foregrounding of explicitly conceptual theoretical frameworks within her poems, using, for example, Empsonian dictionary procedures or Wittgensteinian language games as reflexive poetic contents (Forrest-Thomson 1990). For purists who prefer "poetry" to remain distinct from prose argument, such explicit framing is detrimental to poetry's "autonomy." There are neo-modernists suspicious of any poetry that makes critical theory too explicit within its procedures. For some, especially for those working outside explicitly intellectual contexts, "critical theory" is tainted by its academic mediations, becoming too academic, or too easily accommodated by the institutions of criticism. For others, sometimes even from within academic disciplines, the problem is the way both critical and poetic forms of "theory" lack the substantive depth of the relevant modes of scholarship, science, and philosophy on which such theory draws, becoming a kind of derivative collage. Most neo-modernists nevertheless recognize that claims for poetry's "autonomy" cannot simply be asserted, but have to be argued for. Once such arguments are understood as conceptual parameters integral to the process of writing, and not simply a question of external critical legitimation, then even the idea of "pure" poetry is forced into dialogue with the impurities of theory and poetic materiality. The attempt to keep form open-ended becomes, then, a conceptual orientation, in which poetic improvisation resists being over-determined by restrictive conceptual schema. Any moment of form can become subject to analysis as residual or conceptual content, just as most types of material or content can be understood as residual forms. Put differently, the diversity of poetic production is driven by the transformation of poetic processes into new kinds of conceptual improvisation through writing. Such improvisation differentiates given forms and contents, working through critiques of the socio-linguistic formalisms that inhibit writing's articulation.

Another way of conceiving the limits of formalism, then, is through explicitly or implicitly theorized conceptions of process and procedural parameters. Processes involved in procedural poetics range from the use of found material and chance procedures, to collage assembly and more extended conceptual framing devices. If some such process or procedure is understood as a condition of the possibility of a work, text, or sequence of works, then the terms of construction tend to deconstruct lyric form, conventional referentiality, and the possibility of reference back to a speaking voice. Where principles of construction are relative or arbitrary, perhaps because bound up with different or overlapping contexts generating unpredictable outcomes, then it can become indeterminate whether a text or sequence merely "appears" non-referential or actively invites readerly reconstruction of its conceptual improvisations. The degree to which the conceptual parameters of a written improvisation are made explicit may over-determine the possibility of a reader improvising their own interpretation. Procedural poetics share the more general avant-garde deconstruction of the supposed autonomy of the "artwork." One consequence is the concern that superficially different texts might be generated through radically different methods and with very different claims on the attention of readers. The resulting similarity of textual surfaces embodies different poetics of depth, poetics which may work implicitly or explicitly, but which sustain even poems with opaque but non-hermetic surfaces. One text's conceptually fragmented but highly constrained referentiality might be mistaken for another text's deconstructed play of signification. Beyond the text itself, readers may have only secondary indications of procedure or intention with which to coordinate a reading.

A number of further faultlines begin to emerge. Serial, sequential, or processual works tend to bend or break the discrete authority of lyric forms, delimiting the integrity of the singular or autonomous poem such that "lyric" indicates a generic mode or modality within the open field of a textual or poetic process. Indeed, where poetic practices delimit the types of insight or authority often claimed in the name or idea of "poetry," such practices pose the question whether they might better be understood as the making of texts or writing rather than as poetry. Poetic practices which question the significance of poetry's historical forms and concepts work analogously to art practices which question what art is, what might constitute art now. The determining questions of meaning, rhetoric, and power might then be understood as sharing theoretical problems with the Wittgensteinian investigations of the conceptual artists "Art and Language" (cf. Art and Language 1980; Harrison 2001; see also Perloff 1996); or, alternatively, the poststructuralist theoretical work of the conceptual artist Victor Burgin (Burgin 1986). An important faultline divides writers who readily recognize such affinities and the validity of theoretical poetics, as opposed to those poets who conceive poetry through resistance to theory and who, informed by the work of Heidegger or Merleau-Ponty, might claim to prioritize perceptual or experiential reflections over the articulation of language's conceptual, discursive, or textual parameters (Merleau-Ponty 1962; Heidegger 1993). Categories of perception and experience are nevertheless historical, with implicit theoretical and conceptual entailments, even if some poets speculate on the possibilities of pre-conceptual or non-conceptual modes of cognition. The phenomenology of perception, moreover, was displaced within the work of Heidegger and then Jacques Derrida, by questions of language and writing (see especially Derrida 1976; Lafont 2000; Milne 2003). Shifts in the development of Continental philosophy and critical theory can be mapped onto generational divides. A writer informed by Roland Barthes' essays is more likely to acknowledge parallels between poststructuralist poetics and "theory," along with post-punk musical politics. An earlier generation might mediate cultural analogies suggested by existentialism, abstract expressionism, pop art, and jazz.

These different types of construction and process tend to make much of the poetry associated with neo-modernism resistant to formalist close reading and the protocols of practical criticism. This resistance to close reading reflects differentiations of conceptuality, differentiations which work as constructive taboos within different networks and taste formations. Predictable horizons of interpretation also need to be circumvented: a poem too easily assimilated by existing modes of criticism forgoes some of its claim to avant-garde radicalism. Neo-modernist poems often need to be read as part of a larger texture, sequence, or book of differentially organized poems. Sometimes the governing procedures of construction are relatively inaccessible. Sometimes a poetic practice involves the reader in their own, more writerly and less "passive," construction of the text. The polemical emphasis underlying Rod Mengham's formulations emerges as a considered judgment, a judgment which traces the faultline where poetics might break with traditional models of "lyric." The stress on lyric impulse nevertheless misrepresents some of the radical poetics through which many poets in *Vanishing Points* generate their writing. Neo-modernist poetry resists assimilation through the traditional categories of "lyric poetry" and the "poem." The articulation of differences between poetry, prose, poetics, visual arts, and critical theory becomes another key faultline.

Given the different ways in which superficial difficulties might be generated, characterizations of avant-garde writing as "experimental," "difficult," or formally innovative usually make sense only as sociological markers of affiliation. By way of illustration, although the cumbersome term "linguistically innovative poetry" was first proposed to identify British avant-garde writing practices as opposed to American "Language" writing, the term is prominently featured in the subtitle of *Out of Everywhere* (O'Sullivan 1996). As with *Vanishing Points*, Maggie O'Sullivan's anthology finds transatlantic affinities. The attempt to name shared criteria for a virtual collective, such as the pursuit of procedural or open-ended forms, both bridges and obscures the differences involved. One supplementary symptom of the awkwardness of formalist or technique-based accounts of innovative, radical, or avant-garde poetry is the difficulty in understanding different strategies of informality (for contrast see Bois & Krauss 2000). Attitudes and pre-judices towards form and formalism are constitutive for different emphases in avant-garde orientations, often functioning as surprisingly violent taboos around, say, the use of personal pronouns. An intrigu-ing faultline, even among British poets who would articulate their work through Anglo-American modernism, is the way passionate engage-ment with a particular American poet might generate very different affiliations from those assumed to be conventional or reasonable in North American contexts. Andrew Crozier and Tim Longville remark of the writers anthologized in *A Various Art*, that:

> one of the means by which many of the poets in this anthology were identifiable to one another was an interest in a particular aspect of post-war American poetry, and the tradition that lay behind it – not that of Pound and Eliot but that of Pound and Williams. (Crozier & Longville 1987: 12)

Introducing a younger group of writers, Ken Edwards suggests that this shared sense of literary tradition might be approached indirectly through various mediating influences:

> Poets outside the mainstream in the late 50s and 60s were faced with the daunting task of making their poetry in what must often have seemed at the outset a cultural vacuum. The dominance of The Movement poets had resulted in the suppression of parts of English poetry's past; American post-war culture (music and painting as well as poetry) provided an alternative set of possibilities to explore; so did post-war European literary and anti-literary phenomena, such as the sound/text/concrete movement or the writings of the French Tel Quel group. But more recent generations of poets working within similar aesthetic paradigms have not been so handicapped. For now they have the previous generation's work to refer to: a body of specifically British but non-parochial writing. . . . Many of the poets at the younger end of this selection have started by discovering the work of Prynne, Mottram, Raworth, Harwood, Cobbing or Roy Fisher, only then proceeding back-wards through these to Pound, Williams, Olson, Ashbery or O'Hara, and then perhaps on to the current work being done in America or Europe. (Edwards 1988: 267)

The need to demonize the largely unread work of Movement poets recurs, along with the difficult negotiation of a specifically British neo-modernism amid overlapping European and American affiliations.

170

The potential reorientation of poetry through analogies with other aesthetic paradigms becomes a recurrent horizon for neo-modernists. Among writers who might be included in this historical circulation of influences, Gertrude Stein remains a curiously decisive and divisive figure, but perhaps no less decisive and divisive than Joyce or Beckett. The reconfigurations of neo-modernism are often synthesized blends rather than purist distillations. Hugh MacDiarmid's postwar neo-modernism is evidently indebted to both Ezra Pound and James Joyce. Brian Catling's work, among other qualities, could be described as Beckettian (see, for example, Catling 1990). Miles Champion's poetry reworks a range of American poets from the 1970s, notably Clark Coolidge, with more than a nod to Tom Raworth (Champion 1996, 2000). For some poets, the influence of modernist prose is sidelined, while others develop a conception of poetry's autonomy less engaged with prose forms. The commitment to poetry as opposed to the variety of avant-garde prose poetics becomes another indicative faultline.

With different modernist approaches and formal strategies widely understood and variously returned to and reworked, new conditions of affiliation are facilitated by the range of work already in circulation. Modes of circulation and distribution are also assisted and mediated by recent information technologies, above all email and internet publication, which have rapidly transformed the possible forms of poetic dialogue. Despite enormous potential, digital poetics, hypertext, and forms of writing without embodiment on the page nevertheless remain somewhat marginal. Amid a rapid expansion in the quantity of poetic "information" now available, the quality of assimilation often remains surprisingly local, not least through the experience of poetry readings. Interpretation of writing as writing nevertheless overlaps across fields of language use that are more global. There may be important new dimensions emerging amid globalized electronic communication, but it remains to be shown how far these are different in kind from the modes of internationalism and localized poetic practice developed by earlier modernists.

The tendency to construct geographical "traditions" needs to be resisted, then, but so too does the desire to construct an international avant-garde on the model of a singular "avant-garde." More nuanced strategies of criticism and understanding are needed to interpret modernist and neo-modernist poetry, incorporating awareness of the procedural poetics, intertextual dialogues and modes of conceptual improvisation sketched here. Although widely used across neo-modernist affiliations, the term "avant-garde" risks becoming fossilized unless understood as an orientation and set of affiliations. Charles Jencks, a postmodernist too keen to abandon the politics of avant-garde aesthetics, suggests that:

> One reason there is no longer an artistic avant-garde, in the traditional Modern sense, is that there is no identifiable front line to advance in the world village, no group or movement that cuts across all the arts, no enemy to conquer, no coherent bourgeoisie to fight, no established salon to enter. (Jencks 1989: 44)

The bourgeoisie may be incoherent, but they remain powerful, and there are plenty of enemies, including Jencks himself, lined up against the political and aesthetic projects of neo-modernism. The bourgeois salon may have become chimerical, but there are cultural institutions and arts councils of many kinds seeking to patronize, fund, divert, and otherwise re-educate avant-garde energies. There are also the so-called "media" and the global academic salons of universities, generating new conflicts and contradictions with which radical poetics continues to struggle. Given the complexity of the many overlapping sites of struggle, it can be difficult to distinguish viable avant-gardism from forms of historical pastiche that merely recycle old forms. The waning of explicit avant-gardes akin to earlier, historical models does not mean that avant-gardism has ceased to exist, however, but that new conditions have seen avant-gardism develop new strategies, becoming recognizable as orientations rather than as programs and positions.

Any attempt to revisit neo-modernism through familiar debates regarding the historical avant-garde has the twin effect of revealing how unsatisfactory such accounts are when applied to British modernism, and how tenuous the theory of the historical "avant-garde" appears in relation to contemporary affiliations (Poggioli 1968; Bürger 1984; Calinescu 1987; Compagnon 1994; Murphy 1998). The identifiable historical avant-gardes were often short-lived, if lived at all, and often with a rather belated, derivative, or secondary impact. From imagism and vorticism through Dada and surrealism to Black Mountain, Fluxus, or Tel Quel, what is most evident is the way in which the terms of avant-garde theory, organization, and social practice have been so systematically resisted in Britain. And yet, many British poets, especially poets of more than local ambition, have found it necessary to inform themselves regarding European or American avant-garde precedents and also the range of avant-garde procedures in one or more non-literary media, such as music, visual art, film, or performance.

Almost all of the contributors included in *Vanishing Points* would be able to give some account of their interest in earlier avant-gardes, and could be said to share an avant-garde orientation, but almost all would also distance themselves from any too explicit affiliation with a group label, school, movement, or ism. Lest this seem like a particular feature of contemporary neo-modernist poetry, something similar is true of the way in which many earlier modernist and neo-modernist poets in Britain and Ireland have worked through an awareness of historical avant-garde formations but without allowing their work to be easily located within any particular avant-garde. Even among writers who might be construed as avant-garde in orientation and sympathetic to modernism, there has been deep resistance to avant-garde organization, with the possible exception of explicitly political rather than aesthetic avant-garde movements, such as Marxism and feminism. A degree of historical awareness of earlier models is usually combined with an avant-garde orientation to other modes of writing and art. A virtual collective of shared avant-garde orientations coexists with a marked absence of actual avant-gardes. Another way of putting this is that many writers recognize the need for avant-garde strategies while protecting their individual autonomy as neo-modernist writers. The absence of consensus around terms such as "neo-modernism" to describe existing affiliations can be taken as evidence of the shared resistance to avant-gardism even among poets quick to assert their interest in modernism or the historical avant-garde. Individual writers negotiate the pressure to be, in effect, one-person avant-gardes; sufficiently resourceful to negotiate the existing networks of production and distribution, while nevertheless working within a loosely shared assertion of difference from supposed pre-modernist or anti-modernist orthodoxies. The self-made neo-modernist poet risks reasserting the very modes of individualism, networking, and self-promotion otherwise derided when pursued by mainstream versifiers. The variety of projects engaged in renewing modernist tendencies suggests the need to develop critical models for reading postwar poetry as the uneven diffusion of neo-modernist poetics. While there is a marked absence of anything resembling the historical avant-gardes, the persistence of terms such as "experimental" and "innovative" points to the difficulty of providing more than indicative outlines of key tendencies. Such outlines are often better understood as maps of relevant faultlines, which, when questioned, reveal tensions at work in contemporary poetic practices. Strategies of differentiation from pre-modern and anti-modernist poetics nevertheless continue to develop avant-garde orientations in the face of new conditions. The variety of neo-modernist poetic practices can be glimpsed in a number of anthologies[1] and through web-based resources,[2] though the texture of printed forms, publishing strategies, and extended critical argument is often obscured by such sampling. There is nevertheless substantial evidence available to show that British and Irish neo-modernist poetry has developed projects and poetics that are distinct from European or North American models, but no less engaged and engaging.

Further Reading

Allen, Tim and Duncan, Andrew (eds) (2007). *Don't Start Me Talking: Interviews with Contemporary Poets*. Cambridge: Salt Studies in Contemporary Poetry.

Crozier, Andrew (1983). Thrills and Frills: Poetry as Figures of Empirical Lyricism. In Alan Sinfield (ed.), *Society and Literature 1945–1970*. London: Methuen, pp. 199–233.

Davis, Alex (2000). *A Broken Line: Denis Devlin and Irish Poetic Modernism*. Dublin: University College Dublin Press.

Forrest-Thomson, Veronica (1978). *Poetic Artifice: A Theory of Twentieth-Century Poetry*. Manchester: Manchester University Press.

Gish, Nancy (ed.) (1993). *Hugh MacDiarmid: Man and Poet*. Orono: National Poetry Foundation, Inc., University of Maine; & Edinburgh: Edinburgh University Press.

[1] See, for example, *The New British Poetry, 1968–88*, Allnutt, D'Aguiar, Edwards and Mottram, eds (1988); *A Various Art*, Crozier and Longville, eds. (1990); *Floating Capital: new poets from London*, Clarke and Sheppard, eds. (1991); *Conductors of Chaos*, Sinclair, ed. (1996); *Out of Everywhere: Linguistically innovative poetry by women in North America & the UK*, O'Sullivan, ed. (1996); *A State of Independence*, Frazer, ed. (1998); *Other: British and Irish Poetry since 1970*, Caddel and Quartermain, eds. (1999); *Foil: defining poetry 1985–2000*, Johnson, ed. (2000); and *Vanishing Points: New Modernist Poems*, Mengham and Kinsella, eds. (2004).

[2] See, for example, Archive of the Now: <http://www.archiveofthenow. com/>; HOW2: <http://www.asu.edu/pipercwcenter/how2journal/>; Jacket magazine: <http://jacketmagazine.com/00/home.shtml>; PENNsound: <http://www.writing.upenn.edu/pennsound/>; Salt Publishing: <http://www. saltpublishing.com/>; and Ubuweb: <http://www.ubu.com/>.

Hampson, Robert and Barry, Peter (eds) (1993). *The New British Poetries: The Scope of the Possible.* Manchester: Manchester University Press.

Huk, Romana (ed.) (2003). *Assembling Alternatives: Reading Postmodern Poetries Transnationally.* Middletown, Connecticut: Wesleyan University Press.

Milne, Drew (1993). Agoraphobia and the embarrassment of manifestoes: notes towards a community of risk. *Parataxis: modernism and modern writing*, 3, 25–40.

Riley, Denise (ed.) (1992). *Poets on Writing: Britain, 1970–1991.* London, Macmillan.

Riley, Denise (2000). *The Words of Selves: Identification, Solidarity, Irony.* Stanford, CA: Stanford University Press.

Terrell, Carroll (ed.) (1981). *Basil Bunting: Man and Poet.* Orono, ME: National Poetry Foundation.

Tuma, Keith (1998). *Fishing by Obstinate Isles: Modern and Postmodern British Poetry and American Readers.* Evanston, Illinois.: Northwestern University Press.

Wilkinson, John (2007). *The Lyric Touch: Essays on the Poetry of Excess.* Cambridge: Salt.

Chapter 9

Contemporary British Women Poets and the Lyric Subject

Linda A. Kinnahan

Beginning in the 1980s and building in the 1990s, anthologies and critical collections focusing on contemporary women's poetry in Britain have galvanized attention for a diversely inventive but too easily neglected body of writing (see Further Reading, below). While various anthologies spurred by the women's movement and its aftermath introduced many women poets to the reading public, the extraordinarily meager critical discussion of women poets writing at that moment made small headway against a tenaciously held assumption that the great British poetic tradition and the vocation of poetry were best occupied by men. Against the long-standing reluctance to allow women onto this hallowed ground, the poetry of contemporary women has sought to challenge the versions of literary history that ignore their female predecessors and to address, in their own poetry, the ideologies of gender fueling masculine models of tradition, poetry, and the poet. By the mid-1990s, feminist critics, editors, and poets themselves aimed to make a difference through launching projects that would bring contemporary women poets into greater visibility by illuminating elided traditions of women's poetry and through theorizing new ways of thinking about poetry, language, and gender, often from a feminist critical perspective.

The lyric remains an important site for discussions of poetic tradition, language, form, and subject matter. Heralded within the British tradition, the lyric maintains an authority historically barred to women and arguably silencing them through its gendered conventions. However, in its foregrounding of the speaking "I," the lyric offers a subversive mechanism of intervention, a possibility for reformulating the lyric subject through negotiating, exposing, and critiquing the cultural systems that authorize and privilege the masculine subject in both poetic utterance and social materiality.

The Lyric "I"

Most fundamentally, contemporary revisions of the lyric self within women's poetry involve, on some explicit or implicit level, a confrontation with poetic tradition and the conventions of the lyric, particularly as they come into the twentieth century from a Romantic heritage. With an emphasis upon the self's capacity for knowledge of itself and the world, through operations of the imagination, the Romantic aura of lyric authenticity assumes a poetic process in which individual, autonomous experience is transformed into the universal and transcendent voice of the poet. The speaking subject of the Romantic lyric, historically considered male, attains and expresses through direct, coherent means the unity of self through which the world is apprehended. Within this tradition, emerging from the humanist Enlightenment, the private utterance of the lyric "I" is transformed through the operations of the poetic imagination into a universal, transcendent expression (as in Wordsworth's formulation of "the spontaneous overflow of powerful feelings recollected in tranquility"). The lyric's transcendental ego resides outside of a reality that can be communicated through language, a medium imagined as a pure, transparent means for accessing "truth" and speaking it to a listening public.

Within this model of poetic subjectivity, authority rests within the poem's ability to create an impression of the "authentic self," appearing unique, natural, and coherent to itself. The refusal of sociopolitical forces in shaping the self (for then, it is not "authentic") or its vision and expression renders this model problematic from numerous contemporary perspectives. The American poet-critic Charles Bernstein, whose poetry and essays often dispute the heritage of the Romantic lyric "I" – the "primacy of the individual voice, fanned by a gentile inspiration" (1992: 2) – describes a "Romantic poetics of sincerity" that evokes "the poet's lyric address to the human-eternal, to the Imagination, what seems to allow the poem to appear to transcend the partiality of its origin. Thus the poet is able to speak for the 'human' by refusing markers that would pull against the universality of 'his' address" (1990: 236, 238). Such markers – of social position, raced or gendered identity, or historical context, for example – make themselves most visible (and therefore non-transcendent) within the poetic construction of voice constructing white maleness as "universal," a process depending upon an understanding of *race* as *non-white* and of *gender* as *non-male*. The "markers" of social and material specificity for whiteness and/or maleness attain invisibility within a framework equating westernized white male experience with the universal human condition, echoing the Enlightenment subject celebrated as an autonomous and self-directed individuality but historically available only to a particular group endowed with certain powers. Within this construction, the voice marking itself as non-white or non-male inherently narrows the frame of experience within the boundaries of a specific group rather than speaking for and to the "universal" human.

As a contemporary manifestation of the coherent and recognizable self, the "representative man" finds modern poetic expression in Britain's post-World War II "Movement," regarded as the dominant British poetry of the 1950s and 1960s and extending its influence through the following decades. Gaining the label in the 1950s and associated with a revolt against the experiments of modernism and perceptions of an overly gentile and provincial domesticity of the postwar, the Movement encompassed a range of poets whose work variously encouraged the concept of a native British tradition sustained by a "continuity of spirit" (Morley, quoted by Doyle 1989: 83) and "an essential and continuous Englishness" (Doyle 1989: 92) from Anglo-Saxon culture to the present. For Philip Larkin, this nativism translated itself through an insistence upon a populist "common style" of language and form, albeit polished, fashioned as a form of civic address to the public to encourage a unity of culture (or bitterly disparage its lack). The Movement's public voice, associated with the rational man speaking in plain language to his fellow men, models what Andrew Crozier describes as "the authoritative self discoursing in a world of banal, empirically derived objects and relations," or the "guiding and controlling presence of a speaking subject constructing the poem's framework of interpretation around its personal authority" (1983: 229, 228). While the model of subjectivity in this poetry signals itself both in terms of class (working or middle, anti-aristocratic) and gender, its claim to a universal expressiveness elides the charge of specificity, privacy, and narrowness leveled at poetry employing a feminine-marked voice or perception.

The British tradition of poetry, emphatically male, presents a dilemma for the woman poet both in her reception through literary history and her construction, as a figure, through lyric practice. The women poet, burdened with the accolade of the "poetess," writes within and against a long history of preconceptions and gender biases throughout the nineteenth and twentieth centuries, even while the lyric has offered a culturally sanctioned space for expressions of emotion, inspiration, and interiority. However, the lyric as practiced by women has suffered diminutive status alongside the more "universalizing" and philosophical high lyric, particularly as modeled by the male Romantics. While the lyric has traditionally been offered as an appropriate poetic form for women, the circumscription of subject matter, language, and form for the woman lyricist has produced a body of poetry routinely collapsed under such derogatory labels as sentimental, trivial, narrow, domestic – the domain of the "poetess." The critically debased history of women's lyrical practice continues to inform attitudes toward self-expression in women's poetry, so that to be too lyrical for a woman means too feminine, too emotional, too solipsistic rather than too humanistically unified and coherent.

The construction of the "universal" and the "human" underlying the unified Enlightenment subject long barred women from participation in legal, social, political, and religious institutions. The lyric tradition, through its transmission of the universal, coherent, and autonomous "I," enacts a gendered authority derived from such exclusive histories and dynamics. Naturalizing the male as the active maker, the "I" who imagines, observes, writes, and makes culture, the lyric positions the figure of the female more passively: as muse and inspiration to the (male) poet, as subject to the (male) poet's gaze, as a silent cultural object upon which the male operates to create both masculine self and art. Feminist critics like Rachel Blau DuPlessis, Susan Stanford Friedman, and Margaret Homans have argued that the lyric's ideological encodings of gender underlie the voicing of the "I" in poetry and the assumptions (derived from the Romantic tradition in particular) of the expressive self. As a genre, "poetry activates notable master plots, ideologies, and moves fundamentally inflected with gender relations," constituting a "cluster of foundational materials with a gender cast built into the heart of the lyric. The foundational cluster concerns voice (and silencing), power (appropriation and transcendence), nature (as opposed to formation and culture), gaze (framing, specularity, fragmentation), and the sources of poetic matter – narratives of romance, of the sublime, scenes of inspiration, the muse as conduit" (DuPlessis 1994: 71).

The masculine-based notion of subjectivity underlying the voicing of a true, sincere, unitary self lodged within the center of the lyric derived from the Romantic tradition operates to exclude women from the lyric "I" or to shape the female "I" in limited ways. The figuring of the woman as land or nation (as in Irish tradition, most emphatically) renders her silent and shaped by the masculine perspective; the female object of the love lyric is made visible through the desiring gaze of the male; the equation of traditional woman's experience with trivial, overly private, and overly emotional sensibilities has served to denigrate particular sources of art and forms of expression; the delineation of particular genres as most suitable for the woman poet – such as the love lyric – has restricted the female "I" in relation to intimate matters that in turn serve arguments about the limited realm of women's experience and voice. The British lyric tradition has prohibited women, by and large, from the claims made by its most heralded figures (men speaking to men), just as women's access to selfhood in Western culture has not equaled that of men. For women of color, such exclusion is doubled. Under the pressure of the lived histories of non-white and/or non-male groups, the lyric "I" often emerges for many poets as a necessary formulation of a suppressed or erased identity. Unwilling to give up a claim to self that history has too long denied but aware of the trappings of an essentialized and unitary self, women poets have reinvented the female-marked "I" in myriad ways to suggest models of subjectivity that are variously fluid, multiple, permeable, and contingent, inherently disrupting a male tradition of the lyric subject and its attendant ideologies of gender privilege.

Reframing the Self

The first inkling in the postwar period of a newly gendered lyric arrives with the insistence upon poetry that reveals women's experiences through women's voices, in defiance of the establishment tenets of the Movement and the evolution of the British tradition through primarily male exemplars. During the 1960s and 1970s, social revolts against traditional gender roles and ideas fueled women's poetry. Often referred to in critical discussions as the "expressive" mode of contemporary feminist poetics, this flowering of poetry by women characteristically featured a lyric "I" speaking directly and accessibly of her life as a woman, bringing culturally muted issues and topics, such as sexuality, violence, or motherhood, into public discourse and poetic consideration (Wills 1994). Just as the women's movement of the 1970s raised urgent questions about women's voice, identity, and experience, the explosive upsurge of poetry by women at this time asserted the legitimacy of the female-marked "I" of the lyric poem, directly challenging condescending attitudes toward women's poetry as narrow, trivial, emotional, sentimental, home-bound, or private (and not "universal" in its focus on female spheres or activities). Indeed, the work of poets consciously responding to the women's movement aggressively sought to correct long-standing equations of the female poetic voice with the frail "poetess," while staking a claim for the reporting of women's experiences as a way of realizing that "the personal is political." In the process, the deliberate use of the female "I" exposed the falsely universalizing gesture of the lyric "I" as ideologically (in content and form) masculine, an ideology dependent upon the silencing of woman in the lyric through figuring her as muse, nature, body (or body parts) – the mute, gazed-upon object mirroring back to the masculine "I" his essential identity and significance.

While in North America poets identifying themselves with this expressive feminist project met both popular success and academic acclaim (such as Adrienne Rich, Audre Lorde, Marilyn Hacker, Marge Piercy, and Alice Walker), feminist poets in Britain, such as Michèlene Wandor, Michèle Roberts, Alison Fell, Judith Kazantzis, Mary Dorcy, and Stef Pixner, remained little known except in feminist circles. In part, this marginalization of self-identifying feminist poets has had to do with the tenacious longevity of a masculine poetic tradition in Britain, more insistently male and more resistant to challenge than in America. The "systematic exclusion of women poets from literary history" argued by Claire Buck (1996: 81), among many feminist critics, doubly marginalizes those women poets with self-declared feminist persuasions, such as the women included in the groundbreaking anthology *One Foot on the Mountain*, edited by Lilian Mohin (1980), and making one of the first claims in postwar Britain for women's poetry in general and for feminist poetry in particular (for a history and critical assessment of the poetry of the women's movement, see Buck especially).

Shaping their aesthetics upon the ideas of consciousness raising and personal expression to reveal daily life, feminist poets of the 1960s and 1970s relied upon the lyric use of first-person to enhance a kinetic sense of identification between reader and poet and to claim a knowledge of the self – and the right to express that knowledge in unmediated form – suppressed by patriarchal culture. An accessible and direct use of language and form supported the imperative to reach a broad audience as the poem itself functioned as a form of consciousness raising and political action. Within the context of 1970s feminist publishing and poetry, the female-marked lyric "I" becomes a source of self-empowerment – of speaking oneself into being as a fully dimensional being rather than a prescribed set of gendered roles – and a conduit for interaction with others. Rather than the autonomous individual of Enlightenment heritage, defined by feminist thought as masculine in its structures of separation and independence, the feminist lyric "I" or self "is distinguished and specified in terms of a particular feminist agenda of self and liberation, in which the self is individualized but distinguished from a negatively conceived model of selfhood" that distinguishes "between self and other as the ground for a self-contained and authoritative selfhood"; instead, the lyric subject "depends on, and is produced through, interdependence," opposing a "masculine and individualist model of selfhood with a model conceived in terms of relationship and a feminist political community" (Buck 1996: 89–90).

During the 1970s, the expressive lyric model served feminist goals in advancing political action and consciousness raising through the medium of poetry and through challenging the naturalized assumption of the poet as a man. At the same time, other women poets with feminist allegiances were exploring different poetic routes that excluded them from the reading and writing communities committed to the expressive mode. Veronica Forrest-Thompson, Carlyle Reedy, Wendy Mulford, and Denise Riley exemplify some of the women poets of the 1960s and 1970s whose work continues a modernist or avant-garde foregrounding experimentation with language and form, counter to the accessibility demanded of both the Movement and the expressive strain of feminist poetics. Often associated with the activities and effects of the British poetry revival of the 1960s (which challenged the Movement's nativist stance and restrictive aesthetics) and with small-press publication (Middleton 1993; Mottram 1993), women involved with the experimental "alternative poetry scene" were often not included in feminist anthologies or publications, nor were they readily acknowledged in discussions of experimental, small-press poetry activity in Britain. Until recently, feminists and/or women whose explorations of lyric subjectivity concentrate on how language processes attenuate identity formation have met with marginalization, invisibility, and neglect from varied camps.

The feminist 1970s also marginalized women of color, centering the expressive lyric upon the experiences of white women. The claim to female experience, without consideration of race or ethnicity, unconsciously replicated the universalizing aspect of the Romantic lyric and (also unconsciously) reflected the British habit of thought that assumed a white national identity. A racially homogeneous society until the late 1940s, Britain's sense of national identity presumed whiteness until post-empire immigration from the Caribbean, Asia, and Africa brought the "British subject" face to face with its multicultural – and multi-racial – complexion. During the 1970s, women of color began to give voice to their own particular experiences within categories of race and gender produced, in part, by the post-empire dynamics of immigration, citizenry, and political debate.

Lyric Strains

Poets who began publishing work in the 1980s have inherited both the ease of using the female-marked "I" and the unease of assuming its stability or unity or collective capacity in speaking as "woman." They also signal a keen recognition of the positioning of the female self in poetic tradition as well as social discourse. And, significantly, these poets both experience and explore the changing racial and ethnic demographics of British society, altered definitions of national and Commonwealth citizenship, and the rise of new national configurations within the British Isles. The breakup of the British Empire and the influx of immigrants to Britain from previous colonies and Commonwealth nations not only has changed the face of the "British subject" but has complicated notions of national identity. The growing right-wing discourse on the "individual," emerging in the face of increasing immigration during the 1960s and 1970s and reaching a high pitch during the Thatcher years, raised controversial questions of national identity and the "self" associated with nation. The regressive turn to traditional ideas of womanhood marking public commentary in these years brought new urgency to the public and social possibilities for the lyric as a mode of answering, interrupting, and critiquing the model of autonomous individuality increasingly espoused in support of political and economic policy under Thatcher.

If, during the 1970s, the lyric's potential to claim women's experiences through a woman's voice becomes realized in the expressive mode, by the 1980s, this lyric voice of female authenticity is itself resisted

and complicated by poetry increasingly attentive to discursive, institutional, and representational forces constructing notions of the
"authentic self" in an increasingly multicultural Britain that, nonetheless, undergoes the mediating impact of nationalistic claims to
specifically English, Scottish, Irish, and Welsh identity.

Writing within the context of changing ideas and forms of nationalism within the British Isles (for example, the establishment of
Welsh and Northern Ireland Assemblies in Parliament and of an
independent Scottish Parliament), accompanied by the intensification
of discourses of nationalism, Gillian Clarke joins other poets such as
Eavan Boland, Liz Lochhead, and Kathleen Jamie in considering the
construction of female identity in relation to ideologies of national
identity. Born in Wales in 1937, Clarke takes up the question of
Welsh identity in poetry that focuses intently on rural place and the
everyday experience of her life there, building the lyric as a "place
of solidarity and connectedness" (Dowson & Entwistle 2005: 247).
Her poetry directly engages with Romantic conventions of the lyric,
particularly in her emphasis on nature; however, in this engagement
with Romanticism, Clarke regenders the lyric self and its operations.
Her first volume, *The Sundial* (1978), joins with the voices of other
women poets in the 1970s in celebrating the domestic cycles of life
and death, particularly through weaving image-based connections
between the maternal body and the natural environment, as in the
speaker's claim to a shared circumference with a sea bird and her
nest of eggs in "Curlew":

> Dusk blurs
> circle within circle till there's nothing left
> but the egg pulsing in the dark against her ribs.
> for each of us the possessed space contracts
> to the nest's heat, the blood's small circuit.
> (1997: 25–6)

These early poems of domestic and maternal experience, placed
precisely within the rural spaces of Wales around her, variously
emphasize the relation of community, nature, and speaker in ways
that extend through time to consider, as in "Lunchtime Lecture," the
imagined life of past women. Attending the presentation of a talk on
fossil remains, the speaker stares at a female skull "from the second
or third millennium / B.C.," a cranium that "would fit the palm / Of
a man's hand. Some plague or violence / Destroyed her" (1997: 20).
By the poem's end, the speaking "I" is not merely the observer, but

begins to imagine herself subtly as a point of connection with the ancient female and her buried life:

> I, at some other season, illustrate the tree
> Fleshed, with woman's hair and colours and the rustling
> Blood, the troubled mind that she has overthrown.
> We stare at each other, dark into sightless
> Dark, seeing only ourselves in the black pools,
> Gulping the risen sea that booms in the shell.
>
> (1997: 21)

Clarke's handling of the lyric increasingly positions the "I" as a chronicler of women's lives, both those lost to history and those lost in her own personal life. Joining a collective effort by poets (and feminists across the board) to reclaim women's lives and histories, Clarke's early poems nonetheless begin to display a distinction arising from the positioning of the "I" in a specific place that has a specific history, often hidden, buried, or evident in traces. Moreover, the focus on place extends to the lives of women before her who inhabited and shaped specific places; in other words, it is through place that subjectivities emerge across time.

Place grounds Clarke's poems in the landscape and distinguishing features of rural Wales, and it is within such environs that women have traditionally been constrained within the space of home. The gendering of place and space, for Clarke, proves to be a defining feature of the Welsh lyric tradition, and one that her work early speaks to in "Dyddgu Replies to Dafydd." The poem refers to Dafydd ap Gwilym, a fourteenth-century Welsh poet, and Dyddgu, one of the two women he addresses in his poems. In Clarke's imagining of the feminized object of the lyric tradition gaining voice, the lyric voice of Dyddgu registers her confinement in the place of home as a contrast to Dafydd's freedom:

> You are packing your songs
> in a sack, narrowing your
> words, as you stare at the road.
> The feet of young men beat, somewhere far off
> on the mountain. I would women
> had roads to tread in winter
> and other lovers waiting.
>
> (1997: 22)

In a gesture repeated and amplified in later volumes, Clarke's early poems enact a necessary confrontation with the circumscribed, objectified position of "woman" in the male lyric tradition. These confrontations consistently engage the place and history of Wales, retracing the steps of generations before her whose muted subjectivities interweave through the "I" seeking to chronicle the relation of place and gender within Welsh history and literary tradition.

In one of Clarke's most well-known poems, the title poem of her second volume, *Letter from a Far Country* (1982), the poet imagines writing a "letter home from the future" to all of the "husbands, fathers, forefathers" (1997: 45), to warn that the "women are leaving" their well-ordered homes (1997: 54). Launching a "critique of the patriarchal character of Welsh culture," the long poem draws upon a tradition of letter writing, feminized in its historical availability to women when other forms have not been deemed proper, and equally feminized in the diminished regard for the private expressiveness of the epistle (Broom 2006: 24). Indeed, the poem references the masculinely defined notion of "great works" as opposed to the disregard for the private and unfinished markings of women's lives within enforced domesticity: "Our airing cupboards / are full of our satisfactions," yet ironically the "masculine question" refuses to acknowledge the relation of material lives to forms of expression or to value the forms available to women in the domestic sphere, for " 'Where', they call 'are your great works?' " (1997: 49). The deliberate use of the letter refuses this notion of "great works," or of standard expectations of completion or unity provided by the lyric "I" of "great works." Either interrupted by the return of family life and routine or deliberately choosing not to complete the letter, the speaker leaves it "unsigned, / unfinished, unposted," claiming it will not be signed and sent until the "far country" apart from patriarchal structures is realized and reached.

In the course of the letter, the place of home is closely examined, revealed through the ordered linen closets, the alphabetically arranged books, and the organized kitchen shelves that keep the "detritus of a family's / loud life" at bay. Imagining leaving and writing from "far away," the speaker enters "a landscape. Hill country, / essentially feminine," where her "grandmother might have lived" in "[a]ny farm. Any chapel./ Father and minister, on guard, / close the white gates to hold her" (1997: 46). Occupying this "essentially feminine" landscape, the lyric "I" slips from the well-ordered solidity of her domestic constitution, in which the outlines of her identity are shaped and enforced by the needs of family and home, producing the "I" who has mapped and "charted all your needs" (1997: 48). The "feminine" landscape is not a utopian escape, but an intuited, fragmentary chronicle of the "we" who have lived behind the white gates while plagued by many a "question from the mind, / snaking underneath the surfaces," breaking the domestic space "as a small, black, returning doubt" (1997: 46) or, later, "mixing rage with the family bread" (1997: 54). The speaker absorbs the "lost" song:

> All their old conversations
> Collected carefully, faded
> And difficult to read, yet held
> Forever as voices in a well.
>
> (1997: 47)

The poem moves through images of past women's lives – the grand-mother standing before hand-stitched washing, the mother making a laundry list, the pauper and suicide whose names are not recorded "in the black book of this parish / a hundred years ago," the speaker herself as a child longing to carry tea to the men in the fields and take her place in the "feminine privilege, / the male right to the field" that inevitably does violence upon her body:

> Even that small task made me bleed.
> Halfway between the flowered lap
> of my grandmother and the black
> heraldic silhouette of men
> and machines on the golden field,
> I stood crying, my ankle bones
> raw and bleeding like the poppies
> trussed in the corn stooks in their torn
> red silks and soft mascara blacks.
>
> (1997: 50)

Finally, though, it is this body, and the bodies of the "grandmothers," that is the irreconcilable "place" of the self. The poem records the violence – physical and more importantly psychological – that patriarchy renders upon the woman's body, but the final stanzas move toward an alternate notion of body that keeps the women from actually leaving. Pulled like the tide outward, the self is nonetheless scripted to return to the place of home, albeit the place of love:

> We are hawks trained to return
> to the lure from the circle's
> far circumference. Children sing
> that note that only we can hear.

> The baby breaks the waters,
> disorders the blood's tune, sets
> each filament of the senses
> wild. Its cry tugs at flesh, floods
> its mother's milky fields.
> Nightly in white moonlight I wake
> from sleep one whole slow minute
> before the hungry child
> wondering what woke me.
>   (1997: 55)

The poem ends with the final question, "Who will do the loving while we're away?" This seeming equation of women's bodies with a destiny of child-rearing and home-boundness has garnered criticism, although close attention to the language of the self's construction renders a different view of the body as a place within which ideological conflicts emerge, both across time and in a specific time. The lyric "I" works to uncover the ideological underpinnings of gender relations in Welsh history, as suggested through careful choices like the word "trained," for, as Sarah Broom argues, "the first image of hawks *trained* to return to the lure complicates" any reading of an essential female self:

> Clarke's description of the values of traditional Welsh society exposes an ideological link between woman and home, woman and farm, woman and place, which acts to create a pressure on women to remain the stable connector between people and the land in a context where movement away from the family land for the purposes of employment, as well as actual emigration, are experienced as a threat to Welsh nationhood. Clarke's evocation of this ideology is relatively straightforward; what makes her poem more complex is the self-conscious probing of the extent to which *the speaking woman's construction of self* is imbricated with these kinds of ideas. (Broom 2006: 128, emphasis added)

Clarke returns repeatedly to the long-poem form to explore the ideological operations of history within a defined place, experimenting with the lyric sequence to locate the "I" in relation to genealogy, language, and land. In both "Cofiant" (in the 1989 *Letting in the Rumour*) and "The King of Britain's Daughter" (in the 1993 volume of the same name), the lyric subject intermingles biography and autobiography, the "I" both shaping and constituted by facts of lineage that merge with gendered ideologies of power, authority, and recognition. The lineage of male dominance and inheritance finds itself interrupted by the lyric "I" of the female and the insertion of the daughter into a lineage typically erasing or omitting women. "Cofiant," a Welsh word for biography, signifies a practice beginning in the nineteenth century through which a subject's life (usually a male preacher) was told through accounts of his life, examples of sermons, letters, and tributes (Clarke 1989: 121). Taking up this hybrid form, Clarke includes multiple lyric speakers from generations in her family reaching back to the Welsh tribesman Gruffyd in 1047 and forward to her own parents. Although the standard *cofiant* would not include much accounting of women, this *cofiant* inserts the stories of mothers and grandmothers alongside those of the men. The "I" emerges through layers of family stories, like the "margins of books, poems printed / on foxed, beveled pages; under the shelf / where we peeled back the old wallpaper; / lists; old letters; diaries; notebooks" that are written in her father's hand, the marginal forms of writing constituting the history as the "I" putting together the history does so through challenging the norms of the *cofiant* in drawing upon the margins of lives and writings. The poem also signals its own incompletion and lack of final authority, for like the sea on the coastline, it "drafts and re-drafts the coast / and is never done / writing at the edge" (1989: 135). The poem ends with a list of ancestors, arranged with one exception as an accounting of sons that descend back to "Gwaethfoed of Cibwr in Gwent and Morfudd, d. of Ynyr Ddu" (1989: 136). The exception is the drafter at the edges of the *cofiant*, the "Daughter of Penri Williams, wireless engineer of Carmarthenshire and Ceinwen Evans of Denbighshire," the poet herself who, throughout the poem, discovers her ancestors' places of life and death and her own place – as chronicler of the edges of place and history – in this genealogy of Welsh patriarchy.

As with Clarke's unsettling of Welsh lyric traditions as they sustain a male-centered narrative of national identity, other poets address the intersections of a feminized land, muse, mythic figure, or object of desire marking lyric traditions with both prior and emergent nationalist ideologies. The clash, however, of the idea of nation as empire and the idea of nation in the post-imperial period (which according to many social critiques produces an idea of nation as ethnicity within discourses of "pure" British stock, i.e. white [see Goulbourne 1991]), emerges forcefully to reshape lyric conventions of self and voice in the poetry of immigrant women of color. Among poets in Britain with a "familial connection to a non-Western culture," the Caribbean community "has been the most prominent in the poetry scene, and British poets of Caribbean origin have consistently made issues of race, ethnicity and culture central to their writing" (Broom 2006: 50, 51). Developing a poetry characterized by language hybridities that mix standard English with Caribbean Creoles and that foreground orality, poets such as Jean "Binta" Breeze (born and raised in Jamaica) and Grace Nichols (born and raised in Guyana) explore the potential for lyric identities to perform as "carriers of a specifically Caribbean female history" (Innes 1996: 318) and to explore cultural systems of "womanhood" attenuating the African Caribbean woman's experience of subjectivity in its encounter with geographic movement into the British isles. Nichols' long poem sequence, *i is a long memoried woman*, winning the Commonwealth Poetry Prize in 1983, foregrounds the gendered experience of slavery, as the "i" – as opposed to the singular, authoritative "I" of British lyric tradition – layers the histories of the Middle Passage and slave existence with an imagined return to Africa.

In asserting the female "i" as integral to understanding this history, the epic exposes oppressive systems of womanhood taught by the dominant white, male culture, and seeks alternatives through celebrating women's powers and imagining their ways of knowing – sexually, bodily, spiritually, maternally, culturally. The work of the lyric subject involves making visible the knowledge and abilities of the "i" who speaks from the margins of patriarchal colonial history; moreover, understanding and challenging the deeply complex ideologies of female and black self-hatred informs the work of the lyric in Nichols' hands. However, in countering these ideologies, Nichols – as does Breeze – resists expressing a unified or essentialized notion of black immigrant womanhood while imagining a collective but pluralistic "we."

Speaking to this collective, pluralistic construction of self, Nichols writes a poem in the early 1980s entitled "Of Course When They Ask For Poems About the 'Realities' of Black Women" and included in *A Dangerous Knowing* (Parmar & Osman 1985), the first collection of poetry by "British based Black women" published in Britain – also including the work of Barbara Burford, Gabriela Pearse, and Jackie Kay – and a self-proclaimed intervention into publishing practices that have rendered the work of black women poets virtually invisible (Parmar & Osman 1985: vii). Later included in *Lazy Thoughts of a Lazy Woman and Other Poems* (1989), this poem registers a central concern of that volume and the one preceding it, *The Fat Black Woman's Poems* (1984), addressing a "more specifically British context" than her first volume and responding to "British (and Western) concepts of feminine beauty and behavior" (Innes 1996: 327). Answering to the dominance of white women's poetry and experiences of the feminist publications of the 1970s, the poem warns against the notion of a single voice speaking for all black women's experiences and, ultimately, against the repetition of simple stereotypes underlying expectations of those anxious to hear of the "realities of black women" while assuming they are all the same. It warns too against the possibility that those realities may only sustain the reader's sense of liberal concern for the "oppressed" while leaving systems of oppression in place. Locating itself clearly within the triply marginalized position of "black women's poetry" at this time – left out of British tradition by virtue of gender and color, left out of 1970s feminist publications by virtue of color, and left out of incipient attention to "black British" poetries by virtue of gender – the poem refuses to play the role of the representative or token black woman's poem:

> what they really want
> at times
> is a specimen
> whose heart is in the dust
>
> a mother-of-sufferer
> trampled/oppressed
> they want a little black blood
> undressed
> and validation
> for the abused stereotype
> already in their heads
>   (Parmar & Osman 1985: 48)

Claiming that she cannot write a "poem big enough / to hold the essence / of a black woman / or a white woman / or a green woman," Nichols dispenses with the universal voice of the lyric, suggestively registering the poem's awareness of the "universal" voice as a tool for perpetuating racial prejudice that ultimately can feed a self-loathing in the particularized woman of color. The poem moves from the speaking "I" who refuses to participate in the racial ideology demanded of the lyric available to her (the feminist lyric of personal experience as well as the universal, transcendent lyric of tradition) to the gesture of coalition at the poem's end:

> maybe this poem is to say
> that I like to see
> we black women
> full-of-we-selves walking

> crushing out
> with each dancing step
>
> the twisted self-negating
> history
> we've inherited
>
> crushing out
> with each dancing step
> (Parmar & Osman 1985: 49–50)

Like Nichols, Jean "Binta" Breeze writes out of her Caribbean experience, often using a hybridized Creole and figuring a subjectivity emerging from the hybridized experiences of a Caribbean upbringing in a colonized space and a relocation to England as a British subject. Particularly known as a dub poet, Breeze concretizes her work's relation to oral traditions of African and Third World cultures through Creolized language and performance. Insisting upon the poem's orality, the interrelatedness between the speaking I, the body, and socio-historical contexts is brought to the foreground on the written page and in the performance of the page. In her first three volumes (*Riddym Raving*, 1988; *Spring Cleaning*, 1992; and *On the Edge of an Island*, 1997), the "I" traverses the constructions of subjectivity as colonized subject and as immigrant in an often inhospitable "mother country" of Britain, conveying the racial dynamic of Britain's immigration polices and debates that altered and/or denied citizenship status to subjects who helped develop the wealth of the empire, and who were taught, within their colonized space, to think of themselves as "British" – a self-identification battered by the experiences of discrimination and exclusion encountered by immigrants of color upon actually moving to Britain.

As does Nichols, Breeze creates a lyric subjectivity that both refuses victimhood and imagines a diverse collectivity, as in "sisters celebration," included in *The Arrival of Brighteye*:

> is lang time now
> we know seh
> han mek fi do
> wat mout talk bout
> so we linking up
> from coas to coas
> seven days a labour
> an yuh wander wat
> we shouting bout
>
> (2000: 40)

Rewriting the earth's creation (the seven days of labor) as a celebration of "woman / jumping up / rubbing up / soaking up / all de music," the poem also revises the exclusion of women's bodies from Christian theologies of creation:

> dem pitch out
> in dem birt scream
> is nat a orgy
> is a mass
> (2000: 40)

The abject becomes sacred – the birth scream rendered as a sacred ritual or "mass" – and the "we" of this female space of communion brings light to the world:

> we lighting lamp
> one by one
> in de sun or
> in de shady
> joy in de making
> home sweet home
> (2000: 40)

Breeze will often interact with narratives of cultural authority in constructing a lyric subject who draws agency from conditions of gender and ethnicity that traditionally have restricted subjectivity for women of color. Chaucer's *Canterbury Tales*, especially in their collusion with scriptural ideas of womanhood, come under fire in one particular instance. Occupying a privileged place in British (and Western) poetic tradition, as well as offering a framework for de-authorizing or debasing women's sexuality, Chaucer's poetry undergoes renovation by the Caribbean and female-marked "I" of "The Wife of Bath Speaks in Brixton Market." The Creolized voice re-reads not only Chaucer but the Christianized conventions of gender shaping his text, beginning with the assertion that "My life is my own bible / wen it come to all de woes / in married life" (2000: 62). Questioning the double standard inscribed by and within the Bible, the voice of the Wife of Bath unravels the artificiality of prohibitions upon sexual pleasure and experience placed upon women, claiming "wat I do wid my body is my personal business" after recounting the sexual privileges allotted to men in scripture:

> Abraham, Joseph
> Nuff adda holy man
> Did have nuff wife
> Whey God forbid dat?
> Yuh see no clear word?
> Where Im ever order virginity
> Dere is no such commandment!
>
> (2000: 62)

The role of the "I" in direct encounter with the authority of scripture undoes the logic of that authoritative claim; moreover, placing Chaucer's English within the Creolized voice of this Wife of Bath suggests the fluid, living changes in language that characterized his own work and that this Creolization carries forward.

The working in, through, and against authoritative discourses renders the lyric more complex in its stance toward the conventions and histories from which it emerges. The final poets that this essay will consider compel the lyric "I" to simultaneously engage with and interrogate lyric traditions, particularly as they are complicit in the constructions of subjectivity through social discourses and through the operations of language. Aware of and influenced to different degrees by variants of poststructural and feminist theories, Carol Ann Duffy and Denise Riley each engage in deliberated and self-conscious ways with the lyric tradition. Duffy's experiments with the dramatic monologue and her insistent positioning of the lyric "I" in relation to economic and nationalistic discourses develops as a poetics of public discourse. Riley's syntactic and linguistic disruptions on the page draw upon interdiscursive constructions of the female self to put the notion of the authentic self under question while refusing to abandon the speaking "I" in acceding to the poststructural and/or avant-garde aversion to the "self." For both poets, awareness of feminist intellectual and political thought undergirds a reluctance to abandon the female-marked "I" that, nonetheless, accompanies a skepticism about the self's authority as free from language. Language, in the extremely different poetries of Duffy and Riley, is seen to operate as a material aspect of the world with material effects on systems of power. The construction of identity within language is explored through lyric innovations of form and a self-referential signaling of how linguistic (including poetic) forms structure meaning.

A Scots-born poet who attended Liverpool University in the 1970s, moving to London and Manchester in the 1980s, Carol Ann Duffy would draw upon these urban, industrial environs undergoing economic changes under Thatcher and altered demographics of race, ethnicity, and class in a post-empire Britain. During the 1980s and 1990s, Duffy's first collections of poetry question how the individual is imagined within economic, nationalist, and socially Conservative discourses arising during the ascendancy of the New Right and Thatcherism; consequently, many of her poems of this period identify and challenge a public rhetoric of selfhood advancing the values of authentic, autonomous, and unified subjectivity, coexisting with "traditional" values of social life. In some poems, such as "The Act of Imagination" (in *The Other Country*, 1990), Duffy cuts across the discursive landscape of Conservative thought through employing a rapid-fire parataxis. Juxtaposed soundbites bombard the lyric subject, dissolving the "self" within discourses of right-wing ascendancy in Western capitalism: listing items that "may be prosecuted for appalling the Imagination," the poem includes "President Quayle," "British Rail," "The Repatriation charter," "A Hubby," "Bedtime with Nancy and Ron," "eating the weakest survivor," "Homeless and down to a fiver" (1990: 25). Metonymically foregrounding social shifts in Britain brought on through the Conservative government's embrace of a free-market economy (through moving from a postwar collectivism to the deregulation of British Rail, a valuing of market individualism, and a retreat from forms of social welfare), concurrent with a call to traditional family values and a renewed nationalism (in response to debates over immigration and repatriation), the poem points to the collusion of economic policy, social control, and national identity. Discourse overcomes the "imagination," thwarting the "lyric tradition in which a single and singular voice struggles to express and defend an authentic 'personality' that stands over against an inauthentic world" (Naylor 1999: 7).

Many of Duffy's poems ask that the reader imagine how a particular "self" comes to understand him or herself through encounters with language naming him/her as "other," as in "Foreign" (*Selling Manhattan*, 1987). Here, rather than the paratactic cataloguing of discursive fragments found in "The Act of Imagination," Duffy uses her signature form, the dramatic monologue. Rather than assuming that the "authentic self" speaks through this form, however, Duffy's dramatic monologues often point to the participation of this lyric convention in maintaining an ideology of selfhood dependent upon the processes of "othering," of rendering subjectivities unrecognizable except within specific, privileged articulations of selfhood, be they sexually defined, racially demarcated, class-linked, or nationalistic.

(Indeed, a range of elided or marginalized subjectivities are addressed in Duffy's poetry, including those that speak to her own self-identifications with lesbianism and nationalistic politics during the dissolution of the United Kingdom.) Speaking in the voice of an immigrant who perceives himself through the "word" labeling him as "alien," the poem registers the experience of apprehending the self through words naming it as other, alien, undesirable, non-British:

> Imagine one night
> You saw a name for yourself sprayed in red
> Against a brick wall. A hate name. Red like blood.
> It is snowing on the streets, under the neon lights,
> As if this place were coming to bits before your eyes.
>
> (1987: 47)

Recalling the rise in white violence in the late 1950s and recurring through the 1970s, the poem suggests how language sustains racially bound dynamics of power, in part through establishing a rhetoric of selfhood in opposition to the "alien." To exist in otherness is to "not translate" except within the language constructed to identify that otherness, to be "inarticulate" within the dominant articulations of self-hood: "And in the delicatessen, from time to time, the coins / in your palm will not translate. Inarticulate, / because this is not home, you point at fruit" (1987: 47).

Although Duffy is considered by many a "mainstream" poet, by virtue of her popularity, awards, and publishing support by major houses, and Denise Riley is associated with a more marginalized "experimental" community in Britain (associated with linguistically innovative poetry, small independent presses, and often an explicitly theoretical inflection), it seems fruitful to set aside such oppositional categories when considering how their poetic efforts constitute a poetic continuum. This continuum, I would argue, is traceable through the explicit focus on the gender-marked lyric genre and the lyric subject as discursive formation, exemplifying varying modes of feminist work exploring the speaking subject in relation to social, public discursive structures.

Denise Riley, characterized by Jane Dowson and Alice Entwistle's history of twentieth-century women poets as a poet of the "disruptive lyric," has shouldered much commentary and controversy about the issue of the lyric, often being accused from an avant-garde perspective as somehow *too lyrical* to be truly experimental (as in focusing upon the "I" and interior emotion). Along with other poets like Wendy Mulford, Geraldine Monk, Caroline Bergvall, and Maggie O'Sullivan, Riley is often discussed in terms of avant-garde, American-influenced, theoretical poets in Britain, whose texts reject conventional forms of language, favoring disruptive, paratactic, associative, and self-referential strategies that emphasize textuality and the materiality of language. As part of an alternative poetry scene in Britain that has variously manifested a poststructural poetics of "I aversion" (as the male British poet cris cheek characterized the poetic avant-garde in post-1980 Britain), these women have nonetheless resisted and questioned the evacuation of the "I" as predominately privileging men without considering the historical uncertainty of subjectivity held by women (see especially the discussion of Riley's relation to the avant-garde and feminist poetry communities in Kinnahan 2004). Nonetheless, Riley and others knowingly complicate the lyric subject through holding the "I" up for inspection within discursive determinations of identity.

Riley's volume *Mop Mop Georgette* pursues a vexed concern with the lyric, asking at one point, in "A Shortened Set," "I'd thought / to ask around, what's lyric poetry?" (1993: 22). The poem "Dark Looks" intervenes in contemporary theories of subjectivity and writing through relating textuality to gendered authority. Opening with a fashionable dismissal of the author ("Who anyone is or I am is nothing to the work"), the poem goes on to evoke a gender-coded dilemma:

> The writer
> Properly should be the last person that the reader or the listener need
> think about
> Yet the poet with her signature stands up trembling, grateful,
> mortally embarrassed
> And especially embarrassing to herself, patting her hair and twittering
> If, if only
> I need not have a physical appearance! To be sheer air, and
> mousseline!
>
> (1993: 54)

The speaker's concern with her own body counterpoints the initial denial of self in the text, pointing to the danger of erasing the materiality of the female body in embracing certain poststructuralist understandings of "text" and "self." The female body is again evoked in the poem through references to menstrual blood so that we are forced to consider the question of the poetic "I" in relationship to the female body's manifestations in discourse and culture. Within this framework, the speaker queries, "What forces the lyric person to put itself on trial though it must stay rigorously uninteresting?" (1993: 54). Is dullness of self the modern manifestation of Romantic transcendence, covering over the material aspects of the world, providing a "veil for the monomania / which likes to feel itself helpless and touching at times?" (1993: 54). The final lines of the poem re-evaluate the first line's assertion of the author's absence from the text by intoning a humorously desperate plea to the reader not to forsake the "I" in the text": "So take me or leave me. No wait, I didn't mean leave / me, wait, just don't – or don't flick and skim to the foot of the page and then get up to go –" (1993: 54).

Riley, whose work as a theorist is well known and clearly informs her poetry, poses a way to consider the post-1970s feminist work of the lyric, in its many variations. In an essay disclaiming a collective identity for women, she argues that the "question of the politics of identity could be rephrased as a question of rhetoric. Not so much of whether there was for a particular moment any truthful underlying rendition of 'women' or not, but of what the proliferations of addresses, descriptions, and attributions were doing" (1992a: 122). Contemporary women poets, indeed, reinvent the lyric and the potential for the lyric "I" through traversing the "proliferations" of "woman" and refusing to settle in any one spot.

Further Reading

Bertram, Vicki (ed.) (1997). *Kicking Daffodils: Twentieth-Century Women Poets.* Edinburgh: Edinburgh University Press.

Broom, Sarah (2006). *Contemporary British and Irish Poetry.* New York: Palgrave Macmillan.

Dowson, Jane & Entwistle, Alice (2005). *A History of Twentieth-Century British Women's Poetry.* Cambridge: Cambridge University Press.

Kinnahan, Linda (2004). *Lyric Interventions: Feminism, Experimental Poetry, and Contemporary Discourse.* Iowa City, IA: University of Iowa Press.

Mark, Alison & Rees-Jones, Deryn (eds) (2000). *Contemporary Women's Poetry: Reading/Writing/Practice.* London: Macmillan.

Severin, Laura (2004). *Poetry Off the Page: Twentieth-Century British Women Poets in Performance.* Aldershot: Ashgate Press.

Anthologies

Adcock, Fleur (ed.) (1987). *Faber Book of 20th-Century Women's Poetry*. London: Faber & Faber.

Cope, Wendy (ed.) (1989). *Is That the New Moon? Poems by Women Poets*. London: Collins.

Dooley, Maura (1997). *Making for Planet Alice: New Women Poets*. Newcastle upon Tyne: Bloodaxe.

Duffy, Carol Ann (ed.) (1992). *I Wouldn't Thank You for a Valentine: Poems for Young Feminists*. London: Viking.

Dunhill, Christina (ed.) (1994). *As Girls Could Boast: New Poetry by Women*. London: Oscars Press.

France, Linda (ed.) (1993). *Sixty Women Poets*. Newcastle upon Tyne: Bloodaxe.

Mohin, Lilian (ed.) (1980). *One Foot on the Mountain: An Anthology of British Feminist Poetry, 1969–1979*. London: Onlywomen Press.

Mohin, Lilian (ed.) (1986). *Beautiful Barbarians: Lesbian Feminist Poetry*. London: Onlywomen Press.

O'Sullivan, Maggie (ed.) (1996). *Out of Everywhere: linguistically innovative poetry by women in North America and the UK*. London: Reality Street.

Rumens, Carol (ed.) (1985). *Making for the Open: The Chatto Book of Post-Feminist Poetry, 1964–1984*. London: Chatto & Windus.

Chapter 10

Place, Space, and Landscape

Eric Falci

It is no surprise that British and Irish poetry after World War II is fretted with concern about place and space. Massive shifts in geo-politics after 1945, the dissolution of the British Empire and sub-sequent large-scale immigration into Britain, technological advances that allowed for long-range travel to an unprecedented degree and revolutionized global communications, and the destabilizing effect of these and other changes on late capitalist societies and communities have inflected postwar poetry's obsession with location. In "Wherever I Hang," Grace Nichols is sardonically cheerful about postcolonial upheavals when she attempts to elide the conflicts of her "new-world-self" which is "divided to de ocean / Divided to the bone" by embracing an ethos of mobility: "Wherever I hang me knickers – that's my home" (Ramazani et al. 2003: 908). The slip in possessives – from "me" to "my" – is symptomatic of the speaker's continuing divisions. Such mobility, however, becomes a source of anxiety for Derek Mahon in "Afterlives." Returning to Northern Ireland after a time in London, the poet wonders if by staying in Belfast, and living the Troubles "bomb by bomb," he would have "learnt what is meant by home" (1999: 59). While the uneasy half-rhyme on bomb/home perfectly enacts the uneasiness of the speaker, the concluding declamation of Nichols's poem belies its own enthusiasm. The manifold ways in which notions of "home," "place," and "space" have become increasingly burdened in postwar poetry is forecast by Auden's masterpiece, "In Praise of Limestone" (1948), itself multiply displaced. Set in Italy by a peripatetic

English poet who became an American citizen a few years before, and who was traveling in Florence but thinking back to his home turf in Yorkshire, the poem begins with a sidelong thesis about a limestone landscape:

> If it form the one landscape that we the inconstant ones
> Are constantly homesick for, this is chiefly
> Because it dissolves in water.
>
> (Ramazani et al. 2003: 806)

This passage, with its "inconstant ones" and their constant longings, and its "one landscape" that barely qualifies, sets up a usable figure for this essay. A landscape gives way to its opposite. The poetry of the period is filled with such dissolving landscapes, places that open underfoot into murky indeterminacies, and spaces made and unmade by modernity's alterations, accidents, and disasters.

A great deal of attention has been paid to matters of spatiality and location in late twentieth-century critical thought. The intellectual revolutions of the late nineteenth and early twentieth centuries generally resulted in startling reconceptions of time and historicity, whether it was the Hegelian time of dialectical history, the Marxist time of revolution, the Darwinian time of evolution, the Freudian time of the psyche and its processes, the Einsteinian time of space-time, or the Fordist time of economic production. As a result, temporality was privileged as the active agent in human affairs, and space was regulated to the role of static frame, where time happened. In the final third of the century, space and place began to re-emerge as conceptual problems, most prominently in the fields of phenomenology, epistemology, social theory, and political economy. The assumed immobility of place was infused with the indeterminacy and activity of space. Space was conceived of as having a poetics, and of being a kind of production itself rather than simply occupying the ground where production happened (de Certeau 1984; Lefebvre 1991). Places – actual, virtual, conceptual – became the site of spatial practices and experiences.

An extraordinary range of ideas and writers were consolidated as part of "the spatial turn," which in turn bolstered emerging fields of "postmodern geography" and "human geography." Readings of spaces, spatial forms, spatial systems, spatial practices, and the materiality of space became central to the work of leading theorists and scholars (Soja 1989; Massey 1994). The most celebrated set-piece in Fredric

Jameson's pivotal text, *Postmodernism* (1991), is an extraordinary reading of the Westin Bonaventure Hotel in Los Angeles, a site that forces experiential discontinuities upon its visitors, which Jameson uses as an instance of the process of "cognitive mapping" that he insists upon in his groundbreaking account of postmodernism. One of the surest signs of the importance of spatial thinking in current critical theory is that it does not need to be emphasized anymore; it has submerged itself within various intellectual discourses and fields, and at present is as much a framework for thinking as a topic of it. While "place" has become a fairly unfashionable frame for thinking about poetry, "space" has moved beyond the status of a critical buzzword into a critical tool.

This essay's own place is at the well-traveled intersection of the two concepts, and it is my hope that examining contemporary British and Irish poetry through these seemingly exhausted frames will not result in the production of simply more exhaustion. My sense is that our understanding of "the poetry of place" has worked within a fairly narrow band of analytical concerns. We have read the poetry of place, the place of poetry, and place in poetry, but we have not yet threaded together these only partially compatible modes to see whether postwar poetry does anything with and to place within its own heterogeneous spaces.

As an initial organizational move, we could say that there are two seemingly contrasting impulses in the way late twentieth-century British and Irish poets delineated place and space. The first is excavatory, and the second scopic. This doublet is similar to the one that Peter Barry proposes in *Contemporary British Poetry and the City* (2000), a process of transhistorical seeing he describes as "double visioning" (Barry 2000: 45–8, 226). While these two modes are not mutually exclusive (and are not as utterly determined by the rural–urban binary as Barry suggests), and while the ultimate utility of such a binary is in locating all of its leaks, it does serve to establish a range. These contrasting impulses do not establish an axis so much as outline a constellated set of mechanisms, effects, structures, and perspectives, each of which operates in conjunction with the others. Seeing is always a seeing into. Looking always has seeing as a desired object and a vanishing point. For many poets, some more obviously and more insistently than others, the scope is a shovel.

For the majority of people, place and space are first experienced visually, and only then further sensualized and conceptualized. The pastoral tradition in English poetry is predicated on the act of seeing, and much twentieth-century urban poetry could be described as a poetry of looking. The tendency of poets after the war to work archaeologically indicates an additional framework for thinking about space. And while not necessarily original – archaeology has long been a favored site for finding subjects – the sheer volume of important postwar British and Irish poetry that imagines itself as proceeding archaeologically is of great interest. While rural and pseudo-rural sites have been popular staging areas for much of this work, I will pay more attention to urban archaeologies here. Further, a poetics of excavation does not preclude a simultaneous poetics of seeing. Indeed, excavatory poetics could be thought of as a corollary to scopic poetics, rather than opposed to it, and the poets I will eventually highlight in this chapter – Roy Fisher, Ciaran Carson, and Eiléan Ní Chuilleanáin – are not representative of either impulse, rather incorporating and/or eschewing both. By testing the terms upon which "place poetry" operates, these poets emphasize the array of lenses that mediate any act of poetic seeing, thereby accounting more fully for the rich materiality of the local places their poems envisage and assemble.

The importance of locality in later modernism, as a counterweight to the perceived internationalism of high modernism, has been stressed by a good deal of recent scholarship (see particularly Alderman & Blanton 2000; Davis & Jenkins 2000). Such poetic regionalism – as practiced in Britain and Ireland by such figures as Basil Bunting, John Hewitt, Patrick Kavanagh, Hugh MacDiarmid, and David Jones – was a mechanism for consolidating and extending the gains of modernist poetry within an alternate frame, while also offering a looping path back to certain aspects of English pastoral poetry, particularly the work of William Wordsworth and Thomas Hardy, central avatars of place poetry in English. The non-metropolitan locales of many of these poems could therefore be read as both a species of reaction and continuity. Patrick Kavanagh's cranky and prescient 1952 distinction between "parochialism" and "provincialism" continues to have purchase in this sense. While the "provincial" poet (and for Kavanagh, Ireland was provincial) "has no mind of his own" and depends on the view from the metropolis for all of his opinions, the "parochial" poet "is never in any doubt about the social and artistic validity of his parish," and therefore "all great civilizations are based on parochialism – Greek, Israelite, English" (Kavanagh 2003: 237). As an attempt to short-circuit the center–periphery model by re-centering the periphery, Kavanagh's oft-quoted view becomes a powerful heuristic if we mute the rancor. Such "regional modernisms" do not merely trade the metropolitan internationalism of high modernism for a poetry of the hinterlands. Poets like Basil Bunting and David Jones should not be simply placed in an adjacent canonical space. Instead, the complex refiguring embedded – however unwittingly – in Kavanagh's notion of "parochialism" can be applied to them as to other works and figures. The "region" becomes not only the zone for an alternate politics, but also an imaginative space that can be made to enact temporalities and scales that differ from metropolitan rhythms. Regionality becomes a stance for poetry as well as a site for poems.

At the same time that a good deal of poetry of the period placed itself very carefully within a precise grid of locations, the countervailing impulse was toward the derealization, or the multiplication, of places. While such an impulse is central to many modernist works – the "Unreal City" of *The Waste Land* is "Jerusalem Athens Alexandria / Vienna" as well as London (Eliot 1991: 67) – the quality of such moves in later poetry tends to mute the mythical abstractions of an Eliotic method. The different ways in which much late century poetry figures space should be set against the scholarly shifts I mentioned at the outset. The dominant metaphors of the "spatial turn" in the 1980s and 1990s had to do with "reading" landscapes, cityscapes, and architectures, and many poets anticipated and manipulated such conceptual models. While the notion of "reading" landscape and space was clearly not invented in the 1980s – "nature" has been figured, allegorized, and textualized for millennia – the concatenation of postmodern approaches to meaning and signification, the increasing interest in space in the latter part of the century as an object of inquiry, and the emphasis on locality and regionality (even within an increasingly global late capitalist system that weakened the specific textures of such locations) resulted in a heterogeneous body of work that has been tagged with the backhandedly dismissive phrase, "the poetry of place." Place became an increasingly popular area of poetic exploration (and fetishization), at the same time that the space of poetry became more heavily influenced by postmodern tendencies toward open forms, non-hierarchical structures, associative contents, lexical and semantic play, and figural flexibility. Notions of place – as it was delineated in poetry – became both more and less rooted at the same time.

Much of the poetry of place that seems to be centered in the 1970s sets itself within these diverging convergences, so that the cluster of significant poems of place in the latter third of the twentieth century is a product of many, not always complementary, traditions and genealogies. Contributing to the excavatory tendency are the increased interest in local histories (a much more dangerously politicized endeavor in Ireland than in England, Wales, or even Scotland); the skepticism with which grand narratives (often embedded in the discursive and institutional structures articulated by metropolitan centers) were treated within late century critical thought; a poetic retrenchment, whereby late modern, anti-modern, or postmodern writers attempted to fix their ground, as compared to the seeming deracinations of the high modernists; and a refurbishment of the Romantic notion of the poet as seer, diviner, and mystic, although now such personae were stripped of some privilege, and reduced to diggers, archivists, excavators, and trackers. The scopic nature of much of this work was conditioned by the ocular bearing of most of the poetry belonging to the English pastoral tradition, although postmodern reconceptions of seeing and subjectivity also contributed to the attention given to the problematic of seeing within place poetry of the period.

Seamus Heaney's work of the 1970s is indexical of the excavatory approach. Celebrated from the beginning for his hyper-rich descriptions of rural life, Heaney's work of the 1970s became increasingly indebted to the mechanism of linguistic excavation central to the Irish poetic tradition of *dinnseanchas*, even as it staked out a place apart from but adjacent to the mainstream of Wordsworthian pastoral poetry (Longley 2000a: 90–133). *Dinnseanchas*, which is usually translated as "place-name lore," refers both to the importance in the oral traditions of interpreting the history of a place by unpacking the etymology of its name, and to the written incarnations of these narratives. Such tales occur in collections of prose pieces or poems devoted exclusively to giving the history of places in relation to their names, or as important digressions in many of the key literary texts of early Ireland, most famously in *Táin Bó Cúailnge* ("The Cattle Raid of Cooley") and *Acallam na Senórach* ("The Colloquy of the Ancients" or, as it has been most recently translated, "Tales of the Elders of Ireland"). As practiced by poets in medieval Ireland, *dinnseanchas* poems were a means to narrativize and historicize the Irish ground, to explain it via either mythology, dynastic politics, or social history (MacGiolla Léith 1991). Taken up by later twentieth-century poets in both Irish and English, *dinnseanchas* became a way to think through Ireland's imperial and linguistic dispossession by the English. The prevailing tendency among Irish writers in English has been to metaphorize the loss of Gaelic culture and tradition by way of the figure of *dinnseanchas*, although for poets in Irish *dinnseanchas* has become a way to assert cultural and poetic continuity (Ní Dhomhnaill 2005: 25–42, 156–70). As the violence of the Troubles in Northern Ireland worsened, and the prerogatives of poetry in a place of strife became a prominent theme, Heaney's poetry began to complicate the sonic and imagistic density of its descriptions by digging into their social, linguistic, and political foundations. *Dinnseanchas* can structure such an imaginative task: the seeing of place becomes a way to see into its history. Heaney's 1974 lecture "Feeling into Words" summarizes this approach. In it Heaney espouses a view of poetry "as divination, poetry as revelation of the self to the self, as restoration of the culture to itself; poems as elements of continuity, with the aura and authenticity of archaeological finds, where the buried shard has an importance that is not diminished by the importance of the buried city; poetry as a dig, a dig for finds that end up being plants" (1980b: 41). Heaney's most famous examples of *dinnseanchas* – poems like "Anahorish," "Broagh," and "Toome" – undertake such a project, attempting to "bed the locale / in the utterance," bodying out the place-name by reconstructing it sonically (1972: 25).

An equally important instance of such an approach, one that again sets itself in the midst of violence in Northern Ireland, is John Montague's *The Rough Field*. A densely arranged sequence written over the course of a decade and first published as a whole in 1972, *The Rough Field* strews its multi-tracked pages with autobiographical pieces, political screeds, found texts, emblems of the long political struggle in the North, and various other quarry, so that the text becomes the fractured landscape it so assiduously details. It attempts to simultaneously enact a modern *dinnseanchas* and lament the cultural unity that underwrote the tradition, fundamentally hobbling any such attempt:

> The whole landscape a manuscript
> We had lost the skill to read,
> A part of our past disinherited
> (1972: 30)

The Rough Field (an Anglicization of the Irish name of Montague's ancestral turf, Garvaghey in County Tyrone) is in some ways the archetypical contemporary place poem: an extended sequence that attempts to remap physical space as textual space, its pages strewn with archeo-textual finds, mimicking the embattled fields in Northern Ireland whose history they describe.

Though rarely using the *dinnseanchas* tradition as explicitly in his poetry as Heaney or Montague (though see his wonderfully arch "The Route of the *Táin*" [1973] for a counter-*dinnseanchas* poem), Thomas Kinsella has perhaps done more than any other recent poet in English to spur the re-immersion in early Irish texts and locales that has characterized the postwar period, mainly through his landmark translation of the central Irish epic – the aforementioned *Táin Bó Cúailnge*, which Kinsella published as the *Táin* in 1969 – as well as several other major translation projects, but also through the incorporation of material from the cruces of early Irish history and myth, most notably the pseudo-history origins of Ireland, *Lebor Gabála Érenn* ("The Book of Invasions of Ireland"). As he abandoned the formal shapeliness that earned him early praise, in favor of Poundian sequences and open works, early Irish mythical material became both structural scaffolding and narrative germs in major texts such as *Notes from the Land of the Dead* (1973) and *One* (1974). These "landscapes with ancient figures" often work as hinges into more abstract or personal terrain (Kinsella 1996: 86), and it is generally true that in his work through the 1980s physical places serve as antechambers into the "saturated depths" of the psyche's interior spaces (Kinsella 1996: 89).

However, his use of Jungian archetypes has become more subdued in his work of the past several decades, which has foregrounded another aspect of his poetry that had been there, though obscured, all along. As we will see with Fisher and Birmingham as well as Carson and Belfast, Kinsella has used Dublin – especially the area near the Guinness Brewery where he spent much of his early life – to think with (Fisher 2005: 285). The dark and sometimes terrifying psychic landscapes that characterize much of his best work often arise out of specific Dublin locations and scenes. Eschewing a Joycean encyclopedic reconstruction of his home city (yet utterly indebted to Joyce's monumental projects), Kinsella uses Dublin-specific details sparsely while indicating clearly that his body of poetry is intimately connected to it. Especially in his recent work, poems are launched from Dublin environs (*St Catherine's Clock*, 1987 and *Poems from Centre City*, 1990), outline routes taken through the city ("To the Coffee Shop" and "To the Pen Shop," 1997), remember the Dublin of the poet's childhood ("Settings," 1985), or satirize the city from within its borders (*One Fond Embrace*, 1988 and *Open Court*, 1991). Dublin becomes even more central when we examine his particular publishing circumstances. In 1972 Kinsella began Peppercanister Press in order to issue regular chapbooks of his own work, naming it after the local nickname for

St Stephen's Church near Merrion Square. So far, there have been 27 Peppercanister volumes (as of June 2007), and even though he taught for many years in the United States and his work is regularly collected and published by major presses on both sides of the Atlantic, this publication mechanism has emphasized not only the inter-connectedness of Kinsella's body of work, but also its Dublin roots. Though rarely "about" Dublin as such, Kinsella's ongoing network of poems constitutes a *dinnseanchas* of a different, and perhaps more significant, sort.

While the Irish *dinnseanchas* tradition gave Irish poets a framework for their articulations of place poetry, and while the worsening violence in the North resulted in the complex politicization of such varieties of blasted pastoral, this is not to say that Irish poets in the postwar period had exclusive rights on "the poetry of place." Perhaps the major achievement in twentieth-century English poetry is catalyzed by its specific location in Northumbria. Basil Bunting's *Briggflatts*, pub-lished in 1965 after a long silence, is an intensely rooted poem, and uses the histories, mythologies, and geographies of Northumberland to evoke an "archipelago of galaxies" that encompasses a millen-nium and ranges from the farthest edges of the Celtic fringes and Scandinavia through southern Europe to Asia (Bunting 2001: 70). Its investment in the linguistic registers and vocabularies of Northern England, its sharply carved stanzas and lines, and its harmonic densities make *Briggflatts* into a kind of sedimented epic, wherein the poem mimics a geological formation to an extent unseen in other twentieth-century poetry.

In Bunting's wake came a series of important works in the 1970s and 1980s that reconceptualized poetry's involvement with the land-scapes and locations of "coiled, entrenched England" (Hill 2000: 112). Geoffrey Hill's *Mercian Hymns* (1971) travels "tracks of ancient occupa-tion" as it reconstitutes the ground of King Offa's eighth-century kingdom of Mercia within the late twentieth-century Midlands (2000: 120). *Place* (1971–1980), Allen Fisher's multivolume project, turns the poetic text into a trawler to excavate the histories, archives, and arch-aeologies of South London. Finally, Peter Riley's continuing series of Midland and Northern topographies – *Lines on the Liver* (1981), *Tracks and Mineshafts* (1983), *Alstonefield* (2003), and *Excavations* (2004) – may end up constituting the most significant engagement with location and landscape in twentieth-century British poetry. In turning now to the work of Roy Fisher, Ciaran Carson, and Eiléan Ní Chuilleanáin, I want to highlight several varieties of "place poetry" that tend to be much less sure of their own practices of marking space than, say, Heaney's prototypical place poems, and which prove to generatively complicate postwar poetry's relationship to place.

Perhaps the most important aspect of Roy Fisher's poetry for the concerns of this essay is that he insistently questions the conceptual bedrock underlying much of the more archetypical place poetry, such as Heaney's or Montague's. Fisher's poetry continually tests Montague's assumption – subtended, perhaps contradictorily, by the long tradition of Irish place poetry as well as postmodern denaturalizations of place – that the landscape is readable: if we have lost the skill to read the landscape's manuscript, this necessarily assumes that we once could. Additionally, his poetry negotiates the split between poetry and the pastoral. This is not to say that Fisher's work is strictly anti-pastoral, notwithstanding Peter Barry's descriptions of him as "laureate of the urban-prosaic . . . the quintessential city poet" (2000: 9). Rather, his poetry is a kind of evacuated pastoral, gazing at landscapes unmade and remade by industry and unmoored by tourism and the heritage industry, as well as critiquing the structure of the gaze that provides for such asymmetrical relations between humans and the land on which and off which we live.

Fisher's writings, many of which are constituted by collaged acts of seeing, enact a long-range meditation on the place of the human within spaces that are themselves shot through with human agency and action (Gregson 1996; O'Brien 1998; Kerrigan 2000). One of his best such poems, "Wonders of Obligation" (1979), folds a poignant confession into its visual motions: "I'm obsessed / with cambered tarmac, concretes, / the washings of rain" (Fisher 2005: 20). Central to such an obsession is the rearrangements it enacts upon its objects. The slightly convex "cambered tarmac" (either designed as such to encourage drainage or warped by the elements), gives way to its presumed substance (concrete). The odd plural form both defamiliarizes concrete and places it in several unaccustomed categories. "Concretes," what we might call a faulty plural, operates in two ways depending on what kind of analogues we use to read the word. Either we read the world as suggesting multiples of a discrete object called "concrete," or a mass plural that designates an uncountable substance (like "waters" or "lands"). Like the word "sand," "concrete" is a mass plural that usually does not take the "s." Attaching the "s" occludes the usual lexical workings as well as the perceptual mechanisms encoded within the lexis.

This tiny bit of "making strange" is only activated because of its strong semantic and contextual gravitation to the phrases on either side of it. The "cambered tarmac" may be made of concrete, a substance that first is grammatically undone, and then elementally eroded, worn away by the "washings of rain" which may have caused the cambering of the tarmac in the first place. The point of such microscopic obsessions on my part is to show that while Fisher's poetry is very often scopically driven, it does not simply describe perceptions. Often, as in the small passage above, a micro-environment is assembled, one which sees and re-sees the landscapes that its own seeing has made, and which interrogates the processes that go into such a making. The interplay of various ecologies, "unseparable, interfolded," is central to Fisher's poetics of location (Fisher 2005: 280).

Fisher's first significant work, the "assemblage" (2000: 69) of poetry and prose published in 1961 as *City*, gains much of its energy not simply from the strength of its descriptions of post-industrial Birmingham, but rather from the way it continually questions the "readability" of the city. The text – compiled from various loose poems and prose fragments by the poet's friend and editor of Migrant Press, Michael Shayer – does not narrate the city, or even the poet's perambulations through it. Rather, *City* presents an array of multi-generic texts that end up reproducing the non-narrative space of the city itself, the assemblage of micro-processes and micro-narratives produced by and productive of the hegemony of institutions, political power, and the deployments of capital. Fisher's *City* is a space of tactics, strategies, and practices.

City continually unpacks its own processes, most poignantly in the movements from discrete poems to units of prose, from individually titled pieces to untitled parts. Much of the pleasure and interest of the text comes from watching local bits fail to map onto other local bits, and from the oddly jarring way in which certain of the poems (especially "The Entertainment of War" and "The Park") seem out of place, too traditional for the poetic fabric into which they are stitched. At the same time, the way in which short lyrics like "North Area," "By the Pond," and "The Sun Hacks" simply give way to untitled prose blocks suggests that this array of textual spaces is miming an actual city's often unplanned amalgams.

At times the descriptions of mid-century Birmingham seem to be channeling early Eliot (especially in "Lullaby and Exhortation for the Unwilling Hero"), while at others they are much more comfortable interleaving the pastoral and the post-industrial: "The society of singing birds and the society of mechanical planners inhabit the world together, slightly ruffled and confined by each other's presence"

(Fisher 2005: 35). This is not to deny that the poem presents a degraded city. It sets itself squarely in a mid-century Birmingham wrecked by the war, abandoned by industry, and wrecked again by ill-conceived projects of urban renewal, and it sometimes meta-morphoses its inhabitants into "a composite monster" (2005: 37). Nevertheless, this consummate text of urban decay often reads against its own grain, incorporating pastoral cues that are not simply emptied of significance, even if such redemptive tags are severely atten-uated. It evokes the "bombed city" of Birmingham as a razed site of death and waste, but the poem does not exchange an Eliotic "unreal" London for an "unreal" Birmingham (2005: 31), or attempt to recu-perate the city via a mode of diminished pastoral. Additionally, it is not simply that Fisher masterfully documents and describes the city's degradation. Rather, the structure of the piece works against any singular hermeneutical reading. The multiple, palimpsestic space of *City* – "the ghost of the older one still lies among the spokes of the new" (2005: 32) – resists narration. Such a counter-teleology frustrates the poem's strongly scopic urge: the sureness of the descriptive texture is again and again undercut by its large-scale construction. The weirdly hybrid quasi-industrial sites that populate the poem – an imagined "North Area" which has "dunes with cement walks" and "much glass to reflect the clouds"; fields impinged upon by "prefabricated work-shops"; a pond-side space that improbably houses both a "fishermen's shack" and a "pit-mound"; a "tree" made from "steel stakes" (2005: 34, 35, 40) – replicate the dueling tendencies of the poem's concep-tual urges.

The importance of *City* within the body of postwar place poetry is that it delineates a poetics of urban experience that invests fully in neither a pastoral tradition of Wordsworthian ambulatory remembrance nor an Eliotic one of apocalyptic spectatorship. Neither does it allow itself the kind of interpretive understanding that will be the goal and troubled achievement of later place poets like Heaney. Rather, in sinking each of these modes into a poetic construction that allows free play to none of them, Fisher writes a place poetry constantly re-energized by renovating its own perceptual apparatus.

Such an approach continues throughout his body of work, and while *City* may not have an authorial shape, it is as shapely as anything in his oeuvre. Fisher's poems are more formally open than Heaney's tight sonic clusters or Hill's dense structures, and as an increasing facility with a poetics of process – no doubt influenced by Fisher's other life as a jazz pianist – interacted with his scopic style, the poems became more like collages of seeing. The sequences that are the major achievements of such a mode – "Glenthorne Poems" (1970), "Matrix" (1970), "Diversions" (1976), "Handsworth Liberties" (1974–8), "Wonders of Obligation" (1979), "Texts for a Film" (1991), "It Follows That" (1993–4), and "The Dow Low Drop" (1994–2000) – uncoil their materials in fluctuating, bifurcating strands, constantly opening spaces into others. In *A Furnace* (1986), the perceptual apparatus at the core of his poetics undergoes its most radical transformation. Every location in this poem's series of superimposing landscapes becomes both estranged and manifold, "repeatedly elsewhere," through a series of substitutions and displacements that catalyze the text's hyperspace, its "trodden city" (2005: 56, 132).

In moving to another "trodden city," I want to focus on the way in which Ciaran Carson's poetry interweaves various conceptions of place within its stratigraphical textures. Like Fisher with Birmingham and Kinsella with Dublin, Carson localizes his poetry in his home city of Belfast, and, again like both of them, uses malleable formal structures and genres to map out iterating versions of Belfast, within which industry, political strife, British occupation, and sectarian violence have established a highly delineated, multiply signifying, complexly coded cityscape. Partially adapting Seamus Heaney's model of the poet as excavator (although like Paul Muldoon's, Carson's tweaking of Heaney's oeuvre has provided a constant source of compositional energy), but redirecting the model in order to account for the experiential flux of the city as well the multiple narratives and historiographies that constitute it, Carson's Belfast poems enact the vicissitudes of the "city" not only as a discursively composed space but also as a place of human geography intersected by multiple lines of perceptual, political, social, and institutional tension. His well-known line "the city is a map of the city" (Carson 1989: 69) evokes a keen awareness of the slippages that occur between competing representations. And the specific textures of such slippages, the way in which his poems interleave varieties of places and spaces while rarely allowing them to coalesce into an interpretable whole, will be my topic here.

Carson's 1989 volume *Belfast Confetti* is his most sustained attempt to map the overlapping structures and landscapes of Belfast, or at least to thoroughly document the failure of any attempt to map such a heterogeneous place. Just as Fisher describes the city as an ongoing palimpsestic event, so does Carson pay close attention to the way in which "it seems that every inch of Belfast has been written-on, erased, and written on again" (Carson 1989: 52). Every kind of seeing, mapping, reading, and conceptualizing the city are both available and untrustworthy in Carson's work. Such skepticism relies on Heaney's establishment of a poetic stance rooted in place at the same time that it is re-routed, a shift neatly encapsulated in "At Toomebridge":

> Where negative ions in the open air
> Are poetry to me. As once before
> The slime and silver of the fattened eel.
> (Heaney 2001: 3)

The sonic soldering binding these lines belies the airiness they attempt, and while Heaney's poetics are more cryptic than is usually admitted ("the wet centre," after all, is impossibly "bottomless"), they rarely approach the level of contingency and provisionality that catalyzes Carson's work (Kerrigan 1998). And much of these contingent, provisional maneuvers occur as the product and excess of Carson's intensely textured gaze at his home city.

It may help at first to get a sense of the varieties of space in which Carson's Belfast poems work, and then turn to a single poem in order to watch the poetic reactions as they occur. Various mechanisms of perceiving and conceptualizing place and space are interwoven, and each of these models frames a different Belfast. Reading Carson's poems is often a matter of tracing how different frames overlap, leaching into one another as the poem proceeds. The significant amount of leakage that occurs as frames morph results in a syncopated and excessive textual fabric that never establishes a cohesive space or a coherent place. There are several key modes in Carson's figurations of location. One is experiential space, which often takes the form of a "flâneur-in-danger." An inveterate perambulator who never has the freedom of motion and anonymity of the Benjaminian model, the typical narrator is often on the move through Belfast. However, movements through Belfast (especially in the heavily sectarian areas of West Belfast where Carson grew up and lived) were always limited or endangered by institutional and extra-institutional forces, either the British military, the overwhelmingly Protestant Royal Ulster Constabulary, or the Republican and Loyalist paramilitary groups that controlled neighborhoods. Divisions were maintained by material means – barricades, barbed wire, roadblocks, "peace walls," and guns – as well as immaterial and abstract ones. While the dominant metaphor of Carson's poetics is cartographical, material maps are untrustworthy

213

because they "avoid the moment" (Carson 1989: 58). Carson's earlier formula can be inverted to resemble more closely the Borgesian parable from which it descends: the (only believable) map of the city is the city, since actual maps distort the city by shrinking it and by stopping its temporality.

Each of these problems is "solved" in Carson's work with the introduction of two different kinds of maps, each of which constitutes another spatial frame. The first problem is solved through an appeal to "remembered maps," the accumulation of experiences and perceptions that constitute individual, familial, and community memory. Carson's poems often "remember" what a particular bit of Belfast used to be like, sometimes resorting to intertexts to show a previous iteration of the city, and sometimes depending on the memory of the speaking subject. The map of the city becomes a continually uploading – and highly unstable – conceptual document. At the same time, these immaterial micro-maps, assembled from an assortment of evidence and experience (not all of it simply the speaker's alone), prove to be essential in the tense space of Belfast. In the prose piece "Question Time," an encounter with paramilitaries during a bike ride through the most notorious interface in Belfast (where the Protestant-populated Shankill Road and the Catholic-populated Falls Road come together) requires the speaker to "remember" the human geography of the street where he grew up so as to prove his affiliation. After being asked questions like "Where are you from? . . . What was the number of that house? . . . What streets could you see from this house . . . Who lived next door?," the narrator explains that "the map is pieced together bit by bit. I am this map which they examine, checking it for error, hesitation, accuracy; a map which no longer refers to the present world, but to a history, these vanished streets; a map which is this moment, this interrogation, my replies" (Carson 1989: 62–3).

The human map interrogated in "Question Time" finds its inverse in another spatial frame central to Carson's work: the surveillance map. In a city as heavily monitored by military, security, and paramilitary forces as Belfast, the anxiety of surveillance becomes a pressing concern. While maps are generally untrustworthy, the concession made just after the imperative "don't trust maps" is crucial: "Though if there is an ideal map, which shows the city as it is, it may exist in the eye of that helicopter ratcheting overhead, its searchlight fingering and scanning the micro-chip deviations" (Carson 1989: 58). The searchlight is a metonym for the entire security and surveillance apparatus of the modern state: cameras, mirrors, spies, informers, and our own trackable traces. The "place" of seeing here is the divine and digital eye of a computer network.

We can see the interactions of spaces (remembered, perceived, surveilled, represented, embodied) in a textual place by turning briefly to "Turn Again," the first poem in *The Irish for No* (1987). This poem is in the prototypical short form of Carson's work in the 1980s, comprised of two long-lined stanzas of five and four lines. In both *The Irish for No* and *Belfast Confetti*, these short lyrics intersperse the long narrative poems and prose pieces that take up each volume's bulk. "Turn Again" can be read as a primer for much of Carson's work. The first stanza is a micro-meditation on the provisional nature of maps:

There is a map of the city which shows the bridge that was never built.
A map which shows the bridge that collapsed; the streets that never existed.
Ireland's Entry, Elbow Lane, Weigh-house Lane, Back Lane, Stone-Cutter's
    Entry –
Today's plan is already yesterday's – the streets that were there are gone.
And the shape of the jails cannot be shown for security reasons.

(1987: 7)

The "map of the city" fails to show the city, reproducing a bridge that, presumably, only made it to the planning stages, a bridge that is no longer there, and streets that never existed. The third line offers a list of street names which either are on the obsolete map the poet is studying, or are so small that they never made it onto a map, and therefore "never existed." The representation of the city fails to account for all of its places, and is fundamentally unable to because of its static frame. The final two lines of the first stanza introduce two further kinds of space, the nostalgic space of the past ("the streets that were there are gone"), and the hegemonic space of the state ("the shape of the jails cannot be shown for security reasons"). It is not the case that one mode of space gives way to another. Rather, each spatial frame awkwardly overlaps the other, so that place is continually interrupted by incommensurable spaces. We are not sure of the status of the streets. They are present orthographically, but absent from the actual city. They may have never existed, or they may have only ever existed on the map. Or they may have "actually" existed, but only as pieces of local knowledge, evaporated in the motions of cartography.

The second stanza offers additional spatial frames, initially emphasizing the materiality of the map, and metaphorizing the materials in order to trope the strife in West Belfast:

The linen backing is falling apart – the Falls Road hangs by a thread.
When someone asks me where I live, I remember where I used to live.
Someone asks me for directions, and I think again. I turn into
A side-street to try to throw off my shadow, and history is changed.

(1987: 7)

The material map becomes a metaphor, and then an oblique marker of the narrator's own inability to keep his personal map current. The place of memory interrupts the place of the present, and the poem ends by enacting a lived space (for the first time there is a "scene") that presents an oblique danger. The "someone" asking for directions is a potentially dangerous figure in sectarian Belfast, and the poem ends with the poet attempting to escape this alternate variety of surveillance by resorting to the subjective and life-saving map in his head. The figure in the poem becomes an embodied map, although the enjambment slightly masks the double implication of the final lines. "Turn[ing] into / A side-street" could be either an action or a meta-morphosis, and the particular kind of change that "history" under-goes remains inscrutable as the clashing frames of perspective and location result in a spatial fuzz that offers nothing like the solidity of place.

The multiple ramifications of surveillance are a central topic of Carson's poetry, from the long-lined work of the 1980s and 1990s – *The Irish for No* (1987), *Belfast Confetti* (1989), *First Language* (1994), and *Opera Et Cetera* (1996) – that becomes a stylistic trademark to the severely attenuated lines of *Breaking News* (2003). The "ubiquitous surveillant God" (1996: 56) of the state's security apparatus continu-ally plays across the surface of Carson's cartographies, and such multiplying panopticons result in a forceful textual paranoia: "For everything you say is never lost, but hangs on in the starry void / In ghosted thumb-whorl spiral galaxies. Your fingerprints are every-where. *Be Paranoid*" (1996: 46, italics in original). Carson's poetry of place is in some ways more specific than Fisher's, if only because Carson's poems are littered with the markers of Belfast – streets, stores, brands, pubs – but they are also constantly dissolving into the "place-less" places of memory, institutional power, and technology.

Like Fisher's, Carson's poems are interested in superimposing land-scapes, but while Fisher's poems tend to achieve such superimposi-tions by way of juxtaposing modes of perceptions as well as discrete sites, Carson's more insistently foreground the various ways in which places are multiply demarcated, and how perception and agency are impinged upon by such demarcations. Surely much of this is due to the nature of the places about which they write. While Fisher's Birmingham suffered the same kind of mid-century industrial decay and economic malaise as Belfast, the Troubles in Northern Ireland imposed additional (violent, ultra-pressurized) grids and maps upon the city, limiting the on-the-ground freedom of its inhabitants as well as conditioning their modes of agency. Carson's poems anatomize both place and the gaze by showing how multiple frames interact and compete in what Fisher calls "the live map" of the city (2005: 287).

The urban poetry of Carson and Fisher may itself depart from the largely rural scenes that dominate the pastoral tradition in English poetry, but in many ways it continues the project of much of that poetry, even as it renovates the excavatory model favored by Heaney, Montague, and, in a different way, Hill. In turning to Eiléan Ní Chuilleanáin's poetry, I want to emphasize a very different strand of postwar place poetry. The supposed dearth of urban poetry by women has been examined by Peter Barry and others, and the pastoral tradition has been dominated by male writers, but it is not the case that contemporary women poets have avoided or ignored concerns of place and location. Most often, this results in poetry that either emphasizes domestic spheres as a counterweight to the kinds of public, open air places that tend to feature in poetry by men, or resists and rewrites pastoral tropes that gender land, earth, or nation as female. Both of these modes of feminist rewriting work to scramble the procedure by which the male/female binary reinforces and is reinforced by the array of false analogies mapped onto it, thereby short-circuiting patriarchal structures that feed off of such discursive shell-games. Eavan Boland, Carol Ann Duffy, Liz Lochhead, Medbh McGuckian, Nuala Ní Dhomhnaill, and Denise Riley have taken up this project with considerable force. Questions about the politics of space and the constructions of place have been crucial to the work of such poets, especially in Ireland, where gender differences were used to figure colonial relationships (Boland 1995; Batten 2003).

Ní Chuilleanáin, a professor at Trinity College, Dublin who was born in Cork, can be placed within this larger feminist tradition, and she has written powerful revisions of patriarchal structures and myths, most stunningly in "Pygmalion's Image" (1989). But it seems to me that she, especially in the context of this essay, is up to something quite different, and to conclude I would like to suggest that her small and important body of work contains a significant investigation into poetry's ability to represent location. Place, in Ní Chuilleanáin's work, constitutes a fungible, oblique node of entry or access within a network of routes constantly in process. Ní Chuilleanáin's poetry obviously contains a scopic drive, but one that does not work by superimpositions (like Fisher's), excavations (like Heaney's or Hill's), or cartographies (like Carson's). Nonetheless, her poems powerfully cultivate a different kind of spatial poetics, one that is all the more intriguing for being much less place-able.

Throughout her four primary volumes – *The Second Voyage* (1977, rev. 1991), *The Magdalene Sermon and Earlier Poems* (1991), *The Brazen Serpent* (1995), and *The Girl Who Married the Reindeer* (2002) – the places evoked, whether domestic, liturgical, or natural, become staging areas for spatial narratives. Reading Ní Chuilleanáin requires inhabiting a compressed, yet flexible lyric eye that travels "a knowing path / Twisting away" (1977: 5). Her texts' dense lenses contrast with the more torqued-out tendencies of Fisher and Carson. While Ní Chuilleanáin's major thematic clusters – feminism and female life, folklore and myth, monastic and religious life, ritual, architecture, and art – reveal a traditional poetic sensibility, her occluding narratives and local hermeticisms stage a critique of such traditional topoi. This is nowhere more apparent than in her demarcations of space and location. She does not necessarily tighten the focus or see "more" in her poetry than Fisher or Carson, but her particular way of forcing the reader to occupy the intricacies of the text's visual paths suggests a quite different kind of scopic drive.

"River, with Boats," from *The Magdalene Sermon*, exemplifies the spatialities that emerge within her taut lyric frames. After an opening stanza which clearly stations a female figure sleeping in a window-side bed where the "birds hop" and the "boats pass," a longer second stanza specifies what the woman can hear – "the hooters / Down there in a greeting" – and see – "a flash of the river, / A glitter on the ceiling / When the wind blows" and "the high branches of trees" on the opposite side of the river (1991: 23). We are watching the poet watching a woman in her riverside bedroom, and it would seem that the woman's bedroom overlooks the riverside scene (the hooters are "down there"). The first two stanzas outline an almost perfect ocular chain: the reader looks "down" upon the poet, the poet looks "down" and "in" upon the woman sleeping, and the woman "hears" down upon the hooters and sees across to the trees.

The final stanza, however, enacts a fairly significant perspectival shift. The scopic symmetry of the first two stanzas is upended by the third. The river, which up until now had seemed of moderate size, enlarges when we find out that at its "highest tide" the bedroom window is "blocked / By the one framed eye / Of a tethered coaster" (1991: 23). This "tethered coaster" might be a life preserver on the water, and the re-torqued perspective is clinched by the final two lines:

> And the faces of the mariners
> Crowd at the glass like fishes.
> (1991: 23)

The bedroom window has become a kind of porthole, and the commanding sensory vista of the first two stanzas has inverted: now the woman is watched by the mariners. A space of seeming comfort has been transformed into a bubble of surveillance. The reader following the lyric gaze is submerged along with the woman in the final stanza, and while a clear thematic point is being lodged about spectrality and gender, such a lodging only takes effect when the spatiality of the poem is capsized. The lyric gaze – both the reader's and the poet's – is short-circuited, or at least re-routed. The reading eye that has to turn upon itself to manage the final stanza's shift is a subtle and precise unrigging of poetry's scope: a critique of seeing from within the seen.

Ní Chuilleanáin's spatial poetics differ greatly from Fisher's or Carson's, but they are all skeptical of the ease of visuality. Postwar "poetry of place" – a term needing both evacuation and reinvigoration – is most powerful when it pushes hard against the places it represents and the spaces it constructs. The excavatory tendency among poets such as Heaney or Montague has come under strenuous and necessary critique for its presumptions and evasions, just as the scopic drive among all the poets mentioned here has been a continual site of anxiety. And yet both modes continue in much of the most recent and bracing place poems, such as Riley's *Excavations*, Muldoon's transatlantic metamorphoses, or Maggie O'Sullivan's linguistic re-carvings that so often engage the material of the natural world. As globalization continues to refigure the meaning of location and the texture of place, the space of poetry will absorb and refract such reconfigurations. Place will not dissolve into the virtualities of space, but location – as a constellation of forces, pressures, openings, borders, and passages – will become both more and less defined by its surface topographies. This incommensurable scenario, in which place will become both thicker and more placeless, is given a wonderful turn in the final line of Derek Mahon's "A Garage in Co. Cork": "We might be anywhere, but are in one place only" (1999: 131). The tug between the conditional and the present tense, as well as the friction between "anywhere" and "one place," signals the bifurcations implicit in our sense of location, and the contradictions that structure the space where we are.

Further Reading

Allen, Nicolas & Kelly, Aaron (eds) (2003). *The Cities of Belfast*. Dublin: Four Courts Press.

Bachelard, Gaston (1969). *The Poetics of Space*, trans. Maria Jolas. Boston, MA: Beacon Press.

Barry, Peter (2000). *Contemporary British Poetry and the City*. Manchester: Manchester University Press.

Davis, Alex & Jenkins, L. M. (eds) (2000). *Locations of Literary Modernism: Region and Nation in British and American Modernist Poetry*. Cambridge: Cambridge University Press.

de Certeau, Michel (1984). *The Practice of Everyday Life*, trans. S. Rendall. Berkeley, CA: University of California Press.

Hooker, Jeremy (1982). *Poetry of Place: Essays and Reviews, 1970–1981*. Manchester: Carcanet.

Jameson, Fredric (1991). *Postmodernism, or, The Cultural Logic of Late Capitalism*. Durham, NC: Duke University Press.

Kaplan, Caren (1996). *Questions of Travel: Postmodern Discourses of Displacement*. Durham, NC: Duke University Press.

Kirkland, Richard (1996). *Literature and Culture in Northern Ireland since 1965: Moments of Danger*. London: Longman.

Lefebvre, Henri (1991). *The Production of Space*, trans. Donald Nicholson-Smith. Oxford: Blackwell.

Massey, Doreen (1994). *Space, Place, and Gender*. Cambridge: Polity Press.

Tuan, Yi-Fu (1977). *Space and Place: The Perspective of Experience*. Minneapolis, MN: University of Minnesota Press.

Williams, Raymond (1973). *The Country and the City*. Oxford: Oxford University Press.

Chapter 11

Poetry and Religion

Romana Huk

The topic of this chapter may seem unnecessary in a book about writing after modernism. As quintessential modernist T. S. Eliot put it in 1932, more than a decade in advance of the date that frames this anthology, "for the great majority of people who love poetry, *'religious poetry'* is a variety of minor poetry" (1936: 96). The very term *religious poetry* suggests the secularizing effects of modernization since the Enlightenment; the Middle Ages would have found it tautological. Yet it is precisely its antithetical relationship to modernism that has, in highly revised versions, given religion a new and critical relevance for postwar poetry.

I need to unpack that statement rather quickly here, moving through an abbreviated consideration of everything from the renegotiation of Judeo-Christian orthodoxies to the recovery of ancient forms of mystical revolt to counter the modern era's invented certainties. Some forms of postwar religious revival are relatively predictable and reactionary; others coincide with the crises and opportunities of a postcolonial or devolving "kingdom." Still others offer so sympathetic a response to broader mid-century philosophy that they begin to resemble deconstructive theory. Taken together, these poetries evidence what Gianni Vattimo would, by the century's end, call "the return of religion in our culture" (1999: 25), or the dawn of a post-rational, "post-secular" age. Many poets in the first phase of the postwar period revived what Paul Fussell identified as modernism's myth-making impulse in response to historical crisis (1975: 131), and in defiance of the

Enlightenment's demythologizing project. But the second phase has conducted, in concert with the linguistic turn in philosophy, what maverick bishop John Robinson controversially advocated as "reluctant revolution" from within: the "demythologizing" of religion itself (1963: 11) at the risk of losing the plot, meaning, and way altogether in the dark wood of postwar history. Motivated by that history to construct a poetics in pursuit of otherness, and a theology based, improbably, on doubt and absence, recent poets have re-trod the *via negativa* with some rather surprising, post-postmodern results.

I

Like the Great War, which inspired many conversions, World War II proved a spiritual turning point for a host of writers. As Auden later suggested, Hitler's domination of Europe in the 1930s had signaled a decisive failure of human "reason," "liberal humanism," and secular progress as conceived by the Enlightenment's descendants (1956: 40). For Auden the recognition that, as he wrote in 1941, "the whole trend of liberal thought . . . has been to undermine faith in the absolute" (1941b: 50) demanded a return to absolute faith in God, an embrasure of purgative "myths and rites" and even of St Anselm's famous medieval formulation of *a priori* reasoning: *credo ut intelligam* ("I believe in order that I may understand," Auden 1941a: 31), because "absolute and irrational belief permits, because it goes beyond, the exercise and play of that most human of faculties, the reason that accompanies understanding" (Reeves 2004: 191, 189). In other words, reason must be used to get beyond reason – or rather, in Auden's new Kierkegaardian formula, "Christianity paradoxically requires the exhaustion of all reasonable explanations and a leap of faith into the unknown and unreasonable" (Reeves 2004: 189). Such reversals allowed Auden to relegate the Freudian and Marxist systems he had adapted in the 1930s to the status of "Christian heresies" (1956: 38), to be reabsorbed into the mysterious oneness of the same Christianity he had earlier found wanting as a systemic response to the modern world's social ills.

Some poets in the 1940s would take a more holistic route toward a reversal of the previous decade's "urge to make politics a secular religion" (Strong 1997: 155). Most interesting among them was J. F. Hendry, whose short-lived "New Apocalypse" forged links between surrealist, Freudian, Marxist, and mystical "New Romantic" visions.

Rejecting (as had Freud) "institutional" religion as the "neurosis of mankind" (1941: 155) and even as fascism's double, Hendry nonetheless argued that myth-making's "liberation of 'conative energy', of imagination, of religion" (in truer, "organic" forms) affords "emergence from group psychology" or "Hitlerism" (1941: 158). Yet Hendry also exhibits post-Nietzschian suspicions about language in his insistence that new instantiations of such "religion" must evolve through a permanent revolution among competing, "socially useful" mythologies, in an ongoing "process of breaking-down," applied "to state authority as well as to inner beliefs," themselves "submitted to be make-shift . . . and subject to constant revision" (1941: 165–6). Unlike Robert Graves, who felt that it was time for poets to oppose the "damned, illogical, faked, fifth-rate pseudo-mystery that [theologians had] made of religion" with "the *real* truth . . . in poetry" (Lloyd 1983: 118), Hendry did not merely substitute one set of mythologized beliefs for another. And unlike Dylan Thomas, palpably absent in the group's major anthology (perhaps because, as Seamus Heaney puts it, he "continued to place a too unenlightened trust" in language [1995: 144]), Hendry's own poems, like "Europe: 1939," would offer myth's fulfillment only at arm's length, by rechanneling complicit speech through the neo-surrealist, suffering body in wartime: "Their unbelief is death, and all these dead now walk up out / Of my speech of hands where love and living plead and bleed" (1941: 63).

But Hendry's proleptic argument for a Lyotardian trade of historical *grands récits* for provisional *petits récits* was largely ignored in his day, overwhelmed by responses like Auden's return to the *via negativa*, to negative theology's "exhaustion of all reasonable explanations" in order to glimpse what lies "beyond." An implicit response to the many calls for poetry's silence after Auschwitz – made most famously by Theodor Adorno and George Steiner – Auden's (like Samuel Beckett's and, later, Jacques Derrida's) paradoxical postwar choice to write against writing finds echoes in other kinds of cultural work for the remainder of the century. But conceptions of that unnamable "otherness" that lies beyond reason and representation differ. And Auden, like Eliot, and most of the late-modernists treated below, would ultimately if ironically return to traditional models for understanding and even universalizing it – to *"religious* poetry," as Eliot defined it – when teetering on the abyss into which their constructions must fall.

Whereas the young Eliot pursued an understanding of Indic religions in admiration of their fearlessness in "looking into a dark and vertiginous abyss" rather than at a comforting image of godhead, "[h]is mature religious faith . . . represented a retrenchment from his Eastern interests, a step back from the 'abyss' of heretical and bewildering points of view into the discipline of a single faith, dogma and practice" (Kearns 1987: 162, 139). Such resolutions illuminate his *ars poetical* assertion in *Four Quartets* (1942) that writing must offer "An easy commerce of the old and the new, / The common word exact without vulgarity, / The formal word precise but not pedantic" (1991: 207–8). The poem's clarity of construction – despite the mystical processes of negation that underpin it – allows its troubling backdrop of war to be absorbed, ultimately, into the timeless peace of Little Gidding, an Anglican religious community that survived destruction by the Puritans to resurrect in the eighteenth and again in the nineteenth century. Likewise, the later Auden's negative theological processes ultimately resolve themselves within Anglican liturgical frameworks, as in "Horae Canonicae," structured by the canonical hours, or daily prayers specified by canon rule. Yet Auden steps a fraction further than Eliot toward the negation of poetry's solutions – even insisting on the impossibility of this poem's subject, Good Friday, for poets: "Christmas and Easter can be subjects for poetry, but Good Friday, like Auschwitz, cannot" (1974: 168). As Gareth Reeves suggests, illuminating the ultimate use to which Auden would put his earlier psychoanalytic tools,

> the larger implication is that this is what happens every day of our lives: we do not, we cannot, because it is "so horrible", think about Christ's martyrdom, even though, or indeed because, it informs everything we do and are. (2004: 193)

This ancient, unspeakable pain and guilt underwrites *all* speech and action in Auden's Christianization of Freud's theories. The poem is therefore set in the canonical hours of any day, as well as those of Good Friday and each subsequent year's (impossible) commemoration of the same. The heart of the sequence, "Nones" (pronounced "knowns") – referring to prayers sung at 3 p.m., the time of Christ's death on the Cross – begins by undoing itself (as its title punningly suggests), announcing "What we know to be not possible" (1991: 634). The poem is littered with departures from Auden's earlier poems, from "a room, / Lit by one weak bulb, where our Double sits / Writing and does not look up" (1991: 636) – in short, from his own *doppelgänger*, because all writings and selves will be turned inside out when that "meaning" that "Waits for our lives" (1991: 635) prevails. Yet Auden gestures silently toward an ultimate order in established ritual even as the writing negates itself. He only shifts "Lauds," sung at sunrise, to the end of the poem, so that he, like the Eliot of "East Coker," may find his end in his beginning.

In similarly updated versions of modernism's epiphanic spatializations of time, numerous postwar poems also collapse the age's violence into an eternal "now" where the crucifixion, the war, and the Holocaust merge – so that redemption, however mysterious, is made possible again. Among them is "Still Falls the Rain," Edith Sitwell's 1942 piece about the London Blitz:

> He bears in His Heart all wounds . . .
> See, see where Christ's blood streames in the firmament:
> It flows from the Brow we nailed upon the tree
> Deep to the dying, to the thirsting heart
> That holds the fires of the world.
>
> (Sitwell 1979: 272–3)

So strikingly different from her irreverently experimental work of the 1920s, Sitwell's suddenly popular poems of the 1940s have "an unexpected gentleness and compassion, marking what one can only describe as conversion" (Bennett 2001: 194). Sitwell's reference to the damned Dr Faustus's vision of Christ's blood flooding the four corners of the sky suggests her sense of complicity in Europe's world-engulfing theater of war and her kindred vision of Eliot's fires and purgation. Yet these images that Sitwell weds, with phrases like "[d]eep to the dying," to poems by her frequent wartime guest Dylan Thomas, demonstrate the powerful, universalizing impulse that would briefly subsume the "New Apocalyptic" and the orthodox within the same camp. Even Kathleen Raine – best-known as mid-century poetry's most vocal proponent for the eclectic, ultimately neo-Platonic, universal tradition of the *Sophia Perennis* that she and her set (including Thomas Blackburn, Jeremy Reed, David Gascoyne, and Vernon Watkins) inherited from Egyptian hermetic and Indic traditions as well as classical Jewish Kabbalah, Plotinus, and various other Gnostic sources – converted to Roman Catholicism in the 1940s. Before renouncing her conversion, she took Sitwell's topics to heart, as in the poem "See, See Christ's Blood Streams in the Firmament" in *Stone and Flower: Poems 1935–43*, a poem that demonstrates much of Raine's "perennial philosophy" concerning the veil of life's illusions and, beyond it, the unrepresentable divinity glimpsed in nature's Pythagorean correspondences and geometries. Yet in this war poem, such illusions figure in a cosmic crucifixion, with Raine's

Anglo-Saxonish neologisms underscoring the poem's connection to the anonymous medieval Christian poem "Dream of the Rood" and signaling its return to that era's propensity for heroic myth-making.

Such works also illuminate the all-embracing vision with which David Jones began and encircled his late epic, *The Anathemata*. The poem's meditation on "Fore-Time," including the whole of ancient and modern Western history, is folded into instantaneousness, into the moment of the Catholic priest's "lift[ing] up an efficacious sign" (1952: 49): the host at Mass, simultaneously signaling Christ's incarnation and his redemption of time. Jones's title itself functions as a sign of the "impossible" unity we find in Auden's "Nones" and in Eliot's *Quartets*. As Jones explains, the word "anathemata" means "something holy" in the Old Testament and just the opposite in the New Testament (1952: 27–8). Jones nonetheless departs significantly in his neo-Thomistic views of writing and the writer. Indeed, some have suggested that this particular kind of British Catholic writing perpetuates an "Elizabethan tradition of recusancy" that engendered allegiances to the Church abroad and an "aware[ness] of European thought to a degree unusual among Anglo-Catholic and English protestant" writers (Ward 1983: 48). Certainly Jones and his modernist Catholic brethren were students of the work of Jacques Maritain, the French theologian and art critic who interwove the Church's late-nineteenth-century Thomist revival with the modern philosophy and science it was meant to trump. Because Thomism stresses "that sense-experience forms the starting point for all . . . knowledge, and that in this life [man] cannot know anything, except what is divinely revealed, without the use of images" (Copleston 1965: 167) and "through a repercussion of his knowledge of the world of things" (Maritain 1953: 114), the *via negativa* offers no path to its artists. Indeed, Maritain would vilify the extremes of "pure art," condemning abstraction that reaches fully out of the world for what he called "experience of the void" (1953: 137).

Such ideas fostered Jones's sacramental world view, his conviction that "the Catholic Church commits its adherents . . . to the body and the embodied; hence to history, to locality, to epoch and site, to sense-perception, to the contactual, the known, the felt, the seen," as he put it in "A Christmas Message" in 1960 (Ward 1983: 32). As he wrote in 1971, "[t]he insistence that a [post-impressionist] painting must be a thing and not the impression of something has an affinity with what the Church said of the Mass" (Williams 2005), by which he means that the Mass functions through *anamnesis* to "re-present before God an event in the past [like the Last Supper] so that it becomes *here and now operative by its effects*" (1952: 205). Jones's poem, like the Mass itself, becomes "'a recalling of all the dead', 'of all times and places'" (Hooker 1989: 267). Claiming that such regard for the "particular genius of places, men, trees, animals [with] yet . . . a pervading sense of metamorphosis and mutability" was further born of a deeply Celtic persuasion in his work (Williams 2005), Jones argued that the poet must "re-*present*" (in Poundian fashion), rather than *represent*, things and history as dynamic, interconnected, and always in excess of what we see and understand, like the raised bread of the host.

Even the material word "anathemata" signals excess, suggesting the fullness of the cultural text should opposing definitions be refolded. It was broken in two (Old Testament, New) at the Incarnation, Jones explains, and daily "at the point of the Mass called the Fraction," the framing occasion of his poem. To be regathered in that chalice (an image that features importantly in Jones's painting as well), the enormous shifting body of this work struggles to reunite its broken parts – though it necessarily remains "fragments of an attempted writing," as the book's subtitle insists, because the Mass's mysterious act of recalling all things is effected by divine intervention only. Jones's work, unlike that of the later Eliot and Auden, has often seemed "so experimental as to repel most readers" (Ward 1983: 134) because it takes a different route around modern rationality. Rather than *thematizing* negation from a position of transcendence, this kind of form is *doing* something from *within* words, is itself a messy "act" not of purgation but of anamnesis – accumulative and celebratory but fractured in acknowledgment of its worldly limitations. Things obscured by partial or imperial vision, like Jones's Welsh history, must be (impossibly) refolded into cultural memory for its wholeness to appear. Welsh memory and language are therefore imaged in Heraclitean rivers, like the Dee (in Welsh, "Dyfrdwy," which "some have interpreted . . . as meaning the 'divine water'" [Jones 1952: 69]), allegorically reunited with land masses by the end of the poem. There, questions about "Who primordially separated / this simple and fecund creature," water, from the land, like the halves of the host, are made to divulge their own answers, when we *remember* that the "who" of such interrogatives in the poem's final litany-like structure had earlier served as relative pronouns, in glacially accumulating lines that identify the "loosener of the naiad girdles" as "He whose greater signs are '*per creaturam aquam*'" – the God who "made water to be the foundation" of the "greatest sacraments" (1952: 234). As we hear a last description of the priest's framing act we understand Jones's project, like his, has been one of administering a sacrament, of *re-presenting* the "otherness" that underwrites the wholeness of history and "the word."

In this Jones is deeply related to the greatest of Scottish modernists, Hugh MacDiarmid, who (in a quotation of Jones) also attended to the "Celtic cycle that lies, a subterranean influence as a deep water tumbling under every tump of this island" (Hooker 1989). In MacDiarmid's case too, "an encyclopedic inclusiveness of detail" pervades the late work, along with deepening spiritual convictions (Gish 1984: 180). But MacDiarmid's growing ambition to return to the authoritative vision his countryman Hendry had qualified, to demonstrate "the *absolute* coherence of the writer's intellectual quest" for "the international of the spirit" (Gish 1984: 206, my emphasis) folds difference back into sameness – linking, for example, the vibrantly revisionary, mystically oriented, *fin-de-siècle* Eastern Orthodox philosophy of Vladimir Sergeevich Soloviev with Scottish innovativeness, through the "organically evolving" nature of the Orthodox Church's "free theocracy" (Williams 1997: 501). Soloviev's figure of Sophia, echoing various forms of Gnostic and Jewish mystical thought, represents the spilt divinity who nonetheless takes atemporal part in a transcendent unity, maintaining "being" as well as "becoming": a dynamic of opposites, rhyming with that essentialized "Caledo-nian anti-syzygy" or self-contradictory energy which both negates and unifies and which MacDiarmid had made central to his poetics. Envisioning such correspondences *between mythologies of contradiction* led him to what may be the grandest imaginable project of modernist transcendence, far more ambitious than any discussed above, achieved by climbing the Scottish hills in *Dìreadh I* (1974) to an international purview that could then be negated in order "to soar beyond conventional wisdom" *and* the Pascalian abyss: "So, we scale the summit and leap into the abyss, / And lo! we have wings" (1978: 1,174). Fantastically combining accumulative and apophatic procedures, MacDiarmid best exhibits the unresolved clash of desires apparent in mid-century work with his documentation of all that "becomes known" in unknowing, an oxymoronic mythology of negation's fruits.

II

Such overweening, late-modernist metaphysical speculation was not an option, however, for poets just beginning their careers after the war. Patricia Waugh suggests that "mythic vision" began by the 1960s to seem "a Fascistic invocation of art to redeem politics in a seductive vision of reparative return to the pure and whole" (1989: 74). Or, as Thomas Merton, the Trappist monk, poet, critic, and friend of artists from Ad Reinhardt to Ian Hamilton Finlay analogously suggested, "in an age of concentration camps and atomic bombs, religious and artistic sincerity will certainly exclude all 'prettiness' or . . . cold, academic perfectionism . . . [and] be characterized by a certain poverty, grimness and roughness which correspond to the violent realities of a cruel age" (1953: 164). Hendry and company had considered what such art might look like, but the new generation saw few differences among these various spiritual initiatives given the mythologizing impulse those projects had shared.

This is perhaps one reason that the formally conservative "Movement" of the 1950s looked suspiciously upon belief in general, rejecting what it lumped together as the mystical departures of poets like Thomas, Gascoyne, and Hendry, even linking their quasi-surrealist experiments of the early 1940s to the ideological excesses of the "Red Decade" before them. Movement poets preferred to think of theirs as an age of *The Less Deceived*, as Philip Larkin's 1955 collection would name it, its fear of any sort of flight of emotion or vision justified by Donald Davie in his famous "Rejoinder to a Critic": "Be dumb! / . . . How dare we now be anything but numb?" (1983: 74). Loosely defining themselves against the American "New Romantics" (who were beginning to get high on Far Eastern and other "foreign" belief systems), they also dismissed those at home who – like Ted Hughes, Penelope Shuttle, Peter Redgrove, even the early J. H. Prynne – would dabble in shamanism. Rather than questioning modern rationality, or interrogating language as rationality's tool, the Movement sought to erect an Augustan clarity of speech as a *barrier* against mid-century irruptions of the irrational. What Davie would refer to, in ironically biblical language, as the new "chastity in poetic diction" was born of a deeper sense of complicity in Europe's ideological excesses than Americans could possibly have registered, alongside an awakened sense of social morality and responsibility (Davie 1952). The latter resounded in famous poems of the period, like Larkin's "Church Going," whose punning title implies that "superstition, like belief, must die" even while the socially binding (and chastising) *structures* of culture remain, because "[a] serious house on serious earth it is" (Larkin 2003: 59). Such emphases (which found lighter expression in the dozens of *Church Poems* [collected in 1981] by future Poet Laureate

John Betjeman) transformed the work of poets like Stephen Spender and powered the philosophy of influential writers like Iris Murdoch, driving spiritual poetry (whether conservative *or* experimental) perpetually back down to earth, into the realm of the social.

And yet Waugh makes a corollary statement: "It had become evident that Enlightenment reason could [not] . . . contain the human impulse toward transcendent meaning: more than ever from the sixties, it seemed imperative that literature address such absences" (1989: 71). Indeed there are few postwar poets who do *not* return to religion at some point in their career. Davie himself would move toward a late poetry "intent on expressing . . . a firm sense of religious belief" (Schirmer 1983: 129), attributing his initial attraction to the eighteenth century to the fact that it was, in his view, "a religious century" (Davie 1982: 164). In this he resembles C. H. Sisson, whose many poems with religious themes, like "An Essay on God and Man," welter in times less principled and rational than Alexander Pope's, when Descartes' "cogitat has only been a wince" (1984: 156). Deeply affected by his residence in the 1950s in Ireland, Davie came to think it a place that had not "been secularised" (1989: 12), one that might prove a conduit for the return of Britain's religious belief, primarily through the work of Austin Clarke, whose religious poetry (reviled by the likes of Beckett) often explored the medieval, monastic world of the Irish Romanesque (Martin 1993: 51). Yet Davie continued to argue with familiar Movement fervor that "the only language proper for [religious poetry] is a language stripped of fripperies and seductive indulgences, the most direct and unswerving English" (1981: xxix), and the only proper attitude an all but dumb submission to our earthly state. In "Having No Ear," he expresses gratitude for God's "giving, in default / Of a true ear or of true holiness, / This trained and special gift of knowing when / Religious poets speak themselves to God, / And when, to men" (1990: 352). The resignation to a plodding thud of repetition in the final line substitutes "having no ear" for the "stillness" Auden was listening for in "Horae Canonicae." Davie's own comical poem by the same name pictures, in *his* sub-section entitled "Nones," a figure "[s]oggy with gin" thinking it "hardly worth / Living in a world so full of changes / And revolutions" – in other words, Auden himself, whose "dozy," disillusioned, and irresponsible thought is deemed "hardly 'prayer'" (1990: 298).

Murdoch follows suit in her philosophy of the period, stressing the insufficiency of individualized vision as well as the dozy kind of mysticism that becomes self-negating "masochism": "[I]s the *via negativa* of the will . . . the only or most considerable conscious power we can exert?" (1998: 356). Longing for what she calls a "practical mysticism," she despairs of finding answers in an existentialist thinking that she considers "nothing more than a form of romantic self-assertion . . . or else something positively Luciferian," even parenthetically speculating that "[p]ossibly *Heidegger is Lucifer in person*" (1998: 226, 358–9). Murdoch exemplifies her era's Movement-like suspicion that such "models of consciousness [like Sartre's] were abstractions, dogmatic mythologies of closure," as opposed to usable faith in "ordinary being." Through her conflict we might also understand the work of Elizabeth Jennings, a Movement poet but one so profoundly interested in mysticism that she published, in 1961, a book called *Every Changing Shape: Mystical Experience and the Making of Poems*. Yet in it she argues mightily that rather than undermining human knowledge, mysticism yields "patterns" of "universal application" that can indeed be communicated in verse (1996: 29–30). Though her woman-centered reading runs in a subversive sidebar throughout this text, going so far as to declare intimations of Wisdom in medieval mystical works to be "God herself," Jennings's self-contradictory mini-revolution from within Movement confines also continually asserts that the best mystics never stray beyond "orthodox theology." Language emerges as the "unfailing instrument of truth" (1996: 38) when, as in "Little Gidding," "the common word" is chosen to communicate mystical epiphany so that the poet's ends become our beginnings, ensuring that we always already arrive where we started. Though in supple, largely free-verse pieces like "Let Things Alone" she suggests the need to "learn it all over again, / The words, the sounds, almost the whole language / . . . With shock, then dark," in most of her rigorously formal *Collected Poems* she suggests just the opposite: that "ideas cannot come / As barren notions" and that tradition's "hardest creeds" are what she "need[s] // . . . for [her speaker's] heart to leap to God" (2002: 297).

But popular theology of the time was readier to embrace the linguistic turn and its emergent deconstructive tendencies, as evidenced by *Honest to God*, the 1963 volume by John Robinson, Bishop of Woolwich, which sold 300,000 copies in two years. As Waugh writes, Robinson "offended orthodox Anglicans by suggesting that the time had come to reconceptualise God in metaphors of depth or ground rather than those of transcendence" (1989: 65). He was one of the first clergymen to deconstruct the "homely literality" foisted on the Bible through "crudely" spatializing metaphors of a "God 'up there'" (Robinson 1963: 3):

Suppose belief in God does not, indeed cannot, mean being persuaded
of the "existence" of some entity, even a supreme entity, which might
or might not be there, like life on Mars? Suppose the atheists are right
– but that this is no more the end or denial of Christianity than the discrediting of the God "up there", which must in its time have seemed
the contradiction of all that the Bible said? Suppose that all such athe-
ism does is to destroy an idol, and that . . . such a God – the God of
traditional popular theology – *is* a [Freudian] projection, and perhaps
we are being called to live without that projection in any form.
(Robinson 1963: 6)

Drawn from Heideggerian reconsiderations of the divine – as "not a
projection 'out there', but manifest in every particular 'thou' encountered through love" (Waugh 1989: 66) – Robinson's thought reflects
the shift toward new forms of near-atheistic questioning that would,
paradoxically, identify the next generation of postwar "religious" poetry.

Matching the Movement in concerns about morality, social justice,
and ethics, the precursors of that next generation nonetheless
complicated such imperatives with interests in existentialism and
phenomenology that had converged with political and linguistic
philosophy in the "linguistic turn," rendering their demythologizations
of religion even more radical than Robinson's. Whereas their contemporary Ted Hughes would reject Movement conservatism by
burrowing back into pre-Christian England like a latter-day shaman
in order to re-"create" language like a new age Adam (even conducting
experiments with Adamic language in *Orghast*, his collaboration with
theatre director Peter Brook), these poets were cut off from such vatic
ventures by an increasing sense of being mired in history's atrocities,
enforced through poetry's own medium: words. Among them was Ian
Hamilton Finlay, one of the world's best-known concrete poets, who
wrote that "consecutive sentences are the beginning of the secular"
and defined the concrete poem as a "a model of order . . . set in a space
full of doubt" (Clark 1995: 136). Also among them is Basil Bunting,
who repudiated the "[h]ierarchy and order, the virtues of the neo-
Platonic quasi-religion" that he felt "were prime virtues . . . to Yeats,
Pound and Eliot" (1989: 3). Bunting had no use at all for neo-Platonic
theories; his sense of form arose from the opposite: *de*-transcendence,
and attention to particulars, the unresolved complexities of the everyday. He downplayed any comparison between his most famous poem,
Briggflatts (named for a Quaker hamlet and meeting house in Cumbria),
and Eliot's "Little Gidding," modeling his speaker's progress after
that of the lowest of the low, the "quietest attitude" (pun no doubt

intended) of the poem's "slowworm." Its undiscriminating and lingering perspectives offer "Lindisfarnian illuminations," bright embroideries *upon* words, rather than conventional meanings, that interlace in his sonata (as he referred to it) but offer no visions of ends or beginnings. Instead, its coda veers into the unknown, and "[b]lind we follow / rain slant, spray flick / to fields we do not know" (2001: 79).

In postwar deconstructive philosophy, the opening up of such gaps or breaks within culture's tightly woven syntax offered hope for an exit from the linguistic imbrications of history. Some poets recognized, long before Derrida, the relation between the two. Thus we find that in Geoffrey Hill's poetry political crimes and devotional practice meet in the secular sentences of history even as their collision opens a way out of *aporia*, toward an unimaginable "atonement" that paradoxically depends upon the lack of linguistic or aesthetic resolution for its potential. As he puts it in *Canaan*, "I say it is not faithless / to stand without faith, keeping open / vigil at the site" (1997: 9), attentive at the empty tomb of otherness "sentenced" and crucified by historical overdeterminacy, waiting for, by analogy, what Derrida described as "*l'invention de l'autre*." Hill recently distanced himself from both Eliot and the Movement by arguing against Christopher Ricks' celebration of *Four Quartets* for wielding "confidence" in the "good sense" and "generous common humanity" of "clichés": "The residual beneficiaries have been Larkin and Anglican literary 'spirituality', two seeming incompatibles fostered by a common species of torpor" (2003: 158–9).

Hill has summarized his own more restive poems as "a heretic's dream of salvation expressed in the images of the orthodoxy from which he is excommunicate" (Haffenden 1981: 98). Like Stevie Smith (with whom he shares more than most realize), Hill might best be described as a "backslider as a non-believer," drawn to the beautiful clichés of culture and worship but "disenchanted" (as Smith put it in her controversial poems of the 1960s) with the discrepancies between enchanting myths promulgated by doctrine and doctrine's entanglement with discourses of power and violence (Huk 2005: 292–5). As Hill puts it in "Annunciations," "The Word has been abroad, is back, with a tanned look / From its subsistence in the stiffening-mire. / Cleansing has become killing." Or, in an attempted address to the Virgin,

> Nor is language, now, what it once was
> even in – wait a tick – nineteen hundred and forty-
> five of the common era, when your blast-scarred face
> appeared staring, seemingly in disbelief,

shocked beyond recognition, unable to recognize
the mighty and the tender salutations
that slowly, with innumerable false starts, the ages
had put together for your glory
in words and in the harmonies of stone.
But you have long known and endured all things
Since you first suffered the Incarnation:
Endless the extortions, endless the dragging
In of your name. *Vergine bella*

(Hill 1998: 28)

Though Hill's speakers often address the beloved divine with seeming intimacy and confidence, they constantly collide with the "extortions" of a history whose "false starts" at "saluting" the holy are caught up, even in such words, in the violence that altered language itself, the poet suggests, by 1945. The poem continues with another such start by "dragging in" that "name" yet again above, dramatizing its complicity in a co-option that it simultaneously exposes and evades by breaking up false "harmonies [written] in stone."

Jon Silkin, Hill's one-time student and colleague at Leeds, and one of the few poets writing from an explicitly Jewish perspective just after the war (alongside Elaine Feinstein, Denise Levertov, and others), also breaks up the seeming harmonies of both poetry and history that owe their "generous common humanity" to exclusions of otherness, whether repressed or openly advocated, as in Eliot's later essays. He does so most famously in "Astringencies," which recalls the fact that in neighboring York "there has been / No synagogue since eleven ninety / When eight hundred Jews / Took each other's lives / To escape christian death" (1980: 27), or forcible conversion. The disavowed or forgotten continues to shape both thought and action in these poems, as in Auden's: "All Europe is touched / With some of frigid York, / As York is now by Europe" (Silkin 1980: 28). Silkin had learned much from Hill, whose "idea of history was harder, grittier and more painful than polished like myth" of which, he recalls, he had become "wary" (conversation with the author, 1988).

Yet Silkin's demythologizing poems, which nonetheless maintain *devekuth* (or adhesive practice) by borrowing the Old Testament's parallel forms, unfold very differently, in moment-by-moment, tactile movements through the world. "In Judaic terms," Silkin writes, "although the soul may be nucleated by God's essences, humanity can only experience these through the body, that is, the total being" (1980: 52). Interestingly, Jewish, neo-Thomist, and feminist theologies (among others) began to converge postwar, in part due to their recuperations of the bodily experience that both religious and philosophical archives of knowing had for so long bypassed; its otherness to linguistic perception, both as perceiver and as perceived, displaces the naming, classing, distancing, and disavowing of relation between self and other that language enables and indeed promotes. Yet Jewish traditions have long eschewed the Christian mystic's, "personal" union with God in order to prioritize the *first* experience of humans, as Jewish philosophers like Emmanuel Levinas understand it: intrinsic responsibility to the presence of the other. For Levinas, ethical relation is the starting point for apprehension of what transcends it, rather than isolated experience. This near-rhymes with the postwar thought of Murdoch, whose impatience with what she saw as existential self-centredness mirrored Levinas' dismissal of philosophy's "alchemy by which otherness is transmuted into sameness by means of the philosopher's stone of the knowing ego" (Putnam 2002: 17). Levinas' "Abrahamic" thought privileges diasporic experience instead – movement, like Bunting's, into the unknown.

Silkin's poems *enact* such movement, shifting constantly into proximity with "somethings" like his own mute, incomprehensible, and short-lived child in perhaps his most powerful poem, "Death of a Son." Refusing translation of otherness into sameness *or* sublimity, he writes: "Something has ceased to come along with me / Something like a person: something very like one. / And there was no nobility in it / Or anything like that" (1980: 7). Proceeding via indenting lines that inch forward by also stepping back, lines filled with deictics that point to difference without naming it, Silkin's work confers a dignity upon the unknown that approximates his relationship with the unnamable divine:

> This was something else, this was
> Hearing and speaking though he was a house drawn
> Into silence, this was
> Something religious in his silence
>
> (1980: 7)

Not positioned, like his modernist forebears, to construct ultimate eschatological "meaning" from such silence, Silkin's speakers, in works like *The Peaceable Kingdom*, move tentatively (if not without Hill-like, self-reflexive humor) into forms of caring relation instead. In "A Death to Us," for example, the death of a fly on the poet's page becomes allegorical in its suggestion of the "infinite responsibility," as Levinas would have it, one bears to another: ". . . his purpose became, in dying, a demand // . . . So I must carry his death about me / Like a large fly, like a large frail purpose" (1980: 4). Like Bunting, Silkin encounters the very large only in the very small; but more than that, the "demand" here is that caring witness become action, become physically "carried" as an impossible, oxymoronic, "large frail purpose," indefinite but transformative in its inversion of familiar hierarchies. In effect, the purpose of much postwar work that rejects the solutions of Eliotic or Movement aesthetics is to reject the familiar for forms of uncertainty that invite *difference* in as incremental revelation.

III

Hill rebukes the late century "religious" poetry of others in his recent book, *Style and Faith*: "one recognizes that the general drift of the tendency has been towards an effusive post-Symbolism . . . which coy and prurient exercises in the 'confessional' mode have further dissipated" (2003: 139). Though harsh, this assessment might win agreement from those allergic to the increasingly self-serving (therefore "prurient"), vague (and thus vaguely Symbolist, without Symbolism's goals) professions of faith in countless recent poems, many of them testifying to neo-Romantic experiences with a now uncapitalized nature. For Hill, such dilutions and anachronisms constitute a misconnection of sellable "style" and rigorous spiritual questing, a "fundamental idleness impossible to reconcile with the workings of good faith" (2003: xiv). Those who *have* pursued the mid-century project of rigorously rethinking "religious poetry" have tended to come from outside the narrower authorized tradition, matching style and faith in increasingly complicated, often highly innovative forms.

Among them are postcolonial writers, both those who arrived during the postwar's waves of immigration and those later born in the UK. The first generation's demythologizations usually turned on pluralizing *remythologizations* of the Christian story alongside older African ones, as in the work of Wole Soyinka – well known as a playwright but largely forgotten as a poet. In *Idanre* (whose title refers to a town and natural sacred site in Nigeria), Soyinka, like Derek Walcott, connects his culture's complex pantheon of gods to that of the Greeks. Yet his title poem's re-encounter with the creation myth of the Yoruban god Ogun resolves with an "All hail" to not only "Saint

Atunda," the "First revolutionary" – who smashed his master, the first god, into the bits that became the Yoruban pantheon – but also to "the rest in logic / Zeus, Osiris, Jahweh, Christ in trifoliate / Pact with creation, and the wisdom of Orunmila, Ifa / Divining eyes, multiform // Evolution of the self-devouring snake to spatials / New in symbol, banked loop of the 'Mobius Strip'" (1967: 83). Understanding spirituality as necessarily caught in the realm of the symbolic – producing "kinks" in the strip's otherwise self-destructive, independently generating links – Soyinka foregrounds linguistic faultlines in his work, reminding us here and again in his notes that his is "only an illusion but a poetic one, for the Mobius strip is a very simple figure of aesthetic and scientific truths and contradictions" (1967: 87–8). In this tradition of linking together "othered" mythologies and dominant ones to highlight the potential truths and illusions in both, one might also place poets like James Berry, Grace Nichols, Jean "Binta" Breeze, and Benjamin Zephaniah. And on the other end of the spectrum, harnessing deconstructive fervor to Catholic sensibility, is David Marriott, whose formally radical poems interrogate not only the gaps in secular sentences but also the lost place of blackness in the "Names of the Fathers," or theological/patriarchal discourse that disavows its fear of racial as well as sexual otherness. Self-blessing or "crossing oneself" begins with the words, "In the name of the father." But in this poem, where "we are born knowing / that in my father's house darkness can't be forgiven . . . / Exile is a story not not to be passed on . . . ," the gesture becomes one of crossing oneself out, even though the double negative suggests the inevitable inscription of the disavowed within dominating mythologies.

Like him, Irish poet Brian Coffey incorporates fewer localized references, history, and mythic framings than the other postcolonial, devolving, or northern poets thus far discussed, focusing instead on the operations of symbols and all that they have obscured. A student of Maritain's in the 1930s, Coffey demonstrates a clear connection to Jones, his near contemporary, if far less modernist confidence in the "efficacious sign." His late epic poem, *Advent* (1975) – "the *Briggflatts* of Irish poetry," as J. C. C. Mays declared on its jacket – begins with Jonesian desire to access a sacramentalized world, laying its "prestress primal slime" and "saurian ease" alongside its accumulating history and mythologized memory, but can only interrogate such things from within a self-replicating house of words made "darkness solid," where even Mallarmé's "chance" is only "dice dead" (1986: 5). Certainly Coffey avoided easy myth-remaking in part because the Irish revival had already made such pursuits nearly *de rigueur* in popular poetry like Clarke's – so much so that Samuel Beckett famously suggested Coffey, Denis Devlin, and Thomas MacGreevy were the only hope Ireland had for the development of a modern poetics (1984: 70). Beckett welcomed these poets' "awareness of the new thing that has happened, . . . namely the breakdown of the object, whether current, historical, mythical or spook" and our resultant "rupture in communication." He also suggested that "All poetry, as discriminated from the various paradigms of prosody, is prayer" (1984: 68), meaning perhaps that poetry substitutes "objective" writing with solicitous *action*. Admitting "break-down of the object" in writing permits what Derrida calls a "quasi-transcendental condition" of open-endedness, a condition that deconstruction shares with the "yes," the "come" of prayer (1993: 32) – avoiding the location of the divine in the sphere of predication, of prayer within the payback economy of discursive ends.

Advent makes clear that it is actually an extended prayer. It ends in the isolated line "so be it," a translation of the Aramaic "Amen" (1986: 42). Rather than striving, like Jones, to reconnect parts of the cultural text, Coffey longs for further break-up. The first scene, filled with "so many sleepers" responding through "hard habit" to Beckettian "sudden garden bell[s]," offers an Eliotic vision of upside-down broken towers with no tarot card to reveal apocalypse, but only a world of reified secular sentences, a prison-house of language that prevents any "incoming of the other":

> From tumbled citadel one stared at air
> shaped by walls   rigid like frozen speech
> Unsafe unhappy chance   promised no joy no egress
> it is constraint to narrowness it's patience
> with need with sentence   no angel calls here
>   (1986: 5–6)

The "need" for knowable shapes, safety and "narrowness" – the "sentence" above, imprisonment by pun – pre-empts desire, a Blakean "Want want want want want" (1986: 11). By the poem's end, an exit from the near palindromic sentences of history ("Slaves with tyrants beget tyrants with slaves") is only "for us surely / where friend gives greatest gift." It is an *act*, recalling the axiom about "no greater love" than in giving one's life for one's friend. The suggestion is that the poet *gives himself*, or gives over his own ending as well as language's rational categories, in a Christ-like act that "saves [us] from bondage" (1986: 41). This allegorically sacrificial invocation of 'otherness' in prayer signals a radical unknowing or open-endedness quite unlike Eliot's confident reconciliation of opposites, fire and rose.

Similarly, John Riley, a Leeds poet of Scottish heritage, drawn like MacDiarmid to Eastern Orthodoxy (converting just before his early death), re-interpreted its mystical ideas as offering no clear leap into transcendence. Michael Grant quotes from St Basil in the "Afterword" to Riley's *Selected Poems*: "We know our God from His energies, but we do not claim that we can draw near to His essence" (1995: 138). Eastern Orthodoxy's depiction of divinity in iconography eschews "knowable" realism for abstraction, its goldwork attracting divinity as energy or *effect* instead: light, the invisible illuminator that renders the world fleetingly intelligible, both physically and metaphysically. Aligning his work with the early avant-garde's rethinking of the finished, timeless art-object, the "verbal icon," Riley sets himself the task of giving form to *presently* evolving "energy" in what he called "apophatic icons" (1980: 38): poems that acknowledge the materiality of their medium by disturbing the realistic illusion. Such poems, he wrote, "reveal the brokenness and imperfection of human utterance" in order to make "the Word, the Logos, . . . participate in the death and resurrection" (1995: 134).

Riley's best-known work, "Czargrad" (whose title calls up Constantinople and other doomed utopias), begins by dying, as a writing, in the solitary confinement of reiterating textual/temporal structures, of "book[s] of hours, meanings, hierarchies" (1980: 155). Unlike Auden but like Coffey, Riley images such structures as a darkened house in which his speaker writes until the next arrival of the irritating "bloody sun" (or son), a crucifixion image which disrupts "words / hissed out in avoidance of error" (1980: 159) and folds them into its necessary death. The poem *advocates* encountering "error" in all its senses – from that of "wrongdoing" ("the stink of colossal crime / still on West Europe") to that of its oldest denotation, "wandering," what Derrida calls "desert errancy" (Derrida 1999: 188) – to encounter what has been impeded by such processes of correction. The poem becomes one long (erring) locution, its opening, "to get to know," succeeded by fragments beginning with "that." The last fragment, "that all that is done," reverberates with paradox; it both remains incomplete and affirms Christ's last words, "it is finished," suggesting that such understanding builds only through continued "doing" and wandering into what the poem's last words offer with no end-stop: "next field."

Like neo-Thomist Coffey, Riley places us "always in human circumstances / no angels and prone to forget / we can work only from point to point" (Coffey 1986: 41). The increasing confluence of theologies in poetic approaches to the divine is in part due to their agreement upon a postmodern humility that has labored to connect deconstructive apophatics with non-transcendence. Yet many of the most interesting "*post*-postmodern" innovations have tended to come from women writers who re-enter the realm of (sexist, inhospitable) mythology as postcolonial writers have done, by pluralizing it. Pauline Stainer, for example, the maverick of the "New Generation" poets of the late-1980s, "flouted Larkin by dipping voluptuously into the European myth kitty" (Morley 2003). In her best-known poem, "The Ice Pilot Speaks," Stainer adapts yet another ancient poetic trope, beyond erring, for twenty-first-century work: weltering (like "The Wanderer" in one of the oldest Christian poems), though her speaker does so on a now-frozen sea of mythic imaginings that both provide and threaten her survival. She plays Arctic explorer on this textual map frozen like Coffey's house but negotiable by her form of oxymoronic, neo-empirical "Protestant mysticism" (Duncan 2003). As she puts it in "Frequencies," we receive many competing mediations at once, none fully "true" or "real" yet *all* constitutive of the reality we make, like alchemists, from what we touch. The poem's third section, a palindrome entitled "Mirror-Canon," updates Bunting's sonata forms, invoking the complications and repetitions of nature with *this* musical form that strictly replicates by mirroring (its punning title recalling the strict religious rule of "canons"). In sync with post-modern suspicions about romantic access to the "real," the poem's mirrors displace its subjects into figures of speech that endlessly weave and reweave frameworks of perception, so that even Christ in its central line is nested in metaphor: "love as a bundle of myrrh between the breasts": a gentle image arriving through others, like "tapestries flow[ing] like plainsong / in the cleansing river" into "a window embrasure . . . refracted / through [his] halo" (2003: 79). Stainer is interested in how even divine subjects refract metonymically, often violently, over time and within everything from our ecclesiastical to military "embrasures" (a pun on crenels in a military wall). Still, she leaves the divine in the palindrome's pivotal line because, as her first and last lines optimistically have it, "There is some kind of exchange always."

It may be that, like their postcolonial counterparts, women poets tend to see the history of "knowing" not so much as a linear progression to impasse but rather as a crumbling bulwark against what has *been* active and potentially enabling all along, though "othered" within it. Both Stainer and experimental poet Wendy Mulford return to ancient stories or seeming "still-lives," like the enigmatic "Lady and the Unicorn" tapestries at the Musée de Cluny, illuminated from other perspectives – or, as Stainer puts it in the poem above (rewriting Coffey's image of the death of Mallarméan chance), "light plays on the still life with dice." Stainer's title *The Lady and the Hare* recalls these tapestries, which Wendy Mulford also contemplates at the heart of her poem "La Pitié-Salpétrière" (originally a prison for prostitutes and a poor-house for women and other outcasts, later an insane asylum, and now a hospital). Mulford's Lady is, as in the tapestries, connected to the five senses, the body – long associated with femininity, as opposed to "intellect" – but also with Ahasver, the figure who, by legend, refused to help Christ carry the cross and became "the wandering Jew." His "crime is the first crime" and everyone's, projected upon him; his "sentence" (and everyone's) to be caught in the linguistic entrapments of a falsifying logic that cruelly scapegoats otherness to save itself: "Sentenced of a sentence. In the doom of repetition." "May the Lady release us," the poem prays (2002: 143), alluding to the sixth tapestry that shows her giving back her jewel (read by many as the gift of the senses). Mulford reinterprets this sacrifice not as election of virginity but as *giving back life* (like that woman in Christian history, Mary). Here, in the "grey morning," it means skirting the sentence with an alternative story, open-ended and sensually rich like the *millefleurs* tapestry, told to children who are "deiparous" (bearing, or bringing forth, a god) (2002: 147). As a result, "[t]he lady and the unicorn awake" (2002: 148): representation becomes action, "delivered up" with "Cagot love" or release of otherness from *inner*-exile. Theirs is movement past what both reification of myths *and* asceticism have reduced to grayness through refusal of the gift, *already given*, of uncontainable life.

What I think my own narrative maps is a trajectory that begins with mid-century negation and closes with twenty-first-century erring and excess, both of which seem revelatory of what postmodern philosophy, too, has acknowledged it longs for: the "possible impossible." The late-modern choice of adapting ancient mysticism's rejection of representation to its own negative way, a path of rejection and transcendence of the postwar world, paralleled in uncanny ways the deconstructive path blazed by philosophers with their "linguistic turn" from the road of enlightened progress. Since then, such transcendent positioning for either poets or philosophers has come to seem precisely like the sort of myth-making that requires excision from the surprisingly resilient *activity* we name "belief."

Further Reading

Lawson, Peter (2006). *Anglo-Jewish Poetry from Isaac Rosenberg to Elaine Feinstein*. Edgware, Middlesex: Vallentine Mitchell.

Lazer, Hank (2008). *Lyric & Spirit*. Richmond, CA: Omnidawn.

Maritain, Jacques (1953). *Creative Intuition in Art and Poetry*. New York: Pantheon.

Mellors, Anthony (2005). *Late Modernist Poetics: from Pound to Prynne*. Manchester: Manchester University Press.

Robinson, John (1963). *Honest to God*. London: SCM Press.

Waugh, Patricia (1989). *The Harvest of the Sixties: English Literature and its Background, 1960–1990*. Oxford: Oxford University Press.

Williams, Rowan (2005) *Grace, Necessity and Imagination: Reflections on Art and Love*. Harrisburg, PA: Morehouse.

Chapter 12

Institutions of Poetry in Postwar Britain

Peter Middleton

Poetry may be, in the words of Hugh MacDiarmid's encyclopedic poem *In Memoriam James Joyce*, "human existence come to life" in "the flower and fruit, the meaning and goal, / Which won all else is needs removed by the knife," but as the metaphor suggests, the fruit or flower depends on the plant on which it grew even if the roots and leaves have to be cut away to be displayed or eaten (MacDiarmid 1978: 757). Literary criticism of poetry tends to treat the poem as if its roots in publishing, the funding bodies that fertilized its growth, the readership that supported it, and the other institutions that made it possible could all be cut away without losing any of the significance of the poem itself. This idealization of the poem is usually visualized as a black text printed on the white page of a book of related poems by a single author. Critical analysis and literary history are composed in terms of the cognitive and affective decisions that make this facture possible, interpretations based largely on the critic's introspective attention to the readerly responses that are assumed to be typically elicited by its hermeneutic codes. In MacDiarmid's poem the speaker goes on to narrate a walk through woodland in which he sees beautiful trees still uncut and the imagery invites reflection on the implications of tearing the poem away from its sites of production and reception. Although MacDiarmid himself is merely being playful with traditional metaphors in order to heighten awareness of the historical contexts of poetry rather than making a point about the material cultures of poetry, these images are helpful for understanding the relation between poetry and the institutions that support it. The poem published in a discrete collection of one author's poems remains the gold standard of poetic achievement even though the important literary transactions have increasingly taken place off the page. The typical page poem in a book by a leading postwar publisher of poetry such as Faber & Faber is reassuringly similar to the poetry of the past several hundred years, and this appearance of continuity may be the most important feature of the printed poem, almost its reason for being. Behind the page are other practices that mark a deep divide between the early Enlightenment and the world of late modernity, and actually make this page less intelligible as an artifact than its centuries-old precursor. To understand why, we need to look at what has happened to readers, writers, and the dissemination of poetry during the past fifty years.

Scenes of aesthetic innovation and the generation of the poem's semantic repertoire often take place at other sites than the book-length collection of poems: the new communications media made possible by the transistor; education's classroom pedagogies and textbooks; performance by the author either live, on radio, or on a recording; and the transformations of publishing that have been driven by evolving technologies (ranging from affordable hand-operated machines such as the stencil duplicator and the desktop computer to the latest digital print-on-demand systems that can produce perfect bound copies in any run required). Transistorized technologies required new forms of content and created networks of listeners and readers with a very different relation to the text than those constructed by the institution of the book. The 1944 Education Act enfranchised succeeding generations who previously would never have had any higher education, as well as vastly extending the numbers taking a General Certificate of Secondary Education (GCSE) in English at sixteen and Advanced Level examinations at eighteen, and stimulating further, higher, and adult education in English as well. These students required poetry for study. Philip Larkin's poem "Church Going" could be described by Anthony Thwaite as "a poem that has been much chewed over in W.E.A. [Workers Educational Association] classes and that sort of thing" (Thwaite & Silkin 1963: 11). A tough economic reality creates the landscape in which all these institutions operate to make poetry as a public art possible. Book and magazine sales are not sufficient to pay for the costs of production, let alone to pay adequate salaries to poets, and the result has been a growing dependence of poets, poetry publishers, and the organizers of public readings on public funding.

Government intervention in poetry production has increased steadily throughout the period as the Arts Council, the British Council, and local government agencies have taken over the responsibility for financing poetry. These organizations cannot subsidize just anything they like; they have policy targets to meet. In 2005 the Arts Council, according to its website, had to ensure that all grant funding met some of these following five objectives: "supporting the artist, enabling organisations to thrive, not just survive, championing cultural diversity, offering opportunities for young people, and encouraging growth." Poetry that obviously meets several of these developmental criteria is therefore much more likely to flourish than work whose rationale cannot easily be paraphrased in such terms.

We can best trace these transformations in poetry brought about by the developments in communication media, education, leisure industries, and print technology that have given form to the economic forces at work, through study of the long biography of specific poems. Below I shall follow the publication history of three representative poems in some detail. Although there are some lesser areas of recent institutional practice that these poems do not readily reveal (such as the dependence of poetry on the markets of the art world evident in the history of concrete poetry, poetry's alignment with the popularity of other types of participant theatre such as stand-up comedy, and the importance of the political campaigns of new social movements as sites for the creation of poetry audiences with strong if partial investments in specific types of poetry), taken together their histories exemplify the main economic and social contexts that have shaped recent British poetry.

Andrew Motion's poem "The Dying Race" is an apparently autobiographical poem, in the first person, confronting memories of the house where he grew up with speculations about his father's regular drive to the "humid ward" in the hospital where his mother lives. Its first version was first published in the 65-page issue of *PN Review* no. 3 in 1976. *PN Review* had just become an A4 large-format magazine with double columns under the joint editorship of Donald Davie, Michael Schmidt, and C. H. Sisson. Looking back on the magazine about fifteen years later, Schmidt, who eventually emerged as the main editor, was adamant that this was not a "little magazine" nor a "magazine of record or a mere anthology of new poetry" but rather "a forum for new writing and for the exchange of ideas: a meeting place, a stimulant, a catalyst for writers and readers" (Görtschacher 1993: 408). It is well printed in a small clear typeface that projects

245

intellectual seriousness and a commitment to using every inch of space, suggesting that there is much work to be done in supporting poetry. Sisson's editorial explains that they are trying to avoid politics and concentrate on the "less popular" aim of "giving good circulation to good writing, and the discussion of ideas which get less than their share of exercise in other fora" (Sisson 1976). The magazine was subsidized by the Arts Council (*PN Review* has been one of the best funded clients of the Arts Council's Literature Department; when Schmidt was asked whether *PN Review* could be self-supporting, he said that it would need to treble its subscription list since it had very few sales in the shops [Görtschacher 1993: 407]). Funding alone made the magazine possible, and Sisson admits in his editorial that "our problem is therefore with an audience which is not yet there or – less ambitiously – with one which is just beginning to appear, here and there, in a scattered way" (Sisson 1976: 1). Motion's poem sits in the right-hand column alongside the final paragraphs of a review by Michael Hamburger of an anthology of German Democratic Republic (GDR) poetry. This issue continued the international scope of the new magazine: in addition to Hamburger's discussion of GDR poetry, there was an essay on Russian poetry, a translation by Samuel Beckett of the French poet Alain Bosquet, and reviews of Eugenio Montale and George Seferis. Motion's poem could be read as part of this company, making its range of significance much wider than the middle-class Home Counties family history it might have appeared to offer in another context. Here the mention of "derelict pill-boxes" and even the way his memory shows him the house as if it were lit by lightning both evoke a world still haunted by war.

The poem first appeared in book form in *The Pleasure Steamers* (1978) published by Carcanet, who decided to emulate the austere page design of Faber & Faber that had become the norm for the presentation of poetry, though the result was better designed than the average Faber volume. Credits are given to magazines such as *Agenda*, *Outposts*, *Poetry Book Society Supplement*, *PN Review*, *Stand*, *The Honest Ulsterman*, *The Listener*, and *The Times Literary Supplement* – a collection of the leading venues in which to publish poetry. Throughout the postwar period publication in leading poetry and literary magazines has been a necessary step toward achieving a book contract with a commercial publisher, usually coupled with extensive performance. The book also records another achievement that, at that time, was more unusual than it is today, the award of a poetry prize, in this case the long-established Oxford University Newdigate Prize of 1975 for the poem that makes up the middle section of *The Pleasure Steamers*. Today there are many poetry prizes of all kinds and winning them has become another route to a book contract, although the common pattern is not based on the restriction to a specific constituency as in the case of the Newdigate but to invite anyone to apply and charge an entry fee that will help fund the award. The most prestigious prizes can attract tens of thousands of entries, testifying to the popularity of writing (though not necessarily of reading) poetry. Motion's win pointed to the future. He became one of the most influential figures in British poetry – editor of *Poetry Review* in the 1980s, then Poet Laureate in 1999.

Motion revised the poem for this volume. Magazine publication can be a trial run of a poem, and the poet can respond to comment from readers as well as to his or her own reflections consequent on seeing the poem more objectively once in print. He deleted various phrases and lines, shortening the poem overall from five to four stanzas. Out went the inadvertent pun on his father's surname ("you moving / invisibly"), and so too did the recognition that "your wife" is also the narrator's mother. Most significantly, the poem is presented as the first in a series that comprises the final section of the book, devoted to memories of his mother. These poems document years of visits to his comatose mother and conclude the book with the poem "The Legacy," in which he attributes his ability and permission to write to her: "I sit down to write / at the desk she willed me" (Motion 1978: 58).

"The Dying Race" is a poem that works hard to elicit a reader's trust that the words are honest and the content truthful. It is immediately striking for its apparent lack of intimacy with the parents; it uses disconcertingly anonymous pronouns and circumlocutions (his father is only identified as "you," and his mother is "your wife"). Poems about parents had already launched other careers, notably Seamus Heaney's, and have been a staple of the dominant form of postwar British poetry, the personal lyric. The problem of establishing the right to be heard in public culture is negotiated through an allegory in which the poetic persona establishes its authority by enacting its filiation in terms that heavily stress authenticity by drawing on credible details of personal memory, and this authenticity then underwrites the extensions of the poet's discourse into other areas of judgment and assertion. Most authors of the personal lyric have written such parent poems, a prevalence that suggests that poetry as an institution now lacks authority in its own practice, and that neither the recognizable appearance of poetic form, nor the use of poetic diction, nor the legitimacy provided by a format or publisher can wholly make up for this. Authority may have to be grafted on to the poem and, as in the case of Motion's poem, much of its legitimation will have to be the internal work of the poem's content.

"The Dying Race" later appeared as the first poem in a Faber book, his *Selected Poems: 1976–1997* (it proudly announces Motion's laureateship in later printings). The poem had been revised again. The house is no longer "elegant" and is reached by a "lane" not a "drive," taking out any risk of seeming to boast about his family estate at the moment when a new Labour government had been elected on an egalitarian platform after a long period of Conservative government. Line breaks were made more effective. A "selected poems" is a mark that a poet now has a substantial body of work deserving the advertisement of a trailer of highlights for potential newcomers and a useful summary for existing devotees. Motion's representation on the Faber & Faber roster of poets tacitly emphasized his new eminence.

Faber & Faber dominated the publication of postwar British poetry. By having most of the leading modernist poets on their list, and many of the poets (mostly outside the modernist tradition) who had established major reputations since, they have largely defined what constitutes good poetry. Their uniform house style, which reached its apogee with the cover design of a repeating pattern of monochrome small double "f"s in various colors on the paperbacks of the past decade, strongly projected the impression that this was not just ordinary poetry, this was Faber poetry, poetry of a reliable type and circumscribed mode, above all a poetry of high standards rooted in, but having grown beyond, modernism. The economics of their business depended on steady sales of poetry by Eliot (himself one of the directors until the 1950s), Ezra Pound, Wallace Stevens, W. H. Auden, and other modernists. These leading modernists, followed by leading 1930s poets and a good cross-section of the new modernist poets of the 1940s, had all been taken up by the firm, and the result might have been a publisher with the same sort of profile as New Directions in America, one based on a commitment to the intellectual ambitions of avant-garde poetics. Eliot himself, however, began moving away from literary radicalism during the 1940s, and as a director of the company most involved in poetry editing slowly took the publisher in the 1950s in the new direction of a growing conservatism heralded in the poetry world by the emergence of Robert Conquest's *New Lines* in 1956. In 1951 Faber still had a considerable roster of modernists alongside some more formalist poets: George Barker, Roy Campbell,

Lawrence Durrell, William Empson, W. S. Graham (who would become the only postwar modernist to go on publishing new work with the publisher), Robert Lowell, Edwin Muir, Louis MacNeice (a substantial list by him), Norman Nicholson, Herbert Read, the remarkable Welsh modernist Lynnette Roberts, Stephen Spender, Henry Treece, and Vernon Watkins. A sign of things to come occurred when Basil Bunting offered them a poetry manuscript only to have Eliot turn it down, suspending Bunting's career as a literary figure for a decade – rejection had harsh consequences for some. Over the next two decades they would take on Ted Hughes, Thom Gunn, Sylvia Plath, Seamus Heaney, Paul Muldoon, Craig Raine, Andrew Motion, and Wendy Cope, and move wholly clear from the publishing of newer modernists. Gael Turnbull, J. H. Prynne, Tom Raworth, Lee Harwood, Allen Fisher, Maggie O'Sullivan – these and other major poets would have to look elsewhere because their avant-garde leanings excluded them from acceptability.

Faber & Faber have been influential in another way too. The page design of their poetry books has had a pervasive effect on the way poetry is read because they created a high degree of uniformity that, despite occasional minor changes of font or the addition of modest ornamental capitals for the first letter of each poem (in Seamus Heaney's *Death of a Naturalist* for instance), has set a norm for the appearance of poetry on the page. They have used two basic formats, a taller one for hardbacks and a shorter paperback dimension, formats that closely approximate the standard size of fiction hardbacks and paperbacks. These were books designed for the mass-market bookshop and were not going to alter flexibly to match the design ambitions of open field poetry or visual experimentation. The layout of Motion's *Selected Poems* demands that "A Dying Race" begins so far down the page that three lines are left to linger alone on the reverse, where the Carcanet edition had neatly placed the entire poem on one page and still managed to use a slightly larger, more readable font. The holding over of these final three lines ("the hair from her desperate face / I might have discovered by now / the way love looks, its harrowing clarity") to the following page in order to fit the format tacitly conveys the message that the publishing format overrides any demands the poem itself might make. This standardized format became a key signifier of the well-made poem. The Faber page is relatively short and will not normally accommodate more than 22 lines of poetry after the title, which is set well above the following text, and does not readily allow for long lines, stepped margins, or more than the most simple visual

patternings, and works best with the internal rectangularities of stanzaic verse. When Heaney writes one long verse paragraph in the title
poem, "Death of a Naturalist," the result is messy in appearance. The
Faber page presentation foregrounds a functionality that directs the
reader to infer that the words should be treated as semantic vehicles
rather than contemplated as aesthetic objects.

New and cheaper technologies of printing have emerged from the
continuing technological revolution of the twentieth century that
enable poets and readers to sidestep such hegemony and produce
magazines, pamphlets, and books that do not require the resources of
a commercial publisher and often not even an arts funding subsidy,
and in doing so allow for ambitious modes of composition and presentation. A typical example is provided by a poem by J. H. Prynne,
"L'Extase de M. Poher," in which skeptical reflections on psychoanalysis
and historical materialism are so rapidly spliced with questions about
urban landscape and its production of garbage that the poem appears
to be the work of what it mockingly calls a "steroid metaphrast" or
over-stimulated reviser of texts.

Prynne's books were published by small independent presses for many
years (even if he had wanted, Faber & Faber would not have published his work given their unwillingness to publish any but first-
generation modernist poets). The words in the first published version
of this poem gleam unevenly with the ink that has pooled as it bled
through the stencil on a hand-operated duplicator used to produce a
stapled A4 magazine, *The Anona Wynn* (its title the name of a singer
and radio personality of the 1950s). "What person could be generalised
/ on a basis of 'specifically' sexual damage," (Prynne 1969) asks the
text, almost becoming a concrete poem at this point because the word
"damage" is damaged to the point where the two "a"s are nearly solid
blots and the entire word heavily over-inked. Such contingent imper-
fections become part of the reading experience of such publications.
Stenciling gives the text an unprinted informality that suggests
improvised production driven by an urgent desire to communicate with
the readership quickly (the magazine's title appears to be written in
red felt tip pen and the magazine has no page numbers), giving such
productions an affinity with both classroom materials and political tracts.
Such facture conveys the tacit message that this is work the publishers
regard as significant enough to volunteer their time and money for:
poetry outside the marketplace. Compare this to the way the text
now appears in a collected edition published by Bloodaxe, a press partly
financed by the Arts Council (Northern Arts), a collection printed on

a paper whose commercial bleached whiteness makes the first show-ing look dirty, and whose sharp typeface is functional and professional.

In between these two showings "L'Extase de M. Poher" appeared in what is surely Prynne's most beautifully printed book, *Brass*, a large-format volume published by Andrew Crozier's Ferry Press, a small press entirely operated (and presumably financed) by Crozier that also published words by Robin Blaser, Steven Jonas, John James, and a few others, including the proprietor. Prynne's inclusion in this series signaled that he too belonged in such carefully chosen company, just as the gathering of poets in *The Anona Wynn* was a deliberate gather-ing of the circle of poets who read and were read by Prynne himself, what one might call the first readership of the poem. Prynne was very conscious of issues of readership arising from forms of publication, as he reveals in a somewhat pessimistic letter to Crozier that was published in a stapled unbound A4 poetry magazine, *The English Intelligencer*, around 1967. Prynne says he values the work of the poets in the magazine but wonders at the apparent lack of commonality.

> What do all these damn neat craftsmen or rowdies *do* with their lives, how do they get on with it, in heaven's name? Do they read? or think, or scheme for the possible world? Who *are* the people as a figure of insistence, as they could go at it, necessary & honourable? . . . I had thought that perhaps something might *move*, if there were perhaps some initial measure of trust, so that the community of risk could hold up the idea of the possible world; we could approximately and in some sense or other mostly be *in* it, or moving in part across the same face, giving out something and who am I to care how it is done? Get back the know-ledge, the purities, the lightness of language, whatever it is. For nothing's more absolutely certain, as I know you at least know, than that no single person could now carry at this in a way likely to be interesting. Some adept little heroism will spring up sooner or later, I suppose, wasting his birthright in the pride of doing it all for himself. But why, after so long, cannot we try to live inside it, a common and undesperate matter, rather than nurse it up intimately within the single thread. (Prynne 1967: 189)

These are questions that go to the heart of the issues involved in publishing poetry in Britain. Different modes elicit different responses and even readerships, yet all committed poets, says Prynne, want not just to be read passively (as a diversion or entertainment) but for their work to encourage transformative action. What the poets need to recognize is that such desired consequences can only be achieved through cooperation. This is a poet's view of what Theodor Adorno says about the best modern lyric poetry, that when it is at its most individual it is "most deeply grounded in society" (Adorno 1991: 43).

Brass appears to set aside all such doubts in the brassy confidence of its large-format volume, which has a deep red cover with just the title in gold. No author's name is to be seen until the book is opened. Ferry Press printed an edition of 250 copies, a number that sounds small unless you know that this is about the number of copies that any poetry book by a relatively unknown poet is likely to sell. There is good anecdotal evidence that poetry sales in the UK for ordinary books of poetry run at between two and three hundred copies irrespective of whether published by a leading trade press or a small independent publisher. Thick paper and a generously scaled version of the Renaissance typeface Garamond all give *Brass* something of the look of an anonymous eighteenth-century poetry pamphlet. The book's design also had a more recent genealogy in the books of Black Mountain and San Francisco Renaissance poets in the USA, ranging from the Jargon editions of Charles Olson's *Maximus Poems* and Auerhahn Press books published in the Bay Area in the late 1950s and early 1960s, to the more recent UK fine editions produced by Cape Goliard and Fulcrum Press between 1965 and 1973. Between about 1965 and 1974 poetry publishing flourished briefly in Britain and showed what was missing when publishing became over-standardized. These publishers recognized that the quality of the paper, the size of the page, the choice of typeface, and the design of the page all contributed to the meaningfulness of the poetry. Cape Goliard's edition of Charles Olson's *Archeologist of Morning* has pages the scale of those in an art book, uses a thick textured paper, and can accommodate lines as long as sixteen words and the staggered margins of open field and projective verse. Fulcrum's edition of Lee Harwood's *The White Room* (1968) was printed in two editions, a trade edition and a collector's version in 100 copies "on grey glastonbury antique laid paper" signed by the author. Many publishers of poetry had found that the way to profitability was to create a special collector's edition alongside a more affordable trade edition, using more expensive paper, elaborate binding, an author's signature, and sometimes holograph material too. Ferry Press only produced the one edition of *Brass* but probably calculated that high production values would pay for themselves by attracting collectors as well as poetry readers. *Brass* was making a brassy statement by its very appearance, implying that the poetry belonged in the company of the leading avant-garde American and British poets, and also carried on a long poetic tradition reaching back to eighteenth-century satirical verse.

After *Brass* the poem next appeared in the first collected edition, produced by Anthony Barnett and his small independent press, Agneau 2. This is an edition that shows many signs of its limited budget yet manages to create an impression of high seriousness and to reveal the extent of Prynne's body of work. Looking back over these four showings of the poem, it is possible to see the implications of the production values by looking at the way each publication chooses a different solution to the problem of presenting a poem that extends over two pages. The first version chooses to divide the poem after the line "your right thumb. Freudian history again makes," giving the reader a sense of slight arbitrariness, though the play on Freudian readings of the thumb is made appropriately prominent. *Brass* makes the page cut in the poem with the entirely cryptic line "a/c payee only, reduce to" but then the next page begins with the line "now   what" (the two words are separated by a space equaling about three missing words), as if the poem were making a new start. In Anthony Barnett's edition the poem occupies a double spread and comes into its own as a readable text as a result, and this time he breaks ingeniously after the "now   what" (the two words are separated by a wide space), further underscoring the way Prynne's poem dramatizes an internal moment of radical uncertainty induced by the thought of the monetarization of social relations. Now what will the reader find over the page? In the current trade edition from Bloodaxe these solutions are forgotten, and the poem breaks for a turning of the page much further down the poem at the line, "or grass etc, hay as a touch of the," a line that does not appear to have been chosen with any conscious purpose as the seam between one page and the next. The poem is subordinated to the overall aim of an economic assemblage of the texts without any investment in the integration of textual semantics and design values.

What is necessary for Prynne's poem to be readable? In addition to the construction of bibliographic codes that will enable readers to infer its meanings with satisfying complexity, the poem also presupposes a reader with a university level education in literature. It expects the reader to want to decode its glancing allusions (to wonder who M. Poher was, for instance – Alain Poher became the interim French president for three months in 1969 after the resignation of Charles de Gaulle) and to recognize its aesthetics of rapid montage as having a modernist genealogy. The following passage from the poem not only tacitly instructs its readers, almost certainly sending them to the dictionary to find out the meaning of "metaphrast" (a translator who transposes verse forms or turns prose into verse) and reference books on steroids or entomology, it also assumes that readers will be familiar enough with various philosophies of history and theories of culture, sufficient to pick up the metaphoric argument. The poem also specifically reflects on the whole question of what a poem needs to attempt if it is not to become consoling entertainment in a culture where poetry is no longer "instrumental" to the knowledge economy. It cannot take for granted that its audience will simply watch its channel:

> No
> poetic gabble will survive which fails
> to collide head-on with the unwitty circus:
> . . . . .
> we are too kissed & fondled,
> no longer instrumental
> to culture in "this" sense or
> any free-range system of time:
> 1. Steroid metaphrast
> 2. Hyper-bonding of the insect
> 3. 6% memory, etc
> any other rubbish is mere political rhapsody, the
> gallant lyricism of the select, breasts & elbows
> (Prynne 1999: 162)

The phrase "steroid metaphrast" is indexical of the poem's dilemmas. Can the reception, the metaphrasis of this verse into the reader's prose, be helpful in the manner of the remarkable curative properties of steroids, or will there be damaging side-effects as the poem hints? The poem doubts its own capacity to effect its communicative and analytic aims. Susan Stewart's observation that in a poem "every formal feature is . . . a social-historical feature and at the same time makes possible links and adaptations between and across social and historical contexts" (Stewart 2002: 252) points in the direction that a critical response might develop. Such disjunctive surfaces and impeded referentiality are the understitching of a dominant pattern of verbal communication from which most hegemonic poetry diverts attention.

Since the publication of the poems by Motion and Prynne, arts funding has become even more pervasive and the mission statements of the main organizations have become unavoidable. This is particularly clear in my third example of the workings of the institutions of recent UK poetry, Lavinia Greenlaw's poem "Guidebooks to the Alhambra." Greenlaw has established a reputation as a poet interested in history and science and this was very much on show when she published three poems in the "New Generation" issue of *Poetry Review* in 1994. "New Generation" was an enterprise to raise public awareness of new poetry that was organized by a committee of poets, publishers, book-sellers, and funding agencies, who chose twenty poets from a list of over a hundred and then promoted their books heavily in bookshops and the mass media (even alongside pop music on BBC Radio One). It worked. Many of the poets have gone on to become powerful figures in the poetry world. No independent publishers were involved, and no modernist poets were on the panel. One judge, Michael Longley, sounded a note of uncertainty about the direction of this effort, saying: "The publicity has so far played down what I enjoy most in many of the poets: tense formality, learned knottiness, abstruse vocab-ularies, strange noises. I'm not sure that I want poetry to be the new rock 'n' roll" (Longley 1994: 52). It is all the more striking in the face of this concerted publicity to be told by one of the organizers, Peter Forbes, the editor of *Poetry Review*, that "only one key institution has played a significant role in the rise of the New Generation (besides this magazine, of course): Bloodaxe Books" (Forbes 1994: 6). Such unwillingness to recognize the power of state institutions of arts fund-ing and education for the maintenance of poetry is widespread and probably helps their ascendancy.

Greenlaw's poem "Guidebooks to the Alhambra" is one of three she published in this issue of *Poetry Review*, and it appears on what seems a crowded page after the clean spaces of the books and magazines dis-cussed earlier. The top of the page has the words "New Generation Poets" in white caps on a black banner (every page bears this title as if it were a logo), and the title of the magazine appears at the bottom of the page. Introducing the selection of poem is not a simple name as in the other magazines I have described, but an elaborate news-paper style page giving a long biographical and critical note, a personal statement, a list of three favorite books of poetry, and a personal note. "I don't know where poems come from," she tells the reader, "Now I've moved back to within a mile of where I was born. I need more sleep" (Greenlaw 1994: 101). This provides a strong frame for read-ing the poem's opening lines as authentic confessional autobiography (rather than, for instance, a poem about the sleep of reason or political apathy, or the elaboration of a fictional conceit):

> Things change, become home and we must leave them.
> What do you want? An untouchable sleep
> in which I cannot touch you. This heat
>
> (Greenlaw 1997: 9)

The introductory note further prepares the reader by saying that "Greenlaw's sensitivity to *change* is her finest quality." As a result of this critical steer it may be difficult to perceive other themes in the poem, such as the oblique threats of violence made by the speaker as she recounts guidebook stories of adultery and infanticide to a second person we assume is her lover. "My tongue hesitates on the delicate erosion / of your shoulders and lower back," she tells him, and this hesitation of erotic caress and articulation is haunted by the dangerous grandeur of the palace. This poem offers itself as an overheard intimacy between two lovers, and the effect is to circumvent the question of poetic audience that so bothered Prynne by creating the illusion that there is no theatricality here, that our presence is not registered by the lovers whose exchange we witness, as the speaker addresses her lover. We are given an image of love in our time that claims, despite the artifice of the speaker's poetic conversation, to be an authentic photograph of actual lovers in the act of kissing and fondling. The public sphere turns out to be composed of private worlds of memory and intimacy.

*   *   *

These three biographies of poems that have made some mark on recent literary history all manifest the effects of the straitened economics of poetry production. Poets cannot earn enough from publication and have to augment their income from other jobs, typically in teaching, writing for the media, or arts management, and many augment their income by extensive live performance (some poets now manage a modest income from regular visits to schools, libraries, and local festivals of literature, where they run workshops as well as reading their work). Most publishers cannot run poetry lists without subsidy of some kind. The result has been twofold: the growing importance of national bodies disbursing government funds to support publishing, performance, and arts education, and the proliferation of independent small presses reliant on various combinations of cheap printing and the patronage of owners or subscribers. The deep divisions between modernist and non-modernist poetry that we can see even in these three examples are partially sustained by these economic conditions that then play out in the institutions of the media, education, and performance, and in struggles over funding. (Peter Barry's *Poetry Wars* [2006] chronicles the sometimes bitter conflict over what sort of poetry should appear in the Poetry Society's Arts Council funded magazine *Poetry Review* and the long cultural memories it left behind.) Poetic composition has been pushed in specific directions: toward shorter self-contained poems permeated by authorial presence in the form of emotional display and personal history as well as a performative rhythm and visible poeticality; and toward experiment with modes that signify negation of these values or toward the use of visual and performative elements that signify an originality that can justify the relatively expensive investment of unsubsidized time, labor, and materials.

All three of the poems I have chosen require some education in the reading of poetry, and for almost all postwar readers this has occurred initially at school. The 1944 Education Act made universal free education available to all children up to the age of fifteen, and subsequent investment in sixth-form and higher education beginning in the 1960s greatly widened the possible readership of literature. The teaching of English Literature was burdened for most of the period by the ambition to teach a heritage defined in largely conservative terms that undervalued contemporary writing and especially international writing, which until at least the 1980s was considered a corrosive influence on the traditional pieties of English culture expressed in its literature. Iconic in this regard was the failure to teach any literature after 1832 in Oxford University until the syllabus was reformed at the end of the 1960s. University teaching of English remained resistant to the teaching of contemporary writing, especially poetry, and this meant that whereas departments of music and the visual arts took it for granted that modernism and avant-garde or experimental aesthetics played a central role in their fields, literature departments remained resistant to what was widely derided as sterile intellectual elitism or alien continental traditions (French poetry has surprisingly had very little influence on British poetry despite its geographical proximity).

Education provides a distinctive market for the larger poetry publishers. In addition to teaching anthologies, schools buy large quantities of a tiny handful of specific poetry books that are "set" for national qualifications in English taken at sixteen and eighteen. At any one time there are a handful of syllabi for these assessments, and so if a book by Philip Larkin or Ted Hughes is chosen it is guaranteed an enormous sale and will be imprinted on thousands of youngsters as typifying modern poetry. Look through *The Nation's Favorite Poems* (Jones 1996) compiled from a BBC series and you will see very few contemporary poems, and those by Hughes and Larkin. Almost all the choices are poems taught at school several decades ago. This anthology contains no explanations from readers as to the reasons for their choice, but a somewhat similar, although less widely circulated, collection published in support of the charity Shelter Cymru, *Voices at the Door* (Burt & Jones 1995), which asked well-known Welsh figures to choose a favorite poem, gives useful insight into the influence of education on the readership for British poetry. Glenys Kinnock, the wife of the former Labour Party leader, tells us that Wilfred Owen's "Strange Meeting" is her choice because "this poem still moves me, and it ensured that when I first read it, at the age of fourteen, I would never have any illusions about the nature of war" (Burt & Jones 1995: 149). Peter Hain, a minister in the Labour government, also chooses a poem by Donne because of his school memories. When the readers do choose contemporary poetry, it is either because it is Welsh poetry that is felt to sustain their sense of national identity, or because, as John Puzey explains when he chooses a poem by John Hegley, "Eddie Don't Like Furniture," "I cannot divorce writing from the writer. I need to have some empathy with the outlook and the 'persuasion' of the poet in order really to enjoy the poetry" (Burt & Jones 1995: 206). Emotional empathy ("this poem still moves me") and identification are the main aesthetic and ethical values, as Sheenagh Pugh (herself a poet) explains: "It makes me feel like crying my eyes out, which is part of what I want from a poem. I've no time for what Gillian Clarke calls 'clever young man poems,' which make you think 'how clever that poet is,' rather than 'how profound,' or 'how moving'" (Burt & Jones 1995: 204). Emotional identification, catharsis, and above all emotionally intelligent insight, as well as some recognition of national identity, are what these readers seek in poetry, and too much cognitive mapping will be rejected as facile intellectualizing.

We can also see how these attitudes are formed by looking first at an anthology of poems chosen by children, and then at a typical study guide for the GCSE. The anthology *I Like This Poem* (1979) edited by Kaye Webb, the long-serving editor of Puffin Books (Penguin's children's list), offers brief quotations from named children to accompany popular choices sent in by members of the Puffin clubs in schools. Those few poems that are by living authors were chosen by the younger children for their emotional impact: Spike Milligan's

"Baboon" "because it is funny but is also sad in some ways." Older children also like poems which articulate their dilemmas: one girl of 14 likes Michael Rosen's poem, "My Brother is Making a Protest About Bread" because "I can easily identify with it. I am a long sufferer of wholemeal bread . . . I'm glad someone else shares my point of view" (Webb 1979: 153). The appeal of many contemporary poems is similar. Paul Muldoon's "Quoof" invites identification with family dilemmas, as does Jo Shapcott's amusing anecdote about carrying and spilling her lunch and a plastic cup of hot tea with the problems of the office lunch hour, in "Work in the City" (Webb 1979: 80). A recurrent observation by the children is that, as one girl says about Richard Wilbur's "Boy at the Window," "it makes me feel sad and yet happy as well." Poetry is measured by its emotional force and its opportunity for identification.

This academic year 2005/6 selections by four poets (Simon Armitage, Gillian Clarke, Carol Ann Duffy, and Seamus Heaney) appear in the widely used *AQA Anthology for English Literature* alongside single poems by American, Caribbean, Black British, and South Asian writers. Ten and twenty years from now these poems will remain the paradigm of what poetry should be for the majority of these readers. Carol Ann Duffy "has been on the school syllabus since 1994, which means that for once a poet is being taught whilst the language of the street is still fresh in her lines. Not surprisingly, she is popular in schools, something that wasn't always the case. In 'Head of English', from her first book *Standing Female Nude* (Anvil, 1985), she recorded a gruesome encounter at the chalkface where educational Eng. Lit. and new writers meet and often don't understand each other: 'Today we have a poet in the class. / A real live poet with a published book. / Notice the ink-stained fingers girls. Perhaps / we're going to witness verse hot from the press'" (Forbes 2002).

A guide for students and teachers accompanies the anthology. Students are taken almost line by line through a poem such as Seamus Heaney's "Death of a Naturalist," and taught about the importance of sound, sensory images, assonance, and alliteration. Throughout this commentary it is strongly assumed that the poem recounts an experience and that the task of the reader is to enter its verbal recreation as fully as possible: "How does the poet convey the strength of the speaker's fear and revulsion? Look at line 31." Although there is a brief mention of the use of a "military word" and an invitation to find others, the commentary steers well away from any discussion of the allusions to Irish politics that invest the poem with much of its meaning. There is no suggestion that the poem might owe its ideas to a tradition running from Wordsworth to Derek Mahon, or that the poem reflects on the growth of self-consciousness to the point where it invites the reader to doubt the reliability of its testimony. The student is instead trained to treat a modern poem as an intense personal experience squeezed out of the language.

Simon Armitage, another of these GCSE poets is, according to a BBC website, "one of the country's best-known poets" and it is explicit about why: "his work is known to hundreds of thousands of children because it has been on the GCSE exam syllabus for several years." From the late 1950s onward the poetry reading became increasingly import-ant as a means of promulgating poetry, to the point where today no poet could hope to build a career without reading extensively. These readings, like many of the magazines and pamphlets in which poetry is published, are mostly heavily subsidized by arts funding organiza-tions. The Poetry Live series run by the publisher Philip Allan, which claims to bring about 70,000 school students each year to large poetry readings held around the country, is an exception. It is effectively subsidized by the examination system because the poets chosen to read are those whose poems appear in anthologies assigned as set books for the GCSE examination.

Education may have been a largely conservative force but it has been offset by the growth of the new communications media, especially radio and the internet, which have had a significant influence on the history of poetry over the past fifty years, though it is a history that still remains largely unwritten. Writing in 1943, George Orwell described a wartime project to broadcast a literary program to India as an opportunity to learn more about the possibilities of putting poetry on the radio: "One must remember that extremely little in the way of broadcasting poetry has been done in England, and that many people who write verse have never even considered the idea of read-ing it aloud" (Orwell 1994: 240). Over the next few decades many poets, such as Louis MacNeice and Anthony Thwaite, were employed by the BBC as producers and presenters of literary programs still largely under the ethos of the founder Lord Reith. This might mean a lecture on concrete poetry in 1965, or a selective recording of a Cambridge poetry conference in 1987 presented by Michael Schmidt. Many of these programs were broadcast alongside classical music and drama on the arts channel, the Third Programme (later Radio Three), but some went out on the more popular Home Service or Radio Four. Poetry is still regularly broadcast on popular request programs (these helped make the poet Jenny Joseph's poem "Warning," which begins, "When I am an old woman I shall wear purple," the most popular poem in surveys). Basil Bunting's career benefited from the BBC. A selection of his poems was read twice on the Third Programme during the 1950s when he was otherwise virtually unpublished (probably one poem between 1951 and 1965), and then in 1965 he contributed to an 80th birthday celebration of Ezra Pound by reading three Cantos, and in 1967 he read *Briggflatts*. Every year over the next three years he actually appeared at least once on television as well (Guedalla 1978: 84). Bunting's case is particularly striking because of his relative neglect and his association with an earlier generation of modernist poets.

What is surprising is that neither television, vinyl, tape, nor CD recording has become the medium of choice for poetry reception. Recordings of the majority of poets have at one time or another been available and yet they have not been the success story that they might have been: we do not rush out to buy CDs of the new Wendy Cope, Geoffrey Hill, or Maggie O'Sullivan poems the way we buy popular songs (themselves a mutation of poetry that deserves further study). Like radio, they remain almost entirely neglected by literary historians and critics, are generally hard to find, and are usually treated as if they were secondary to the textual publication, and yet it seems a fair speculation that more people will have heard Bunting on the radio than ever read his poems in a book, and one suspects this is true of many poets. Poetry's relatively condensed linguistic artifacts continue to require the backscanning, rereading, and pondering that only visible text can provide as an integral part of their reception: "most contemporary Anglophone poetry is meant to be both read from the page with attention to meaning, spacing, visual appearance, and sonic indeterminacy sharpened by the ease with which one can reread under such conditions, and witnessed in performance" (Middleton 2005b: 10). This probably explains why the internet has not had more impact. Computer screens remain much harder to read than printed text and most sites do not yet integrate sound well with the textual display. This failure of new communications media to replace printing should not make us infer that they are of no importance, however. "Poetry readings emerge from a long history of the oral performance of written texts which reaches back through the renaissance and medieval cultures to the classical world. Until the advent of the new forms of leisure after the first world war, ordinary experience for almost everyone, whether rich or poor, included participation in groups listening to texts read aloud" (Middleton 2005a: 74). Since World War II the poetry reading by the author, rather than a reader or actor, has become the norm, and such performance is now integral to the reception of almost all UK poetry.

Arts funding organizations, publishing, education, performance, and the new communications media: these institutions have shaped the landscape of recent British poetry. I want to conclude by saying a little about this concept of institutions that I have used flexibly to cover formally constituted organizations such as publishers, cultural systems such as education, and normative practices such as oral performance. My aim has been to show something of the backstage world of poetry rather than to develop a rigorous theoretical model of this literary genre. The claim that institutions make art possible is often viewed with suspicion. The protagonist of Zadie Smith's novel *On Beauty*, Howard Belsey, is an art historian who challenges the belief that there is a "redemptive humanity" (Smith 2005: 155) in art and scorns the idea of beauty in art and the "mytheme of the artist as autonomous individual with privileged insight into the human" (Smith 2005: 252). This belief that art is determined by institutions leads him to destroy his marriage and ruin his career because it prevents him from recognizing the existence and significance of beauty in those he loves and in the art he tries to understand. Smith's picture is a caricature of what exponents of the institutional theory of art actually claim. George Dickie, for instance, is more circumspect than the fictional critic, careful to say that the theory does not try to explain all aspects of art (Dickie 2000: 102) and would not deny the possibility of beauty or poetic achievement. What this institutional theory of art does argue is that there are no inherent features of a work entirely independent of history and cultural context: "The general claim of the institutional theory is that if we stop looking for exhibited (easily noticed) characteristics of artworks such as representationality, emotional expressivity, and the others that the traditional theorists focused on, and instead look for characteristics that artworks have as a result of their relation to their cultural context, then we can find defining properties" (Dickie 2000: 97). In this chapter I have shown that attention to the institutional contexts of British poetry of the past half century makes intelligible features of this poetry that are otherwise obscure or hidden.

Acknowledgments

With thanks to Alan Halsey and Gavin Selerie.

Further Reading

Barry, Peter (2006). *Poetry Wars: British Poetry of the 1970s and the Battle of Earls Court.* Cambridge: Salt.

Dickie, George (2000). The Institutional Theory of Art. In Noël Carroll (ed.), *Theories of Art Today.* Madison, WI: University of Wisconsin Press, pp. 93–108.

Görtschacher, Wolfgang (1993). *Little Magazine Profiles: The Little Magazines in Great Britain, 1939–1993.* Salzburg: University of Salzburg.

Middleton, Peter (2005). *Distant Reading: Performance, Reading and Consumption in Contemporary Poetry.* Tuscaloosa, AL: University of Alabama Press.

Stewart, Susan (2002). *Poetry and the Fate of the Senses.* Chicago, IL: University of Chicago Press.

References

Acheson, James & Huk, Romana (eds) (1996). *Contemporary British Poetry: Essays in Theory and Criticism*. Albany, NY: State University of New York Press.

Adcock, Fleur (ed.) (1987). *Faber Book of 20th-Century Women's Poetry*. London: Faber & Faber.

Adorno, Theodor, W. (1977). Commitment. In Ernst Bloch, Georg Lukács, Bertolt Brecht, Walter Benjamin, & Theodor Adorno, *Aesthetics and Politics*. London: New Left Books, pp. 177–95.

Adorno, Theodor W. (1991). *Notes to Literature*, vol. 1, trans. Shierry Weber Nicholsen. New York: Columbia University Press.

Adorno, Theodor W. (2002). *Essays on Music*, ed. Richard Leppert. Berkeley, CA: University of California Press.

Alderman, Nigel (1994). "The Life with a Hole in it": Philip Larkin and the Condition of England. *Textual Practice*, 8(2), 279–301.

Alderman, Nigel (2004). Poetry in Review: Philip Larkin. *Yale Review*, 92(3), 170–78.

Alderman, Nigel & Blanton, C. D. (eds) (2000). *Pocket Epics: British Poetry After Modernism*. *Yale Journal of Criticism*, 13(1) (special issue).

Aldred, Nannette (2000). Art in Postwar Britain: A Short History of the ICA. In Alistair Davies & Alan Sinfield (eds), *British Culture of the Postwar. An Introduction to Literature and Society, 1945–1999*. London: Routledge, pp. 146–68.

Ali, Agha Shahid (1997). *The Country Without a Post Office*. New York: Norton.

Allen, Nicolas & Kelly, Aaron (eds) (2003). *The Cities of Belfast*. Dublin: Four Courts Press.

Allen, Tim and Duncan, Andrew (eds) (2007). *Don't Start the Talking: Interviews with Contemporary Poets*. Cambridge: Salt.

Allnutt, Gillian, D'Aguiar, Fred, Edwards, Ken, & Mottram, Eric (eds) (1988). *The New British Poetry, 1968–88*. London: Paladin.

Alvarez, A. (1962). *The New Poetry*. Harmondsworth: Penguin.

Alvarez, A. (1966). *The New Poetry*, rev. edn. Harmondsworth: Penguin.

Amis, Kingsley (1958). *I Like It Here*. New York: Harcourt Brace.

Amis, Kingsley (1967). Why Lucky Jim Turned Right. *Sunday Telegraph*, July 2, p. 7.

Amis, Kingsley (1970). *What Became of Jane Austen? And Other Questions*. London: Jonathan Cape.

Amis, Kingsley (1980). *Collected Poems, 1944–1979*. New York: Viking.

Amis, Kingsley (1991). *Memoirs*. London: Hutchinson.

Amis, Kingsley (1993). *Lucky Jim*. London: Penguin (first published 1954).

Anyidoho, Kofi (1998). Hero and Thief. In Gerald Moore & Ulli Beier (eds), *Penguin Book of Modern African Poetry*, 4th edn. London: Penguin.

Appiah, Kwame Anthony (1992). *In My Father's House: Africa in the Philosophy of Culture*. New York: Oxford University Press.

Armitage, Simon (1989). *ZOOM!* Newcastle upon Tyne: Bloodaxe.

Armitage, Simon (2004). The White Stuff: Interview with Simon Armitage. Available at: www.bbc.co.uk/bradford/culture/words/simon_armitage.shtml, accessed September 15, 2008.

Armitage, Simon & Crawford, Robert (eds) (1998). *The Penguin Book of Poetry from Britain and Ireland since 1945*. London: Viking/Penguin.

Art & Language (1980). *Selected Essays 1966–80*. Eindhoven: Stedelijk Van Abbemuseum.

Auden, W. H. (1941a). *New Year Letter*. London: Faber & Faber.

Auden, W. H. (1941b). Where Are We Now? *Decision*, 1, 49–52.

Auden, W. H. (1956). Untitled. In J. A. Pike (ed.), *Modern Canterbury Pilgrims*. Oxford: A. R. Mowbray & Co., pp. 32–43.

Auden, W. H. (1958). *Collected Shorter Poems, 1927–1957*. New York: Random House.

Auden, W. H. (1974). *A Certain World*. Harmondsworth: Penguin.

Auden, W. H. (1977). *The English Auden: Poems, Essays and Dramatic Writings, 1927–1939*, ed. Edward Mendelson. London: Faber & Faber.

Auden, W. H. (1991). *Collected Poems*, ed. Edward Mendelson. New York: Vintage Books.

Ayer, A. J. (1946). *Language, Truth, and Logic*, 2nd edn. London: Gollancz.

Bachelard, Gaston (1964). *The Poetics of Space*, trans. Maria Jolas. Boston, MA: Beacon Press.

Barry, Peter (2000). *Contemporary British Poetry and the City*. Manchester: Manchester University Press.

Barry, Peter (2006). *Poetry Wars: British Poetry of the 1970s and the Battle of Earls Court*. Cambridge: Salt.

Batten, Guinn (2002). Afterword. In Medbh McGuckian, *The Soldiers of Year II*. Winston-Salem, NC: Wake Forest University Press.

Batten, Guinn (2003). Boland, McGuckian, Ní Chuilleanáin and the body of the nation. In Matthew Campbell (ed.), *Cambridge Companion to Contemporary Irish Poetry*. Cambridge: Cambridge University Press, pp. 169–88.

Beckett, Samuel (1984). *Disjecta*, ed. Ruby Cohn. New York: Grove.

Beckett, Samuel (1990). *As the Story Was Told: Uncollected and Late Prose*. London: John Calder.

Benjamin, Walter (2003). *Selected Writings*, vol. 4: *1938–1940*. Cambridge, MA: Belknap Press.

Bennett, J. A. W. (2001). *Poetry of the Passion: Studies in Twelve Centuries of English Verse*. Oxford: Oxford University Press.

Bennett, Louise (1983). *Selected Poems*, ed. Mervyn Morris. Kingston: Sangster's Book Stores.

Bergvall, Caroline (2005). *Fig*. Cambridge: Salt.

Bernstein, Charles (1990). Comedy and the Poetics of Political Form. In Charles Bernstein (ed.), *The Politics of Poetic Form*. New York: Roof, pp. 235–44.

Bernstein, Charles (1992). *A Poetics*. Cambridge, MA: Harvard University Press.

Bertram, Vicki (ed.) (1997). *Kicking Daffodils: Twentieth-Century Women Poets*. Edinburgh: Edinburgh University Press.

Bhabha, Homi K. (1994). *The Location of Culture*. London: Routledge.

Blanton, C. D. (2000). Nominal Devolutions: Poetic Substance and the Critique of Political Economy. In Nigel Alderman & C. D. Blanton (eds), *Pocket Epics: British Poetry After Modernism. Yale Journal of Criticism*, 13(1) (special issue), 129–52.

Bloom, Harold (1975a). *A Map of Misreading*. New York: Oxford University Press.

Bloom, Harold (1975b). Introduction: The Survival of Strong Poetry. In Geoffrey Hill, *Somewhere Is Such a Kingdom: Poems 1952–1971*. Boston, MA: Houghton Mifflin.

Bois, Yve-Alain & Krauss, Rosalind (2000). *Formless: A User's Guide*. Cambridge, MA: MIT Press.

Boland, Eavan (1995). *Object Lessons: The Life of the Woman and the Poet in Our Times*. New York: Norton.

Bold, Alan (1976). *Thom Gunn and Ted Hughes*. New York: Barnes & Noble.

Brackenbury, Alison (1995). *1829*. Manchester: Carcanet.

Bradley, Jerry (1993). *The Movement: British Poets of the 1950s*. New York: Twayne.

Brathwaite, Edward [Kamau] (1973). *The Arrivants: A New World Trilogy*. Oxford: Oxford University Press.

Breeze, Jean "Binta" (2000). *The Arrival of Brighteye and Other Poems*. Newcastle upon Tyne: Bloodaxe.

Bridgwood, Ann & Hampson, John (eds) (2000). *Rhyme and Reason: Developing Contemporary Poetry. A study carried out by BML and BMRB on behalf of the Arts Council of England*. London: Arts Council of England.

Broom, Sarah (2006). *Contemporary British and Irish Poetry*. New York: Palgrave Macmillan.

Brown, George Mackay (1971). *Poems New and Selected*. London: Hogarth.

Brown, George Mackay (1991). *Selected Poems, 1954–1983*. Edinburgh: John Murray.

Brown, Terence (1988). *Ireland's Literature: Selected Essays*. Totowa, NJ: Barnes & Noble.

Buck, Claire (1996). Poetry and the Women's Movement in Postwar Britain. In James Acheson & Romana Huk (eds), *Contemporary British Poetry: Essays in Theory and Criticism*. Albany, NY: State University of New York Press, pp. 81–111.

Bunting, Basil (2001). *The Complete Poems*. New York: New Directions.

Bunting, Basil (1989). *A Note on Briggflatts*. Durham: Basil Bunting Poetry Archive.

Bürger, Peter (1984). *Theory of the Avant-Garde*, trans. Michael Shaw. Minneapolis, MN: University of Minnesota Press.

Burgess, Mary (2005). Mapping the Narrow Ground: Geography, History, and Partition. *Field Day Review*, 1, 121–31.

Burgin, Victor (1986). *The End of Art Theory: Criticism and Postmodernity*. London: Macmillan.

Bush, Clive (1997). *Out of Dissent: A Study of Five Contemporary British Poets*. London: Talus.

Burt, Owen & Jones, Christine (1995). *Voices at the Door: An Anthology of Favourite Poems*. Cardiff: University of Wales Press/Shelter Cymru.

Caddel, Richard (ed.) (1995). Sharp Study and Long Toil: Basil Bunting special issue. *Durham University Journal*.

Caddel, Richard & Quartermain, Peter (eds) (1999). *Other: British and Irish Poetry since 1970*. Hanover, NH: Wesleyan University Press.

Calinescu, Matei (1987). *Five Faces of Modernity: Modernism, Avant-Garde, Decadence, Kitsch, Postmodernism*. Durham, NC: Duke University Press.

Campbell, Matthew (ed.) (2003). *Cambridge Companion to Contemporary Irish Poetry*. Cambridge: Cambridge University Press.

Carpenter, Humphrey (1981). *W. H. Auden: A Biography*. London: Faber & Faber.

Carpenter, Humphrey (1988). *A Serious Character: The Life of Ezra Pound*. Boston, MA: Houghton Mifflin.

Carson, Ciaran (1975). Escaped from the Massacre? *Honest Ulsterman*, 50, 184–5.

Carson, Ciaran (1976). *The New Estate*. Belfast: Blackstaff Press.

Carson, Ciaran (1978). *The Lost Explorer*. Belfast: Ulsterman.

Carson, Ciaran (1987). *The Irish for No*. Winston-Salem, NC: Wake Forest University Press.

Carson, Ciaran (1989). *Belfast Confetti*. Winston-Salem, NC: Wake Forest University Press.

Carson, Ciaran (1993). *First Language*. Winston-Salem, NC: Wake Forest University Press.

Carson, Ciaran (1996). *Opera Et Cetera*. Winston-Salem, NC: Wake Forest University Press.

Carson, Ciaran (1998). *The Alexandrine Plan*. Winston-Salem, NC: Wake Forest University Press.

Carson, Ciaran (2001). *The Twelfth of Never*. Winston-Salem, NC: Wake Forest University Press.

Catling, Brian (1990). *The Stumbling Block: Its Index*. London: Book Works.

Champion, Miles (1996). *Compositional Bonbons Placate*. Manchester: Carcanet.

Champion, Miles (2000). *Three Bell Zero*. New York: Roof.

Cheney-Coker, Syl (1998). On being a poet in Sierra Leone. In Gerald Moore & Ulli Beier (eds), *Penguin Book of Modern African Poetry*, 4th edn. London: Penguin, pp. 339–40.

Chinitz, David (2003). *T. S. Eliot and the Cultural Divide*. Chicago, IL: University of Chicago Press.

Chinweizu; Jemie, Onwuchekwa & Madubuike, Ihechukwu (1983). *Toward the Decolonization of African Literature*. Washington, DC: Howard University Press.

Clark, Thomas A. (1995). The Idiom of the Universe. In Alec Finlay (ed.), *Wood Notes Wild: Essays on the Poetry and Art of Ian Hamilton Finlay*. Edinburgh: Polygon.

Clarke, Adrian & Sheppard, Robert (eds) (1991). *Floating Capital: New Poets from London*. Elmwood, CT: Potes & Poets.

Clarke, Gillian (1989). *Letting in the Rumour*. Manchester: Carcanet.

Clarke, Gillian (1997). *Collected Poems*. Manchester: Carcanet.

Clifford, James (1997). *Routes: Travel and Translation in the Late Twentieth Century*. Cambridge, MA: Harvard University Press.

Cobbing, Bob & Griffiths, Bill (eds) (1992). *VerbiVisiVoco: A Performance of Poetry*. London: Writers Forum.

Coffey, Brian (1986). *Advent*. London: Menard Press.

Compagnon, Antoine (1994). *Five Paradoxes of Modernity*, trans. Franklin Philip. New York: Columbia University Press.

Conquest, Robert (1955). *Poems*. London: Macmillan.

Conquest, Robert (ed.) (1956). *New Lines*. London: Macmillan.

Conquest, Robert (1982). A Proper Sport. In Anthony Thwaite (ed.), *Larkin at Sixty*. London: Faber & Faber, pp. 31–7.

Conran, Tony (1988). *Blodeuwedd and Other Poems*. Mid Glamorgan: Poetry Wales.

Conran, Tony (1993). *Castles: Variations on an Original Theme*. Llandysul: Gomer.

Cope, Wendy (ed.) (1989). *Is That the New Moon? Poems by Women Poets*. London: Collins.

Copleston, F. C. (1965). *Aquinas*. Harmondsworth: Penguin.

Corcoran, Neil (1993). *English Poetry since 1940*. London: Longman.

Coughlan, Patricia & Davis, Alex (eds) (1995). *Modernism and Ireland: The Poetry of the 1930s*. Cork: University of Cork Press.

Coward, Noël (1983). Mad Dogs and Englishmen. In *The Lyrics of Noël Coward*. London: Methuen, pp. 122–3.

Crozier, Andrew (1983). Thrills and Frills: Poetry as Figures of Empirical Lyricism. In Alan Sinfield (ed.), *Society and Literature 1945–1970*. London: Methuen, pp. 199–233.

Crozier, Andrew (2000). Resting on Laurels. In Alistair Davies & Alan Sinfield (eds), *British Culture of the Postwar. An Introduction to Literature and Society, 1945–1999*. London: Routledge, pp. 192–204.

Crozier, Andrew & Longville, Tim (eds) (1987). *A Various Art*. Manchester: Carcanet.

Davie, Donald (1952). *Purity of Diction in English Verse.* London: Chatto & Windus.

Davie, Donald (1955). *Articulate Energy*, rev. edn. London: Routledge & Kegan Paul.

Davie, Donald (1972). *Thomas Hardy and British Poetry.* New York: Oxford University Press.

Davie, Donald (1973). A Comment. *Poetry Nation*, 1, 54–8.

Davie, Donald (1977). *The Poet in the Imaginary Museum.* Manchester: Carcanet.

Davie, Donald (1981). Introduction. In Donald Davie (ed.), *New Oxford Book of Christian Verse.* Oxford: Oxford University Press, pp. xvii–xxix.

Davie, Donald (1982). *These the Companions: Recollections.* Cambridge: Cambridge University Press.

Davie, Donald (1983). *Collected Poems, 1970–1983.* Manchester: Carcanet.

Davie, Donald (1989). *Under Briggflatts: A History of Poetry in Great Britain, 1960–1988.* Manchester: Carcanet.

Davie, Donald (1990). *Collected Poems.* Chicago, IL: University of Chicago.

Davie, Donald (1998). *With the Grain: Essays on Thomas Hardy and Modern British Poetry.* Manchester: Carcanet.

Davies, Alistair (2000). Faltering at the Line: Auden and Postwar British Culture. In Alistair Davies & Alan Sinfield (eds), *British Culture of the Postwar. An Introduction to Literature and Society, 1945–1999.* London: Routledge, pp. 125–38.

Davies, Alistair & Sinfield, Alan (eds) (2000). *British Culture of the Postwar. An Introduction to Literature and Society, 1945–1999.* London: Routledge.

Davis, Alex (1995). "Poetry is Ontology": Brian Coffey's Poetics. In Patricia Coughlan & Alex Davis (eds), *Modernism and Ireland: The Poetry of the 1930s.* Cork: University of Cork Press.

Davis, Alex (2000). *A Broken Line: Denis Devlin and Irish Poetic Modernism.* Dublin: University College Dublin Press.

Davis, Alex (2003). The Irish Modernists and their Legacy. In Matthew Campbell (ed.), *Cambridge Companion to Contemporary Irish Poetry.* Cambridge: Cambridge University Press, pp. 76–93.

Davis, Alex & Jenkins, L. M. (eds) (2000). *Locations of Literary Modernism: Region and Nation in British and American Modernist Poetry.* Cambridge: Cambridge University Press.

Day, Gary & Docherty, Brian (eds) (1997). *British Poetry from the 1950s to the 1990s: Politics and Art.* Basingstoke: Macmillan.

de Certeau, Michel (1984). *The Practice of Everyday Life*, trans. S. Rendall. Berkeley, CA: University of California Press.

Dekker, George (ed.) (1983). *Donald Davie and the Responsibilities of Literature.* Manchester: Carcanet.

Derrida, Jacques (1976). *Of Grammatology*, trans. Gayatri Chakravorty Spivak. Baltimore, MD: Johns Hopkins University Press.

Derrida, Jacques (1999). On the Gift: A Discussion between Jacques Derrida and Jean-Luc Marion, moderated by Richard Kearny. In John D. Caputo

& Michael Scanlon (eds), *God, the Gift, and Postmodernism.* Bloomington, IN: Indiana University Press.

Derrida, Jacques (1993). *Sauf le nom.* Paris: Galilée.

Dickie, George (2000). The Institutional Theory of Art. In Noël Carroll (ed.), *Theories of Art Today.* Madison, WI: University of Wisconsin Press, pp. 93–108.

Dickie, Margaret (1983). Ted Hughes: The Double Voice. *Contemporary Literature,* 24(1), 57–63.

Dooley, Maura (1997). *Making for Planet Alice: New Women Poets.* Newcastle upon Tyne: Bloodaxe.

Dorn, Edward (1965). *Geography.* London: Fulcrum.

Dorn, Edward (1967). *The North Atlantic Turbine.* London: Fulcrum.

Dorward, Nate (ed.) (2003). *Removed for Further Study: The Poetry of Tom Raworth. The Gig,* 13/14 (special issue).

Dowson, Jane & Entwistle, Alice (2005). *A History of Twentieth-Century British Women's Poetry.* Cambridge: Cambridge University Press.

Doyle, Brian (1989). *English and Englishness.* London: Routledge.

Duffy, Carol Ann (1987). *Selling Manhattan.* London: Anvil Press.

Duffy, Carol Ann (1990). *The Other Country.* London: Anvil Press.

Duffy, Carol Ann (ed.) (1992). *I Wouldn't Thank You for a Valentine: Poems for Young Feminists.* London: Viking.

Duffy, Carol Ann (1999). *The World's Wife.* London: Picador.

Duncan, Andrew (2003). *The Failure of Conservatism in Modern British Poetry.* Cambridge: Salt.

Duncan, Andrew (2004). "A Hoard of Marvels." Review of Pauline Stainer's *The Lady and the Hare: New and Selected Poems. Poetry Review,* 94(1).

Dunhill, Christina (ed.) (1994). *As Girls Could Boast: New Poetry by Women.* London: Oscars Press.

Dunn, Douglas (1986). *Selected Poems, 1964–1983.* London: Faber & Faber.

Dunn, Douglas (ed.) (1992). *Faber Book of Twentieth-Century Scottish Poetry.* London: Faber & Faber.

DuPlessis, Rachel Blau (1994). "Corpses of Poesy": Some Modern Poets and Some Gender Ideologies of Lyric. In Lynn Keller & Cristanne Miller (eds), *Feminist Measures: Soundings in Poetry and Theory.* Ann Arbor, MI: University of Michigan Press.

DuPlessis, Rachel Blau & Quartermain, Peter (eds) (1999). *The Objectivist Nexus: Essays in Cultural Poetics.* Tuscaloosa, AL: University of Alabama Press.

Eagleton, Terry (1990). Nationalism: Irony and Commitment. In Terry Eagleton, Fredric Jameson, & Edward Said, *Nationalism, Colonialism, and Literature.* Minneapolis, MN: University of Minnesota Press, pp. 23–42.

Edwards, Ken (1988). Some Younger Poets. In Gillian Allnutt, Fred D'Aguiar, Ken Edwards, & Eric Mottram (eds), *The New British Poetry, 1968–1988.* London: Paladin, pp. 265–70.

Eliot, T. S. (1936). *Essays Ancient and Modern.* New York: Harcourt, Brace & Co.

Eliot, T. S. (1971). *The Waste Land: A Facsimile and Transcript of the Original Drafts Including the Annotations of Ezra Pound*, ed. Valerie Eliot. New York: Harcourt Brace Jovanovich.

Eliot, T. S. (1975). *Selected Prose of T. S. Eliot*, ed. Frank Kermode. New York: Harcourt Brace Jovanovich.

Eliot, T. S. (1988). *The Letters of T. S. Eliot*, vol. 1: *1898–1922*, ed. Valerie Eliot. London: Faber & Faber.

Eliot, T. S. (1991). *Collected Poems, 1909–1962*. New York: Harcourt Brace & Co.

Eliot, T. S. (1996). *Inventions of the March Hare: Poems, 1909–1917*, ed. Christopher Ricks. New York: Harcourt Brace.

Enright, D. J. (1955). *Poets of the 1950s*. Tokyo: Kenkyusha.

Everett, Barbara (1991). *Poets in Their Time: Essays on English Poetry from Donne to Larkin*. Oxford: Clarendon Press.

Fanon, Frantz (1963). *The Wretched of the Earth*, trans. Constance Farrington. New York: Grove.

Fisher, Roy (1961). *City*. London: Migrant.

Fisher, Roy (1975). *19 Poems and an Interview*. London: Grosseteste.

Fisher, Roy (1986). *A Furnace*. Oxford: Oxford University Press.

Fisher, Roy (2000). *Interviews through Time and Selected Prose*. Devon: Shearsman.

Fisher, Roy (2005). *The Long and the Short of It: Poems 1955–2005*. Tarset: Bloodaxe.

Forbes, Peter (1994). Talking about the New Generation. *Poetry Review*, 84(1), 4–6.

Forbes, Peter (2002). Winning lines. *The Guardian*, August 31, 2002. Available at http://books.guardian.co.uk/poetry/features/0,,902897,00.html, accessed September 15, 2008.

Forrest-Thomson, Veronica (1978). *Poetic Artifice: A Theory of Twentieth-Century Poetry*. Manchester: Manchester University Press.

Forrest-Thomson, Veronica (1990). *Collected Poems and Translations*. Lewes: Allardyce Barnett.

France, Linda (ed.) (1993). *Sixty Women Poets*. Newcastle upon Tyne: Bloodaxe.

Frazer, Tony (ed.) (1998). *A State of Independence*. Exeter: Stride.

Froude, James Anthony (1897). *The English in the West Indies; or, The Bow of Ulysses*. New York: Charles Scribner's Sons (originally published 1887).

Fussell, Paul (1975). *The Great War and Modern Memory*. New York: Oxford University Press.

Fussell, Paul (1994). *The Anti-Egotist: Kingsley Amis, Man of Letters*. New York: Oxford University Press.

Garratt, Robert F. (1989). *Modern Irish Poetry: Tradition and Continuity from Yeats to Heaney*. Berkeley, CA: University of California Press.

Gascoyne, David (1998). *David Gascoyne: Selected Prose, 1934–1996*, ed. Roger Scott. London: Enitharmon.

Giles, Paul (1996). From Myth into History: The Later Poetry of Thom Gunn and Ted Hughes. In James Acheson & Roman Huk (eds), *Contemporary British*

Poetry: Essays in Theory and Criticism. Albany, NY: State University of New York Press, pp. 143–74.

Gish, Nancy K. (1984). *Hugh MacDiarmid: The Man and His Work*. London: Macmillan.

Gish, Nancy (ed.) (1993). *Hugh MacDiarmid: Man and Poet*. Orono: National Poetry Foundation, Inc., University of Maine; & Edinburgh: Edinburgh University Press.

Glob, Peter V. (1969). *The Bog People: Iron Age Man Preserved*. Ithaca, NY: Cornell University Press.

Goodby, John (2000). *Irish Poetry Since 1950: From Stillness into History*. Manchester: Manchester University Press.

Goodison, Lorna (1992). *Selected Poems*. Ann Arbor, MI: University of Michigan Press.

Goodison, Lorna (2005). *Controlling the Silver*. Urbana, IL: University of Illinois Press.

Görtschacher, Wolfgang (1993). *Little Magazine Profiles: The Little Magazines in Great Britain, 1939–1993*. Salzburg: University of Salzburg.

Goulbourne, Harry (1991). *Ethnicity and Nationalism in Post-Imperial Britain*. New York: Cambridge University Press.

Graham, W. S. (1979). *Collected Poems, 1942–1977*. London: Faber & Faber.

Graham, W. S. (2004). *New Collected Poems*, ed. Matthew Francis. London: Faber & Faber.

Greenlaw, Lavinia (1994). The Cost of Getting Lost in Space. *Poetry Review*, 84(1), 101.

Greenlaw, Lavinia (1997). *A World Where News Travelled Slowly*. London: Faber & Faber.

Gregson, Ian (1996). *Contemporary Poetry and Postmodernism*. New York: St Martin's Press.

Grey, Edward (1914). Sir E. Grey's Speech. *Manchester Guardian*, August 4, 1914, pp. 7–8.

Griffiths, Bill & Cobbing, Bob (eds) (1988). *ALP: The first 22$^{1}/_{2}$ years: A PALPI supplement*. London: Association of Little Presses.

Guedalla, Roger (1978). Basil Bunting: A bibliography of works and criticism. In Peter Hodgkiss (ed.) *Poetry Information: Basil Bunting Special Issue*, 19, 73–89.

Gunn, Thom (1982). *The Occasions of Poetry*. Ann Arbor, MI: University of Michigan.

Gunn, Thom (1993). *Shelf Life*. Ann Arbor, MI: University of Michigan.

Gunn, Thom (2000). *Collected Poems*. New York: Farrar, Straus & Giroux.

Haffenden, John (1981). *Viewpoints: Poets in Conversation with John Haffenden*. London: Faber & Faber.

Hampson, Robert & Barry, Peter (ed.) (1993). *The New British Poetries: The Scope of the Possible*. Manchester: Manchester University Press.

Harrison, Charles (2001). *Essays on Art and Language*. Cambridge, MA: MIT Press.

Harrison, Tony (1978). *from The School of Eloquence and Other Poems*. London: Rex Collings.

Harrison, Tony (1987). *Selected Poems*, 2nd edn. London: Penguin.

Harrison, Tony (1991). *V. and Other Poems*. New York: Farrar, Straus & Giroux.

Hartley, Anthony (1954). Poetry of the Fifties. *The Spectator*, August 27, pp. 260–61.

Heaney, Seamus (1966). *Death of a Naturalist*. London: Faber & Faber.

Heaney, Seamus (1969). *Door into the Dark*. London: Faber & Faber.

Heaney, Seamus (1972). *Wintering Out*. London: Faber & Faber.

Heaney, Seamus (1975). *North*. London: Faber & Faber.

Heaney, Seamus (1979). *Field Work*. London: Faber & Faber.

Heaney, Seamus (1980a). *Poems, 1965–1975*. New York: Farrar, Strauss & Giroux.

Heaney, Seamus (1980b). *Preoccupations: Selected Prose, 1968–1978*. New York: Farrar, Strauss & Giroux.

Heaney, Seamus (1984). *Station Island*. London: Faber & Faber.

Heaney, Seamus (1985). An Open Letter. In *Ireland's Field Day*. London: Hutchinson, pp. 23–9 (originally published as *Field Day Pamphlet*, no. 2, Derry, 1983).

Heaney, Seamus (1995). Dylan the Durable? On Dylan Thomas. In *The Redress of Poetry*. London: Faber & Faber, pp. 124–45.

Heaney, Seamus (1998). *Opened Ground: Selected Poems, 1966–1996*. New York: Farrar, Straus & Giroux.

Heaney, Seamus (2001). *Electric Light*. New York: Farrar, Straus & Giroux.

Heaney, Seamus (2002). *Finders Keepers: Selected Prose, 1971–2001*. New York: Farrar, Straus & Giroux.

Hebdige, Dick (1987). *Subculture: The Meaning of Style*. London: Routledge.

Heidegger, Martin (1993). *Basic Writings: From "Being and Time" (1927) to "The Task of Thinking" (1964)*, ed. David Farrell Krell. London: Routledge.

Hendriks, Arthur Lemiere & Lindo, Cedric (eds) (1962). *The Independence Anthology of Jamaican Literature*. Kingston: Arts Celebration Committee of the Ministry of Development and Welfare.

Hendry, J. F. (ed.) (1940). *The New Apocalypse: An Anthology of Criticism, Poems and Stories*. London: Fortune.

Hendry, J. F. (1941). Myth and Social Integration. In J. F. Hendry & Henry Treece (eds), *The White Horseman: Prose and Verse of the New Apocalypse*. London: Routledge.

Hewison, Robert (1981). *In Anger: British Culture in the Cold War, 1945–1960*. New York: Oxford University Press.

Hewison, Robert (1986). *Too Much: Art and Society in the Sixties, 1960–75*. London: Methuen.

Hewitt, John (2007). *Selected Poems*, ed. Michael Longley & Frank Ormsby. Belfast: Blackstaff Press.

Hill, Geoffrey (1968). *King Log*. London: Andre Deutsch.

Hill, Geoffrey (1971). *Mercian Hymns*. London: Andre Deutsch.

Hill, Geoffrey (1997). *Canaan*. Boston, MA: Houghton Mifflin.

Hill, Geoffrey (1998). *The Triumph of Love*. Boston, MA: Houghton Mifflin.

Hill, Geoffrey (2000). *New and Collected Poems, 1952–1992*. New York: Mariner Books.

Hill, Geoffrey (2003). *Style and Faith*. New York: Counterpoint.

Hobhouse, L. T. (1910). *Liberalism*. London: Williams & Norgate.

Hollander, John (1981). *The Figure of Echo: A Mode of Allusion in Milton and After*. Berkeley, CA: University of California Press.

Homberger, Eric (1977). *The Art of the Real: Poetry in England and America since 1939*. London: Dent.

Hooker, Jeremy (1982). *Poetry of Place: Essays and Reviews, 1970–1981*. Manchester: Carcanet.

Hooker, Jeremy (1989). In the Labyrinth: An Exploration of *The Anathemata*. In John Matthias (ed.), *David Jones: Man and Poet*. Orono, MN: National Poetry Foundation, University of Maine, pp. 263–84.

Hornsby, Roger A. & Brogan, T. V. F. (1993). Catalog. In Alex Preminger & T. V. F. Brogan (eds), *The New Princeton Encyclopedia of Poetry and Poetics*, 2nd edn. Princeton, NJ: Princeton University Press, p. 174.

Horovitz, Michael (ed.) (1969). *Children of Albion: Poetry of the Underground in Britain*. Harmondsworth: Penguin.

Hughes, Langston (1926). The Negro Artist and the Racial Mountain. *The Nation*, 122(3181), 692–95.

Hughes, Langston (1995). *The Collected Poems of Langston Hughes*, ed. Arnold Rampersad. New York: Random House.

Hughes, Ted (1970). *Crow: From the Life and Songs of the Crow*. London: Faber & Faber.

Hughes, Ted (1994). *Winter Pollen: Occasional Prose*, ed. William Scammel. London: Faber & Faber.

Hughes, Ted (2003). *Collected Poems*. New York: Farrar, Straus & Giroux.

Huk, Romana (2005). *Stevie Smith: Between the Lines*. London: Palgrave.

Huk, Romana (ed.) (2003). *Assembling Alternatives: Reading Postmodern Poetics Transnationally*. Middletown, CT: Wesleyan University Press.

Innes, C. L. (1996). Accent and Identity: Women Poets of Many Parts. In James Acheson & Romana Huk (eds), *Contemporary British Poetry: Essays in Theory and Criticism*. Albany: State University of New York Press, pp. 315–42.

Jameson, Fredric (1988). *The Ideologies of Theory: Essays 1971–1986*, vol. 2: *Syntax of History*. Minneapolis. MN: University of Minnesota Press.

Jameson, Fredric (1991). *Postmodernism, or, The Cultural Logic of Late Capitalism*. Durham, NC: Duke University Press.

Jameson, Fredric (2007). *The Modernist Papers*. London: Verso.

Jamie, Kathleen (2002). *Mr and Mrs Scotland Are Dead: Poems, 1980–1994*. Tarset: Bloodaxe.

Jencks, Charles (1989). *What is Post-Modernism?* 3rd edn rev. London: Academy.

Jenkins, Nigel (1990). *Acts of Union: Selected Poems, 1974–1989*. Llandysul: Gomer.

Jennings, Elizabeth (1966). *The Mind Has Mountains*. London: Macmillan.

Jennings, Elizabeth (1967). *Collected Poems*. Chester Springs, PA: Dufour.

Jennings, Elizabeth (1996). *Every Changing Shape: Mystical Experience and the Making of Poems*. Manchester: Carcanet.

Jennings, Elizabeth (2002). *New Collected Poems*, ed. Michael Schmidt. Manchester: Carcanet.

Johnson, Linton Kwesi (2002). *Mi Revalueshanary Fren: Selected Poems*. London: Penguin.

Johnson, Nicholas (ed.) (2000). *Foil: defining poetry, 1985–2000*. Buckfastleigh, Etruscan.

Johnston, Dillon (1998). *Irish Poetry after Joyce*, 2nd edn. Syracuse, NY: Syracuse University Press (originally published 1985).

Jones, David (1952). *The Anathemata: Fragments of an attempted writing*. London: Faber & Faber.

Jones, David (1963). *In Parenthesis*. London: Faber & Faber (originally published 1937).

Jones, Griff Rhys (ed.) (1996). *The Nation's Favourite Poems*. London: BBC Books.

Joyce, James (1961). *Ulysses*. New York: Vintage.

Joyce, Trevor (2001). *with the first dream of fire they hunt the cold: A Body of Work, 1966/2000*. Exeter: Shearsman Books.

Judt, Tony (2005). *Postwar: A History of Europe since 1945*. New York: Penguin.

Kant, Immanuel (1951). *Critique of Judgment*, trans. J. H. Bernard. London: Hafner-Macmillan.

Kaplan, Caren (1996). *Questions of Travel: Postmodern Discourses of Displacement*. Durham, NC: Duke University Press.

Kavanagh, Patrick (2003). *A Poet's Country: Selected Prose*, ed. A. Quinn. Dublin: Lilliput Press.

Kearns, Cleo McNelly (1987). *T. S. Eliot and Indic Traditions: A Study in Poetry and Belief*. Cambridge: Cambridge University Press.

Keats, John (1958). *The Letters of John Keats*, 2nd edn, ed. Hyder E. Rollins. Cambridge, MA: Harvard University Press.

Kennedy, David (1996). *New Relations: The Refashioning of British Poetry, 1980–1994*. Bridgend: Poetry Wales Press.

Kenner, Hugh (1988). *A Sinking Island: The Modern English Writers*. New York: Knopf.

Kermode, Frank (1967). *The Sense of an Ending: Studies in the Theory of Fiction*. Oxford: Oxford University Press.

Kerrigan, John (1998). Earthwriting: Seamus Heaney and Ciaran Carson. *Essays in Criticism*, 48(2), 144–68.

Kerrigan, John (2000). Roy Fisher on Location. In John Kerrigan & Peter Robinson (eds), *The Thing about Roy Fisher: Critical Studies*. Liverpool: Liverpool University Press, pp. 16–46.

Kerrigan, John (2000b). Divided Kingdoms and the Local Epic: *Mercian Hymns* to *The King of Britain's Daughter*. In Nigel Alderman & C. D. Blanton (eds), *Pocket Epics: British Poetry After Modernism*. *Yale Journal of Criticism*, 13(1) (special issue), 3–22.

Kiberd, Declan (1995). *Inventing Ireland*. Cambridge, MA: Harvard University Press.

Kidd, Helen (1993). The Paper City: Women, Writing, and Experience. In Robert Hampson & Peter Barry (eds), *New British Poetries: The Scope of the Possible*. Manchester: Manchester University Press, pp. 156–79.

Kinnahan, Linda (2004). *Lyric Interventions: Feminism, Experimental Poetry, and Contemporary Discourse*. Iowa City, IA: University of Iowa Press.

Kinsella, Thomas (1996). *Collected Poems, 1956–1994*. Oxford: Oxford University Press.

Kirkland, Richard (1996). *Literature and Culture in Northern Ireland since 1965: Moments of Danger*. London: Longman.

Kolocotroni, Vassiliki, Goldman, Jane, & Taxidou, Olga (eds) (1998). *Modernism: An Anthology of Sources and Documents*. Edinburgh: Edinburgh University Press.

Lafont, Cristina (2000). *Heidegger, Language and World-Disclosure*, trans. Graham Harman. Cambridge: Cambridge University Press.

Larkin, Philip (1960). What's Become of Wystan?, *The Spectator*, 205, July 15.

Larkin, Philip (ed.) (1972). *Oxford Book of Twentieth-Century English Verse*. Oxford: Oxford University Press.

Larkin, Philip (1982). *Required Writing*. London: Faber & Faber.

Larkin, Philip (1988). *Collected Poems*, ed. Anthony Thwaite. London: Faber & Faber.

Larkin, Philip (1999). *Selected Letters*, ed. Anthony Thwaite. London: Faber & Faber.

Larkin, Philip (2001). *Further Requirements*, ed. Anthony Thwaite. London: Faber & Faber.

Larkin, Philip (2002). *Trouble at Willow Gables*, ed. James Booth. London: Faber & Faber.

Larkin, Philip (2003). *Collected Poems*, ed. Anthony Thwaite. New York: Farrar, Straus & Giroux.

Lawson, Peter (2006). *Anglo-Jewish Poetry from Isaac Rosenberg to Elaine Feinstein*. Edgware, Middlesex: Valentine Mitchell.

Lazer, Hank (2008). *Lyric & Spirit*. Richmond, CA: Omnidawn.

Leavis, F. R. (1932). *New Bearings in English Poetry: A Study of the Contemporary Situation*. London: Chatto & Windus.

Lefebvre, Henri (1991). *The Production of Space*, trans. Donald Nicholson-Smith. Oxford: Blackwell.

Lehman, David (1998). *The Last Avant-Garde: The Making of the New York School of Poets*. New York: Doubleday.

Leonard, Tom (1984). *Intimate Voices: Selected Work, 1965–1983*. Swansea: Galloping Dog Press.

Levertov, Denise (1970). *Relearning the Alphabet*. New York: Norton.

Lewis, Wyndham (ed.) (2000). *BLAST 2*. Santa Rosa, CA: Black Sparrow Press (originally published 1915).

Lewis, Wyndham (ed.) (2002). *BLAST 1*. Santa Rosa, CA: Black Sparrow Press (originally published 1914).

Lloyd, David (1993). *Anomalous States: Irish Writing and the Post-Colonial Moment*. Durham, NC: Duke University Press.

Lloyd, David T. (1994). *The Urgency of Identity: Contemporary English-Language Poetry from Wales*. Evanston, IL: Triquarterly.

Lloyd, Joanna (1983). The Correspondence between Robert Graves and Lynette Roberts, 1943–1952. *Poetry Wales*, 19(2), 55–122.

Longenbach, James (1987). *Modernist Poetics of History: Pound, Eliot, and the Sense of the Past*. Princeton, NJ: Princeton University Press.

Longley, Edna (2000a). *Poetry and Posterity*. Tarset: Bloodaxe.

Longley, Edna (2000b). *Bloodaxe Book of 20th Century Poetry: from Britain and Ireland*. Tarset: Bloodaxe.

Longley, Michael (1991). *Gorse Fires*. Winston-Salem, NC: Wake Forest University Press.

Longley, Michael (1994). Michael Longley Writes on Being a New Generation Judge. *Poetry Review*, 84(1), 52.

Longley, Michael (1998). *Selected Poems*. Winston-Salem, NC: Wake Forest University Press.

Longley, Michael (2004). *Snow Water*. Winston-Salem, NC: Wake Forest University Press.

Lopez, Tony (2006). *Meaning Performance*. Cambridge: Salt.

MacDiarmid, Hugh (1978). *The Complete Poems*, 2 vols, ed. Michael Grieve & W. R. Aitken. London: Martin Brian & O'Keefe.

MacGiolla Léith, C. (1991). Dinnseanchas and Modern Gaelic Poetry. In Gerald Dawe & John Wilson Foster (eds), *The Poet's Place: Ulster Literature and Society, Essays in Honour of John Hewitt, 1907–1987*. Belfast: Institute of Irish Studies, pp. 157–68.

MacNeice, Louis (1966). *Collected Poems*. London: Faber & Faber.

Mahon, Derek (1968). *Night Crossing*. Oxford: Oxford University Press.

Mahon, Derek (1981). *Courtyards in Delft*. Winston-Salem, NC: Wake Forest University Press.

Mahon, Derek (1999). *Collected Poems*. Loughcrew: Gallery Press.

Mahon, Derek (2005). *Harbour Lights*. Loughcrew: Gallery Press.

Malpas, J. E. (1999). *Place and Experience: A Philosophical Topography*. Cambridge: Cambridge University Press.

Manchester Guardian (1914). Peace or War? August 4, 1914, p. 6.

Maritain, Jacques (1953). *Creative Intuition in Art and Poetry*. New York: Pantheon.

Mark, Alison & Rees-Jones, Deryn (eds) (2000). *Contemporary Women's Poetry: Reading/Writing/Practice*. London: Macmillan.

Martin, Augustine (1983). Donald Davie and Ireland. In George Dekker (ed.), *Donald Davie and the Responsibilities of Literature*. Manchester: Carcanet, pp. 49–63.

Marwick, Arthur (1998). *The Sixties: Cultural Revolution in Britain, France, Italy, and the United States, c. 1958–c. 1974*. Oxford: Oxford University Press.

Massey, Doreen (1994). *Space, Place, and Gender*. Cambridge: Polity Press.

Matthias, John (ed.) (1971). Contemporary British Poetry. *TriQuarterly*, 21 (special issue).

Mayer, Peter (1974). *Bob Cobbing and Writers Forum*, 2nd edn. London: Writers Forum.

McDonald, Peter (1997). *Mistaken Identities: Poetry and Northern Ireland*. New York: Oxford University Press.

McGuckian, Medbh (1989). *On Ballycastle Beach*. Loughcrew: Gallery Press.

McGuckian, Medbh (1998). *Shelmalier*. Winston-Salem, NC: Wake Forest University Press.

McGuckian, Medbh (2002). *The Soldiers of Year II*. Winston-Salem, NC: Wake Forest University Press.

McGuckian, Medbh (2003). *Had I a Thousand Lives*. Winston-Salem, NC: Wake Forest University Press.

McLeod, John (2004). *Postcolonial London: Rewriting the Metropolis*. London: Routledge.

Mellors, Anthony (2005). *Late Modernist Poetics: from Pound to Prynne*. Manchester: Manchester University Press.

Mendelson, Edward (1999). *Later Auden*. New York: Farrar, Straus & Giroux.

Mengham, Rod (2004). Introduction. In Rod Mengham & John Kinsella (eds), *Vanishing Points: New Modernist Poems*. Cambridge: Salt, pp. xvii–xix.

Merleau-Ponty, Maurice (1962). *The Phenomenology of Perception*, trans. Colin Smith. London: Routledge.

Merton, Thomas (1953). Sacred Art and the Spiritual Life. In *Disputed Questions*. New York: Harvest, pp. 151–64.

Middleton, Peter (1993). Who Am I to Speak? The Politics of Subjectivity in Recent British Poetry. In Robert Hampson & Peter Barry (eds), *New British Poetries: The Scope of the Possible*. Manchester: Manchester University Press, pp. 107–33.

Middleton, Peter (2003). Imagined Readerships and Poetic Innovation in UK Poetry. In Romana Huk (ed.), *Assembling Alternatives: Reading Postmodern Poetries Transnationally*. Middletown, CT: Wesleyan University Press, pp. 128–42.

Middleton, Peter (2005a). *Distant Reading: Performance, Reading and Consumption in Contemporary Poetry*. Tuscaloosa, AL: University of Alabama Press.

Middleton, Peter (2005b). How to Read a Reading of a Written Poem. *Oral Tradition*, 20(1), 7–34.

Miller, Tyrus (1999). *Late Modernism: Politics, Fiction and the Arts between the World Wars*. Berkeley, CA: University of California Press.

Milne, Drew (1993). Agoraphobia and the embarrassment of manifestoes: notes towards a community of risk. *Parataxis: modernism and modern writing*, 3, 25–40.

Milne, Drew (ed.) (2003). *Modern Critical Thought*. Oxford: Blackwell.

Minhinnick, Robert (1989). *The Looters*. Brigend: Seren.

Mohin, Lilian (ed.) (1980). *One Foot on the Mountain: An Anthology of British Feminist Poetry, 1969–1979*. London: Onlywomen Press.

Mohin, Lilian (ed.) (1986). *Beautiful Barbarians: Lesbian Feminist Poetry*. London: Onlywomen Press.

Montague, John (1972). *The Rough Field*. Winston-Salem, NC: Wake Forest University Press.

Montague, John (1979). *The Rough Field*. Dublin: Dolmen.

Montague, John (1984). *The Dead Kingdom*. Winston-Salem, NC: Wake Forest University Press.

Montague, John (1989). *The Rough Field*, 5th edn. Winston-Salem, NC: Wake Forest University Press.

Montague, John (1998). *Drunken Sailor*. Winston-Salem, NC: Wake Forest University Press.

Montague, John (2003). *Smashing The Piano*. Winston-Salem, NC: Wake Forest University Press.

Moore, Gerald & Beier, Ulli (eds) (1998). *Penguin Book of Modern African Poetry*, 4th edn. London: Penguin.

Morel, E. D. (1916). *Truth and the War*. London: National Labour Press.

Morgan, Edwin (1990). *Collected Poems*. Manchester: Carcanet.

Morley, David (2003). A spring in her heels. Review of Pauline Stainer's *The Lady and the Hare: New and Selected Poems*. Guardian Unlimited (online), Saturday November 22, 2003. Available at http://books.guardian.co.uk/review/story/0,,1089333,00.html, accessed September 15, 2008.

Morrison, Blake (1980). *The Movement: English Poetry and Fiction of the 1950s*. Oxford: Oxford University Press.

Morrison, Blake & Motion, Andrew (eds) (1982). *Penguin Book of Contemporary British Poetry*. Harmondsworth: Penguin.

Motion, Andrew (1978). *The Pleasure Steamers*. Manchester: Carcanet.

Motion, Andrew (1993). *Philip Larkin: A Writer's Life*. New York: Farrar, Straus & Giroux.

Motion, Andrew (1998). *Selected Poems, 1976–1997*. London: Faber & Faber.

Mottram, Eric (1993). The British Poetry Revival, 1960–1975. In Robert Hampson & Peter Barry (eds), *New British Poetries: The Scope of the Possible*. Manchester: Manchester University Press, pp. 15–50.

Muldoon, Paul (1973). *New Weather*. London: Faber & Faber.

Muldoon, Paul (1977). *Mules*. London: Faber & Faber.

Muldoon, Paul (1980). *Why Brownlee Left*. Winston-Salem, NC: Wake Forest University Press.

Muldoon, Paul (1983). *Quoof*. Winston-Salem, NC: Wake Forest University Press.

Muldoon, Paul (1990). *Madoc: A Mystery*. London: Faber & Faber.

Muldoon, Paul (1995). *Six Honest Serving Men*. Loughcrew: Gallery Press.

Muldoon, Paul (2001). *Poems 1968–1998*. New York: Farrar, Strauss & Giroux.

Muldoon, Paul (2006). *Horse Latitudes*. New York: Farrar, Straus & Giroux.

Mulford, Wendy (2002). *and suddenly, supposing: Selected Poems*. Buckfastleigh: Etruscan.

Murdoch, Iris (1998). *Existentialists and Mystics: Writings on Philosophy and Literature*. New York: Penguin.

Murphy, Richard (1998). *Theorizing the Avant-Garde: Modernism, Expressionism, and the Problem of Postmodernity*. Cambridge: Cambridge University Press.

Nairn, Tom (1977). *The Break-Up of Britain: Crisis and Neo-Nationalism*. London: New Left Books.

Naylor, Paul (1999). *Poetic Investigations: Singing the Holes in History*. Tuscaloosa, AL: University of Alabama Press.

Ngũgĩ wa Thiong'o (1986). *Decolonising the Mind: The Politics of Language in African Literature*. Portsmouth, NH: Heinemann.

Ní Chuilleanáin, Eiléan (1977). *The Second Voyage*. Winston-Salem, NC: Wake Forest University Press.

Ní Chuilleanáin, Eiléan (1991). *The Magdalene Sermon and Earlier Poems*. Winston-Salem, NC: Wake Forest University Press.

Ní Dhomhnaill, Nuala (2005). *Selected Essays*, ed. Oona Frawley. Dublin: New Island.

Nicholls, Peter (1995). *Modernisms: A Literary Guide*. London: Palgrave Macmillan.

North, Michael (1987). The Word as Bond: Money and Performative Language in Hill's *Mercian Hymns*. *ELH*, 54(2), 463–81.

North, Michael (1994). *The Dialect of Modernism: Race, Language, and Twentieth-Century Literature*. New York: Oxford University Press.

O'Brien, Sean (1998). *The Deregulated Muse*. Newcastle upon Tyne: Bloodaxe.

Okigbo, Christopher (1971). *Labyrinths, with Path of Thunder*. New York: Africana.

Okot p'Bitek (1984). *"Song of Lawino" and "Song of Ocol."* Oxford: Heinemann.

Okri, Ben (1998). On Edge of Time Future. In Gerald Moore & Ulli Beier (eds), *Penguin Book of Modern African Poetry*, 4th edn. London: Penguin, pp. 302–4.

Olsen, Redell (2004). *Secure Portable Space*. London: Reality Street.

Olson, Charles (1966). *Selected Writings*, ed. Robert Creeley. New York: New Directions.

Orwell, George (1994). *Essays*. Harmondsworth: Penguin.

O'Sullivan, Maggie (ed.) (1996). *Out of Everywhere: linguistically innovative poetry by women in North America and the UK*. London: Reality Street.

Parmar, Pratibha & Osman, Sona (eds) (1985). *A Dangerous Knowing: Four Black Women Poets*. London: Sheba Feminist Press.

Paterson, Don (2001). The Legacy of NewGen. *Poetry Review*, 91, 1.

Peach, Linden (1992). *Ancestral Lines: Culture and Identity in the Work of Six Contemporary Poets*. Bridgend: Seron.

Perloff, Marjorie (1985). *Dance of the Intellect: Studies in the Poetry of the Pound Tradition*. Evanston, IL: Northwestern University Press.

Perloff, Marjorie (1996). *Wittgenstein's Ladder: Poetic Language and the Strangeness of the Ordinary*. Chicago, IL: University of Chicago Press.

Perloff, Marjorie (2002). *21st-Century Modernism: The "New" Poetics*. Oxford: Blackwell.

Plath, Sylvia (1981). *The Collected Poems*, ed. Ted Hughes. London: Faber & Faber.

Poggioli, Renato (1968). *The Theory of the Avant-Garde*, trans. Gerald Fitzgerald. Cambridge, MA: Harvard University Press.

Pound, Ezra (1917). Studies in Contemporary Mentality, IV: The "Spectator." *New Age*, September 6.

Pound, Ezra (1968). *Literary Essays of Ezra Pound*. New York: New Directions.

Pound, Ezra (1971). *Selected Letters of Ezra Pound, 1907–1941*, ed. D. D. Paige. New York: New Directions.

Pound, Ezra (1973). *Selected Prose, 1909–1965*, ed. William Cookson. New York: New Directions.

Pound, Ezra (1990). *Personae: Collected Shorter Poems of Ezra Pound*, rev. ed. Lea Baechler & A. Walton Litz. New York: New Directions.

Pound, Ezra (1998). *The Cantos of Ezra Pound*. New York: New Directions.

Prynne, J. H. (1967). Letter. *The English Intelligencer*, series 1, 189–90.

Prynne, J. H. (1969). L'Extase de M. Poher. In Wendy Mulford (ed.), *The Anona Wynn*. Cambridge: n.p. [no issue number given: only one issue believed to have been produced].

Prynne, J. H. (1971). *Brass*. London: Ferry Press.

Prynne, J. H. (1982). *Poems*. Edinburgh: Agneau 2.

Prynne, J. H. (1999). *Poems*. Newcastle upon Tyne: Bloodaxe.

Prynne, J. H. (2005). *Poems*, 2nd edn. Newcastle upon Tyne: Bloodaxe.

Putnam, Hillary (2002). Levinas and Judaism. In Simon Critchley & Robert Bernasconi (eds), *Cambridge Companion to Levinas*. Cambridge: Cambridge University Press.

Rainey, Lawrence (1998). *Institutions of Modernism: Literary Elites and Public Culture*. New Haven, CT: Yale University Press.

Rainey, Lawrence (ed.) (2005). *Modernism: An Anthology*. Oxford: Blackwell.

Ramazani, Jahan (1994). *Poetry of Mourning: The Modern Elegy from Hardy to Heaney*. Chicago, IL: University of Chicago Press.

Ramazani, Jahan (2001). *The Hybrid Muse: Postcolonial Poetry in English*. Chicago, IL: University of Chicago Press.

Ramazani, Jahan (2009). *A Transnational Poetics*. Chicago, IL: University of Chicago Press.

Ramazani, Jahan, Ellmann, Richard, & O'Clair, Robert (2003). *Norton Anthology of Modern and Contemporary Poetry*, 3rd edn. New York: Norton.

Rawls, John (1996). *Political Liberalism*. New York: Columbia University Press.

Reeves, Gareth (2004). Auden and Religion. In Stan Smith (ed.), *Cambridge Companion to W. H. Auden*. Cambridge: Cambridge University Press.

Reynolds, Oliver (1985). *Skevington's Daughter*. London: Faber & Faber.

Richards, I. A. (1926). *Science and Poetry*. New York: Norton.

Ricks, Christopher (1984). *The Force of Poetry*. Oxford: Clarendon Press.

Riley, Denise (1992a). A Short History of Some Preoccupations. In Judith Butler & Joan W. Scott (eds), *Feminists Theorize the Political*. New York: Routledge, pp. 121–9.

Riley, Denise (ed.) (1992b). *Poets on Writing: Britain, 1970–1991*. London: Macmillan.

Riley, Denise (1993). *Mop Mop Georgette: New and Selected Poems, 1986–1993*. London: Reality Street.

Riley, Denise (2000). *The Words of Selves: Identification, Solidarity, Irony*. Stanford, CA: Stanford University Press.

Riley, John (1980). *Collected Works*, ed. Tim Longville. Cambridge: Grosseteste Press.

Riley, John (1995). *Selected Poems*, ed. Michael Grant. Manchester: Carcanet.

Roberts, Michael (ed.) (1932). *New Signatures: Poems by Several Hands*. London: Hogarth.

Roberts, Neil (1999). *Narrative and Voice in Postwar Poetry*. London: Addison Wesley Longman.

Robinson, John (1963). *Honest to God*. London: SCM Press.

Rumens, Carol (ed.) (1985). *Making for the Open: The Chatto Book of Post-Feminist Poetry, 1964–1984*. London: Chatto & Windus.

Ruthven, K. K. (1969). *A Guide to Ezra Pound's "Personae" 1926*. Berkeley, CA: University of California Press.

Ryan, Ray (2002). *Ireland & Scotland: Literature and Culture, State and Nation, 1966–2000*. Oxford: Clarendon Press.

Sagar, Keith M. (2000). *The Laughter of Foxes: A Study of Ted Hughes*. Liverpool: Liverpool University Press.

Said, Edward W. (1993). *Culture and Imperialism*. New York: Knopf.

Schirmer, Gregory A. (1983). "This That I Am Heir To": Donald Davie and Religion. In George Dekker (ed.), *Donald Davie and the Responsibilities of Literature*. Manchester: Carcanet, pp. 129–42.

Schmidt, Michael (1973). The Politics of Form. *Poetry Nation*, 1, 49–53.

Schwitters, Kurt (1993). *Poems, Performance Pieces, Proses, Plays, Poetics*, ed. trans. Jerome Rothenberg & Pierre Joris. Philadelphia, PA: Temple University Press.

Scott, J. D. (1954). In the Movement. *The Spectator*, October 1, pp. 399–400.

Scupham, Peter (1990). *Selected Poems, 1972–1990*. Manchester: Carcanet.

Severin, Laura (2004). *Poetry Off the Page: Twentieth-Century British Women Poets in Performance*. Aldershot: Ashgate Press.

Sherry, Vincent (2003). *The Great War and the Language of Modernism*. New York: Oxford University Press.

Silkin, Jon (1972). The Poetry of Geoffrey Hill. In Michael Schmidt & Grevel Lindop (eds), *British Poetry since 1960: A Critical Survey*. Oxford: Carcanet, pp. 143–64.

Silkin, Jon (ed.) (1979). *Penguin Book of First World War Poetry*. Harmondsworth: Penguin.

Silkin, Jon (1980). *Selected Poems*. London: Routledge & Kegan Paul.

Sinclair, Iain (ed.) (1996). *Conductors of Chaos*. London: Picador.

Sinfield, Alan (1992). *Faultlines: Cultural Materialism and the Politics of Dissident Reading*. Oxford: Clarendon Press.

Sinfield, Alan (2004). *Literature, Politics and Culture in Postwar Britain*. London: Continuum.

Sisson, C. H. (1976). Editorial. *PN Review*, 3, 1.

Sisson, C. H. (1984). *Collected Poems, 1943–1983*. Manchester: Carcanet.

Sitwell, Edith (1979). *Collected Poems*. London: Macmillan.

Skelt, Peterjon (1991). *Prospect into Breath: Interviews with North and South Writers*. Twickenham: North & South.

Smith, Iain Crichton (1965). *The Law and the Grace*. London: Eyre & Spottiswood.

Smith, Iain Crichton (1981). *Selected Poems, 1955–1980*. Edinburgh: Macdonald.

Smith, Iain Crichton (1989). *A Life*. Manchester: Carcanet.

Smith, Stan (1982). *Inviolable Voice: History and 20th-Century Poetry*. Dublin: Gill & Macmillan.

Smith, Stan (2005). *Irish Poetry and the Construction of Modern Identity: Ireland Between Fantasy and History*. Dublin: Irish Academic Press.

Smith, Zadie (2005). *On Beauty*. London: Penguin.

Smyth, Gerry (2001). *Space and the Irish Cultural Imagination*. New York: Palgrave.

Soja, Edward W. (1989). *Postmodern Geographies: The Reassertion of Space in Critical Social Theory*. London: Verso.

Soyinka, Wole (1967). *Idanre and Other Poems*. London: Methuen.

Spender, Stephen (1946). *Poetry since 1939*. London: Longmans, Green, & Co.

Spender, Stephen (1974). *Love–Hate Relations: English and American Sensibilities*. New York: Random House.

Spivak, Gayatri Chakravorty (1999). *A Critique of Postcolonial Reason*. Cambridge, MA: Harvard University Press.

Stainer, Pauline (2003). *The Lady and the Hare*. Newcastle upon Tyne: Bloodaxe.

Stevenson, Randall (2004). *The Last of England?* Oxford English Literary History, vol. 12: *1960–2000*. Oxford: Oxford University Press.

Stewart, Susan (2002). *Poetry and the Fate of the Senses*. Chicago, IL: University of Chicago Press.

Strong, Beret E. (1997). *Poetic Avant-Garde: The Groups of Borges, Auden and Breton*. Evanston, IL: Northwestern University Press.

Sullivan, J. P. (1964). *Ezra Pound and Sextus Propertius: A Study in Creative Translation*. Austin, TX: University of Texas Press.

Swarbrick, Andrew (1995). *Out of Reach: The Poetry of Philip Larkin*. Basingstoke: Macmillan.

Terrell, Carroll (ed.) (1981). *Basil Bunting: Man and Poet*. Orono, ME: National Poetry Foundation.

Thomas, R. S. (1986). *Selected Poems, 1946–1968*. Newcastle upon Tyne: Bloodaxe.

Thurston, Michael (2003). Writing at the Edge: Gillian Clarke's *Cofiant*. *Contemporary Literature*, 44(2), 275–300.

Thwaite, Anthony & Silkin, Jon (1963). No Politics, No Poetry? *Stand*, 6(2), 7–23.

Tomlinson, Charles (2001). *American Essays: Making it New*. Manchester: Carcanet.

Tomlinson, Charles (2003). *Metamorphoses: Poetry and Translation*. Manchester: Carcanet.

Tuan, Yi-Fu (1977). *Space and Place: The Perspective of Experience*. Minneapolis, MN: University of Minnesota Press.

Tuma, Keith (1998). *Fishing by Obstinate Isles: Modern and Postmodern British Poetry and American Readers*. Evanston, IL: Northwestern University Press.

Tuma, Keith (ed.) (2001). *Anthology of Twentieth-Century British and Irish Poetry*. New York: Oxford University Press.

United Nations (2000–2008a). The United Nations and Decolonization: History. Available at www.un.org/Depts/dpi/decolonization/history.htm, accessed August 26, 2008.

United Nations (2000–2008b). The United Nations and Decolonization: Trust and non-self-governing territories, 1945–1999. Available at www.un.org/Depts/dpi/decolonization/trust2.htm#uk, accessed August 26, 2008.

United Nations (1960). Resolution 1514 of the General Assembly. Declaration on the Granting of Independence to Colonial Countries and Peoples. Available at www.un.org/Depts/dpi/decolonization/declaration.htm, accessed August 26, 2008.

Vattimo, Gianni (1999). *Belief*, trans. Luca D'Isanto & David Webb. Cambridge: Polity Press.

Von Hendy, Andrew (2002). *The Modern Construction of Myth*. Bloomington, IN: Indiana University Press.

Walcott, Derek (1973). *Another Life*. London: Jonathan Cape.

Walcott, Derek (1986). *Collected Poems, 1948–1984*. New York: Farrar, Straus & Giroux.

Walcott, Derek (1987). *The Arkansas Testament*. New York: Farrar, Straus & Giroux.

Ward, Elizabeth (1983). *David Jones: Mythmaker*. Manchester: Manchester University Press.

Ward, Geoff (2000). *Statutes of Liberty: The New York School of Poets*, rev. edn. New York: St Martin's Press.

Waugh, Patricia (1989). *The Harvest of the Sixties: English Literature and its Background, 1960–1990*. Oxford: Oxford University Press.

Webb, Kaye (1979). *I Like This Poem*. Harmondsworth: Penguin.

Westminster Gazette (1914). A Dramatic Scene: The House and Sir Edward Grey's Statement. Logic of events. August 4, 1914, p. 10.

Whelan, Kevin (1992). The Power of Place. *Irish Review*, 12, 13–20.

Wilkinson, John (2007). *The Lyric Touch: Essays on the Poetry of Excess*. Cambridge: Salt.

Williams, Raymond (1973). *The Country and the City*. Oxford: Oxford University Press.

Williams, Raymond (1977). *Marxism and Literature*. New York: Oxford University Press.

Williams, Raymond (1989). *The Politics of Modernism: Against the New Conformists*, ed. Tony Pinkney. London: Verso.

Williams, Rowan (1997). Eastern Orthodox Theology. In David Ford (ed.), *The Modern Theologians*, 2nd edn. Malden, MA: Blackwell, pp. 499–513.

Williams, Rowan (2005). *Grace, Necessity and Imagination: Reflections on Art and Love*. Harrisburg, PA: Morehouse.

Wills, Clair (1993). *Improprieties: Politics and Sexuality in Northern Irish Poetry*. Oxford: Clarendon Press.

Wills, Clair (1994). Contemporary Women's Poetry: Experimentalism and the Expressive Voice. *Critical Quarterly*, 36(3), 434–52.

Wills, Clair (1998). *Reading Paul Muldoon*. Newcastle upon Tyne: Bloodaxe.

Yeats, W. B. (1989). *The Poems* rev. ed., Richard J. Finneran, vol. 1 of *The Collected Works of W. B. Yeats*, ed. Richard J. Finneran and George Mills Harper. New York: Macmillan. vol. 1. New York: Macmillan.

Young, Alan (1981). *Dada and After: Extremist Modernism and English Literature*. Manchester: Manchester University Press.

Index

Page numbers in *italics* indicate extensive/in-depth discussion of the topic